The Word-Lover's Lexicon

THE WORD-LOVER'S LEXICON

A Whimsical Collection of Uncommon, Amusing, and Useful Words

(Including the Ones You Meant to Look Up but Didn't)

by Michael Laser

DB

DANA
BOOKS

This book is affectionately dedicated to
_____ _____ *(your name here):*
a lover of words,
or perhaps a person who is about to become one.

"Midway on the road of life, I found myself in a dark wood,
full of words I had seen before,
whose meanings I did not know."

Contents

Introduction

Quick-Start Guide

You don't have to read these introductory pages if you'd rather not. Just start browsing. The words and the quotations speak for themselves.

But if you'd like to know *why* I put this book together, read on.

•

Take a look at these sentences, which come from three very different sources:

- "I don't want any more of your meretricious persiflage." — from *Women in Love*, by D.H. Lawrence, 1920
- "The famously callipygian television personality Kim Kardashian makes frequent requests for free Spanx." — from an article in the *New Yorker*, 2011
- "What is proposed is like a monstrous carbuncle on the face of a much-loved and elegant friend." — Prince Charles, commenting on a proposed extension for London's National Gallery, 1984

If you know the words *meretricious, persiflage, callipygian, and carbuncle*, you're probably smiling. Even if you have no idea what *meretricious persiflage* is, you may have found the words intriguing. And doesn't the line about Kim Kardashian and her Spanx make you *want* to know what *callipygian* could possibly mean? As for that *carbuncle*... the context gives you a pretty good idea of what Prince Charles is saying.

Let me clue you in. *Meretricious* means "whore-like," among other things. *Persiflage* is teasing banter. A person who is *callipygian* has a shapely behind. And we should pity the possessor of a *carbuncle*, which is a painful cluster of boils.

Now give those sentences another try. They're much more entertaining once you know the words.

You could express the same ideas with more ordinary words. It would sound something like this: "I don't want any more of your whorish banter." "The television personality Kim Kardashian, she of the famously shapely derrière, makes frequent requests for free Spanx." "What is proposed is like a monstrous cluster of boils on the face of a much-loved and elegant friend." Something is lost, though. There's a subtle magic in the originals. Uncommon words like these are worth knowing, and worth reviving.

You're holding in your hands a collection of fascinating words that have fallen out of use. These aren't obscure oddities found only in unabridged dictionaries: they're words I encountered in books and articles over the last forty-odd years.

To me, they're treasures. They name and describe things and people with admirable precision. They contain implied meanings that simpler words don't. And they're fun. Even before you know what they mean, they tease you with their mystery.

Another thing they have in common: they're all in danger of extinction.

Our language has grown steadily simpler over the past hundred and fifty years. The average sentence shrank from 50 words in Shakespeare's day to 23 words in 1893,[1] and was estimated at 15 to 20 words in 2017.[2] Older words are falling out of use faster than new words are entering the language.[3] If you compare paragraphs from *Moby-Dick* (1851), *The Great Gatsby* (1925), and a random novel of the past few years, you'll see these trends instantly. Or plug the words in this book into the Google Books Ngram Viewer (which counts occurrences of words over time and graphs the data), and you'll see, in most cases, mountains on the left giving way to low floodplains on the right.

My purpose isn't to bemoan simplification. I admire lean, lucid prose. But there's more than one way to write. Even as Hemingway's muscular simplicity was edging out Faulkner's challenging vocabulary and syntax in popularity, a defiant minority of writers insisted on using words that must have baffled many of their readers:

 • "I noticed that whenever he felt his enigmas were becoming too recondite, even for such a solver as I, he would lure me back with an easy one." — Vladimir Nabokov, *Lolita* (1955)

---

[1] Sherman, Lucius Adelno, 1893. *Analytics of literature: A manual for the objective study of English prose and poetry*. Boston: Ginn and Co.

[2] The Acropolitan, 2017. "Sentence Length Has Declined 75% in the Past 500 Years," on Medium.com.

[3] Statistical Laws Governing Fluctuations in Word Use from Word Birth to Word Death, *Scientific Reports* 2, Article number 313, doi:10.1038/srep00313

- "He crossed swiftly to the dressing table... and discovered a message, neatly indited on scented note paper, for him..." — Thomas Pynchon, *V.* (1963)
- "He's projected a sort of white-collar attitude of cheery competence and sangfroid." — David Foster Wallace, *Infinite Jest* (1996)

Recondite, indite, sangfroid. Pat yourself on the back if you know these words. Most English-speakers don't.

And it's not just the literary elite who inject unusual words into their prose:

- "This has always been a nation willing to sell out its past for putative progress." — from a column in *Newsweek*, 2002
- "In the contest between erosion and orogeny, erosion never loses." — from an article in the *New Yorker*, 1986
- "...seminude invaders among smoldering monuments, preening with bloodlust and concupiscence." — from a review of the book *Alaric the Goth* in *The Atlantic*, 2020

Putative, orogeny, concupiscence. Good, useful words. Let's not lose them.

•

Our brains are wired to use language, and to delight in it. There's a special satisfaction in reading a sentence that precisely captures something we've seen or experienced. There's also pleasure in playing with words. A clever rhyme makes everyone smile. ("Dear kindly social worker / They say go earn some dough / Like be a soda jerker / Which means like be a schmo": that's Stephen Sondheim's "Gee, Officer Krupke," from *West Side Story*.) Puns make people groan, but a great one deserves applause. ("Did you hear about the guy who fell into the upholstery machine? He's completely recovered.") We play word games like Scrabble and Dictionary—or, more recently, Words With Friends and Wordle. Even nonsense words tickle us, so much that we remember them better than our friends' birthdays. The proof: you can probably spell *supercalifragilisticexpialidocious* correctly, give or take a letter.

Discovering a word you've never seen before ranks as another pleasure. If you picked up this book, there's a good chance you've browsed in a dictionary at least once, and that you came up with something fascinating or amusing. Some words— like *lickspittle*, "a fawning, flattering toady"—call up vivid images. Others are just fun to say out loud. (*Picaroon! Hobbledehoy!*) Words like *mondegreen* and

Waldeinsamkeit name phenomena that we might not have noticed without them. Others, like *curare* and *bolide*, make us aware of things we didn't know existed. (At least, I didn't.)

You'll find hundreds of words like those here. You'll also find...

☞ Insults. Many of the personality types included here are the opposite of flattering:

- *miscreant*: a lawbreaker, evildoer, villain, or one who behaves badly

- *pilgarlic*: a bald-headed man, regarded with mild contempt (from "peeled garlic," believe it or not)

- *myrmidon*: a follower who carries out orders without question

☞ Things you've seen or experienced, but probably didn't know the names for:

- *lunula*: the pale, half-moon-shaped area at the base of a fingernail

- *burladero*: a wooden barrier in a bullring, behind which bullfighters can hide when chased

- *horripilation*: the bristling of hair (on the head or the body) as a result of fear or cold

☞ Things you don't run into every day:

- *hoodoo*: a column of rock, shaped by weathering, as seen in Bryce Canyon and the Badlands

- *yurt*: a round tent on a collapsible frame, used by nomads, especially in Mongolia

- *charango*: a small guitar-like instrument used in Andean music, traditionally made from an armadillo shell

☞ Strange or appealing concepts:

- *nepenthe*: a mythical drug that induces forgetfulness, and thereby removes pain or suffering

- *lagniappe*: an extra or unexpected gift; a small gift given to a customer with a purchase

- *frottage*: the technique of rubbing (as with a pencil on a paper covering something with a raised surface) to transfer an image; or the act of rubbing against a clothed stranger in public for sexual pleasure

☞ Foreign words and phrases.

- *sub specie aeternitatis* (Latin): viewed from the perspective of eternity; from a universal perspective

- *l'esprit d'escalier* (French): "staircase wit": the perfect retort that comes to you only after you've left the party, when you're going down the stairs

- *hygge* (Danish/Norwegian): a feeling of comfort and contentment, especially with friends or family; as an adjective, the word can describe a setting that creates this feeling

☞ Words from law, medicine, architecture, art, and music:

- *coverture*: the legal status of a married woman, who was considered to be under her husband's protection and authority: though women in the U.S. have most of the rights they were formerly denied, coverture has not been officially abolished here

- *strabismus*: a defect in which the eyes can't look in the same direction at the same time

- *lintel*: a horizontal piece of wood, stone, steel, or concrete that spans the top of a door or window and supports the materials above it

- *contrapposto*: a position in which most of the weight rests on one leg: a relaxed, natural pose, used by sculptors in ancient Greece and revived in the Italian Renaissance

- *fermata*: a musical symbol that tells the performer to hold the note as long as s/he would like—i.e., longer than the written note value

.

If you want to use a word that's new to you, it's important to learn *how* to use it. Otherwise, you might end up writing, *I intercalated myself into the F train.* Why not, since *intercalate* means "to insert between other things"?*

To help you avoid that sort of misstep, I've included exemplary quotations for most of the words in this book. These aren't dull,

* Here's why you shouldn't write that sentence: or, no, on second thought, I'll let you figure it out for yourself.

pointless sentences, invented as if by a grudging student for homework. ("Wow, Maya, you sure look *lissome* today.") I've chosen these quotations for their grace, their wit, or the surprising information they contain. Turn to any page and you'll find something worth reading out loud to a friend.

•

One could assemble a book like this by combing through an unabridged dictionary and listing obscure words, such as *lestrigon* and *mentagra*. But I've never seen either of those words in print.

I put this collection together a different way. Every word comes from a book or article I read. Here's how it all began:

After grad school, as I set out to become a famous novelist, it occurred to me that I ought to know the meanings of the words in the books I read. I started underlining the ones that were unfamiliar and writing them on the last page of each book, along with the page number. When I finished the book, I looked up the words and wrote the definitions on a separate sheet of paper.

Lolita, Ulysses, Murphy (by Beckett), *V.* (Pynchon), *Ada* (Nabokov), *The Rainbow* (D.H. Lawrence), and *Tristram Shandy*: all of these required multiple pages.

The lists piled up. In seven years, I accumulated more than a hundred pages of them. Like Richard Dreyfuss in *Close Encounters of the Third Kind,* shaping a Devil's Tower of mashed potatoes, I felt inexplicably compelled to build my little mountain, without knowing exactly why.

In 1984, having learned word processing, I organized the words in categories. The collection kept growing. I've refined the definitions by consulting multiple dictionaries, and added sample quotations and pronunciation guides (except where that's obvious). I've even added some jokes. (No, *celerity* doesn't come from *celery*, that fast-growing vegetable. Celery doesn't even grow that quickly!)

How to Use This Book

- Read it for pleasure: read a page a night before going to sleep, or read it on the train to work, or before dinner, with a cocktail in hand. If you wish, you may keep a copy in the john.

- Browse here and there, opening to a random page when you feel the need to be amused.

- Mark the words you already know, for a sense of satisfaction. Or, mark the ones you've been running across for years, and learn them.
- Familiarize yourself with these words and then read any 19th-century novel.
- Write a story or book in the style of Nabokov or Pynchon, amazing readers with your wordplay and reviving words long thought defunct.
- If you're a journalist, do your part and inject some of these words into your reporting, so they'll live again.
- Give copies of this book to your children, or favorite nieces and nephews. Explain that English has more riches in it than they've ever dreamed.
- Win at Scrabble.

•

Treat this lexicon as you would Aladdin's treasure cave. See which rutilant gems appeal to you, and help yourself. Use whichever words you like most: in letters to the editor or to old friends, in memos to the CEO, in notes tucked into your fifth-grader's lunch box.

Or, the next time someone refers to *meretricious persiflage*, just enjoy knowing what the words mean.

heritage in his own way.

November 12, 1956

228 logodaedaly, ergomancy
" undinist
recondite
237 Mimir
258 lithophanic
267 penele
273 flavid
274 Vibissa
278 plangent
281 aurock

41 pavonian   76 alembic   218 alembics
   glovine   103 lentigo   224 maquette
42 nictating   111 lentor   225 telestically
51 ulliulations   134 persnginity
53 pedejour   instar
56 friable   136 trochaic
64 incarnadine   140 inutile
   eructation   143 camrigo
75 congeneric   145 viatic
76 saporous   148 nativudinal
80 aclosonic   150 pavonine
88 olisbos   151 nacreous
                    152 liporine

The back page of my paperback *Lolita*.

- X -

From the Hoi Polloi to the Hoity-Toity: People

Rascals, fools, lovers, unfortunates, youths and elders, big shots and underlings—the planet has more than seven billion people roaming around on it, and our language has words to describe most of them. Will you find yourself here? I hope you will... but not among the miscreants and popinjays.

Personality Types and More: Nouns

Rotten people come in many varieties: villains, cowards, scoundrels, traitors. How can I insult thee? Let me count the ways.

miscreant ("MISS-kree-ənt") a lawbreaker, evildoer, villain, or one who behaves badly (The word can also be used as an adjective.)

> "Mr Duterte's hard line on drug dealers and other miscreants was at the core of his election campaign." — from an article in *The Economist*, 2020

recreant ("REK-ree-ənt") one who is cowardly, or unfaithful to a belief or cause

> "Like the recreant... who, lying in the ditch while the battle raged, came out afterwards and boasted of his courage." — S. J. Weyman, *Under Red Robe*

poltroon ("pahl-TROON" or "pole-TROON") (archaic or humorous) a contemptible coward

> "Did I not know thee brave as fearless fire... I could swear thou wert a poltroon." — Herman Melville, *Moby-Dick*

caitiff (KAY-təff") (archaic) a despicable, contemptible, or cowardly person

> Although the word packs a strong dose of disdain, it originally expressed sympathy—because it derives from *captive,* i.e., a weak, wretched prisoner.

scapegrace (archaic) an incorrigible, unprincipled rascal, or a mischievous person, especially a young one

> "He... was the most charming young scapegrace in the army." — William Makepeace Thackeray, *Henry Esmond*

reprobate ("REP-rə-bait") an unprincipled scoundrel (often used humorously)

"In the penitentiaries, when men are flogged, the most hardened reprobates will blubber like little children." — Thomas Mann, *The Magic Mountain* (translated by H.T. Lowe-Porter)

"Who are you calling a scapegrace, you reprobate?"

picaroon (archaic) a rogue, adventurer, thief, or vagabond

"Soon after Major André's execution, the picaroon Joseph Whaland reappear'd down in the Maryland marshes and renew'd his piratical depredations on behalf of the British." — John Barth, *Letters*

apostate ("ə-POSS-tait") one who abandons a religious faith—or, by extension, a cause or political belief

"[Sarah] Longwell is far from the only Republican in town who's publicly criticized Trump, but she's been more open about it than most. She described herself as an 'apostate Republican' in a piece in *The Atlantic*..." — from an article on the website Politico.com, 2019

recusant ("rək-YOO-zənt") one who refuses to submit to authority or obey a rule; a dissenter or nonconformist

Originally, the word referred to a Catholic who refused to attend Church of England services.

Not all who wander are lost

flâneur ("flah-NURR") one who wanders about idly; a loafer (but the word also has this connotation: one who walks in a city in order to observe and experience it)

"Adept of the joys of watching, connoisseur of empathy, the flâneur finds the world 'picturesque.'" — Susan Sontag, *On Photography*

2

Nasty women. You'll notice that many of these words are archaic. That may be because tossing them about recklessly proved dangerous.

harridan ("HAR-ih- dən," the first A pronounced as in *cat*) an unpleasant, aggressive, scolding old woman

> "The nymphs, with whom you first began,
> Are each become a harridan." — Jonathan Swift, "The Birthday Verses on Mr. Ford"

virago ("vih-RAH-go") a loud, domineering, bad-tempered woman; a scold

> Virago Press, founded in 1973, publishes feminist books by women: a fine example of turning a slur upside down and inside out.

vixen a quarrelsome, shrewish, hot-tempered, or malicious woman; or a female fox

> This centuries-old word has taken on a different meaning in recent decades: an attractive, flirtatious, sexually active woman.

termagant ("TER-mə-ghənt") a harsh, shrill, willful woman; a shrew

> "What!—me a termagant!—me a vixen!—I'll pull your eyes out, you white-livered villain." — Harry Rowe, *No Cure No Pay*

fustilugs ("FUSS-tih-lugs") (archaic) a fat, untidy, unattractive woman

> "Every Lover admires his mistris, though shee be... a vast virago, or... a fat fustilugs." — Robert Burton, *The Anatomy of Melancholy* (1638)

slattern ("SLAT-ərn") (archaic) a slovenly, lazy woman who cares little about her appearance or the cleanliness of her home

> "...I am surprised that the place is so clean; I imagined her a slattern, leaving pans unwashed and plates stacked in the sink and long black hairs in the cake mixture." — Joanne Harris, *Chocolat*

beldam ("BELL-dəm") (archaic) any old woman; or an ugly, malicious, witch-like one

trollop ("TRAHL-əp") (archaic, now used humorously) a promiscuous or immoral woman, or a prostitute

> "...that impudent Trollop, who is with Child by you..." — Henry Fielding, *Joseph Andrews*

demirep ("DEM-ee-rep") (archaic) a woman with a bad reputation, because of suspected promiscuity

"…he had no Knowledge of that Character which is vulgarly called a Demirep; that is to say, a Woman who intrigues with every Man she likes, under the Name and Appearance of Virtue… in short, whom every Body knows to be what no Body calls her." — Henry Fielding, *Tom Jones*

demimondaine ("DEM-ee-mahn-DANE") a woman who belongs to the demimonde: i.e., on the margin of respectable society, supported by a wealthy lover

"The object of Christian's adoration is Satine, a nightclub chanteuse and demimondaine, almost past her prime and riddled with consumption." — from a review of *Moulin Rouge! The Musical,* in the *New York Times,* 2019

A few ridiculous and contemptible types, for your amusement

popinjay ("POP-in-jay") a vain, talkative person who dresses and/or behaves in an attention-getting way (originally, a parrot)

"…the writer drew on fact-inspired legends like… novelist Baroness Orczy's entirely fictional Scarlet Pimpernel, the secret identity of the British popinjay who saves French aristocrats from the Reign of Terror." — from an article in the *Washington Post,* 2021

punchinello ("Pun-chə-NELL-oh") (archaic) a short, stout buffoon, or clown (from a character in traditional Italian puppet shows)

"I saw Ludovic at an upper window, hanging over the sill in a limp manner resembling a punchinello at a puppet show." — Margaret Kennedy, *Troy Chimneys*

momus ("MOH-məss") (rare/literary) one who is quick to criticize; a faultfinder

This word derives from Momus, the Greek god of censure and mockery, who was banished from Olympus for criticizing the other gods.

pilgarlic ("pill-GAR-lick") a bald-headed man, regarded with mild contempt

Etymology: from "peeled garlic," believe it or not. Does a bald head really resemble a naked garlic clove? Seems a bit cruel to me.

lickspittle a servile flatterer or toady; one who fawns on the powerful

Let's pause a moment to admire the vivid picture this word creates. (Sorry. Gross!)

peckerwood (pejorative) a rural white Southerner: the term is used most commonly by African Americans, and implies that the person is poor, uneducated, and bigoted

> "Don't you call me that, you little tin weasel peckerwood loony's son." — from the movie *Stand By Me*, 1986

gaby ("GAY-bee") (British dialect) a foolish person, or simpleton

> "She is still whimpering after that gaby of a husband—dead (and served right!) these fifteen years." — William Makepeace Thackeray, *Vanity Fair*

looby a big, clumsy person, especially one who is stupid or lazy

> "[These] are all convincing Arguments to a Country Looby." — Richard Steele, *The Englishman*

Underlings and followers

minion ("MIN-yən") an underling, especially an unimportant or servile one

> The animated film *Despicable Me* gave the name *minions* to those yellow, goggled creatures shaped like medicine capsules, who carry out the orders of the villainous protagonist, Gru.

myrmidon ("MER-mə-dahn") a follower who carries out orders without question

> Why does this word have the same root as the Greek word for *ant, myrmex*? It's because, in Greek myth, Zeus transformed a nest of ants to create the Myrmidons, a warlike people. They later faithfully followed Achilles in the Trojan War.

votary (VOH-tə-ree") a devoted follower of a religion, a leader, or a pursuit; one who is bound by religious vows

> "We are votaries to freedom of speech and expression." — from an article in *Economic and Political Weekly*, 1991

> Rhetorical question: Can a notary be a votary of the Rotary?

subaltern a subordinate

> This word has an additional meaning for Marxist and post-colonial theorists: as an adjective, it describes a class of people (usually workers or peasants) dominated by a more powerful class.

> "An effort is made to allow the conscious, individualized subaltern to speak, unfettered by the western Self's political shackles." — from an essay in the book *Women, Culture, and International Relations*

epigone ("EP-ə-gohn") a second-rate imitator or follower, especially of an artist or philosopher

> "Thus, by an irony of history Stalin's epigones began the liquidation of Stalinism and thereby carried out, *malgré eux-mêmes*, part of Trotsky's political testament." — Michael Harrington (quoting Isaac Deutscher), *Socialism*

Names in the news, several centuries ago

Nimrod a skilled hunter: often used ironically (from a descendant of Noah, mentioned in *Genesis*)

> In a Looney Tune, Daffy Duck addresses Elmer Fudd as "my little Nimrod." Audiences didn't recognize the Biblical/literary reference, and understood the word to mean "inept fool." It has had that additional meaning ever since.

Keen-eyed Nimrod has sighted his prey.
Take care where you aim your weapon, noble hunter!

Maecenas ("mih-SEE-nəs") a wealthy, generous benefactor who supports artists, etc.

The original Maecenas was a Roman statesman, a friend of Horace and Virgil, and a patron of literature.

"The Mæcenas of the last century did influence literature and art; the Mæcenas of to-day cannot." — from an article in *Belgravia*, 1875

Croesus ("CREE-səs") an extremely rich man

Croesus was the king of Lydia, in what is now Turkey. He lived in the 6th Century B.C., and was famed for his wealth. If you encounter his name, chances are it will be preceded by *rich as*.

"There he was, rich as Crœsus, and dictating to the government." — James Truslow Adams, *The Epic of America*

Boeotian ("bee-OH-sh'n") a dull, stupid person

Boeotia was a region in Greece, west of Athens. The sharp-witted Athenians supposedly considered their country neighbors dull— the same way some New Yorkers view everyone west of the Hudson.

Lovers, of various ilks

paramour ("PAR-ə-moor," rhymes with "Farrah poor") (archaic) a lover, male or female, especially the secret lover of a married person

"A paramour comes in handy when you need to cut the grass." If Groucho never said this, he should have.

cicisbeo ("CHEE-chiz-BAY-oh") the lover or male companion of a married woman

Having such a companion seems to have been a common, open practice among the nobility in Northern Italian cities in the 1700s. In Sheridan's play, *School for Scandal*, he refers to the non-sexual variety: "…a mere platonic Cicisbeo, what every London wife is entitled to."

leman ("LEM-ən," like the fruit) (archaic) a sweetheart or lover; especially, a mistress

"He… offred kingdoms vnto her in vew, / To be his Leman and his Lady trew." — Edmund Spenser, *The Faerie Queene* (1590)

gallant ("GAL-ənt" or "ghəl-ONT") a lover, ladies' man, or suitor

"O, wicked, wicked world! One that is well-nigh worn to pieces with age to show himself a young gallant!" — William Shakespeare, *The Merry Wives of Windsor*

"My Lady, your gallant is here. Shall I send him up, or shoot him?"

Girls, spirited and saucy

gamine ("GAM-een" or gam-EEN") a girl or young woman with boyish, mischievous appeal, often petite and short-haired; formerly, a female street urchin

> In Charlie Chaplin's *Modern Times,* Paulette Goddard's character is called, simply, the gamine. (Spelled *gamin* in the title card— but that means a male street urchin.)

> "The puckish gamine who, alas, sometimes enjoyed teasing and tormenting him." — Iris Murdoch, *An Unofficial Rose*

hoyden ("HOY-dn") (archaic) a high-spirited, carefree girl or woman, often loud or impudent; a tomboy

> "…sometimes hoydens behaved in ways that are rude by today's standards—a girl who pushed another out of her seat at school was a hoyden in 1865." — from an article in the *Christian Science Monitor,* 2018

soubrette ("soo-BRETT") a saucy, coquettish lady's maid in comic operas and plays; or an actress playing such a part

Just as I suspected: someone had the clever idea of naming a business Sue Brett. "In 1946, [Jack Baker] went into business... in the dress trade. He chose the name Sue Brett, which is derived from the French 'soubrette'..." — from an article in the *New York Times*, 1971

Spirited and young, of either gender

hellion ("HELL-yən") a mischievous, unrestrainable person, especially a child

> "Watching those little hellions scamper around in a state of high-scream would be enough to mute even the loudest biological clock." — from an article in the *Toronto Star*, 2005

Unusual women

houri ("HOO-ree") in Islam, a beautiful virgin companion for a faithful Muslim in paradise; or any beautiful, voluptuous young woman

> "They shall recline on jewelled couches face to face, and there shall wait on them immortal youths with bowls and ewers and a cup of purest wine... And theirs shall be the dark-eyed houris, chaste as hidden pearls: a guerdon for their deeds... We created the houris and made them virgins, loving companions for those on the right hand..." — *The Koran,* translated by N.J. Dawood

> "What is she, Isaac? Thy wife or thy daughter, that Eastern houri that thou lockest under thy arm?" — Sir Walter Scott, *Ivanhoe*

sibyl ("SIB-əl") a woman who can foretell the future

> The original sibyls were prophetesses who spoke in riddles, which priests then interpreted. The most famous was the Sibyl of Cumae in Italy, an old woman who advises Aeneas in *The Aeneid* and guides him through the underworld.

> "The spirit of deep prophecy she hath, / Exceeding the nine sibyls of old Rome." — William Shakespeare, *Henry VI, Part One*

There are some people you'd rather not spend time with

Dutch uncle someone who lectures, advises, or scolds bluntly and unsparingly

"… now let me talk to you like a Dutch uncle for a moment Mister Bast because I must be frank to tell you I feel you've been spreading yourself a bit too thin." — William Gaddis, *JR*

nark (British) an informer, or stool pigeon

> The American term *narc* (narcotics agent) came along at least a century later than the British version. The two are homophones, but I believe that's just a coincidence.

The unfortunate ones

tatterdemalion ("tat-ər-də-MALE-yən") a person in torn, ragged clothes

> "Mrs. Bramble, turning from him, said she had never seen such a filthy tatterdemalion, and bid him begone; observing that he would fill the room with vermin." — Tobias Smollett, *Humphry Clinker*

lazar ("LAZE-ər") (archaic) a poor, diseased person, especially a leper; or a diseased beggar

> "He did not scowl, the Galilaean mild, / Who met the Lazar turned from rich man's doors, / And called him Friend, and wept upon his sores!" — Samuel Taylor Coleridge, "Sonnet V (Sweet Mercy)

spado ("SPAY-doh") a neutered person or animal; or, in law, a person who is unable to reproduce, especially because of impotence

Some are exceedingly healthy, while others...

mesomorph ("MEZZ-ə-morf") a powerful, muscular person of medium stature

> "Behold the manly mesomorph / Showing his splendid biceps off." — W.H. Auden, *Nones*

> Contrasting with the mesomorph are the *ectomorph* (lean, delicate) and the *endomorph* (soft, round).

valetudinarian a chronic invalid, especially one who is morbidly anxious about his or her health

> "...having been a valetudinarian all his life, without activity of mind or body, he was a much older man in ways than in years..." — Jane Austen, *Emma*

"I'm sick as a dog," said Dr. Glump, valetudinarian and veterinarian.
"Not all dogs is sick, Sir," said his nurse.
"Away with you, quibbler!"

trencherman ("TRENCH-ər-mən") (humorous) a person who eats a lot, heartily; or (archaic) a guest who eats often at someone else's home

> "Everybody knew old Pen, regular old trencher-man at Gaunt House, notorious old bore, regular old fogy." — William Makepeace Thackeray, *Pendennis*

"You're not from around here, are you?"

zingaro ("ZIN-gah-roh") (Italian) a Gypsy, i.e., one of the Roma people (the word is considered offensive by some)

> "I am a Zingaro, a Bohemian, an Egyptian, or whatever the Europeans, in their different languages, may chuse to call our people, but I have no country." — Sir Walter Scott, *Quentin Durward*

fellah ("FELL-ə") a peasant or farm worker in an Arab country (plural: *fellahin*)

> "His family were fellahin and, like Nasser, he preserved an instinctive sympathy for the peasant society from which he sprang." — from an obituary in the *Times* of London, 2016, about Egyptian journalist Mohamed Hassanein Heikal

blackamoor (archaic) any dark-skinned person, especially an African: often used with contempt, and now considered offensive

> "A barrister who called a solicitor's clerk a 'blackamoor' was found guilty of race discrimination yesterday and suspended for a

year by a Bar disciplinary tribunal." — from the *Times* of London, 2002

mestizo ("mess-TEE-zoh") a person of mixed blood: especially, in Latin America, someone of mixed Spanish and indigenous ancestry

"In Brazil... half the population is white, but Indians predominate in the interior, mestizos in the north, and the negro element is strong in Bahia." — Robert A. Humphreys, *Latin America*

"Actually, I am from around here."

autochthon ("aw-TOK-thən") a native: one who was born where he or she lives; or an aborigine, i.e., one of an area's earliest inhabitants (adjective form: *autochthonous*)

"The cattle business has also supplied the West's autochthonous festival, the rodeo." — from an article in *Harper's* magazine, 1946

Elders

centenarian ("sent-ə-NAIR-ee-ən") a person who is a hundred years old, or older

Willard Scott, the TV weatherman, used to send out birthday greetings to centenarians on the *Today* show. Al Roker continued the tradition.

"Now, the centenarian can continue to get behind the wheel until at least 2024, when the license expires." — from an article in *USA Today*, 2022

gaffer an old man, especially from the country (from "godfather"): originally a term of respect, later used humorously or contemptuously; or, in movie/TV production, the head electrician

If you're one of those people who sticks around after a movie and reads the credits, you've seen the term *gaffer* many times. You've also seen (and probably snickered at) the credit for Best Boy: i.e., the Gaffer's assistant.

gammer (archaic) an old woman, especially from the country (from "godmother": the feminine version of "gaffer")

"The gaffers and gammers of the quarter... gossiped Tuscan-wise on their doorsteps." — Thomas Trollope, *Marietta*

paladin ("PAL-ə-dn") a paragon of knighthood, heroic and chivalrous; or a strong defender of a cause

> The twelve knights who served Charlemagne (in legend, not fact) were called paladins; they appear in *The Song of Roland*.

> More recently, on the TV show *Have Gun—Will Travel* (1957-1963), the hero's calling card used a chess knight as a logo and instructed potential clients to "Wire Paladin." As a boy, I thought Wire was his first name.

> "President Donald Trump, who has seized on the protests to recast himself as a paladin of order, said in a tweet Tuesday afternoon that the incursion was reason to bring soldiers into the city." — from an article on Bloomberg.com, 2020

nob (slang) a wealthy person, or one possessing high social status

> Nob Hill, in San Francisco, is one of the wealthiest neighborhoods in the U.S. Its representative in Congress is Nancy Pelosi. The name originated in the 1850s, when four of the country's wealthiest railroad tycoons built mansions there.

bellwether a person or thing that leads a trend: by observing the bellwether, you can see where the trend is heading

> Originally, a bellwether was a sheep with a bell hung from its neck, followed by the rest of the flock. (A *wether* is a castrated ram.)

> "Iowa has been a bellwether state in recent presidential elections." — from an article on Vox.com, 2020

bashaw ("bə-SHAW") an important (or self-important) person, especially an official (an early form of the Turkish title *pasha*)

> "You've taken to being a nob, buying land, being a country bashaw." — George Eliot, *Middlemarch*

doyen/doyenne ("doy-ENN") the oldest, most prominent, or most respected member of a group or profession (male/female)

> "Mahon, long considered the doyenne of San Diego's ballet community, started California Ballet Company more than 50 years ago." — from an article in the *San Diego Union-Tribune*, 2020

arbiter ("AR-bə-tər") a person authorized to judge or decide: the ultimate authority

> "*Vogue* magazine, perhaps the world's top arbiter of style, is making a statement about its own models: Too young and too

thin is no longer in." — from a Facebook post by WTEN, News 10, 2012

A few political types

mugwump any independent person, especially in politics (In 1884, the term referred to Republicans who switched parties and supported Grover Cleveland.)

> "But now she calls herself a mugwump and opposes the President's proposal as highly dangerous to freedom." — from an article in *Life* magazine, 1937

> The word also has a negative connotation: a person who remains neutral to the point of refusing to commit to any position.

physiocrat a believer in the economic theory (developed by François Quesnay in the 18th Century) that land and agriculture are the only real sources of wealth, and that government shouldn't interfere with free trade

> "…the belief of Turgot and the physiocrats that by removing restraints on trade a multitude of individual efforts would… create a larger quantity of wealth than any effort at mercantilist regulation." — Lewis Mumford, *Condition of Man*

Locofoco a member of a radical faction in New York that opposed the more conservative mainstream Democratic party, starting in 1835

> The Locofocos spoke up for social justice and opposed monopolies and banks. But where does the name come from? From a type of match they used to light candles after Tammany Hall goons turned off the gaslights to disrupt the meeting.

What is the plural of "smartypants"?

polymath one who is learned in many fields

> "If being a generalist was so ineffective, why are the founders of the five largest companies in the world—Bill Gates, Steve Jobs, Warren Buffett, Larry Page, and Jeff Bezos—all polymaths?" — from an article on the Observer website, 2018

savant ("sah-VONT") a scholar; one who is renowned for deep knowledge of a field

> The word *savant* has also come to mean a person with a developmental disability (such as autism) who shows exceptional brilliance in a particular field, often music or math. Formerly, the

term for such a person was *idiot savant*; for obvious reasons, this phrase is now rarely heard.

"What did the European savants of Existentialism understand about *la condition humaine* that Ma Rainey did not?" — from an article in the *New Yorker,* 1996

Ah, youth!

ephebe/ephebus ("ə-feeb" or "ə-FEEB" / "ə-FEEB-əss") in ancient Greece, a youth: especially one 18 to 20 years old, in training for full citizenship

"I'm in the class of fussy bimanists. / As a discreet ephebe in tights assists / A female in an acrobatic dance, / My left hand helps, and holds, and shifts its stance." — Vladimir Nabokov, *Pale Fire*

hobbledehoy ("HOB-əl-dee-HOY") (colloquial) a gawky or awkward youth, no longer a boy, not quite a man

"James, then a hobbledehoy, was now become a young man, having had the benefits of a university education, and acquired the inestimable polish which is gained by living in a fast set at a small college, and contracting debts…" — William Makepeace Thackeray, *Vanity Fair*

abecedarian ("EY-BEE-SEE-dair-ee-ən") a novice; someone who is learning the basics, e.g., the rudiments of the alphabet

"It would be consummate folly to put Homer, Virgil, or Horace, into the hands of the young Tyro, or Abecedarian in the Latin and Greek languages, before he has previously gone through his inferiour classics." — A.G. Sinclair, *Artis Medicinae Vera Explanatio* (1791)

"I coulda been a contender!"

___ **manqué** ("mahn-KAY") unfulfilled, would-be, or unsuccessful

This French word is an adjective, commonly used in English in combination with a noun, e.g., an artist manqué, an actress manqué.

"Casaubon… is an intellectual *manqué*." — F.R. Leavis, *The Great Tradition* (referring to a character in *Middlemarch*)

And then there are those who refused to neatly fit in any of the previous categories

quidnunc ("KWID-nunk") (archaic) ("What now?") a busybody, someone who tries to keep up with all the latest gossip

"A quintessential quidnunc chronicles his continent-hopping capers as photographer to the stars and the royals… and as a fox in Celebrity's henhouse." — from a review of the book *Beaton in the Sixties: The Cecil Beaton Diaries as He Wrote Them, 1965-1969*, in *Kirkus Reviews*

The quidnuncs listened, agog, as Benny Bilge reported on the progress of the Third Reform Act through the Lower House.

sybarite ("SIB-ə-rite") a person devoted to luxury and sensual pleasure: the word sometimes implies effeminacy

"The lords of Lacedemon were true soldiers, / But ours are Sybarites." — Lord Byron, *Marino Faliero, Doge of Venice*

chatelaine ("SHAT-ə-lane") the wife of a castle's owner; a woman in charge of a château or large household

Chatelaine is the name of a Canadian women's magazine, one of the country's most popular. It has been published since 1928.

grisette ("grih-ZETT") (French) (archaic) a girl or young woman of the working class

16

The word comes from *gris* (gray), because that was the color of the cheap fabric these young women's dresses were made of. *Grisette* also came to mean a part-time prostitute.

"That pretty, neat appearance which one sees in French girls of a class just a little above the grisette." — Mary Elizabeth Braddon, *Wyllard's Weird*

grass widow a woman who is divorced or separated from her husband, or whose husband is away

"What about coming round on Tuesday and cheering me up when I'm a grass widow." — Kingsley Amis, *Take a Girl Like You*

punter one who gambles, especially betting against the bank (as in faro or baccarat); or one who makes a risky investment

Or, in the U.S., the player who punts the football... or, at Oxford or Cambridge, someone who propels a flat boat on the Thames by pushing a pole... or, in England, a prostitute's client. This word has so many jobs to do!

Word Play

Match the people and characters on the left with the words on the right that best describe them.

Thomas Jefferson	miscreant
Mr. Burns from *The Simpsons*	gallant
Cary Grant	myrmidon
Imperial Storm Trooper from *Star Wars*	Croesus
Gregory Peck as Atticus Finch	pilgarlic
Charlie Chaplin	paladin
Loki from *The Avengers*	polymath
Jeff Bezos	tatterdemalion

Personality Types, Temporary States, etc.: Adjectives

Flaubert, advising De Maupassant, urged the younger writer to show vividly how a particular grocer or concierge is different from all other grocers or concierges—and to do it succinctly. There are many ways to achieve the goal. The following adjectives may help.

Pray that your biographer doesn't use these words to describe you

unctuous ("UNK-chew-əss") insincerely flattering, ingratiating, or pious, in an oily way

> I wonder if Charles Dickens created the character Uriah Heep (in *David Copperfield*) as the personification of the word *unctuous*.

> "Gail, you know that whenever you mention the name of the junior senator from Texas, I think: Eddie Haskell wasn't *that* unctuous." — from an op-ed dialogue in the *New York Times*, 2021: this is Bret Stephens, addressing Gail Collins, comparing Ted Cruz unfavorably to the famously insincere character on *Leave It to Beaver*

Pecksniffian ("Peck-SNIFF-ee-ən") hypocritically pretending to benevolence or lofty morality

> The word derives from Mr. Pecksniff, a treacherous hypocrite in *Martin Chuzzlewit,* by Charles Dickens.

> "*Rolling Stone*'s sneering 2011 insistence that [Ron] Swanson is 'the perfect depiction of aggrieved American manhood at the twilight of the empire' may have pleased the magazine's Pecksniffian audience. But it misses the mark." — from an article in *National Review,* 2014

mendacious tending to lie or deceive habitually (or, if said of a statement, untrue)

> "A great line of poetry, albeit by a mendacious fascist, will outlast... the most sanctified of good deeds." — from an article in the *Times Literary Supplement,* 1988

overweening arrogant, overconfident, insolent

> "Engaged. Donald Trump, 45, overweening casino developer, and Marla Maples, 27, his on-again, off-again girlfriend." — *Time* magazine, 1991

orgulous ("OR-gyə-ləss") proud; haughty

One can be proud without being arrogant, but this word seems to bear a tinge of disapproval more often than not. (Compare with the Spanish word for *proud, orgulloso,* which usually has a positive connotation.)

"Many people find Layton... too loud, pushy, orgulous and self-referential for comfort." — from an article in *Matrix*, 1992

bumptious ("BUMP-shəss") disagreeably pushy, aggressive, confident

"That eternal scapegrace of the humorous writer, the ill-bred and bumptious rich American tourist." — from an article in *Travel* magazine, 1929

malapert ("MAL-ə-pərt") (archaic) impudent, presumptuously bold

"You are too malapert for a young maiden." — Sir Walter Scott, *The Betrothed*

hoity-toity highfalutin, condescending, snooty, superior in attitude, especially without justification

Some people are hoity-toity; so are some buildings.

"They put me in a freight elevator surrounded by steel plates and plywood, with a hard-hat operator... That's how I went up to my hoity-toity apartment before closing." — from an article in the *New York Times*, 2021, about disgruntled buyers of multimillion-dollar apartments at 432 Park Avenue, a slender tower nearly 1,400 feet tall

sententious ("sen-TEN-shəss") tending to speak in aphorisms, or to moralize pompously (can also refer to a style of speech or writing)

"Lord Mahon is also a little too fond of uttering moral reflections in a style too sententious and oracular." — Thomas Macaulay, *War of the Succession in Spain*

pharisaical/pharisaic ("farrah-SAY-ə-kəl"/"-ək") hypocritically self-righteous; observing the letter of religious law but not the spirit

"There are vast multitudes of Pharisaical hypocrites among baptized Christians." — Cardinal Newman, *Parochial Sermons*

venal ("VEEN-əl") corruptible; willing to accept a bribe

"We are all venal Cowards, except some few." — from a letter by Andrew Marvell (1670)

Don't confuse *venal* with *venial,* which (in Christian theology) describes sins that are minor and forgivable, as distinct from mortal sins. Here's a question for theologians: Is venality a venial sin?

flagitious ("flə-JIH-shəss") villainous; criminal; heinous (can refer to a person or an action)

"Our king... may deserve the reproach of lewdness, but he is an undoubted catholic; and his faith is pure, though his manners are flagitious." — Edward Gibbon, *The Decline and Fall of the Roman Empire*

peccant ("PECK-ənt") (archaic) sinful, guilty of a moral offense

"...the brilliant (if morally peccant) young politician from Arkansas discovered Washington DC to be, in his own words, 'a goddamned jungle, a sick perverted place.'" — from an article about Bill Clinton in the *Independent*, 2003

rebarbative ("rə-BAR-bə-tiv") extremely unattractive, repellent

"Still, everyone appeared to be extremely nice, except that that Dr. Greenfield man was a trifle rebarbative. (This was a word which Toby had recently learnt at school and could not now conceive of doing without.)" — Iris Murdoch, *The Bell*

anthropoid resembling an ape; or, if said of an ape, resembling a human being

"For an Irish girl, Miss Counihan was quite exceptionally anthropoid." — Samuel Beckett, *Murphy*

gibbous ("GIB-əss") hunchbacked; or, if said of an object, rounded, convex; or, if said of the moon, more than half full

"She is liable to the same variety of changes as the Moon, sometimes almost Full, at other times Gibbous." — William Leybourn, *Cursus Mathematicus* (1690) (The title means *Mathematical Course*, not *Curse Math*, as I supposed.)

feckless lacking strength, initiative, purpose, or character; ineffective; irresponsible

"Bertha despised the gentry. They were feckless; they couldn't do a hand's turn for themselves." — Dorothy Whipple, *The Priory*

Don't you wish *feckful* were a word? Well, it is, according to the *OED*. Just as you'd expect, it's the opposite of feckless. But it's "chiefly regional," in Northern England and Scotland, or else used humorously.

asthenic ("ass-THEN-ik," with the TH pronounced as in *thick*) pathologically weak

This word means "suffering from asthenia," a medical term for abnormal weakness or lack of energy, or loss of strength or energy

neurasthenic ("noo-rəs-THEN-ik") (dated) suffering from neurasthenia, a medical condition characterized by exhaustion, thought to be related to depression or stress—possibly an earlier name for what's now called chronic fatigue syndrome

> "Many characters in fiction of [the 19th century] were neurasthenic, and portrayed positively. This attitude made the diagnosis desirable and some patients sought it out." — from an article in the *Atlantic*, 2016

> "Some of the caddies were poor as sin and lived in one-room houses with a neurasthenic cow in the front yard..." — F. Scott Fitzgerald, "Winter Dreams"

jejune ("djə-DJOON") insipid; naïve, unsophisticated, childish; or uninteresting

> "Gradus had long been a member of all sorts of jejune leftist organizations." — Vladimir Nabokov, *Pale Fire*

fatuous ("FA-choo-əss," with the A pronounced as in *have*) foolish, or pointless, especially in an oblivious or smug way; can also refer to speech or writing

> "In other words, McConnell is just engaging in fatuous blather." — from an opinion column in the *Los Angeles Times*, 2020

footling ("FOO-tə-ling") lacking in judgment; or inept, or (referring to something other than a person) pointless

> "They are paraphrases of great works, made by footling people." — George Bernard Shaw, from an article in the *Daily Chronicle*

> "You do talk the most footling rot." — W. Somerset Maugham, *The Bread-Winner*

lubberly (archaic) big and clumsy

> A *lubber*—as you might have guessed—is a big, clumsy person.

> "'I did that, sir,' said a great lubberly fellow, stepping forward." — Charles Dickens, *Oliver Twist*

Some types you'd rather not argue with—or hire

contumacious ("kahn-too-MAY-shəss") stubbornly rebellious or resistant to authority

> "Contumacious prisoners were put to a dreadful torture." — Nathaniel Hawthorne, *The French and Italian Notebooks*

froward ("FROH-ərd") contrary, willful, hard to deal with

"[Johnson:] A Judge may become froward from age." — James Boswell, *The Life of Samuel Johnson*

fractious ("FRAK-shəss") rebellious; cranky; unruly (often refers to children)

"Yes, everyone should shop for major appliances now and then, just to leave behind our fractious political cacophony! Just kidding. Everything is political. Tell people you're looking at a new fridge, and you'll start an argument." — from an article in *National Review*, 2020

bellicose ("BELL-ih-kohss") aggressive, inclined to fight

"Hillary Clinton, Barbed and Bellicose" — title of a column in the *New York Times*, 2014

"Bellicose, you say? I'll show you bellicose! Here, eat this candle, you puny popinjay!"

restive unable to keep still; impatient with restraint; on edge; hard to control

"Such music is not for the piano, and her audience began to get restive." — E.M. Forster, *A Room With a View*

thersitical ("thur-SIT-ih-kəl") loud and abusive, foul-mouthed

The word derives from Thersites, a loud, ugly, abusive Greek soldier killed by Achilles in the Trojan War.

"...there is a pelting kind of thersitical satire, as black as the very ink 'tis wrote with..." — Laurence Sterne, *Tristram Shandy*

recalcitrant ("ree-KAL-sih-trənt") stubbornly uncooperative; defiant of authority

"You are not the kind of person who beats on recalcitrant vending machines." — Jay McInerney, *Bright Lights, Big City*

refractory ("rə-FRAK-tə-ree") stubborn, hard to manage

"...mother and daughter in Mr. Wilding's absence pleaded his cause with his refractory bride-elect." — Rafael Sabatini, *Mistress Wilding*

"Refractory, that's what that horse is. He's refractory, all right. Most refractory beast I've seen in a while. Recalcitrant, too."

captious ("KAP-shəss") inclined to criticize in a petty way; fault-finding

"The human sweetness in him was half dried up, and a misanthropy, so new and alien to him, made him querulous and captious." — Bolton King, *The Life of Mazzini*

bilious ("BILL-ee-əss") peevish, bad-tempered; of a sickly color (from "bile")

Remember the four "humors"—black bile, yellow bile, phlegm, and blood—and the belief that a person's temperament depends on which one dominates? Supposedly, if you're bilious, it's because you suffer from an excess of yellow bile.

"Mr. Wrench was a small, neat, bilious man, with a well-dressed wig, he had… an irascible temper, a lymphatic wife, and seven children, and he was already rather late…" — George Eliot, *Middlemarch*

querulous ("KWER-yoo-ləss") inclined to complain, petulant

"The bigger the project, the greater the outcry, intelligent or otherwise, that is sure to arise from a querulous citizenry." — from an article in the *New York Sun*, 2006

persnickety ("per-SNIK-it-ee") (informal) fussy; insisting on careful attention to trivial details

"Few debates over Latin American literatures devolve into persnickety hair-splitting more quickly than quarrels over the question of what constitutes magical realism." — from an article on BostonGlobe.com, 2021

finical ("FIN-ik-əl") (British) fussy, overly fastidious or particular

Or, to put it more concisely: *finicky*. But which came first? *Finical* first appears in the late 1500s; *finicky* in the mid-1700s.

Fortunately, some people are more pleasant to be around

ebullient ("ih-BOOL-yənt" or "ə-BUHL-yənt") energetically enthusiastic; overflowing with exuberance or excitement

Originally, this word meant *boiling over.*

"As that huge crowd headed back to their buses and cars and trains, the mood was ebullient." — from an article about the 1963 March on Washington, on the Daily Beast website, 2013

sanguine ("SANG-gwin") optimistic, cheerful, confident (even in a difficult situation)

Like *bilious,* this word derives from the belief that the four humors determine human temperament. A sanguine personality is one dominated by blood (from the Latin root *sang-*), and is characterized by a ruddy complexion and a hopeful nature.

"How could a man of his caliber be this sanguine about a war we had barely begun to fight?" — Neil Sheehan, *A Bright Shining Lie*

avuncular ("ə-VUNK-yoo-lər") of or like an uncle, especially a genial, benevolent one

"Two weeks of poker had led to his writing to his uncle a distressed, but confident, request for more funds; and the avuncular foot had come down with a joyous bang." — P.G. Wodehouse, *The Intrusion of Jimmy*

equable ("EK-wə-bəl") even-tempered, not easily upset

"The equable-nerd manner that colleagues once noted in Alito deserted him soon after Barack Obama became President." — from an article in the *New Yorker*, 2022

Then again...

saturnine ("SAT-ər-nine") gloomy, surly, sluggish, and/or taciturn

"How evil he looked! The face was saturnine and swarthy, and the sensual lips seemed to be twisted with disdain." — Oscar Wilde, *The Picture of Dorian Gray*

atrabilious ("at-rə-BILL-yəss") (rare) melancholy, gloomy; irritable

We're back to the four humors again. This word derives from "black bile": the humor that produces this type of temperament, according to medieval physiology. By the way, the word *melancholy* itself comes from the Greek words for black bile.

"It was his wife, Petronille, still young and passing handsome, but of atrabilious and harsh mien." — Eugene Sue, *The Iron Trevet, or Jocelyn the Champion*

abject ("AB-jekt") wretched, contemptible, lacking self-respect; or (when referring to an undesirable condition) extreme, e.g., *abject poverty*

"I know nothing so abject as the behaviour of a man canvassing for a seat in parliament." — Tobias Smollett, *Humphry Clinker*

impassive ("im-PASS-iv") emotionless, or seeming to be so

"Even the impassive Chesterfield cried in despair, 'We are no longer a nation.'" — John Richard Green, *A Short History of the English People*

dubitative inclined to doubt; or feeling or expressing doubt

"Stephen's face gave back the priest's indulgent smile and, not being anxious to give an opinion, he made a slight dubitative movement with his lips." — James Joyce, *A Portrait of the Artist as a Young Man*

Sex! Lust! Passion!

concupiscent ("kahn-KYOO-pəss-ənt") lustful

The noun form is *concupiscence:* "…seminude invaders among smoldering monuments, preening with bloodlust and concupiscence." — from a review of *Alaric the Goth* in *The Atlantic,* 2020

lubricious ("loo-BRISH-əss") lewd, intended to arouse lust; lecherous, showing sexual desire; smooth or slippery, especially with oil

"…Silver arrives with every noir mystery woman's attendant clichés: a lubricious walk, a wad of cash in the bosom of her complicated lingerie, a languorous way of lighting cigarettes— and a gun." — from a review of *Paradise Blue* in the *New York Times,* 2018

Most Likely to Succeed

sedulous ("SEDJ-yoo-ləss") persistent, diligent; can refer to a person, or to an effort

"…the entire sexual life of young men was supposed to be conducted out of sight… The dangers to which a young man would expose himself did not matter… and his mentors at school and at home sedulously refrained from explaining anything about that to him." — Stefan Zweig, *The World of Yesterday* (translated by Anthea Bell)

doughty ("DAO-tee," the first syllable rhyming with *cow*) (archaic, used for humorous effect) steadfast, brave, strong

"Mr. Rodgers is a doughty fighter for the moderate cause." — from an article in the *Times* of London, 1977 (When I read this sentence, I assumed the article referred to *our* Mister Rogers—it certainly seems to describe him—but no, this was a Mr. William Rodgers, spelled with a D, a leader in England's Labour Party.)

puissant ("PWEE-sənt") (archaic) powerful, potent, wielding authority

"…the puissante Mrs. Estée Lauder, who is currently presenting a store promotion throughout Harrods…" — from an article in the *Times* of London (whose editor chose to embellish the word with a French/feminine final -*e*), 1978

Do not confuse *puissant* with *pissant*, a vulgar insult meaning "a thoroughly contemptible, insignificant person."

redoubtable ("rih-DOWT-ə-bəl" or "ree-") formidable; illustrious; worthy of awe or reverence

"She was gutsy, brave, talented and skilled beyond measure in the art of self-promotion. She was, in a word, redoubtable." — from an article in the *Brantford* (Ontario) *Expositor*, 2006

Well, what do you know?

prescient ("PREH-shənt") having knowledge of what will happen before it happens

Note the root, *scien-*, which is shared with *science, omniscient, conscience,* and *nescient.* The root derives from the Latin word that means *to know.*

"…twenty-one years after he penned these words, they seem positively prescient as a description of Hollywood's reigning aesthetic." — Michael Medved, *Hollywood vs. America*, referring to Frank Capra's denunciation of sex, violence, etc. in the movies, circa 1971.

sapient ("SAY-pee-ənt") wise, discerning

(used ironically) "…the economy which has been introduced by the virtuous and sapient assembly, makes amends for the losses sustained in the receipt of revenue." — Edmund Burke, *Reflections on the Revolution in France*

sentient ("SEN-shənt") capable of perception through the senses; conscious

"The possibility that Ellen DeGeneres might not be the nicest person in Hollywood should never have been a complete surprise to any sentient observer of television, famous people or human behavior." — from an article in the *Washington Post,* 2020

nescient ("NESH-ee-ənt") ignorant; or lacking awareness

"…the lethargy of nescient matter: the apathy of the stars." — James Joyce, *Ulysses*

benighted ("bə-NITE-əd") ignorant, either intellectually or morally; unenlightened

"Women will no longer have control over their own bodies in half of this benighted country." — from a column in the Boston Globe, 2022

muzzy (colloquial) confused, befuddled; or (referring to thinking/writing) imprecise, muddled, unclear

"I… have developed a violent cold in the head which perhaps accounts for why I felt so muzzy in the brain." — Leonard Woolf, *Letters*

purblind ("PUR-blind") (literary) having poor vision; or lacking in understanding

"…impressions from their previous endearments seemed to hustle away into the corner of their brains, repeating themselves as echoes from a time of supremely purblind foolishness." — Thomas Hardy, *Tess of the D'Urbervilles*

"I've always been SHY!!"

diffident ("DIFF-ə-dənt") timid, lacking self-confidence

"Nursing under a diffident manner a considerable amount of secret arrogance." — Joseph Conrad, *Chance*

Shall we bring this product to market? *Diffident*: the toothpaste for insecure people.

farouche ("fə-ROOSH") sullen, shy, unsociable; lacking social graces

"The younger girl was a lithe, farouche animal, who mistrusted all approach, and would have none of the petty secrecies and jealousies of schoolgirl intimacy." — D.H. Lawrence, *The Rainbow*

Let's get physical

sylphlike ("SILF-like") slim, graceful (said of girls or women)

A sylph is a mythical being that lives in the air. Ariel in Pope's "The Rape of the Lock" is a sylph; and Ariel in Shakespeare's *The Tempest* could be described as one, too. The word has also been used ironically when describing characters who are far from graceful or slender.

"Tall and sylphlike… she changes clothes behind a privacy curtain in the girls' locker room at her high school. But just being allowed to set foot in that locker room was a huge victory for the girl. She is transgender." — from an article in the *New York Times*, 2017

callipygian ("kal-ə-PIDG-ee-ən") having shapely buttocks

I wondered when any writer would have occasion to use this word. Then I took a wild guess, which proved correct: "The famously callipygian television personality Kim Kardashian makes frequent requests for free Spanx." — from an article in the *New Yorker*, 2011

What bird would dare befoul this comely creation?
A callow pigeon, perhaps.

lissome/lissom ("LISS-əm") supple, slender, agile, graceful

"… A daughter of our meadows, yet not coarse; / Straight, but as lissome as a hazel wand…" — Alfred, Lord Tennyson, "The Brook"

gracile ("GRASS-əl" or "GRASS-ile") attractively slender

"He thought her body beautiful, fine and gracile." — Anita Brookner, *Fraud*

brachycephalic ("brak-ee-sə-PHALL-ik") having a short, wide head: most commonly referring to dogs, e.g., pugs

> Strictly speaking, a skull must have a width more than four-fifths of its length for its owner to be considered brachycephalic.

> "United [Airlines] officially stopped flying brachycephalic breeds (more commonly known as snub-nosed dogs or cats) last June, as the dogs' compressed facial structure can compromise their ability to breathe." — from an article in the *New York Times*, 2019

prognathous ("PROG-nə-thəss") having a protruding jaw, i.e., one that projects forward more than average

> "The whole universe is under attack from Thanos, an infinitely villainous villain sporting a multicleft, prognathous chin." — from a review of *Avengers: Infinity War* in the *Wall Street Journal*, 2018

rugose ("ROO-gose") wrinkled

> The word is most often used in scientific literature—but not exclusively: "...representatives of the Rolling Stones said yesterday that the rugose rockers would be performing [in Hong Kong] on Nov. 7 and 9." — from an article in the *New York Times*, 2003

rubicund ("ROO-bih-kənd") ruddy, having a reddish complexion

> "The English face, now turned up toward him, was rubicund, merry, kindly, but worried..." — Malcolm Lowry, *Under the Volcano*

glabrous ("GLAY-brəss") smooth and hairless: said of skin or leaves

> The term is more often used in science, but can be used less formally as well: "...an old man, / wearing a fringe of long white hair, bareheaded, / his glabrous skull reflecting the sun's / light..." — William Carlos Williams, "Sunday in the Park"

From hunger

ravening ("RA-vən-ing": the A is pronounced like the A in *have*) fiercely hungry and searching for prey; voracious

> "Beware of false prophets, which come to you in sheep's clothing, but inwardly they are ravening wolves." — *The Book of Matthew*, 7:15 (King James Version)

esurient ("ə-SOOR-ee-ənt") (archaic) very hungry; or greedy

It's not easy to find a good example of this word in a sentence. The best I could do was this one, from an article about taking a standardized test in middle age: "In truth, I hadn't incorporated G.R.E. vocabulary favorites like 'esurient' and 'vitiate'..." — from the *New York Times,* 2011

edacious ("ə-DAY-shəss") gluttonous, voracious; or related to eating

The word is now used mainly for humorous effect, but has also been used to refer to merciless Time: "Concord Bridge had long since yielded to the edacious tooth of Time." — James Russell Lowell, *The Bigelow Papers*

anthropophagous ("an-throw-PAH-fə-ghəss") cannibalistic, i.e., eating human flesh

"The victims of anthropophagous activities included—and most usually were—accused and executed sorcerers or witches." — Thomas M. Ernst, in *The Anthropology of Cannibalism*, edited by Laurence R. Goldman

Nothing exceeds like excess

prodigal ("PRAH-də-ghəl") spending recklessly and wastefully

In the Book of Luke, the Prodigal Son was the one who squandered his inheritance and then returned to his father, repentant. The phrase "Prodigal Son" refers to his irresponsible ways, not his remorseful return.

However, the Oxford English Dictionary acknowledges the confusion and allows the alternate meaning, "that has lived a reckless or extravagant life away from home, but subsequently made a repentant return," as in this line from *Dombey and Son, by* Charles Dickens: "The prodigal son was evidently nervous of visiting the parental abode."

crapulous ("KRAH-pyə-ləss") tending to drink or eat excessively; or, drunk

The word seems to suggest something different. But mature lexicographers will refrain from commenting.

"The crapulous eructations of a drunken cobbler." — Sydney Smith, *Works*

bibulous ("BIB-yoo-ləss") overly fond of (or addicted to) alcohol

In the 1902 silent comedy "The Bibulous Wire Walker," a man coming home drunk with a friend has a run-in with a clothesline and climbs onto it, imagining that he's a tightrope walker.

Prudent types

provident ("PRAHV-ə-dənt") frugal; making foresightful arrangements for future needs

> "My suspender broke and had it not been for my provident habit of carrying a supply of safety pins with me, I should have had an awkward day of it." — from a letter written by Vanessa Bell, in her *Selected Letters*

abstemious characterized by restraint, especially in the consuming of food or alcohol

> "...a whore, it seemed to me, had no right to be sitting there like a lady, waiting timidly for someone to approach and all the while abstemiously sipping her *chocolat.*" — Henry Miller, *Tropic of Cancer*

The bold and the reckless

temerarious ("tem-ər-AIR-ee-əss") reckless; presumptuously bold

> This is the adjective form of *temerity*, which means *audacity*.
>
> "The King was one of the first that entered [the breach], choosing rather to be thought temerarious then timorous." — John Speed, *The History of Great Britaine Under the Conquests of ye Romans, Saxons, Danes and Normans* (1611)

horn-mad enraged; furious enough to gore, like a bull; or (obsolete) mad with jealousy because one has been cuckolded

> "A loose wife makes her husband horn-mad and heart-sad." — Ovid, *Invective Against Ibis*, translated by John Jones

pot-valiant brave or bold from drunkenness

> "...my sister Tabby provoked me into a transport of passion; during which, like a man who has drank himself pot-valiant, I talked to her in such a stile of authority and resolution, as produced a most blessed effect. She and her dog have been remarkably quiet and orderly ever since this expostulation." — Tobias Smollett, *Humphry Clinker*

Alas! A lack.

penurious ("pə-NOO-ree-əss" or "pə-NYOO-ree-əss") very poor; or stingy

Penury means extreme poverty. You would think, therefore, that *penurious* would mean, simply, *very poor*. It also has a different shade of meaning, however: tight-fisted.

"One of his acquaintance, a penurious young poet, who, having nothing in his pockets but the… potential gold of manuscript verses, would have grasped so eagerly… at the elegant outsides of life…" — Walter Pater, *Imaginary Portraits*

impecunious ("im-pə-KYOO-nee-əss") poor; having little or no money, either chronically or temporarily

"Once the pioneers of modern design on the Vineyard were impecunious architects and academics, while today only the very wealthy can afford to build on what has become incredibly desirable real estate." — from an article on BostonGlobe.com, 2021

The impecunious fop struck a poignant pose,
having spent his last farthing on fashionable finery.

Natty, and beyond

soigné/soignée (masculine/feminine) ("swan-YAY") elegantly dressed; sleek

"William Powell is of course William Powell—suave and *soigné* and perfectly poised." — from an article in *Punch*, 1936

trig trim, neat; or precise

"She really looked very smart and trig and jaunty." — John Strange Winter, *Aunt Johnnie*

bedizened (bə-DIE-zənd") dressed (or adorned) in a gaudy, showy, or vulgar way

> "Do you ever suppose that Jesus walked about bedizened in priestly robes and a crown, and with yon jewels on his breast, and a gilt aureole round his head?" — Thomas Carlyle, commenting on the painting, *The Light of the World,* by William Holman Hunt

Parenthood

progenitive ("pro-JEN-ih-tiv") capable of reproducing

> "Augustus John had an enormous number of illegitimate children... And Lucian [Freud]'s progenitive performance must be damned near equal to John's." — art critic Robert Hughes, quoted in an article in *Vanity Fair*, 1993

gravid ("GRA-vəd," with the A pronounced as in *have*) pregnant, or distended by pregnancy, or full of eggs; or (figuratively) full of something

> "Heritage Restaurant & Caviar Bar opened in early August, the week of the Sturgeon Moon, which is when the Algonquins believed the Great Lakes teemed with gravid fish." — from article in *Chicago Reader*, 2017

enceinte ("on-SANT") pregnant

> "We pass over the time between the marriage and when the Princess Charlotte was declared *enceinte*." — Lady Anne Hamilton, *Secret History of the Court of England*

nulliparous ("nə-LIH-pə-rəss") having never given birth to a child

> "His ability to guess what was wrong with Gwen and to discuss her being nulliparous... is not the breakthrough he had in mind." — from a book review in the *New York Times*, 2008

Etc.

uxorious ("ək-SOR-ee-əss") excessively devoted to or fond of one's wife; or submissive to her wishes

> "The uxorious Hoosier, whose political career seemed deader than Lazarus or Myspace two years ago, is now a heartbeat... away from being leader of the free world." — from an article about Mike Pence in *Newsweek*, 2017

spoony/spooney (dated, informal) sentimental or foolish, especially in love (can refer to a person or a thing, e.g., a letter)

"It's not a spooney, love-lorn effusion, but a good, rational, amusing letter." — Bithia Mary Croker, *Proper Pride*

epicene ("EPP-ih-seen") effeminate; or lacking the typical characteristics of one's gender

> "*[WILLIAM F.] BUCKLEY ASSAILS VIETNAM PROTEST; Condemns Marchers Here as 'Young Slobs' Strutting 'Epicene Resentment'*" — headline in the *New York Times*, 1965

logy ("LOW-ghee") sluggish, lethargic, groggy

> "And do you feel run down at the end of the day? that dull logy tired feeling that just seems to creep through you?" — William Gaddis, *The Recognitions*

oscitant ("AH-sə-tənt") yawning; drowsy; inattentive

> "Southey, who has been my corrector, has been strangely oscitant, or... has not understood the sentences." — Samuel Taylor Coleridge, from his *Letters*

agog ("ə-GAHG") in a state of eager anticipation or interest

> "She was agog to hear and I was agog to tell." — Marian Keyes, *This Charming Man*

costive ("KOSS-tiv") constipated, or tending to be constipated; or (figuratively) stingy or taciturn

> "His companions had once persuaded the very young and costive Babbington that he was going to have a baby." — Patrick O'Brian, *Reverse of Medal*

tabescent ("tə-BESS-ənt") (rare) wasting away

> The word derives from *tabes*, a medical term for the emaciation that accompanies a disease. I wonder if the person who named Tab, the diet cola, was really a subversive prankster.

> (I went hunting just now, and found no evidence to support my theory. I did, however, learn that some people think the name is an acronym for "Totally Artificial Beverage." According to Snopes.com, that rumor is false.)

puisne ("PYOO-nee") (British) inferior in rank (refers specifically to certain judges in England)

> Did you notice that this word is pronounced the same way as *puny*, meaning "small and/or weak"? That's because *puny* derives directly from *puisne*.

Word Play

Fill in the most (or least) appropriate word, and see what happens. *

The _____ (saturnine, feckless) thug sneered at Rick _____
(biliously, concupiscently). "You think you're _____ (redoubtable,
avuncular), don't you?"

But the _____ (temerarious, abstemious) café owner had seen the
_____ (bellicose, epicene) gunsel's type before. "I think you're a
_____ (nescient, hoity-toity) fool, is what I think," he retorted. "Now if
you wouldn't mind pointing that roscoe in some other direction."

At that moment, a _____ (sylphlike, rebarbative) woman in spike
heels burst into the room. "You _____ (venal, overweening) little
crabcake," she hissed.

The two men eyed each other _____ (querulously, unctuously).
"Do you know this _____ (thersitical, anthropophagous) dame?" Rick
asked.

Before the _____ (mendacious, diffident) malefactor could reply,
an explosion sent the three diving under a table for shelter. _____
(Agog, Ebullient), they picked glass shards from their hair. Rick
addressed the _____ (meretricious, pharisaical) intruder: "You were
saying?"

---

*In case you weren't sure, this is an excellent example of how *not* to use the
words in this book.

Nouns that Capture Character

complaisance ("kəm-PLAY-sənss") a desire to please; an obliging, agreeable disposition

> The adjective form, *complaisant*, might be confused with its homophone, *complacent*, i.e., self-satisfied, feeling no need to try harder. Don't make that mistake!

> "What is lost is the look of complaisance that defines young founders looking for capital." — from an article in *Wired*, 2021

mansuetude ("man-SOO-ə-tood") (archaic) gentleness; or meekness

> "Our Lord Himself, made up of mansuetude... received / Opprobrium, contumely, and buffeting / Without complaint..." — Robert Browning, *The Ring and the Book*

hebetude ("HEB-ə-tood") lethargy, or mental dullness

> "The leaden weight of an irremediable idleness descended upon General Feraud, who having no resources within himself sank into a state of awe-inspiring hebetude." — Joseph Conrad, "The Duel"

muliebrity ("myoo-lee-EB-rə-tee") (literary) femininity

> Perhaps the reason we don't hear this word often is that it sounds anything but feminine. If you had to guess its meaning, you might say, "annoying stubbornness, like a mule's." It comes to us from the Latin word *muliebritas,* "womanliness."

> "She was one of those women who are wanting in—what is the word?—muliebrity." — H.G. Wells, *The New Machiavelli*

pulchritude ("PUL-krə-tood," with the first U pronounced as in *nut*) (literary) beauty, especially a woman's

> "...The alleged lack of pulchritude among the young ladies of the radical movement in New York." — from an ad in *The American Mercury*, 1927

ataraxy/ataraxia ("AT-ə-raks-ee"/"at-ə-RAKS-ee-uh") calmness of the mind and emotions

> This was the ideal and the goal of the Stoic philosophers.

> "...I grew calm again and was restored, in the face of nature's pranks, to my old ataraxy, for what it was worth." — Samuel Beckett, *Molloy*

Professions

Skilled workers

sempster (archaic) a tailor, i.e., a male seamstress

> "…as the fellow was well-beloved in the regiment… my uncle Toby took him for his servant; and of an excellent use was he, attending my uncle Toby… as a valet groom, barber, cook, sempster, and nurse…" — Laurence Sterne, *Tristram Shandy*

fuller one who "fulls" cloth, especially wool

> Fulling is a process, now obsolete, that included cleaning and thickening cloth. The surnames Fuller, Tucker, and Walker all derive from parts of this process.

cordwainer (archaic) a worker who makes shoes with new leather, especially cordovan leather

> In the Middle Ages, Cordoba, Spain, was noted for its fine leather, which the English called *cordwain.* This leather became the preferred choice for making fine footwear. (A *cobbler*, as distinct from a cordwainer, repairs old shoes.)

steeplejack (dated) a person who builds, paints, or repairs steeples, smokestacks, towers, etc.

> "When City Hall's flagpole ropes busted two weeks ago, maintenance supervisor Daynon Arrington couldn't find a steeplejack in Kansas City." — from an article on KansasCity.com, 2017

They shoe horses, don't they?

farrier ("FAR-ee-ər," with the A pronounced as in *arrow*) a blacksmith; or one who shoes horses and trims their hooves

> This word comes to us, as you may have guessed, from the Latin word for *iron*, which also gives us *ferrous*, and which supplies the words for *railroad* in romance languages, e.g., *ferrocarril* and *ferrovia.*

> "Today, farriers use a dull version of this blade to clean the crud from the underside of horse hooves, but other than that, these tools aren't frequently seen anymore." — from an article in *Popular Science*, 2020

currier a specialist in the finishing of tanned leather; or one who cleans the coats of horses, with a currycomb

Some skills required

powder monkey a boy who brought powder to the guns on a sailing warship; or anyone who works with explosives

> "I would have been rather an English powder-monkey or a swab in that great victory than an emperor out of it." — Lady Hamilton, letter to Horatio Nelson, 1798

roustabout an unskilled worker, hired as needed, for example, by traveling carnivals; or a worker on an oil rig; or a dockworker

> You may remember the "Song of the Roustabouts" from *Dumbo:*
>
> "We work all day, we work all night
> We never learned to read or write
> We're happy-hearted roustabouts."
>
> These characters are also Black, muscular, and mainly faceless, working at night in the rain with sledgehammers: one of a few racially uncomfortable moments in that film.

The healing arts

naprapath one who treats disease with nutritional therapy and by manipulating muscles, joints, etc. to stimulate the body's self-healing processes

> In Studs Terkel's oral history, *Working,* one interview is memorably subtitled "Nun to Naprapath."

accoucheur ("ah-koo-SHURR") a man who assists at childbirths: a male midwife or obstetrician

> "Thou eunuch of language… thou arch-heretic in pronunciation: thou pitch-pipe of affected emphasis: thou carpenter, mortising the awkward joints of jarring sentences… thou murderous accoucheur of infant learnings…" — from a rant by Robert Burns against an unnamed critic in 1791

Merchants

draper a dealer in cloth and dry goods

> But what are "dry goods"? I've always wondered. The phrase refers to merchandise related to apparel, including fabric, thread, and finished articles of clothing.
>
> In England, however, the phrase *dry goods* refers to non-liquid groceries.

costermonger (British, historical) a person who sells things (usually fruits and vegetables) from a cart or street stand

> "But for every costermonger that soaked an orange in hot water to make it swell, there are hundreds who gave an honest deal on any product they sold." — from an article in the *Independent Press-Telegram* (Long Beach, California), 1972

chandler one who makes and sells candles; or one who deals in supplies of a specific type, such as a ship's chandler

Experts and artisans

camoufleur ("cam-ə-FLURR") an expert in camouflage, especially of military equipment

> "Norman Wilkinson… was primarily a marine painter, but also an illustrator, poster artist, and wartime camoufleur." — from Wikipedia

"Our camofleur is a genius."

sommelier ("səm-əl-YAY") the wine steward in a fine restaurant, knowledgeable about serving wines and pairing them with foods

> "He poured the awkward liquid with the skill of a *sommelier*." — Margery Allingham, *The Beckoning Lady*

bricoleur ("brik-ə-lurr") a person who creates things with whatever materials are available: i.e., one who practices *bricolage*; or a person who fixes things ingeniously

"A bricoleur of genius, Katchor works… from things he has seen and heard in the street or bought in junkshops and bargain book racks." — from an article about Ben Katchor in the *New York Review of Books,* 2001

Starting at the bottom

helot ("HELL-ət") a serf or slave; or, in ancient Sparta, a serf owned by the state and assigned to work the land for individual Spartans

"…throughout the afternoon her movements have been heavy and deliberate, like those of a helot after two straight shifts…" — John Barth, *Chimera*

Walter Brennan in *Meet John Doe* gives this word a completely different meaning, and a different pronunciation ("HEEL-ots"). He lectures a couple of men about the misery of owning things: "Then you get a hold of some dough and what happens? All those nice, sweet, lovable people become helots—a lot of heels. They begin creepin' up on ya, trying to sell ya something. They get long claws, and they get a strangle-hold on ya… "

scullion ("SKULL-yən") a servant who does menial, unskilled work in a kitchen

"Ay, it's the way with them all, from the scullion to the privy-counsellor. If they have a bad master, they keep quarreling with him; if they have a good master they keep quarreling with one another." — Oliver Goldsmith, *The Good-Natur'd Man*

Quite respectable

syndic ("SIN-dik") a government official or representative (people with this title have different responsibilities in different countries)

Have you ever seen a box of Dutch Masters cigars? The image on the box is taken from Rembrandt's painting, *Syndics of the Drapers' Guild.* (Of course, it has a different name in Dutch: *De waardijns van het Amsterdamse lakenbereidersgilde.*)

sachem ("SAY-chəm") a chief, in some North American Indian tribes; (informal) a leader

"[Governor William] Bradford called in a favor from his main indigenous ally, Massasoit, the Wampanoag sachem…" — from an article in *Smithsonian* magazine, 2020

Tammany Hall, New York City's now-defunct political machine, used this word to refer to its bosses.

plenipotentiary ("plen-ə-poh-TEN-shər-ee") a diplomatic agent fully authorized to act independently on behalf of his/her government; or anyone who has the power to act on someone else's behalf

> "After nearly a decade as Russia's ambassador extraordinary and plenipotentiary, arguably his country's most critical foreign emissary, the sixty-six-year-old [Sergey Kislyak] is now a pariah in Washington." — from an article in *Esquire*, 2017

Somewhat respectable

franklin one who was born a free man but not a noble: a member of the class just below the gentry

> Have you noticed how many of the words in this section became surnames? Who knew that Benjamin Franklin's name had this meaning?

burgher ("BƏRG-ər") a resident of a town or city; or a prosperous member of the middle class

> "But El Paso's burghers had visions for a different Duranguito." — from an article in the *Los Angeles Times*, 2020

Less respectable

ward heeler a worker who performs menial tasks, including canvassing, for an urban political boss (the term is contemptuous)

> "[Al] Smith, an eighth-grade dropout who went to work at 15 to support his widowed mother, was deemed by most a coarse ward heeler beholden to the Tammany Hall satraps who anointed him." — from an article in the *Wall Street Journal,* 2018

picaro ("PEEK-ə-roh" or "PICK-ə-roh") an adventurer or rogue

> The adjective *picaresque,* describing a genre of fiction—in which a roguish but appealing hero has a series of adventures—comes from this word.

> "The cast of characters encompasses a broad series of anti-heroic figures, picaros and politicians, ... taxi drivers and taxidermists." — from a review in *Book* magazine, 2000

bravo a hired killer, or desperado; or a daring villain

> "These are the hired bravos who defend / The tyrant's throne." — Percy Bysshe Shelley, *Queen Mab*

knight of the post (archaic) a professional perjurer, hired by dishonest litigants to give false evidence

> "A Knight of the post... a fellow that will sweare you any thing for twelue pence." — Thomas Nashe, *Pierce Penilesse* (1592)

doxy ("DOK-see") a prostitute; or a floozy; or a mistress

> "'Who the devil would you have me leave my money to?' cried Mr. Treverton... 'To my brother, who thinks me a brute... and who would ... [spend] all my money among doxies and strolling players?'" — Wilkie Collins, *The Dead Secret*

cocotte ("koh-KAHT") prostitute

> "... Count Henkel Donnersmark, the German nobleman who was a wild young diplomat in Paris ... [who] astonished the world by marrying the cocotte La Païva, and changed into a sober and far-seeing industrialist on the grand scale." — Rebecca West, *Black Lamb and Grey Falcon*

> If you want to read a juicy historical tale, look up the life of La Païva. I'm not aware of any novels about her, but it's only a matter of time.

> P.S. Do not confuse *cocotte* with *coquette:* a flirtatious woman, one who seeks the attention and admiration of men by feigning sexual interest.

Entertainers

histrio an actor

> From the same root comes the word *histrionic*, i.e., excessively theatrical.

> "Think how juries bring out the worst in histrionic, gallery-playing lawyers." — from an article by Richard Dawkins in *The Observer*, 1997

mummer (archaic) an actor on the stage; or, an actor in a pantomime, wearing a mask and/or costume

> In Philadelphia's Mummers Parade, held each New Year's Day, clubs compete in gaudy costumes, playing musical instruments.

jongleur ("ZHON-glurr") (historical) a wandering performer in medieval England or France, who entertained with songs, storytelling, juggling, or tumbling

> *Jongleur* and *juggler* come from the same Latin word, *joculare*, to jest, but a *jongleur* can do much more than juggle.

"[A] jongleur… with a small lute slung round him, was making his way… through the throng." — Edward Bulwer-Lytton, *Rienzi*

If you like horsing around

(h)ostler one who takes charge of horses, as at an inn

"But presently he had gone back to the hotel and given his horse into the charge of an ostler and had gone off with the girl into the woods, not quite knowing where he was or what he was doing." — D.H. Lawrence, *The Rainbow*

postilion ("poh-STILL-yən") one who rides the left-hand horse of a team drawing a carriage, especially one without a driver

If you've heard this word before, it was probably in the phrase *My postilion has been struck by lightning*—which for many years enjoyed some fame as the foremost example of preposterously unhelpful sentences to be found in travelers' phrase books. James Thurber alluded to it in an article in the *New Yorker*, and the actor Dirk Bogarde called his autobiography *A Postillion Struck By Lightning.*

equerry ("EK-wə-ree") formerly, an officer in charge of the horses of a royal or noble household; currently, an officer who attends members of the British royal family

"As the royals travel frequently and only stay two days in one area, they have a set routine down… In the morning, expect to hear helicopters arriving to take the family to their next appointment. But no need to rush—the equerry and personal protection officers will gather the luggage while everyone finishes breakfast." — from an article in *Town & Country* magazine, 2019

What's the use? It's all feudal.

liege ("LEEZH" or "LEEJ") a feudal lord to whom allegiance or service is due

"My liege, do not believe it! I am yours— / Yours ever… / To the death, yours!" — Robert Browning, *Strafford*

seneschal ("SEN-ə-shəl") the official in charge of servants in a noble household (during medieval times); a steward

"The seneschal… deigned not to take notice of the groups of inferior guests who were perpetually entering and withdrawing, unless so far as was necessary to preserve order…" — Sir Walter Scott, *Ivanhoe*

sewer a servant of high rank in charge of serving meals in a medieval household

> "Let the master of my lord's household see that both clerk and sewer taste the dishes which the one dresses and the other serves." —Sir Walter Scott, *Kenilworth*

vassal ("VASS-əl") one who receives protection and the use of land from a feudal lord, and in return performs military or other service when required; or any servant or subordinate

> "Presumptuous vassals, are you not asham'd, / With this immodest clamorous outrage / To trouble and disturb the King and us?" — William Shakespeare, *Henry IV, Part I*

yeoman ("YOH-mən") a farmer who works his own land, usually a small holding; or an attendant in a noble or royal household

> The word also serves as an adjective, meaning "loyal, and requiring diligent effort": "Wherever the fleets and armies of England have won renown, there stalwart sons of the Browns have done yeomen's work." — Thomas Hughes, *Tom Brown's School Days*

donzel ("DON-zəl") (archaic) a squire; or a young gentleman who is being trained for knighthood

> "But I, donzel, wear the spurs of knighthood, and to succour the distressed is a duty my oath will not let me swerve from." — Edward Bulwer-Lytton, *The Last of the Barons*

villein (VILL-ən") a serf, partially free but under legal obligation to his feudal lord

> A comment on the connection between villeins and villains: "Villain derives from the Middle English villein… It's a pejorative etymology that illustrates… the anxieties around those who were poor yet free, a state considered suspect. Thus, villeins were blamed for the evils disrupting an otherwise peaceful world." — Marisha Pessl, in the *New York Times*, 2017

Oh, to sit back and watch the money pour in

rentier ("RON-tyay") one who earns all or most of his/her income from property rentals or investments

> "Indeed, mainstream economics has become a celebration of the wealthy *rentier* class for a century now…" — from the website Evonomics.com, 2016

If you meet one of these, let me know

tedder a person (or a machine) that spreads new-cut grass for drying

> "The mowers and tedders, sitting in the shade with their bread and cheese and beer, call out to the idler as he passes..." — Philip Robinson, *The Valley of Teetotum Trees*

They also serve who serve

famulus ("FAM-yə-ləss") an assistant or attendant, especially to a sorcerer

> Here, deployed allegorically, is a depiction of a scene you may recognize: "Such is the fortune of war, especially of revolution... It is a dangerous thing such magic. The Magician's Famulus got hold of the forbidden Book, and summoned a goblin: ... What is your will? said the Goblin. The Famulus... bade him fetch water: the swift goblin fetched it, pail in each hand; but lo, would not cease fetching it! Desperate, the Famulus shrieks at him, smites at him, cuts him in two; lo, *two* goblin water-carriers ply; and the house will be swum away in... Deluges." — Thomas Carlyle, *The French Revolution*

factotum ("fak-TOH-təm") (Latin: "do everything") an employee or assistant who does all kinds of work

> "...Detroit Tigers reliever Buck Farmer, the factotum of the bullpen." — from an article in the *Detroit Free Press*, 2021

> I worked as a secretary in the office of Columbia University's Philosophy Department long ago. When there was no work to be done, I would read or write. One of the graduate students, who often found me thus (un)employed, coined a title for me: *facnihil,* or Do Nothing.

servitor ("SERV-ə-tər") an adherent or follower; a servant or attendant

> "The Lord Mayor of London has his own toastmaster as well as his individual liveried servitor who attends and serves him when he dines." — from an article in *The Bellman* magazine, 1918

pursuivant ("PER-swə-vənt") an attendant or follower; or a junior officer of arms (i.e., one who takes part in state or other institutional ceremonies)

> "In all the land that falcon was the best, / The master's pride and passion and delight, / And the sole pursuivant of this poor

knight." — Henry Wadsworth Longfellow, *Tales of a Wayside Inn*

abigail a lady's personal maid

> "…the Master of the Ceremonies leading, with great solemnity, … an antiquated Abigail, dressed in her lady's cast-clothes; whom he (I suppose) mistook for some countess just arrived at the Bath." — Tobias Smollett, *Humphry Clinker*

Opportunities in the religious field

apostle ("ə-POSS-əl") someone sent out on a special mission or as a preacher; or (with a capital A) one of the twelve men Jesus sent out into the world to preach his Gospel

> "Who has not heard of… Miss Nightingale and Miss Garrett as apostles of hospital nursing?" — Samuel Smiles, *Character*

hierophant ("HAI-rə-fant") an interpreter of sacred mysteries (especially in ancient Greece) or esoteric principles

> The first hierophants were the priests who presided over the Eleusinian Mysteries: the annual initiations into the cult of Demeter and Persephone in Eleusis, near Athens.

> "The journalist Ron Rosenbaum, the unofficial grand vizier and first hierophant of Portis admirers, has called him 'perhaps the most original, indescribable sui generis talent overlooked by literary culture in America.'"— from an article about Charles Portis, author of *True Grit*, in the *New York Times*, 2010

mystagogue ("MISS-tə-gog") one who initiates others into a religious or mystical order, or teaches others in preparation for initiation; or (pejoratively) someone who creates or exploits mystery

> "She is… a common mystagogue. She does not, like a decent demagogue, wish to make people understand; she wishes to make them painfully conscious of not understanding." — G.K. Chesterton, *All Things Considered*

nuncio ("NUN-see-oh") the papal ambassador to a foreign government; or any messenger

> "On Saturday, the Vatican announced that the Nicaraguan government had expelled the papal nuncio, … who had mediated in talks between the government and opposition…" — from an article in the *Washington Post*, 2022

verger a person who takes care of the interior of a church; or an official who carries a rod (or other symbol of office) before dignitaries of a church or university

> "How splendid an opportunity for architectural study is afforded by the Abbey, if only the vergers would allow anyone to enjoy it." — from an article in the *Saturday Review*, 1861

postulant a candidate for membership in a religious order

> "She trembled like a postulant when she wrote the Greek alphabet for the first time." — D.H. Lawrence, *The Rainbow*

beadle a minor parish officer in the Church of England, who keeps order in church

> In *Oliver Twist* (and in the musical *Oliver!*), Mr. Bumble, the Beadle, has a memorable scene. Blaming his transgressions on his wife ("She *would* do it"), he is told that "the law supposes that your wife acts under your direction." Mr. Bumble replies indignantly, "If the law supposes that… the law is a ass—a idiot."

eremite ("ERR-ə-mite") a religious recluse

> "The Thoreau-style hermit claims to be concerned only for his or her individual salvation, but also wants to be admired and even emulated. *Walden*, after all, is a kind of how-to guide, a self-help book for aspiring eremites." — from an article in *The New Republic*, 2017

> Note that *eremite* and *hermit* come from the same root, and mean almost the same thing.

anchorite ("ANG-kə-rite") an eremite; or a solitary, unsocial person

> "You live the life of an anchorite here, never coming to the city, and I remain in retirement, scarcely ever going from the city." — John Lesperance, *The Bastonnais*

cenobite ("SEH-nə-bite") a member of a religious order living in a monastery or convent

> "The anchorites and cœnobites were drawn by the sight of these wild mountains." — Arthur Stanley, *Sinai and Palestine*

trilobite ("TRY-lə-bite") an extinct arthropod of the Paleozoic era

> Sorry, I couldn't resist.

To divine is to err

rhabdomancer one who divines (i.e., predicts the future or seeks hidden knowledge) using a rod, wand, or stick

"Although my aura supposedly measured only a few inches, after I had compliantly meditated for a few moments, it expanded to several feet—or so the rhabdomancer claimed." — Joe Nickell, *Real-Life X Files*

dowser ("DAO-zər") a person who uses a divining rod (a forked rod, also known as a dowser) to find underground water or minerals

"…an old man… arrived blindfolded with a forked tree branch in hand. He was a dowser, and the branch was his divining rod… It quickly led him to a source of water. The divining rod pulled the dowser up the driveway, past the cabin… and over the full length of our dock to its end, where he—*sploosh!*—fell into four feet of lake water." — from a book review in the *New York Times,* 2017

chiromancer ("KAI-roh-man-sər") one who predicts a person's future by studying the lines on his/her palms: a palm reader

"His pilgrimages ultimately took him to St. Petersburg, which was in the thrall of the occult and the supernatural. Séances were a fad; so were hypnotism, chiromancy and telepathy." — from a review of a biography of Rasputin in the *New York Times,* 2016

"There seems to be a gap in your life line, Frederick."

"That was when the aliens took me."

haruspex ("HAR-ə-spex," with the A pronounced as in *arrow*) in ancient Rome, one who studied the entrails of sacrificial animals to predict the future

"'Am I to be frightened,' he said, in answer to some report of the haruspices, 'because a sheep is without a heart?'" — James Froude, *Caesar: a Sketch*

sortilegist ("SOR-tə-lidg-ist") one who foretells the future by casting lots or drawing objects randomly from a group

> By the way: "The practice of casting lots is mentioned seventy times in the Old Testament and seven times in the New Testament. In spite of the many references to casting lots... nothing is known about the actual lots themselves. They could have been sticks of various lengths, flat stones like coins, or some kind of dice; but their exact nature is unknown. The closest modern practice to casting lots is likely flipping a coin." — from an article on the website GotQuestions.org

oneiromancer ("oh-NYE-roh-man-sər") one who predicts the future by interpreting dreams

> Remember Joseph in the Bible, interpreting the Pharaoh's dreams and predicting seven fat years and seven lean years? He was an oneiromancer!

Opportunities in the Muslim world

mullah ("MULL-ə" or "MOOL-ə") a Muslim teacher or interpreter of religious law; a general title of respect for a man learned in Islamic theology

> "This argument will probably permeate Israeli decision-making as long as Iran is ruled by mullahs and the Revolutionary Guards." — from an article in the *New York Review of Books*, 2020

mufti ("MUFF-tee") a judge who gives rulings on personal and religious matters, based on Muslim law; or civilian clothing, when worn by one who usually wears a uniform, such as a soldier

> How did this word come to serve two such different purposes? The *Oxford English Dictionary* speculates that it may be because a 19th-century British officer's off-duty attire (dressing gown, tasseled smoking cap, slippers) resembled a mufti's—at least, as muftis were portrayed on stage.

> "He looked a little like a dean in mufti on his summer holiday in Switzerland." — W. Somerset Maugham, *Cakes and Ale*

mameluke ("MAM-ə-luke") a military class in medieval Egypt, composed of former slave soldiers, which eventually ruled the country; or, alternately, a slave soldier, or a freed slave

"I shall not tell how that one solitary Mameluke jumped his horse a hundred feet down from the battlements of the citadel and escaped, because I do not think much of that—I could have done it myself." — Mark Twain, *The Innocents Abroad*

Confession: Every time I see this word, I think of the Great Dane in the comic strip *Marmaduke.*

sultana ("səl-TAN-ə") the wife of a sultan (the ruler of a Muslim country); or his mother, sister, daughter, or mistress

The *Sultana* was also the name of a Mississippi steamboat that exploded and burned in 1865, twelve days after Lincoln's assassination. More than 1,000 passengers died, including many released Union prisoners, making this the worst maritime disaster in U.S. history. (Conspiracy theories blaming sabotage have largely been dismissed.)

dragoman ("DRAG-ə-mən") an interpreter or professional guide for travelers in countries speaking Arabic, Turkish, or Persian

"…the 'barbarian' turns out to be a prince, even though Diana Standing (Miss [Myrna] Loy) for some time imagines him to be a mere dragoman…" — from a review of a 1933 movie, *The Barbarian,* in the *New York Times*

See the world: other distant opportunities

muzhik ("moo-ZHEEK") in Czarist Russia, a peasant

"While muzhik historically was the word for a male peasant, in contemporary usage it has the meaning of a 'man's man' or 'tough guy', and implies a simplicity and roughness of character." — from an article in the *St. Petersburg* (Florida, not Russia!) *Times,* 2001

kulak ("koo-LOCK" or "koo-LACK") in Czarist Russia, a peasant rich enough to own his own farm and hire workers

The Russian word *kulak* means "fist."

Under Stalin, huge numbers of kulaks were exiled or murdered. (About two million were sent to Siberia and the north.)

"In 1929 Stalin began to 'eliminate' the *kulaks* as a class." — Michael Harrington, *Socialism*

bonze ("BAHNZ") a Buddhist monk, especially one from East Asia

In South Vietnam in the 1960s, several bonzes set themselves on fire to protest the government's persecution of Buddhists.

Americans who followed the news learned two new words in those days: *bonze* and *self-immolation.*

sirdar ("SƏR-dar") in India, a nobleman, or someone holding an important position

> "Kanchha... saw the teams passing through Namche on their way to the mountain and noticed Tenzing Norgay, the charismatic *sirdar* (foreman) of the expeditions' high-altitude porters." — from an article in *National Geographic,* 2019

lascar ("LASS-kər") a sailor from India, Southeast Asia, or the Arab world

> Lascars worked on European ships from the 1500s to the mid-20th century.

> "... the magic charm of foreign lands... Where the tumbling surf, / O'er the coral reefs of Madagascar, / Washes the feet of the swarthy Lascar, / As he lies alone and asleep on the turf." — Henry Wadsworth Longfellow, "The Building of the Ship"

curé ("kyoo-RAY") in France, a parish priest

> Although this looks like a cognate of the English term *curate*, that word generally refers to clergy who assist the parish priest.

> "...the curé from time to time looked into the church, where the kneeling boys were shouldering one another, and tumbling over like packs of cards." — Gustave Flaubert, *Madame Bovary* (translated by Eleanor Marx-Aveling)

caudillo ("cow-DEE-yoh") a military or political leader in a Spanish-speaking country; or a military dictator

> Spain's Francisco Franco claimed this title for himself in 1938, following the example of Mussolini, who called himself *Il Duce,* and Hitler, who called himself *Der Führer.*

> "In 1988 García Márquez wrote a profile of the 'caudillo' (as he calls [Castro]) that was published as the prologue to *Habla Fidel, or Fidel Speaks...*" — from an article in *The New Republic,* 2009

angakok/angekok ("ANG-gə-kahk") an Eskimo/Inuit shaman: one who is believed to have magical healing powers through contact with spirits

> "The angakok is also called upon to change the weather, prevent or repair injuries... and to enhance personal success in a variety of areas." — Christina Pratt, *An Encyclopedia of Shamanism*

laird in Scotland, the owner of a large estate

Laird derives from the English *Lord,* but is more closely equivalent to an English esquire: above a gentleman, but below a baron.

I love a man in a uniform

hussar ("hə-ZAR") a soldier in a light cavalry regiment, with a bright uniform

> The Hussars originated in Hungary in the 1400s. Their distinctive uniform was imitated by other European armies in later centuries, along with the title.

> "Nesvítski could hardly keep from laughter provoked by a swarthy hussar officer who walked beside him. This hussar, with a grave face and without a smile or a change in the expression of his fixed eyes, watched the regimental commander's back and mimicked his every movement." — Leo Tolstoy, *War and Peace*

dragoon ("drə-GOON") originally, a soldier who could fight either on horseback or on foot; or, as a verb, to force someone to do something

> Dragoons got their name from their muskets, also called dragoons, which "breathed fire" like mythical dragons.

> "He wasn't to be dragooned into doing or not doing anything." — Thomas Hughes, *Tom Brown at Oxford*

chasseur ("SHA-surr," the A pronounced as in *arrow*) a hunter; or a light cavalry soldier, trained and equipped for rapid maneuvering

> This word is also appended to the names of dishes to indicate that they have been cooked in a white wine sauce with mushrooms and shallots, e.g., "rotisserie chicken *chasseur*." That's because the sauce was originally used to cook wild game brought home by hunters.

"Hey, all those soldiers are getting hungry"

sutler ("SUTT-lər") one who sells provisions to soldiers, either in the field or at an army post

> "There were only a few hundred of them [Venezuelans living in Florence, Italy]: they kept to themselves and worked either in the tobacco factory or at the Mercato Centrale, or as sutlers to the Fourth Army Corps..." — Thomas Pynchon, *V.*

vivandière ("vee-vahn-DYAIR") a female sutler, selling food, supplies, and liquor

[During the 1848 revolution in France] "Women went about disguised as *vivandières*, giving poisoned brandy to the soldiers." — Henry Greville, *Diary*

A few odds and ends

goodman ("GOOD-mən") (archaic) a husband, or master of a household

> The term was also used before a man's name—for those below the rank of gentleman—as in "Young Goodman Brown," the title of a famous story by Nathaniel Hawthorne, which tells of a Puritan husband who believes he sees his pious wife and all the town's respectable citizens giving their allegiance to the devil in the woods one night. He is embittered and suspicious forever after.

cicerone (siss-ə-ROH-nee") a guide who explains antiquities or art to visitors, especially in a museum

> The word comes to us from Cicero, the ancient Roman statesman, renowned for his eloquence as an orator.

> But I challenge any American to hear this word and not think of Rice-a-Roni.

poetaster ("POH-ə-tass-tər") a writer of mediocre verse, or a would-be writer; the term implies that the poet has unjustified pretensions to literary excellence

> "Roy Thayer… had squandered a decade of gray life on an erudite work dealing with a forgotten group of unnecessary poetasters…" — Vladimir Nabokov, *Pnin*

interlocutor ("in-tər-LOCK-yə-tər") a person who takes part in a conversation; or, in a minstrel show, the one in the middle who asks questions of the "end man"

> "'It's you, Moss, is it?' said the Colonel, who appeared to know his interlocutor." — William Makepeace Thackeray, *Vanity Fair*

subdeb ("SUB-deb" or "sub-DEB") (informal, for *subdebutante*) a girl in her teens, not yet old enough for her debut into society

> "The season's debutantes danced their way into society while eager sub-debs looked on." — from an article in *Time* magazine, 1947

thaumaturge ("THAW-mə-tərge") a performer of miracles; or a magician

"The message minus the mumbo jumbo: that's what [Thomas] Jefferson was after. The teachings… without the supernatural baggage. Jesus the *ethicist*, Jesus the *philosopher*… Of this Jesus Jefferson was indeed a fan. Of Jesus the dusty thaumaturge, the wandering soul-zapper and self-styled son of God, less so." — from an article in the *Atlantic,* 2020

Multifarious Modifiers: Adjectives

Here you'll find adjectives not primarily associated with people: words that capture everything from light and darkness to excellence and awfulness.

Let there be light!

incandescent ("in-kan-DESS-ənt") shining intensely with heat; very bright; or passionate

> I always assumed this word referred to the new technology used in Edison's light bulb. But no... the first occurrence of the word predates Edison's invention by nearly a century, according to the *Oxford English Dictionary*.

> "The enjoyment of reading The Enchanter is comparable to the one afforded by studying Beethoven's published sketchbooks: seeing the murky and unpromising material out of which the writer and the composer were later able to fashion an incandescent masterpiece." — from a review of a newly translated Nabokov story (an early version of *Lolita*) in the *Washington Post,* 1986

fulgent, refulgent shining brilliantly; dazzling

> "Bestowing upon the locksmith a most refulgent smile, he left them." — Charles Dickens, *Barnaby Rudge*

lambent ("LAM-bənt") luminous; glowing gently; or flickering

> "Finally, a razor-sharp line appeared ahead of us where the lambent sea ended and blackness began." — from an article in *Smithsonian* magazine, 2022

lucent ("LOO-sənt") luminous; or translucent

> AT&T spun off its equipment manufacturing business in 1996 and called the new entity Lucent Technologies. What the word has to do with telephones, I can't say.

rutilant ("ROO-tə-lənt") glowing or glittering with a reddish or golden light

> "He had a round head as bare as a knee, a corpse's button nose, and very white, very limp, very damp hands adorned with rutilant gems." — Vladimir Nabokov, *Ada*

tenebrous ("TEN-ə-brəss") dark, shadowy, gloomy

> "Over their heads the towering and tenebrous boughs of the cypress / Met in a dusky arch..." — Henry Wadsworth Longfellow, *Evangeline*

"Lovely scenery, don't you think?"
"Mm. A bit tenebrous for my taste."

fuliginous ("few-LIDG-ə-nəss") dark; full of smoke or soot (the word derives from the Latin word for soot, *fuligo*)

> "His head like a smoke-jack;—the funnel unswept, and the ideas whirling round and round about in it, all obfuscated and darkened over with fuliginous matter!" — Laurence Sterne, *Tristram Shandy*

caliginous ("kə-LIDG-ə-nəss") dark, shadowy, misty, murky

> "You clinking, clanking, clattering collection of caliginous junk!" — The Wizard of Oz to the Tin Man (He seems to be misusing the word, but it sounds good.)

stygian ("STIDG-ee-ən") dark, hellish; relating to the river Styx, which flows through Hades (in Greek myth, that is)

> "After a five-minute ride through the stygian darkness, the barge eases up to a low dock." — from an article in *Wired* magazine, 2017

subfusc ("sub-FUSK") drab, dark, dull; also, the attire worn at exams and/or formal occasions at some British universities, e.g., Oxford

> "We were in a bleak, subfusc East London world of poverty, crime, stunted ambition and rather good rock music." — from an article in *The Spectator*, 2010

Sounds, resonant and otherwise

plangent ("PLAN-jənt") striking with a deep, reverberating sound; the word often describes a sound expressing sadness

> "Even though his singing is freer and more forward than ever, its plangent timbre always carries at least a trace of pain." — from a review of a posthumously released album by Elliott Smith, in the *Los Angeles Times*, 2004

reboant ("REB-oh-ənt" or "reb-OH-ənt") reverberating loudly

> "I heard myself laugh an ugly, reboant laugh, my mouth widening in a malevolent sneer." — Marilyn Manson and Neil Strauss, *The Long Hard Road Out of Hell*

orotund ("AW-rə-tənd") full, resonant, clear, strong (referring to a voice); the word can also mean showy, pompous, or bombastic (referring to a style of speaking)

> "Such windy eloquence is not poetry: it has nothing of charm, of natural magic... but it has a certain orotund effectiveness." — from an article in the *Daily Chronicle* (London), 1906

purling moving in ripples, or with a soft, murmuring sound; swirling

> "Paris. Paris. Everything happens here... Shutters going up with a bang and little streams purling in the gutters." — Henry Miller, *Tropic of Cancer*

clamant ("KLAY-mənt") noisy; or urgent, pressing

> "And then high up in the firmamental darkness we heard the clamant cries of some great, passing birds." — O. Henry, "The Door of Unrest"

> Cf. *clamorous*, which comes from the same Latin root.

antiphonal ("an-TIFF-ə-nəl") sung or chanted in alternation by two groups, especially as part of Christian ritual

"The couple tell their story through antiphonal narration, or alternating diary entries about their encounters with friends and family who share their shallow values." — from a review of the novel *The Marriage Diaries*, on the website OneMinuteBookReviews.com, 2006

Good things

bodacious ("bo-DAY-shəss") remarkable, excellent; or very attractive

Perhaps because of its first three letters, this word is often used to mean "having a voluptuous body."

"This... fitness diva is more than just a bodacious bod, a megawatt smile and an easy laugh." — from an article in *Muscle & Fitness*, 2003

The word enjoyed a surge in popularity due to its repeated use in the 1989 movie *Bill and Ted's Excellent Adventure.*

ineffable inexpressible in words

Ineffable can also be used as a noun, meaning "that which is inexpressible."

"'Goodbye, romantic moon,' lamented an unknown writer... in 1957. ... Lunar science was tarnishing the perfect pearly light, which bestowed ethereal beauty and inspired contemplations of the ineffable." — from an article in *Popular Science, 2020*

pukka/pukkah ("PUKK-ə") (originally Hindi) genuine, authentic; or high quality

"Mrs. Turton closed her eyes... and remarked that Mr. Fielding wasn't pukka, and had better marry Miss Quested, for she wasn't pukka." — E.M. Forster, *A Passage to India*

eurhythmic ("yoo-RITH-mik," with the TH pronounced either as in *the* or *with*) characterized by harmonious proportions, especially in art or architecture

Related but different: *eurhythmics* refers to a system of music education, pioneered by Émile Jaques-Dalcroze, in which students move spontaneously in response to improvised music, trying to express what they hear. (Look up a picture of M. Jaques-Dalcroze. He had a funny mustache.)

But to anyone who was sentient in the early 1980s, the word (spelled *Eurythmics*) means the band with Annie Lennox, who sang, "Sweet Dreams (Are Made of This)."

egregious ("ə-GREE-jəss") outstanding in a bad way

"... the public perception is that too many corporate executives have committed egregious breaches of trust by cooking the books, shading the truth, and enriching themselves with huge stock-option profits while shareholders suffered breathtaking losses." — from an article in *Business Week*, 2002

Mr. Catania, my sixth-grade teacher, always encouraged his students to expand their vocabularies. At the end of the year, he began his inscription in my autograph book this way: "I would be egregiously remiss in my pedagogical functions if I failed to..."

fulsome ("FULL-səm") excessive, overdone, offensive, sickening; when describing praise, it also implies that the praise is insincere

"Her servility and fulsome compliments when Emmy was in prosperity were not more to that lady's liking." — William Makepeace Thackeray, *Vanity Fair*

meretricious ("mer-ə-TRIH-shəss") attractive but tawdry and without real value or integrity; (archaic) like a prostitute

"All here is false; all is meretricious." — Virginia Wolff, *The Waves*

brummagem ("BRUM-ə-jem" or "-jəm") cheap, gaudy (or, as a noun, anything that's brummagem)

What a strange word! Where did it come from? Answer: from Birmingham, England, in the 1600s, when the locals pronounced the city's name this way. The city was known as a place where counterfeit coins were made—and, later, as the source of cheap jewelry. You can deduce the rest.

"It is not only rococo; it is brummagem rococo." — Edmund Wilson, in a review of the play *Clair de Lune,* featuring John and Ethel Barrymore, 1921

otiose ("OH-tee-ose" or "OH-shee-ose") serving no practical purpose; lazy, ineffectual, idle

"Large sections of the English language were also rendered otiose by replacing long words with small words hyphenated together." — Michael Frayn, *The Tin Men*

carking (poetic/archaic) causing distress, worry

When you see this word, you will usually see the word *care* following it, as in this fragment: "...a sense of something left undone, of some fearful obstacle to be surmounted, of some carking care that would not be driven away..." — Charles Dickens, *The Old Curiosity Shop*

internecine ("in-tər-NEH-seen" or "-NEE-sine" or "-NEE-sən") relating to conflict within a group; or producing great destruction on both sides

Originally, this word simply meant *deadly*. The connotation of casualties on both sides arrived later. Currently, it chiefly refers to conflicts between factions within a group—but most people think it simply means, *very bloody.*

"The story chronicles the rise and fall of the onetime Wall Street powerhouse Lehman Brothers, covering nearly two centuries of bristling ambition, greed, economic history and internecine family warfare." — from roundup of theater reviews in *Time* magazine, 2019 (referring to *The Lehman Trilogy*)

scabrous ("SCAB-rəss," with the A pronounced as in *arrow*, or "SKABE-rəss") scandalous, indecent; or abusive; or rough-textured, as if covered with scabs

"I would ask everyone reading this to ignore the sensationalist, scabrous headlines and focus instead on the joy that Don [McLean]... has given to so many for so long."— from an article in *Rolling Stone*, 2016

helter-skelter in confusion, haste, or disorder; in England, a spiral slide at a fair or amusement park

The phrase can also be used as an adverb: "Away we all went, helter skelter, through the dry grass." — Samuel White Baker, *The Nile Tributaries of Abyssinia and the Sword Hunters of the Hamran Arabs* (Can we pause for a moment and appreciate that title?)

The Beatles song "Helter Skelter," on the White Album, begins, "When I get to the bottom, I go back to the top of the slide..." Charles Manson interpreted the song as a prediction of race war in the U.S. (more evidence that he was insane); he imagined a chain of events in which he and his followers survived and emerged as rulers, a scenario he called Helter Skelter. A book about the Manson case, written by the lead prosecutor, used the phrase as its title.

Hop to it!

exigent ("EKS-ə-jənt") urgently requiring attention; or demanding

When I see this word, I'm transported back to childhood, to the
Savarin coffee commercials featuring El Exigente, the Demanding
One, the exporter's agent who gave the nod to a village's beans.
Approval meant a celebration; I can still hear the melody.

And by the way, when Harvey Keitel sips a cup of coffee in *Pulp
Fiction* and nods his approval, I assume that's Tarantino's nod to
these commercials.

peremptory ("pər-EMP-tə-ree") demanding immediate obedience,
without leaving room for questions, delays, or refusals; or, in law, not
appealable

During jury selection, attorneys are allowed a small number of
peremptory challenges, differing by jurisdiction and type of case:
i.e., the right to reject potential jurors without stating a reason.
"The Court permitted prosecutors and defense attorneys to
engage in covert racial discrimination during jury selection. The
mechanism was a system of peremptory challenges." — from an
article in *The New Republic*, 1992

In its more general usage: "He spoke in a loud
and peremptory voice, using the tone of one in authority who
checks idle prattle and settles a matter forever..." — Booth
Tarkington, *The Magnificent Ambersons*

Unflattering ways to describe writing or talk

tendentious ("ten-DEN-shəss") biased; written or said to promote a
cause, especially a controversial one

"Polls can have their own politics, and media polls are often
accused of being tendentious." — from an opinion essay in the
Wall Street Journal, 2021

sententious ("sen-TEN-shəss") terse or full of aphorisms; or tending
to moralize, especially in a pompous, pretentious way

"I was raised on words... Sententious flotsam from the
Edwardian-era Socialist Party of Great Britain hung around our
kitchen promoting the True Cause." — from an article by Tony
Judt in the *New York Review of Books,* 2010

turgid ("TƏR-jəd") swollen, bloated; or (said of writing) bombastic,
pompous

"His verbose and turgid style, too, is destitute of all genuine
feeling." — Robert A. Vaughan, *Hours With the Mystics*

Note, too, that the playboy general played by George C. Scott in *Dr. Strangelove* was named Buck Turgidson.

specious ("SPEE-shəss") seemingly plausible but actually false or fallacious; deceptive

> "Trump and his allies furiously pressured authorities in those states to replace Biden's electors with ones for him on specious... allegations that his victory was stolen." — from an article in the *Chicago Tribune*, 2022

incondite poorly constructed; unpolished; crude (usually refers to a literary work)

> "The question of arrangement had to be considered; I did not like to offer a mere incondite miscellany." — George Gissing, *The Private Papers of Henry Ryecroft*

agonistic ("agg-ə-NISS-tik") argumentative; polemical; striving to defeat an opponent in argument

> The origin story: in ancient Greece, an *agon* was an athletic competition. Those physical conflicts lent their name to battles of words.

> "Advocates of agonistic rhetoric presume that deliberation among people with different perspectives enables both individuals and communities to understand a topic more thoroughly." — Patricia Roberts-Miller, *Fanatical Schemes: Proslavery Rhetoric and the Tragedy of Consensus*

invidious ("in-VID-ee-əss") tending to arouse resentment or animosity; offensive; or containing a slight

> "The more invidious reason to claim that people are born with certain traits is to avoid having to help people do any better." — from an article about gender stereotypes and mathematical ability, in *Wired* magazine, 2020

This, that, and the other thing

desultory ("DESS-əl-taw-ree") lacking in order or planning; or, describing a conversation, jumping randomly from one topic to another

> "[Malcolm] Muggeridge... studied natural sciences in a desultory way, and graduated with an undistinguished degree and few prospects." — from an article in *National Review*, 2020

excursive rambling; full of digressions

"...he felt a great homesickness for St. Botolphs—for a place whose streets were as excursive and crooked as the human mind..." — John Cheever, *The Wapshot Chronicle*

Sharp

mordacious ("more-DAY-shəss") biting, severely critical, sarcastic

The word can refer to a person or to speech or writing. You can describe someone's wit as mordacious, or you can describe the person him/herself as mordacious. You can even call a dog mordacious, because the word also means *tending to bite.*

"A small-scale L.A. musical in which that mordacious man-about-necks [i.e., Dracula] figures prominently." — from a review in the *Washington Post*, 1978

piquant ("PEE-kənt" or "PEE-kwənt") provocative, in an appealing way; or pleasantly sharp-tasting

"The flavour of her slang was piquant to him." — D.H. Lawrence, *Women in Love*

These imply approval

apposite ("APP-ə-zit") pertinent; or appropriate

"In that regard, Mr. Obama seems an apposite speaker at Mandela's centenary." — from an article in the *Wall Street Journal*, 2018

Its opposite, *inapposite,* means, as you may have guessed, "not pertinent, or inappropriate."

condign ("kən-DINE") well-deserved, or appropriate (most commonly referring to punishment)

"For a Christian, no Beyond is acceptable or imaginable without the participation of God in our eternal destiny, and this in turn implies a condign punishment for every sin, great and small." — Vladimir Nabokov, *Pale Fire* (This quote comes from the commentary of Charles Kinbote, Nabokov's fictional academic.)

irrefragable ("ih-REF-rə-gə-bəl") indisputable; irrefutable

"I look to [the early Italian masters] as in all points of principle... the most irrefragable authorities." — John Ruskin, *Modern Painters*

apodictic ("app-ə-DIK-tik") incontrovertible; proven by evidence

"In the heights of Geometry… there exist truths of apodictic force in Reason, which the mere Understanding strives in vain to comprehend." — Samuel Taylor Coleridge, *The Statesman's Manual*

pellucid ("pə-LOO-sid") very clear, like glass; or clear in meaning, easily understood

> The Latin root *luc-*, which means *to shine*, gives us many words, including *lucid, pellucid, translucent, lucent, elucidate,* and even *lustrous.*

> "Greatest miracle of all, a tiny stream of pellucid water was flowing down the Gulch." — Louis Tracy, *The Terms of Surrender*

daedal ("DEE-dəl") skillfully made, ingenious; or intricate

> This word comes to us from Daedalus, the mythological figure who designed the maze in which the Minotaur lurked, and who later escaped from a prison tower with his son Icarus by making wings with wax and feathers. (Did you ever wonder where he got all the feathers and wax? According to Encyclopedia.com, "Day after day, he collected the feathers of birds. He also gathered wax from a beehive.")

You don't want to find these words in a review of your work

factitious ("fak-TIH-shəss") contrived, artificial, inauthentic

> The first four letters seem to suggest that this word means something like *factual.* How did it come to mean something so nearly opposite? Here's how: its Latin root is *fact-*, meaning manufactured, i.e., not natural.

> "He objects to stage plays, because they arouse in the audience factitious emotion of a hysterical and unprofitable sort." — Rebecca West, *Celebration*

inutile ("in-YOO-təl") useless; not usable; pointless

> "Beyond the tilled plain, beyond the toy roofs, there would be a low suffusion of inutile loveliness, a low sun in a platinum haze with a warm, peeled-peach tinge pervading the upper edge of a two-dimensional, dove-grey cloud fusing with the distant amorous mist." — Vladimir Nabokov, *Lolita*

nugatory ("NOO-gə-taw-ree") worthless; unimportant; useless

> "Mr. Joyboy was not a handsome man… But these physical defects were nugatory when set against his moral earnestness and

the compelling charm of his softly resonant voice." — Evelyn Waugh, *The Loved One*

inchoate ("in-KOH-ət" or "IN-kə-WAIT") not completely formed, because still at an early stage

"To walk the streets of Santiago [Chile] was to read a collective, anonymous scroll of inchoate rage..." — from an article in the *New Yorker,* 2020

Subject to change

labile ("LAY-bile") unstable, apt to change; emotionally unstable

"His moods were certainly labile and when things were going well they could be markedly euphoric." — Ernest Jones, *The Life and Work of Sigmund Freud*

"He seemed to her unstable, off center. The term often used in *Psychology Today* was 'labile.'" — Saul Bellow, *Him With His Foot in His Mouth*

provisory ("prə-VIZE-ə-ree") conditional, temporary, provisional

"A provisory decision was made... to halt payments until it was clear that the money would not end up in terrorist hands." — from an article in the *Jerusalem Post,* 2006

saltatory ("SAWL-tə-taw-ree") moving or changing abruptly; or pertaining to (or adapted for) leaping or dancing

"Nature hates calculators; her methods are saltatory and impulsive." — Ralph Waldo Emerson, "Experience"

deliquescent tending to melt, dissolve, or turn to liquid, especially by absorbing moisture from the air

"...Mrs. O'Callaghan had taken it into her head to give [a Virgin Mary statue] a vigorous scrubbing... and this had taken off the paint. It had also taken off most of the left cheek, so that the Virgin now hoved in her shadowy corner, chalk-white, leperous and deliquescent." — T.H. White, *The Elephant and the Kangaroo*

redux ("ree-DUCKS" or "REE-ducks") brought back; or revisited

This is one of the few adjectives in English that *follow* the nouns they modify: as in the title of John Updike's novel, *Rabbit Redux* (a sequel to *Rabbit, Run*).

"But the 1980s were far more than just the '50s redux." — from an article in *Spy* magazine, 1993

At least these two words will no longer seem abstruse or recondite to you

abstruse unfamiliar to most people; or hard to understand

"If the bank's lawyers are right, the plot was extraordinarily abstruse." — from an article in the *New Yorker*, 2020

Joey found the Harry Potter books somewhat abstruse.

recondite ("REK-ən-dite") abstruse

"I noticed that whenever he felt his enigmas were becoming too recondite, even for such a solver as I, he would lure me back with an easy one." — Vladimir Nabokov, *Lolita*

Complete

compendious comprehensive—especially if concise as well

"…only the most thoroughly documented, compendious account could do justice to the Kochs' bizarre and Byzantine family history and the scale and scope of their influence." — from a review in the *New York Times*, 2016

plenary ("PLEH-nə-ree") complete; or absolute

You will most often see this word used to describe a meeting at which all members are present (even if they usually meet in smaller groups): "At the final plenary session of the Congress, this invitation was accepted." — from an article in *Nature* magazine, 1931."

A surprising pair of opposites

parochial ("pə-ROH-kee-əl) having a narrow outlook; or limited in scope; or relating to a church parish

"Historians… warn us sternly against setting up our parochial values as universally valid." — Isaiah Berlin, *Historical Inevitability*

catholic broad in interests, sympathies, tastes, etc.; inclusive

"… I can read almost anything. I bless my stars for a taste so catholic, so unexcluding." — Charles Lamb, "Detached Thoughts on Books and Reading"

Naming names

onomastic ("ahn-ə-MASS-tik") pertaining to names, or the study of their origins

"In their onomastic vanity, long-distance hauliers tend to name their juggernauts after themselves." — from an article in the *Times* of London, 1999

eponymous ("ə-PAHN-ə-məss," the second syllable rhyming with *gone*) named after a person; or giving one's name to something, e.g., a city, an era, or a television show

Note that the word can describe either the thing named after the person ("Stinky Fensterbaum's eponymous TV show"), or the person who gave his/her name to the thing ("the eponymous star of *The Stinky Fensterbaum Show*").

Among the answers to the crossword clue *eponymous 1990s sitcom* found by the Crossword Solver (on the website wordplays.com) are *Ellen, Cybill,* and *Seinfeld.*

heteronymous having different names (said of corresponding pairs, e.g., niece and nephew, brother and sister, husband and wife)

Sex again!

ribald ("RIB-əld" or "RYE-bald") bawdy: referring to sex, in an amusing or coarse way

> *Playboy* used to publish a feature called "Ribald Classics." Various collections have been published; the publisher of one described the tales as "little risqué stories from all over the world, past and present."

Ha ha

risible ("RIZZ-ə-bəl") laughable, ridiculous; or pertaining to laughter

> "The most risible McConnell argument from 2016, back then, was his indignation against interrupting the sacred process of electing a president with a base partisan battle over a Supreme Court nomination." — from an article in *The New Republic*, 2020

Blowing hot and cold

calescent ("kə-LESS-ənt") growing hot

> "I've tested the misting fan's potency in several clammy places, from subway stations to the congested, calescent queues at Disney World (where, on a stinking-hot day, I'd unwisely worn a boiler suit)." — from an article in *New York* magazine, 2017

sudorific ("soo-də-RIFF-ik") causing sweating (can also be used as a noun, meaning "a drug that causes sweating")

> Knowing Spanish or Italian helps with this one: the words for sweat (the noun) in those languages are *sudor* and *sudore*.

gelid ("JELL-id") very cold; icy

> "A friend of ours called his daughter, a freshman at Bennington, on Washington's Birthday, and inquired of the operator... if holiday rates would apply to his call. 'The Telephone Company recognizes five holidays,' a gelid voice replied. 'Thanksgiving Day, Christmas Day, New Year's Day, Mother's Day, and Father's Day.'" — from a piece in the *New Yorker,* 1961

frigorific ("frigg-ə-RIFF-ik") causing coldness

But doesn't it sound like an old slogan for Frigidaire? "*Frigorific!*" (Perhaps it will have a new life as a shorter way of saying, "Pretty friggin' terrific!")

You never realized there were this many shapes, did you?

annular ("ANN-yə-lər") shaped like (or forming) a ring

Were you confused in elementary school when the teacher mentioned a tree's *annular rings,* which grew annually? These are also called *annual rings,* or *growth rings.* Since the phrase *annular ring* is redundant, I wonder if the person who first used it meant to say *annual.*

"But the smaller, more distant moon in an annular solar eclipse only partially covers the sun, creating a flaming, silhouetted ring." — from an article in *Popular Science,* 2020

armillary consisting of circles or rings; or resembling a ring

An *armillary sphere* is a model showing objects in the heavens. It's made of several rings, with the Earth or the sun at the center.

"The statue's surface is flat and dull. Details like the zodiac signs in the armillary sphere are flaking." — from an article about the statue of Atlas on New York's Fifth Avenue, in the *New York Times,* 2008

anfractuous ("an-FRAK-shoo-əss") winding, tortuous

"Presently, on a constellation of three hills, / We saw crowning the plain / A town from a missal, a huddle of towers and houses, / Mediaeval Siena. / A gorge of a street, anfractuous, narrow." — C. Day Lewis, *An Italian Visit*

flexuous ("FLEK-shoo-əss") sinuous, curving; or unsteady, wavering

"This morning the eye returns involuntarily to the girl in the pink cotton jacket, she being the most flexuous and finely drawn figure of them all." — Thomas Hardy, *Tess of the D'Urbervilles*

bifurcated ("BYE-fər-kate-əd") split in two; divided into two parts or branches

"I could scarcely remember a time when I was not haunted by the idea of slavery, or was not profoundly conscious of the strange bifurcated world of whiteness and blackness in which I was born and reared." — William Styron, *The Confessions of Nat Turner*

reticulate/reticulated resembling or forming a network (used most commonly in botany)

71

"Criss-crossed upon the man's naked shoulder, was the same strange reticulated pattern of red, inflamed lines." — Arthur Conan Doyle, *The Case-Book of Sherlock Holmes*

cuneate ("KYOO-nee-ət") wedge-shaped (used mainly in botany, to describe a leaf's shape)

Looking at this word, you're reminded of another one, aren't you? Yes, that's right: *cuneiform*, the wedge-shaped writing used in ancient Persia and Mesopotamia. (*Cuneus* means *wedge* in Latin.)

nook-shotten (archaic) crooked, irregularly indented with nooks

The first known use of this hyphenated word is in Shakespeare's *Henry V*, when the Duke of Bourbon speaks disdainfully of "that nook-shotten isle of Albion," i.e., England. (Say it out loud. It's fun.)

oblate ("AHB-late" or "ohb-LATE") flattened at the poles (describes a spheroid)

"Because our less-than-perfect world is slightly flattened on top and bottom (an oblate spheroid, should anyone ever ask), a minute of latitude doesn't measure the same at the equator... as it does at the poles." — Mark Dittrick and Diane Dittrick, *No Uncertain Terms*

vermiform shaped like a worm: long and thin

You're most likely to encounter this word as part of the phrase *vermiform appendix*: the full name for that wormish organ we were taught was vestigial and served no purpose. Scientists now think it may actually have a purpose. They're still figuring it out.

acuminate ("ə-KYOO-mə-nət") pointed, tapering to a point (used mainly in botany and zoology)

"The tail-feathers are all extremely narrow and acuminate, even more so than in the Sharp-tailed Finch..." — Elliott Coues, *Birds of the Northwest*

cannular ("KAN-yə-lər") tubular (used mainly in medicine)

"Dr. Cooper and engineers of the Linde Company developed a surgical cannular probe, by which liquid nitrogen can be applied to minute areas of the brain." — from an article in *Bios* magazine, 1964

ventricose ("VEN-trə-kose," to rhyme with *dose*) swollen in the middle, especially on one side (used mainly in botany, zoology and anatomy); or having a big belly

"The Reverend Rory O'Flannigan rose like the full moon... when first she peeps from behind the hill, rubicund, coppery, ventricose." — Francis Paget, *The Warden of Berkingholt*

faveolate ("fə-VEE-ə-late") honeycombed; containing cells (used mainly in medicine and botany)

stellate ("STELL-ət" or "STEH-late") shaped or arranged like a star, radiating from a center (used mainly in the sciences)

ansate ("ANN-sate") having a handle; or pertaining to something handle-like

> An ansate cross, also known as an *ankh*, has a loop above the crosspiece; it was a symbol of life in ancient Egypt.

cornuted ("kor-NYOO-təd") horn-shaped; or having horns

> If you didn't know that *cornu-* is a Latin root meaning *horn,* now you do. Think *cornucopia,* the horn of plenty, and *unicorn.*

> And since most horned animals have not one but two horns, you might also want to know the word *bicornuate,* "having two horns."

unguiform claw-shaped (used mainly in anatomy and zoology)

> Related word: *ungulate*, which means "hoof-shaped" or "having hoofs."

panduriform shaped (roughly) like a violin, with rounded ends and a narrower middle (used mainly in botany, to describe leaf shapes)

> *Oh come on*, you're thinking. *Who made this one up?* I can't say, but I can tell you that the Oxford English Dictionary gives examples of it going back to the 18th century. And *pandura* means *lute* in Latin.

rimose ("rye-MOSE," to rhyme with *dose*) full of cracks or crevices (used mainly in botany, and in describing fungi)

Other shape-words, whose definitions I won't plague you with, include *aciform, plicate, decussate, crispate, auriculate, scaphoid, retiform, falcate, falciform, trichoid, runcinate, pectinate, erose,* and *torose.*

Textures, etc.

squamous ("SKWAY-məs") covered with scales; or scale-like (used mainly in botany, anatomy, and medicine)

> You may recognize this word from *squamous cell carcinoma,* a form of cancer that begins in *squamous cells,* which look like fish scales and are found near the surface of the skin and in the linings of certain organs and tracts.

coriaceous ("kaw-ree-AY-shəss") like leather, in texture or appearance; rough (used mainly in botany)

> Cautionary note: if you use rare words, not everyone will approve. "The authors' taste for highly caffeinated prose can sometimes feel forced (they describe Gov. Christie, for instance, as having a 'capacious personality and a coriaceous hide')..." — from a book review in the *New York Times*, 2013

sabulous ("SAB-yoo-ləss," to rhyme with *fabulous*) sandy; or gritty, like sand (used mainly in science and medicine)

pinguid oily, greasy

> "He held my hand too long in pinguid fingers." — Amanda Craig, *Foreign Bodies*

setaceous ("sih-TAY-shəss") bristly; or resembling a bristle (used mainly in zoology and botany)

> One example from the 1700s refers to "My father's broad, setaceous visage." The *O.E.D.* categorizes this, helpfully, as a jocular usage.

Through thick and thin

viscid ("VISS-id") thick and sticky (said of fluids; used mainly in the sciences)

> How is *viscid* different from *viscous*? The words are used interchangeably, though *viscous* is more common. Use *viscid* only if you want to emphasize the stickiness. (Most people think of *viscous* as meaning simply "thick and slow-flowing.")

> "The secretion from the glands is extremely viscid." — Charles Darwin, *Insectivorous Plants*

glutinous ("GLOO-tə-nəss") sticky; like glue

> Q: Does this word derive from *gluten* or *glue*?

> A: Both derive from the Latin word *gluten*, meaning *glue*.

> "The lime and clay destroy the slimy glutinous character of the sewage 'sludge' and keep the sewer outlet drain free from the festering and putrefying deposit which otherwise tends to choke it." — from an article in *Scientific American*, 2022

inspissated ("in-SPISS-ay-təd") thickened; condensed (by evaporation)

> "Professor Edgeworth, of All Souls', avoided conversational English, persistently using words and phrases that one expects to

meet only in books. One evening, Lawrence returned from a visit to London, and Edgeworth met him at the gate. 'Was it very caliginous in the Metropolis?' 'Somewhat caliginous, but not altogether inspissated,' Lawrence replied gravely." — Robert Graves, *Good-Bye to All That*

rarefied ("RAIR-ə-fide") very thin (referring, especially, to air at high altitudes); or extremely refined or elevated (in manners, intellect, etc.), and therefore remote from the lives of most people

"In Rarefied Air, Rarefied Company" — headline of *New York Times* article about climbers of Mount Everest, 2003

Wings, feathers, webbing

pinnate ("PIN-ate") resembling a feather—especially in that similar parts are arranged along opposite sides

This word is used most commonly to describe foliage consisting of leaflets on opposite sides of a stalk.

alate ("AY-late," to rhyme with "day late") having wings (used mainly to describe insects or seeds)

apteral/apterous ("AP-tə-rəl"/"AP-tə-rəss") having no wings

totipalmate ("toe-tə-PALM-ate") having webbing between all the toes (used in ornithology)

Shall I compare thee to a rock?

marmoreal ("mar-MORE-ee-əl") like marble: cold, smooth, white, hard; or made of marble

"The marmoreal cool of Debbie Harry and the band's razor-sharp duds plastered across TV screens helped define the nascent new wave genre..." — from an article in *Billboard* magazine, 2020

nacreous ("NAY-kree-əss") having the iridescent luster of mother of pearl; or relating to mother of pearl, or made of it

"[Sir Walter] Raleigh could see the waters of Orinoco, as seductively nacreous as the pearl he wore on his ear." — Simon Schama, *Landscape and Memory*

(I just looked at some photos of the Orinoco River, and I don't know what the hell he's talking about. Perhaps it has changed since Sir Walter's time.)

argent silvery white; or (archaic) silver, the metal

I've never seen this word in a book or article, but I wondered where Argent, the band, got its name. What I learned was that its founder and keyboard player was Rod Argent, formerly of the Zombies, the band that gave us "She's Not There."

Shall I compare thee to some other random thing?

limpid ("LIMP-id") transparently clear, like clean glass or water

> "The eyes are of that soft, limpid, turquoise blue, so often sung by the poets." — Wilkie Collins, *The Woman in White*

> And more recently: "…Those cool and limpid green eyes, / A pool wherein my love lies…" — "Green Eyes," a hit song from 1941

hyaline ("HIGH-ə-lən" or (HIGH-ə-line") glass-like, or as transparent as glass (used mainly in medicine and anatomy)

> "…my gaze kept reverting to her, so childishly slight in closefitting grey, and kept observing that carefully waved dark hair, that small, small-flowered hat with a little hyaline veil…" — Vladimir Nabokov, "The Vane Sisters"

albugineous ("al-byoo-JIN-ee-əss") resembling the white of an egg, or the white of the eye

> This word also has a specifically medical meaning: "pertaining to a dense white layer of tissue found in the testicles and ovaries."

> You'll rarely see this word used outside of medicine—but it's available!

cinereous ("sə-NEE-ree-əss") like ashes; or ash gray (sometimes tinged with black or brown)

> This word is most often found in descriptions of birds—but not exclusively: "Little knowest thou of the burning of a World-Phoenix, who fanciest that she must first burn out, and lie as a dead cinereous heap." — Thomas Carlyle, *Sartor Resartus*

Many parts

multifarious ("mull-tə-FAIR-ee-əss" or "mull-tee-") having a great variety, or many different kinds of parts

> "…the Federal Writers Project's greatest gift lay in introducing Americans to their multifarious, astonishing, broken country." — from an article in the *Los Angeles Times,* 2020

concatenate ("kon-KAT-ə-nate") connected or linked in a series

> You're more likely to see the noun form of this word, *concatenation,* meaning a series of linked objects or happenings: "So I think it's a concatenation of factors, but there's not much question what the outcome is." — from an article about inflation and other problems in the economy, quoting former Treasury Secretary Larry Summers, in *Time Magazine,* 2021

serried crowded together; or standing in rows, close together, like soldiers

> "…the deep moan of subterranean waters sounds forever through the silence of the gorges, dark with the serried pines…" — "Ouida" (Marie Louise de la Ramée), *Wanda*

Patterns

tessellated made (or decorated) with tiles that fit together without leaving any gaps; or describing any shapes that fit together this way

> "…her tessellated processions of color are all about beauty—a quality that seems almost archaic today as a measure of worth for art." — from an article in the *New York Times* about abstract painter Alma Thomas, 2019 (Search online for images of her paintings and you'll quickly see what this reporter meant.)

imbricated arranged in a pattern with overlapping edges (e.g., fish scales)

> "…the low white house which was roofed with imbricated flower-pot-colored tiles resembling bisected drainpipes." — Malcolm Lowry, *Under the Volcano*

damascened ("DAM-ə-seend") decorated with a wavy pattern, either inlaid or etched (refers to metalwork)

> "…this volume supplies us with excellent specimens of guns elaborately chased, of daggers with hilts finely worked in jade and ivory, and of swords beautifully damascened in gold." — from an article in the *Saturday Review*, 1880

piebald ("PIE-bald") spotted or patched, especially with black and white (usually refers to horses); or mixed, consisting of very different elements

> "I want a scrubby, ornery, low-down, sniff-dipping, back-woodsy, piebald gang, who never heard of finger bowls…" — O. Henry, "Aristocracy Versus Hash"

Leaves: something to be desired

foliaceous ("foh-lee-AY-shəss") consisting of leaves or thin layers; having leaves; pertaining to leaves

umbrageous ("um-BRAY-jəss") giving shade; or easily offended (inclined to take umbrage)

> "…the umbrageous loveliness of the surrounding country rendered it a spot the most fitted for joyous seclusion." — Percy Bysshe Shelley, *St. Irvyne; or, The Rosicrucian* (a Gothic horror novel written when the poet was a student at Oxford, published anonymously)

> "The people [of Corsica] are idle, haughty, umbrageous, fiery, quarrelsome… and retentive through generations of old feuds and prejudices to an almost inconceivable extent." — John Addington Symonds, *Sketches and Studies in Italy and Greece* (1879)

Made to be broken

frangible ("FRAN-jə-bəl") easily broken; brittle

> "…the frangible (breakable) bullet—a .30-caliber slug that disintegrates into a pinch of powder when it strikes the special armor of a plane." — from an article in the *New York Times,* 1945 (The bullets were used for training, to avoid injuries due to ricochet.)

fissiparous ("fih-SIP-ə-rəss") tending to break or divide into parts

> "When the year began, Nicholas II was clinging to his throne, Lenin was an exile in Zurich and the Bolsheviks were just one faction in a fissiparous revolutionary underground." — from an article in the *Wall Street Journal,* 2017

fissile ("FISS-əl" or "FISS-ile") capable of being split (usually refers to rock); or, capable of undergoing nuclear fission

> "The aging facility about 60 miles north of Pyongyang was once the main source of its fissile material, turning out roughly enough plutonium each year for one atomic bomb." — from an article in the *Washington Post,* 2019

scissile ("SISS- əl" or "SISS-ile") capable of being cut smoothly or split easily (often used to describe chemical bonds; sometimes used figuratively)

> "The first [play] in the series… was…as scissile by commercials as anything on ITV." — from an article in *The Listener,* 1967

sectile ("SEK-təl" or "SEK-tile") capable of being cut or severed smoothly

> "[Gold] is soft, dense, ductile, sectile, highly conductive, all but indestructible and, of course, very beautiful…" — from an article in the *New York Times*, 2005

More -iles

ductile ("DUK-təl" or "DUK-tile") capable of being stretched into wire or thread; or easily manipulated (referring to a person); or moldable

> "… a vast portion of the public feels rather than thinks, a ductile multitude drawn easily by the arts of the demagogue." — Amy Loveman, a writer/editor at the *Saturday Review of Literature*

"How are we doing here, Mr. Blevins?"
(Slight groan.) "So far, so good."
"I must say, you're the most ductile applicant yet."

tensile ("TEN-səl" or "TEN-sile") capable of being stretched out; or pertaining to tension

Tensile strength refers to a material's ability to resist being pulled apart. The tensile strength of wire or rope is the amount of force that must be applied before it breaks.

"Hayashi, who studies the tensile properties of spider silks, now leaves her apartment only to feed her animals." — from an article in the *New Yorker,* 2020

fictile ("FIK-till") moldable

"For ours is a most fictile world; and man is the most... plastic of creatures. A world not fixable; not fathomable!" — Thomas Carlyle, *The French Revolution*

pensile ("PEN-səl") hanging; suspended

"Of our hundreds of species of birds, the vireos alone vie with the oriole in making pensile nests." — Henry Williams, *The Book of Marvels*

I hope I'm not describing your home

mephitic ("mə-FIT-ik") foul-smelling; noxious (usually refers to a gas or vapor)

"Patrick Suskind's novel is a book of smells... and on the first page 18th-century Paris is anatomized into its component stinks. In its most fetid spot, beside a mephitic cemetery and beneath a fish stall, the hero of 'Perfume'... is born." — from a book review in the *New York Times,* 1986

feculent ("FEK-yoo-lənt") filthy, impure, foul (like feces); containing dirt or waste

"Mr. Swinburne deliberately selects the most depraved stories of the ancient world, and the most feculent corruptions of modern civilization, and dwells upon them with a passionate zest and long-drawn elaboration of enjoyment..." — from a review of a book by Algernon Charles Swinburne in *London Review,* 1866

About days

diurnal ("dye-ƏR-nəl") daily; or of/during the daytime

When describing animals, *diurnal* means the opposite of *nocturnal,* i.e., active during the daytime.

"Humans are diurnal creatures, meant to be awake during the day and to wind down at night." — from an article in *Wired* magazine, 2021

quotidian ("kwo-TID-ee-ən") recurring daily; or commonplace, ordinary

"Quotidian drudgery, absence of those beautiful things which she loved... had driven a mother to despair." — from an article in the *Indianapolis Star*, 1922

Regarding Le Pain Quotidien, a restaurant chain: I know the name means "Daily Bread" (as in *Give us this day our...*) but every time I see the sign, I think, "What agonies have you got in store for us today?"

circadian ("sər-KAY-dee-ən") recurring every 24 hours (refers especially to bodily processes such as the cycle of sleeping and waking)

"Jet lag upsets the circadian rhythms and plays holy hell with the stewardess's monthlies..." — Stanley Elkin, *The Dick Gibson Show*

matutinal ("mə-TOO-tə-nəl") active/occurring/appearing in the morning

"I don't suppose my children enjoyed my prolonged, matutinal throat-clearings, my cock-crow scrapings and garglings." — Dan Jacobson, *The Rape of Tamar*

crepuscular ("krə-PUS-kyə-lər," the second syllable rhyming with *bus*) of or like twilight; or, in zoology, becoming active at twilight, e.g., birds and insects

"The urban crepuscular mammals [mule deer] often graze on the fairways of the Wilson and Harding golf courses..." — from an article in the *Los Angeles Times*, 2022

vespertine ("VESS-pər-teen" or "-tine") active/occurring/appearing in the evening

Delay, delay, delay!

dilatory ("DILL-ə-taw-ree") tending to delay taking action; or intended to cause delay, especially as a strategy for gaining time

"A Need Unfulfilled: Dilatory Tactics by City Hold Up Playground Development." — headline in the *New York Times*, 1929

cunctative ("KUNK-tə-tiv") (rare) prone to delay, slow, or causing delay

When you're tired of saying "former"

erstwhile former

> "The only area where Trump can legitimately point to peacemaking is between Israel and some of its erstwhile adversaries." — from an article in *The Week*, 2020

quondam ("KWAN-dəm") former

> "A small, peppery man of large contradictions, he was the island's greatest populist leader: a quondam trade unionist who later rode roughshod over unions…" — from an article about Joey Smallwood, long-time premier of Newfoundland, in the *Daily Telegraph* (London), 1991

whilom ("WHY-ləm") (archaic) former

> Whilom can also be used as an adverb: "The Squire himself now sallied forth, and began to roar forth the Name of *Sophia* as loudly… as whileom did *Hercules* that of *Hylas*." — Henry Fielding, *Tom Jones*

Long-lasting

perdurable ("pər-DURE-ə-bəl," the second syllable rhyming with *poor*) extremely durable, or permanent, imperishable

> "This good book reminds us of those small, perdurable realities which the clamour of the state would like us to forget." — from a review of the book *Salt,* by Mark Kurlansky, in the *Evening Standard* (London), 2002

> Also, figuratively: "He had had a wife, as well as a perdurable old mother." — Penelope Fitzgerald, *Offshore*

amaranthine ("am-ə-RAN-thin" or –thine, to rhyme with *mine*) unfading, undying; or purplish-red (after the flowers of the amaranth plant)

> *Amaranth* is a name poets coined for an imaginary flower that would never die. (Its Greek roots mean *immortal flower.*) To confuse us all, an actual plant was given the same name.

> "I also tried some white $790 Fisherman Jeans. The verdict: amaranthine chicness, but too expensive to be worn around fish."

— from a review of a new boutique selling fashion and furnishings, in the *New York Times,* 2017

sempiternal ("sem-pə-TƏR-nəl") everlasting, eternal, unchanging

"Liberty without an acknowledgment of the sempiternal distinction between good and evil was a dead end, one that provided no ground for opposition to modern tyranny and no support for a principled recognition of the inherent dignity of the human person." — from an essay by Daniel J. Mahoney in *Hungarian Review,* 2020

inveterate ("in-VET-ə-rət") habitual, long-standing: usually refers to hard-to-change habits or behavior, e.g., *an inveterate gambler* or *womanizer*

"An Oxford mathematician, [Lewis] Carroll was an inveterate puzzler." — from an article in the *Wall Street Journal,* 2022

Prehistoric

Paleolithic ("PALE-ee-ə-LITH-ik") from (or pertaining to) the beginning of the Stone Age; or, with a small p, primitive, outdated

"You wouldn't think, would you, that *we* were the world power with three hundred and sixty nuclear warheads, and the Soviet Union the power with nine paleolithic atomic bombs?" — William F. Buckley, *Stained Glass*

eolithic ("ee-ə-LITH-ik") from (or pertaining to) the period when crude stone tools were first used, at the very beginning of the Stone Age (even earlier than the Paleolithic period)

An *eolith* is a piece of flint, crudely chipped. Those who study such things now believe that these are not tools at all, but geological specimens.

"We were short of knives, and, after killing the sheep in relay, had recourse to stray flints to cut them up. As men unaccustomed to such expedients, we used them in the eolithic spirit..." — T.E. Lawrence, *Seven Pillars of Wisdom*

Something's coming

nascent ("NAY-sənt") in the process of emerging

"The comic book for example has been seen as a degenerate literary form instead of as a nascent pictorial and dramatic form..." — Marshall McLuhan, from his *Letters,* 1951

florescent flowering; blossoming (literally or figuratively)

It's easy to confuse this one with *fluorescent*—even the *New York Times* has done it, referring to the light bulbs without the crucial 'U.' Be careful.

"There are also florescent details in the halos, drapery, and so forth..." — David Lindsay, *Donatello*

foudroyant ("foo-DROY-ənt") sudden, overwhelming, dazzling (from the French word for *lightning*); or, in medicine, occurring suddenly and with severity (referring to a disease)

The *Foudroyant* was the name of one of Lord Nelson's battleships. Retrofitted as a floating museum, it visited various English seaports—and one night in 1897, someone painted an advertisement for a patent medicine on the hull. The owner of the patent medicine was fined 50 pounds; the painter was fined 40 shillings. The judge declared the deed "an outrageous sacrilege."

Undreamt of in your philosophy, Horatio

anagogic ("an-ə-GAHDG-ik") mystical; or, in psychology, "a term applied by Silberer and Jung to the moral, spiritual, allegorical, or uplifting trends of the unconscious." — Howard C. Warren, *Dictionary of Psychology*

"Professor Ellmann... proposes to define the parts [of Joyce's *Ulysses*]—or what he identifies as the literal, ethical, esthetic and anagogic (meaning, roughly, spiritual) aspects—and add them up to 'a new myth for Ulysses.'" — from a book review in the *New York Times*, 1972

mantic prophetic; or pertaining to prophecy

This word shares its source with the praying mantis. In Greek, *mantis* means "prophet." And those forelegs, because they resemble praying hands, reminded some long-ago insect-namer of a prophet.

"There is the same sort of relation between the soul and the mantic vapour as between the eye and light." — T.R. Glover, *The Conflict of Religions in the Early Roman Empire*

fatidic ("fay-TID-ik") prophetic; or pertaining to prophecy

"When Moses, in the fatidic spirit, foretold the future prosperity of Israel..." — from an article in the *Journal of Sacred Literature*, 1861

vatic ("VAT-ik," to rhyme with *cat-sick*) prophetic; pertaining to a prophet

> "[Robert] Stone's fiction abounds with Delphic oracles and vatic pronouncements like this." — from an article in *The New Republic*, 2020

preternatural ("preh-tər-NATCH-ər-əl" or "pree-") outside the normal course of nature (less occult than *supernatural*, but more mystical than *abnormal*)

> "Mrs. Transome was not observing the two men; rather... she seemed to hear and see what they said and did with preternatural acuteness..." — George Eliot, *Felix Holt, the Radical*

When a raven speaks, that's unusual.
When it stops in mid-air, that's preternatural.

eldritch (Scottish) weird, unnatural, sinister, frightening

> "Pearl, in utter scorn of her mother's attempt to quiet her, gave an eldritch scream..." — Nathaniel Hawthorne, *The Scarlet Letter*

> "The Black Panther's ghost brandished an eldritch cleaver." — from the Ministry of Unforgivable Puns

Not of this world

supernal ("sə-PƏR-nəl") celestial, heavenly; or pertaining to the sky

"[Olivia] De Havilland was capable as few other actors have ever been of expressing a kind of supernal grace and guilelessness." — from an article in the *Christian Science Monitor*, 2020

superlunary ("super-LOO-nə-ree") celestial, not earthly (literally, *above the moon*)

"Mary Renault. The name has never meant for me anything less than a superlunary being." — from an appreciation by novelist Linda Proud, 1999

Of this world

temporal ("TEM-pə-rəl") secular, as opposed to ecclesiastical; or pertaining to worldly life, as opposed to spiritual matters or the afterlife; or pertaining to time

"The quality of mercy is not strained. It droppeth as the gentle rain from heaven upon the place beneath... 'Tis mightiest in the mightiest. It becomes the throned monarch better than his crown. His sceptre shows the force of temporal power, the attribute to awe and majesty... but mercy is above this sceptered sway." — William Shakespeare, *The Merchant of Venice*

sublunary ("səb-LOO-nə-ree") of this world (beneath the moon), as opposed to more spiritual planes (such as heaven)

"You talk about the theatre as if it had some cosmic significance. As a matter of fact it is pathetically sublunary." — George Sanders, in a 1957 letter, published in *Dreadful Man,* Brian Aherne's biography of Sanders

How's the weather over there?

favonian ("fə-VOH-nee-ən") mild, benign; or pertaining to the west wind

"Sunday. Heat ripple still with us; a most favonian week." — Vladimir Nabokov, *Lolita*

pluvious ("PLOO-vee-əss") characterized by heavy rainfall; or pertaining to rain

"In this pluvious country, however, it seems that a little rain must fall on every parade." — from an article about a royal wedding in Belgium, in the *International Herald Tribune,* 1999

Speaking of other places...

tramontane ("trə-MAHN-tane") (archaic) foreign; dwelling beyond the mountains; sweeping down from the mountains (e.g., a wind); or barbarous

> The mountains this word originally referred to were the Alps, from the point of view of Italy, and the people referred to were those who lived north of Italy, beyond the mountainous border.

> "The rustic, or even savage, aspect of those Tramontane warriors, often disguised a simple and merciful disposition." — Edward Gibbon, *The History of the Decline and Fall of the Roman Empire*

hyperborean ("hy-pər-BORE-ee-ən") relating to the northernmost latitudes; or referring to an inhabitant of the Arctic; or frozen

> This word comes to us from Greek myth. It derives from the name given to a mythical people who lived beyond the north wind (*Boreas*), in a supposed region of eternal sun.

jerkwater remote and insignificant: said of a place

> Steam-powered locomotives in the American West needed to refill their boilers with water often. Big towns had water towers alongside the tracks; smaller towns didn't, and trains serving them had to stop to fetch water in buckets. Trains on these rural lines were called "jerkwater trains."

> "I followed the pay-roll aboard the jerkwater train that carried it to the waiting miners." — John Black, *You Can't Win*

Animal behavior and anatomy

raptorial ("rap-TAW-ree-əl") predatory (refers mainly to birds); or (if referring to part of a bird or animal's body) adapted for seizing prey

> "Trogloraptor is not much bigger than most garden spiders, but has remarkably elongated claws. When its legs are extended, it measures one and a half inches wide, and the raptorial claws hint that it is a fierce predator." — from an article in the *New York Times*, 2012

"Because of the strong popular prejudice against raptorial birds in general, laws protecting them are usually not enforced." — Henry S. Fitch, *Observations on the Mississippi Kite in Southwestern Kansas*

prehensile ("prə-HEN-səl") adapted for holding or seizing, e.g., a monkey's tail

Used figuratively: "Retailers have been eying [King] Kong's potential with prehensile enthusiasm." — from an article in *Time* magazine, 1976 (anticipating the release of the remake with Jessica Lange)

scatophagous ("skə-TAH-fə-gəss") feeding on dung (e.g., beetles, flies)

If you feel the need for variety, you can also say *coprophagous:* it means the same thing.

"Wipe that scatophagous grin off your face."

anadromous ("ə-NAD-rə-məss") going upriver to spawn (e.g., salmon)

Here's a fuller explanation, from the website of NOAA's National Marine Fisheries Service: "Anadromous is the term that describes fish born in freshwater who spend most of their lives in saltwater and return to freshwater to spawn…"

testaceous ("tess-TAY-shəss") having a shell; or pertaining to shells; or reddish brown, like a flowerpot

"Now it is an equally incontrovertible fact, that of all offerings to the stomach, there is none more grateful than the testaceous marine animal, known commonly by the vulgar name of Oyster." — Washington Irving, *A History of New York*

When there's a lot and it keeps coming

pullulating ("PUL-yə-late-ing," the first U pronounced as in *pun*) swarming, crowded; or quickly spreading, multiplying

"As sticky, as fertile, as any pullulating little patch of ground that Matthew would have stooped over with his magnifying glass and collecting bottle." — Graham Swift, *Ever After*

feracious ("fə-RAY-shəss") fruitful, producing prolifically

"For the mischief that one blockhead… does, in a world so feracious, teeming with endless results as ours, no ciphering will sum up." — Thomas Carlyle, *Past and Present*

Okay, but when do we get the prand?

preprandial ("PREE-PRAN-dee-əl") before a meal, especially dinner

"They were rich upper-middle-class expatriates accustomed to leisurely breakfasts, walks on the beach, afternoon golf, a preprandial martini or two and evenings with the wireless listening to the BBC..." — from a biography of P.G. Wodehouse, by Robert McCrum

postprandial ("POST-PRAN-dee-əl") after a meal, especially dinner

"Biologists have actually been able to measure this physiological dip in our alertness—what science calls a postprandial dip—through changes in our metabolic system..." — from an article in *Popular Science*, 2017

You may safely eat and drink (but be merry at your own risk)

esculent ("ESS-kyə-lənt") edible

Potato: A History of the Propitious Esculent is the title of a 2009 book by John Reader.

potable ("POH-tə-bəl") safely drinkable; or, as a noun, such a liquid

As anyone who has watched a few episodes of *Jeopardy!* knows, one of the most popular recurring categories is Potent Potables. But more frequently, the word refers to water, as seen here:

"Against the backdrop of Jim Crow segregation, ... black families had very limited options. Often, the only places they could settle were in isolated, waterless communities... The lack of potable water was not just bad luck... Nobody else would live there except those who had no other choice." — from an article in the *New York Times* about California's Central Valley, 2019

Similar or different

congeneric ("kahn-jə-NER-ik") belonging to the same genus; or related in origin

"Reason and action are congeneric and homogenous, two aspects of the same phenomenon." — Ludwig von Mises, *Human Action*

macaronic ("mak-ə-RAHN-ik") composed of a mixture of languages; or jumbled in general

"What she experienced as her mind was the hideously macaronic jumble of the room in which she sat." — Jenny Diski, *Happily Ever After*

Flying, leaping, floating, or not doing much of anything

volitant ("VAHL-ih-tənt") flying, or able to fly; or constantly in motion

"...that snowy mass of cloud... rose from the surface of this brilliant, buoyant, volitant, sea in airy bubbles of vapour..." — George Henry Lewes (long-time partner of George Eliot), *Sea-Side Studies*

saltant ("SAWL-tənt") leaping

"...no professor of the saltant art ever applied himself with greater industry, than the naturalist now used his heels on the ribs of [his donkey]." — James Fenimore Cooper, *The Prairie*

natant ("NAYT-ənt") floating (often refers to aquatic plants); or swimming

"In the lamp glass coconut oil... rested golden-hued on water, a natant disc." — Rohinton Mistry, *Tales from Firozsha Baag*

quiescent ("kwee-ESS-ənt") inactive, still, or at rest; dormant

If you've ever bought a box of Popsicles, you may remember seeing the phrase, *A Quiescently Frozen Confection.* Those words made no sense to me, given the meaning of *quiescent*; they sounded like malarkey, meant to make the humble Popsicle sound impressive. But now I discover that the phrase actually means something: "a frozen, sweetened, flavored product in the manufacture of which freezing has not been accompanied by stirring or agitation." (Thanks for this clarification are due to Virginia's Administrative Code, 2VAC5-510-240.)

Tough... strong... there when you need it (and even when you don't want it)

inexpugnable ("in-ek-SPUG-nə-bəl" or "-SPYOO-nə-bəl") impossible to conquer, overcome, or eradicate

The word originally described fortresses that could not be taken by force. In the centuries since, it has more commonly referred to less concrete things: "For here again our inexpugnable hypocrisy comes in and leads us down to perdition even in our prayers." — Alexander Whyte, *Bunyan Characters* (1893)

indefeasible that cannot be undone or made void

"The great writers... have mostly asserted freedom of conscience as an indefeasible right." — John Stuart Mill, *On Liberty*

How babies are made

viviparous ("və-VIP-ə-rəss" or "VYE-," to rhyme with *eye*) giving birth to living offspring (which have developed within the mother's body)

oviparous ("oh-VIP-ə-rəss") reproducing by means of eggs that hatch outside the parent's body

Another fallacy debunked: "The belief was also long current... that fishes not only did not take care of their young, but were invariably oviparous." — from an article in *The American Naturalist,* 1884

ovoviviparous ("oh-voh-vy-VIP-ə-rəss") producing eggs that develop within the mother's body and hatch either before or just after leaving the mother's body (e.g., some fish and reptiles)

And you thought *viviparous* and *oviparous* covered the entire animal kingdom!

The great (and pretty good) outdoors

bosky ("BAHSK-ee") wooded, covered with trees and shrubs

"In a Bosky Westchester Dell, a Meal With an International Flavor" — headline from the *New York Times,* 1967

Did you read the fifth word as *Deli?* I did. (Hm. A bosky deli: a new concept in dining. We may be onto something.)

villatic ("vih-LAT-ik") rural, rustic; or relating to a farm

"The tame villatic fowl scratches and picks with might and main, converting a thousand refuse things into dainty human food." — from an article in the *Atlantic*, 1866

fenny ("FEN-ee") marshy, boggy (a *fen* is a marsh: low-lying land, partly covered with water)

"Finsbury was so called from the fenny district in which it lay." — Daniel Tuke, *Chapters in the History of the Insane in the British Isles* (What a title!)

sere ("SEER") dry, withered (usually referring to a landscape or vegetation)

> "With thick brushstrokes, Ms. Harricks summons the sere land and low trees of the Australian bush…" — from a review of a children's book in the *Wall Street Journal*, 2019

Claustrophobes, choose one of the following

immured ("ih-MYOORD") imprisoned, entombed—either literally or figuratively behind walls

> There's a good chance that, as soon as you read this word and its definition, you thought of the Edgar Allan Poe story, "The Cask of Amontillado," in which a man takes his revenge on a foe by sealing him behind a wall, brick by brick.

commodious ("kə-MOH-dee-əss") comfortably spacious

> "When you live in a commodious home such as this, you feel like you're in a high-end resort." — from an article in the *Times* (of London) Real Estate section, 2015

Within you and without you

endogenous ("en-DAHJ-ə-nəss") produced within an organism; without an external cause (used mainly in biology, medicine, and psychiatry)

> "Genetic factors are known to be important in the ætiology of so-called endogenous depressions, the predisposition being inherited…" — from an article in *The Lancet*, 1962

exogenous ("eks-AHJ-ə-nəss") caused by something outside the body (a variant is *exogenetic*)

> "…and the depressive illness often being precipitated by other factors which may be physical or exogenous." — from that same article in *The Lancet*, 1962

Tasty!

sapid ("SAP-id") flavorful; or pleasant-tasting; or both

> "If the patient attempts to take any sapid food… the pain and burning in the mouth are intolerable." — Patrick Manson, *Tropical Diseases*

saporous ("SAP-ə-rəss") flavorful; or pleasant-tasting; or pertaining to the sense of taste

> "We read of Manna that it was saporous to all palates." — John Hacket, *A Century of Sermons Upon Several Remarkable Subjects* (1675)

> (And yet, in Numbers 11:5-7, the Israelites complain, "In Egypt we had fish for the asking, cucumbers and watermelons, leeks and onions and garlic. Now… there is nothing wherever we look except this manna.")

A few concepts

untenable ("un-TEN-ə-bəl") not defendable, not justifiable

> "There is no way that business owners, or individual workers or consumers, can fix the crisis. We've been forced into this untenable situation by government incompetence and outright malice." — from an article about the coronavirus pandemic in *The New Republic*, 2020

concomitant ("kon-KAHM-ih-tənt") accompanying; or occurring along with something else

> "…even Sylvester Stallone charms; Christopher Walken delivers his customary edge without any of his clichéd, concomitant weirdness." — from a review of the movie *Antz* in *Entertainment Weekly*, 1999

ineluctable ("in-ə-LUK-tə-bəl") impossible to avoid, change, or overcome; inevitable

> "Ineluctable modality of the visible": so begins the third chapter of James Joyce's *Ulysses*, as Stephen Dedalus observes the constantly changing sea.

adventitious ("ad-ven-TIH-shəss") unplanned; acquired by accident; not inherent

> "People often think of me as an adventurous fellow; nothing could be farther from the truth. My adventures were always adventitious, always thrust on me, always endured rather than undertaken." — Henry Miller, *Tropic of Capricorn*

chimeric/chimerical ("kai-MER-ik"/"kai-MER-ih-kəl") hoped for but unattainable; imaginary; or tending to pursue unrealistic goals

> "As the technology industry faces growing government scrutiny, this may not be the time for a visionary, chimerical CEO." — from an article in the *Washington Post*, 2019

putative ("PYOO-tə-tiv") supposed; commonly believed to be

> "This has always been a nation willing to sell out its past for putative progress." — from a column in *Newsweek*, 2002

adiaphorous ("ad-eye-AF-ə-rəss," with both As pronounced as in *arrow*) morally neutral, neither right nor wrong; or impartial or indifferent; or, in medicine, neither harmful nor helpful

> "There was nothing adiaphorous in the medieval world and everybody was assigned a fixed place in a strictly hierarchical organization." — from an article in the *American Economic Review*, 1953

perfervid ("pər-FƏR-vid") ardent, passionate; overly emotional

> When you want to go a degree beyond *fervent,* reach for *perfervid.*

> "[Karl Marx] passed rapidly from the undigested Judaism of his childhood into a short but perfervid period of Lutheranism." — Malachi Martin, *The Keys of This Blood: The Struggle for World Dominion Between Pope John Paul II, Mikhail Gorbachev, and the Capitalist West* (That title makes one long to see the Marvel Comics movie version.)

Colors: all the hues that are fit to print

puce ("PYOOSE") dark red to purple-brown

> "I want puce gloves and green boots." — James Joyce, *Ulysses*

cerise ("sə-REESE") deep reddish pink

> "...a Poiret-inspired evening dress... beaded all over, covered with a cerise tunic which was drawn in under her breasts, Empire style." — Thomas Pynchon, *V.*

fuchsia ("FEW-shə") purplish red: like the flower of the fuchsia shrub

> "It's that unexpected color, that fuchsia that comes out of nowhere, that's your zinger." — from an article in the *Orlando Sentinel,* 2020

saffron ("SAFF-rən," the first syllable rhyming with *laugh*) orange-yellow; or a flavoring or food coloring of this color, derived from part of a crocus

> "...the monks, with alms-bowls partially hidden by their flowing saffron robes, silently floated through the temple gates." — from an article about Buddhist monks in Thailand, in the *New York Times,* 1972

gamboge ("gam-BOHZH" or "gam-BOHDG") orange to mustard yellow

> "Upon sallying out this morning encountered the old-fashioned pea soup London fog—of a gamboge color." — Herman Melville, *Journal of a Visit to London and the Continent* (written in 1849, and showing the effects of the Industrial Revolution)

buff dull beige to light brown

> The word derives from the color of leather made from buffalo hide. Its more familiar, informal meaning—someone who enthusiastically pursues a particular hobby, e.g., a movie buff—comes from the fact that New York City's volunteer firemen once wore buff-colored uniforms. They were the original buffs, who thrilled at racing to fires and putting them out.

ecru ("EK-roo") a light beige color: that of unbleached linen

> "Just before coming back to college, she had indulged in long ecru suède gloves, which she now drew on silently." — Nell Speed, *Molly Brown's Sophomore Days* (1912)

dun grayish brown

> "...Mondaugen felt little and lost in the dun-colored waste." — Thomas Pynchon, *V.*

ochre/ocher ("OAK-ər") orange yellow

> "Ochre in its various warm tones characterized the urban landscape of Rome until the 1990s." — from the website RomeArtLover.it

sorrel ("SAW-rəl") light reddish brown

> When Gulliver travels to the land of the Houyhnhnms—a race of wise, dignified horses—he also discovers their opposite, the human-like Yahoos: filthy, disgusting beasts. "The master horse ordered a sorrel nag, one of his servants, to untie the largest of these [Yahoos], and take him into the yard." — Jonathan Swift, *Gulliver's Travels*

taupe ("TOHP") brownish gray

> *Taupe* is the French word for *mole:* a small animal that's taupe-colored. You're most likely to encounter it when shopping for stockings or pantyhose.

> "At the doors a taupe-colored dusk and a cold November rain closed round her like a wet blanket." — Fannie Hurst, *Just Around the Corner* (Hurst was a best-selling author in her time; her novels *Imitation of Life, Back Street, Humoresque,* and *Young at Heart* were adapted as movies.)

bister/bistre ("BIH-stər") grayish or yellowish brown

> This won't help you use the word eloquently, but when my wife addresses me in mock irritation, she calls me "Mister Bister."

russet ("RUSS-ət") reddish brown

> "The heroic beasts of burden dominate the painting, their white, tan and russet coats shining in the pale, luminous light." — from an article about the artist Rosa Bonheur, in *Smithsonian* magazine, 2020

cerulean ("sə-ROO-lee-ən") sky blue

> "Vibrant pops of Pepto-Bismol pink, tangy orange, cerulean blue and grass green streak across the six new large-scale paintings in Sue Williams's exhibition..." — from an article in *Art in America*, 2014

sable ("SAY-bəl") black; dark; or a small mammal belonging to the weasel family, with dark brown fur used for coats and for artists' brushes

> "Painted was he with his war-paints, / Stripes of yellow, red, and azure, / Spots of brown and spots of sable..." — Henry Wadsworth Longfellow, *The Song of Hiawatha*

glaucous ("GLAW-kəss") grayish or blueish green

> "The sea, its salt drowned in a solution of rain, is less glaucous than gray with waves too sluggish to break into foam." — Vladimir Nabokov, "Spring in Fialta"

> *Glaucous* also has a more specialized meaning: "covered with a powdery, frost-like coating." You've seen this coating on grapes and plums.

viridian ("və-RID-ee-ən") bluish green

> "In 2010, scientists analyzed the composition of the 1893 and 1910 versions of 'The Scream' and found the pigments used included cadmium yellow, vermillion, ultramarine, and viridian, all common in the 19th century." — from an article on the website *Ars Technica*, 2020

viridescent ("vih-rə-DESS-ənt") greenish, slightly green, or becoming green

> "...the front of the mountain ivied and furred with clinging forest, one viridescent cliff..." — Robert Louis Stevenson, from a letter describing the island of Molokai, in Hawaii, 1889

aeruginous ("ee-ROO-jən-əss") bluish green, like verdigris; or pertaining to verdigris

"His suit was not green, but aeruginous." — Samuel Beckett, *Murphy*

incarnadine ("in-KAR-nə-dine") pinkish, like flesh; or blood red

A collection of poems by Mary Szybist, using this word as its title, won the National Book Award in 2013.

roseate ("ROH-zee-ət" or ("ROH-zee-ate") rose-colored; or rose-like; or optimistic

"Clio's crimson sunshade cast a roseate glow over them both." — Edna Ferber, *Saratoga Trunk*

aureate ("AW-ree-ət" or "AW-ree-ate") golden-colored; or like gold in brilliance or splendor

"Such long and supposedly elegant words have been dubbed 'aureate terms,' because… they represent a kind of verbal gilding of literary style." — J.C. Mendenhall, *Aureate Terms* (Is he referring to the words in *this* book?! No, his subtitle is *A Study in the Literary Diction of the Fifteenth Century*.)

xanthous ("ZAN-thəss") yellow, or yellowish-skinned

Xanthan gum, a thickening agent and stabilizer, has nothing to do with the word *xanthous*. Its name comes from the bacteria used in its production, *Xanthomonas campestris*. However, the bacteria's first name means "yellow entity" in Latin—so I spoke too soon.

tawny ("TAW-nee") light brown or yellowish brown

Dobie Gillis often called a certain girl "my tawny pipit." That girl may have been Thalia Menninger, played by Tuesday Weld. (The tawny pipit is a bird.)

Tawny, Scrawny Lion was a popular children's book: one of those Little Golden Books that were so affordable long ago.

rufous ("ROO-fəss") rust-colored: reddish brown (often used to describe birds' plumage)

"Catbirds give the impression of being entirely slaty gray. With a closer look you'll see a small black cap, blackish tail, and a rich rufous-brown patch under the tail." — from AllAboutBirds.org

ferruginous ("fə-ROO-jən-əss") red-brown, the color of iron rust; or containing iron

Not only is *ferruginous* used to describe birds' plumage—it also lends its name to a few bird species, e.g., the ferruginous duck, the ferruginous hawk, and the ferruginous pygmy owl.

rubescent ("roo-BESS-ənt") becoming red; blushing

"Una in her radiant dress and lipstick seems the room's centre, its wellspring, the source of its crackling energy and rich, rubescent light." — Steven Heighton, *The Shadow Boxer*

albescent ("al-BESS-ənt," the first syllable pronounced like the name, Al) whitish, or becoming white

"The familiar old moon hung up there with a fuzzy corona around it, albescent in the soft black sky." — William Boyd, *Any Human Heart*

Begin each of these definitions with "Of, like, or pertaining to…"

hibernal ("hy-BƏR-nəl"), **hiemal** ("HY-ə-məl") winter

"Hibernal beauty of a water main break" — headline in the *New York Times,* February 2019

vernal ("VƏR-nəl") spring

You know this word because of the vernal equinox. (You can easily remember that *vernal* means "in spring," because the other one is the autumnal equinox.)

A park ranger once pointed out what he called a vernal pool, i.e., a temporary puddle that forms in the spring. I thought he was kidding, but no: "In Massachusetts, an aerial survey in 2000 found 30,000 potential vernal pools, ephemeral wetlands that are dry most of the year and only appear with spring rains." — from an article in *USA Today*, 2020

estival/aestival (like *festival* without the F) summer

"The Principal… indicated that in the course of the aestival recess he might be reconsidering the terms and conditions of my employment." — Julian Barnes, *Talking It Over*

hebdomadal ("heb-DAHM-ə-dəl") a week

This odd word comes from *hepta,* the Greek word for *seven.* Even if you've never seen it before, you may remember something closely related: the French satirical weekly *Charlie Hebdo,* site of a terrorist attack by two Muslim brothers outraged by a cartoon of Mohammad. (The French word for "weekly" is *hebdomadaire.*)

austral ("AW-strəl") the southern hemisphere

"Adult whales socialize at both the Auckland and Campbell Islands during the austral winter." — from an article in *Popular Science*, 2020

boreal ("BORE-ee-əl") the north

This word derives from Boreas, mythological god of the north wind.

"…the fires might also degrade the permafrost by removing upper layers of soil that act as an insulating barrier, a process that has been well documented in boreal forests." — from an article about the Siberian tundra in *National Geographic*, 2020

uranic ("yoo-RAN-ik") the heavens

In modern English, this word usually means "containing uranium."

telluric ("tə-LOO-rik") the Earth

"These uniformitarian assumptions… led geologists and paleontologists… to focus upon telluric influences (like changing climates and sea levels)." — Stephen Jay Gould, *The Structure of Evolutionary Theory*

sidereal ("sy-DEE-ree-əl," the first syllable pronounced like *sigh*) the stars, or measured by means of the stars

"A genuine countertenor voice silences all arguments, its sidereal sweetness shaming our pettiness, like the music of the spheres." — Salman Rushdie, *The Ground Beneath Her Feet*

A *sidereal clock* is one that keeps time by the stars. This system, called *sidereal time*, is based on the time it takes for the Earth to rotate in relation to the stars, as opposed to the sun.

sinistral ("SIN-iss-trəl") the left side (or left-handed)

"Sinistral but nowise sinister, long-haired and ascetic, Drew Mack looks to me less a hippie than a Massachusetts Minuteman in his denims, boots, and homespun shirts…" — John Barth, *Letters*

By the way, *sinister* comes from the same root. Because most people are right-handed, left-handedness has been considered suspicious, unlucky, even evil. If the right side is associated with "rightness," then the left is left with all that's not right.

dextral ("DEK-strəl") the right side (or right-handed)

As the left side has negative associations, the right has positive ones. Thus we have *dexterity*, and the French and Italian words for *right* (*droit* and *derecho*, respectively), which refer to both the right side and what you're legally or morally entitled to.

palpebral ("PAL-pə-brəl") the eyelids

"Despite a slight tendency toward palpebral twitching, her closed eyes had a magic." — David Foster Wallace, *Brief Interviews with Hideous Men*

auricular ("aw-RIK-yoo-lər") ears, or the sense of hearing (or, told privately, as if whispered in the ear)

"Confession with us is auricular and is conducted in a richly ornamented recess..." — Vladimir Nabokov, *Pale Fire*

buccal ("BUCK-əl") the cheek; or the mouth

When Dr. Post, my long-time dentist (much beloved, now retired) used to probe my gums and call out to the hygienist the depth of the pockets, she would clarify which side of the tooth she was talking about by specifying *buccal* or *lingual,* i.e., the tongue-side.

gnathic ("NATH-ik") the jaw

From the same root: *prognathous,* "having a protruding jaw," a word we saw earlier.

carpal ("KAR-pəl") the wrist; or the bones that form the wrist

"[Gala Porras-Kim's] carpal-tunnel-inducing artifact drawings can take three months each to complete, even with a team of four assistants to help with drawing and research." — from an article on Vulture.com, 2021

humeral ("(H)YOO-mər-əl") the shoulder; or the upper arm

The *humerus* is the bone of your upper arm, between your elbow and your shoulder. It's not the same thing as your "funny bone," though we may wish it were. (By the way, your funny bone isn't really a bone: that terrible twinge results when you bump your ulnar nerve against the humerus.)

axillary ("ak-SILL-ə-ree") the armpit

"She smelled of damp cotton, axillary tufts, and nenuphars,* like mad Ophelia." — Vladimir Nabokov, *Ada*

* Water lilies.

ventral ("VEN-trəl") the abdomen; or the underside of an animal or plant

"...he continued at intervals to take his pipe from his mouth in order to wink at an imaginary audience and shake luxuriously with a silent, ventral laughter..." — George Eliot, *Adam Bede*

renal ("REE-nəl") the kidneys

A warning for pet-owners: "Raisins are poisonous to dogs and can lead to renal failure." — from the *Washington Post,* 2020. (The things you learn from the newspaper!)

bathyal ("BATH-ee-əl") the deep sea, where sunlight doesn't reach

neritic ("nə-RIT-ik") the shallow sea, near the coast; i.e., the part of the ocean above the continental shelf

thalassic ("thə-LASS-ik," the TH pronounced as in *with*) the sea, especially smaller or inland seas

benthic ("BƏN-thik") the bottom of the ocean

> "But benthic dwellers are difficult to haul up to the surface alive, let alone chipper." — from an article in the *New York Times*, 2020

"What says the *Benthic Bulletin*, Captain Jack?"
"It says they're turnin' my storied career into a motion picture! Johnny Depp's to star!"

pelagic ("pə-LADJ-ik") the ocean surface, or the water just below it; or the open sea, as opposed to coastal waters

> Pelagic birds—which spend most of their lives on the open ocean and visit land mainly when breeding —include the albatross, the

auk, the booby, the petrel, the puffin, and the frigate bird, among others.

riparian ("rih-PAIR-ee-ən" or "rye-") the banks of rivers; or the wetlands next to rivers

"Tannins and other organic waste from riparian cedar trees combine with iron from the ground water to give the rivers a deep color." — John McPhee, *The Pine Barrens*

paludal ("pə-LOO-dəl") swamps or marshes; especially refers to plants and animals found in these habitats

"Beyond the shack the land grows sodden, paludal, and from the marsh rises a wheel of vegetation." — Nick Cave, *And the Ass Saw the Angel*

lacustrine ("lə-KUSS-trin") lakes

"This book thus represents without doubt the most comprehensive volume about tourism and recreation in lacustrine areas yet." — from a review of *Lake Tourism: An Integrated Approach to Lacustrine Tourism Systems,* on Amazon.com

phreatic ("free-AT-ik") underground waters, especially those below the water table and/or accessible through wells

Useful info from the U.S. Geological Survey: "Phreatic eruptions are steam-driven explosions that occur when water beneath the ground or on the surface is heated by magma, lava, hot rocks, or new volcanic deposits..."

alluvial ("ə-LOO-vee-əl") earth deposited by flowing water (e.g., a river delta)

"Tucker planted tobacco in the rich alluvial soil and thus began to make his fortune." — from an article in *USA Today,* 2019

hypogeal ("HY-pə-GEE-əl") the region below the surface of the earth

"This Roman site... is certain to reveal a rich hypogeal harvest." — from an article in *The Athenaeum* magazine, 1886

chthonic ("THAHN-ik") the underworld (in Greek myth: as opposed to Olympian)

"...the chthonic imagery of Norine's apartment, which, if not exactly a cellar... was black as a coalhole and heated by the furnace of the hostess' unslaked desires..." — Mary McCarthy, *The Group*

vitreous ("VIH-tree-əss") glass; especially, resembling glass

If you've seen this word before, chances are it was followed by either *humor* or *china.* The vitreous humor is the transparent gelatinous material that fills most of the eyeball, between the lens and the retina. Vitreous china is a hard, shiny enamel coating applied to ceramics, especially sinks and toilets.

plumbeous ("PLUM-bee-əss") lead; especially, resembling lead in color

> "The chairman's plumbeous face turned blue." — Brendan Behan, *Confessions of an Irish Rebel*

ferruginous ("fə-ROO-jən-əss") iron (or, the color of iron rust)

thionic ("thigh-AHN-ik") sulfur

cupreous ("KYOO-pree-əss") copper

sagittal ("SADJ-ə-təl") arrows or arrowheads

> But you're more likely to see this word in the phrase *sagittal suture*, which refers to the joint at the top of the skull, which separates the left side from the right.

venatic ("və-NAT-ik") hunting

viatic ("vy-AT-ik") traveling

> "I love the process of settling into viatic quarters—the cool linen of the berth, the slow passage of the station's departing lights." — Vladimir Nabokov, *Details of Sunset*

demotic ("də-MAHT-ik") the common people ("in common use; popular"—referring, especially, to language)

> Note the root: *demos,* the Greek word for "people," which also gives us *democracy.*

> "...he had a knack of speaking what he thought of as American demotic." — C.P. Snow, *Last Things*

biotic ("by-AHT-ik") living things; consisting of living things

> "'It's a true refugia,' ... —an area that serves as a sort of biotic bomb shelter where species can survive geologic upheaval."

> —from an article about a region of Australia, in *Atlantic* magazine, 2020

noetic ("no-ET-ik") the intellect, or reasoning

> "Words are our only source of noetic nutrition. Without them, we suffer anorexia of the mind." — from an article in *Maledicta (The International Journal of Verbal Aggression)*, 1984

gnostic ("NAHS-tik") knowledge (especially mystical knowledge)

With a capital G, this word refers to early Christian sects that claimed special spiritual knowledge.

The Gnostic Gospels, a 1979 book by Elaine Pagels, examines 52 texts discovered in an earthenware jar in Egypt in 1945: the texts include some sayings of Jesus familiar from the New Testament, but also ideas that contradict the traditional understanding of Jesus and his teachings.

sacral ("SAY-krəl" or "SAH-krəl," with the A pronounced as in *arrow*) religious rites, symbols, or observances; or, pertaining to the *sacrum,* the bone at the base of the spine

"[Reverend Sun Myung] Moon recently announced in that sacral third person he uses in public appearances, 'he will go to Germany.'" — from an article in the *New York Review of Books,* 1979

lustral ("LUSS-trəl") ceremonial purification

"The assassin placed the bloody head upon Sulla's banquet-table, and coolly washed his hands in the lustral waters of a neighbouring temple." — Charles Merivale, *The Fall of the Roman Republic*

prelapsarian ("pree-lap-SAIR-ee-ən") the time before the Fall of Man (i.e., in Eden; innocent)

"The vision, which now seems distinctly prelapsarian, was of the Web as a bottom-up phenomenon, with no bosses, and no rewards other than the satisfaction of participating in successful innovation."— from an article in the *New Yorker,* 2020

olfactory ("ohl-FAK-tə-ree") the sense of smell

"Crafted in Spain from a single block of alabaster stone, Cire Trudon's newest candle… is both an olfactory and visual masterpiece." — from an article in *Vogue,* 2020

gustatory ("GUSS-tə-tore-ee") the sense of taste; or eating

"There was a coldness to the experience, a sense that all the sous vide-ing and mise en place-ing and tweezering had somehow frozen the joy, the gustatory pleasure… of cooking." — from an article in *Bon Appetit,* 2017

potatory ("POH-tə-tore-ee") drinking

"A pipe signified a more jolly potatory spirit than a cigar." — Orlo Williams, *Vie de Bohème*

spumous ("SPYOO-məss") froth, foam; or covered with small
bubbles

> "Down upon the river that was black and thick with dye, some
> Coketown boys who were at large... rowed a crazy boat, which
> made a spumous track upon the water..." — Charles Dickens,
> *Hard Times*

puerperal ("pyoo-ƏR-pər-əl") childbirth, or the period following it

> Puerperal fever, also known as childbed fever, was responsible
> for the deaths of many women on maternity wards in the mid-19th
> century.

> "Semmelweiss... demonstrated how doctors spread puerperal
> fever by not washing their hands." — from an article in the *New
> York Review of Books*, 1996

Adjectives from Animals ("Of, like, or pertaining to a...")

anserine ("AN-sər-ine," rhyming with *mine,* or "AN-sər-een") goose
(i.e., silly)

> "The geese take to the air in squadron after squadron, covering
> the sky with a glorious anserine calligraphy." — from an article
> in the *Times* (of London), 2006

> "And all because of his anserine stupidity!" — Harry Greene,
> *Barbara of the Snows*

bovine ("BOH-vine") cow

> Bovine spongiform encephalopathy is better known as mad cow
> disease.

> Here's an awful pun I thought I'd never find a use for: "I see your
> calf is all grown and headed off to college. Where will the heifer
> be studying?" "She's enrolled at the Moo-niversity of Cowifornia
> at Bovine."

cervine ("SƏR-vine") deer

> "...the bubbles contained each letter in the alphabet, in sequence,
> to form an outline that's... definitely cervine..." — from the
> "Wordplay" column in the *New York Times*, 2017 (about a puzzle
> whose theme was Rudolph the Red-Nosed Reindeer)

batrachian ("bə-TRAY-kee-ən") frog or toad

> "...I used to think that the purring of these little creatures
> [crickets], which mingled with the batrachian hymns from the

neighboring swamp, was peculiar to Saturday evenings." —
Oliver Wendell Holmes, *The Autocrat of the Breakfast-Table*

"A letter from the King of Fishes to Baron Batrachian of Frogley Hall."
"Tell your employer that we do not accept unsolicited correspondence."

corvine ("CORE-vine") crow, raven

> "I felt as if I were looking in on a corvine colloquium to which I
> had not been invited." — from a column about loud crows
> overhead, in the *New York Times,* 2013

hircine ("HƏR-sine") goat (especially with the connotation of
"lustful"; or smelling like a goat)

> "...I have learned to love the desert. The spectacular sunrises; ...
> the hircine smell of the camels..." — from a story in the *Saturday
> Evening Post*, 1915

leporine ("LEP-ə-rine") rabbit or hare

> "...succumbing to horrified pride as 'the world's foremost expert
> in human-leporine midwifing,' he... attracts the attention of

prominent London surgeons and even the king, and loses control of events." — from a review of a novel based on a true story of scientific fraud in the 18th century, in the *New York Times,* 2019

lupine ("LOO-pine") wolf

J.K. Rowling gave her werewolf professor the name Remus Lupin: one of her many nudges-in-the-ribs for readers familiar with Latin word roots.

(When pronounced "LOO-pən," the same word serves as the name of a common flowering plant.)

ovine ("OH-vine") sheep

By implication, this word often means "unthinkingly following a leader":

"Subsequent editors… have followed his lead with ovine unanimity." — from an article in *The Classical Review*, 1928

ophidian ("oh-FID-ee-ən") snake, serpent

"Annette would occasionally curb with an opaque, almost ophidian, look, her mother's volubility." — Vladimir Nabokov, *Look at the Harlequins*

pavonine ("PAV-oh-nine") peacock

"…the pavonine sun was all eyes on the gravel under the flowering trees…" — Vladimir Nabokov, *Lolita*

phocine ("FOH-sine") seal

"My darling, my sweetheart… had already… retreated to her mat near her phocine mamma." — Vladimir Nabokov, *Lolita*

saurian ("SAW-ree-ən") lizard; or crocodile; or dinosaur

"Mrs. Beatrice Lestrange Bradley… smiled the saurian smile of the sand lizard and basked in the sun." — Gladys Mitchell, *The Mystery of a Butcher's Shop*

testudinate ("tess-TOOD-ən-ət") tortoise; or, shaped like a tortoise's shell

vespine ("VESS-pine") wasp

"A study… of 18th-century England and of the hard-nosed, vespine little genius who depicted mainly its corruptions." — from a brief description of a biography of the artist William Hogarth, in the *New York Times*, 1997

vulpine ("VULL-pine," the first syllable rhyming with *null*) fox

"Sometimes [a fox] came near to my window, attracted by my light, barked a vulpine curse at me, and then retreated." — Henry David Thoreau, *Walden*

Bonus adjectives (they didn't fit anywhere else)

liminal ("LIM-ə-nəl") transitional: at the boundary between two conditions or stages; or minimal, barely perceptible

> "Airports are places of waiting and uncertainty—liminal, indeterminate spaces, caught between one world and another." — from an article in *Church Times*, 2011

fungible ("FUN-jə-bəl") (usually in law or finance) able to be replaced by an identical thing; freely exchangeable

> "The three of them are sitting in a tiny, unsightly, fungible office in a huge, unsightly, fungible building on the M.I.T. campus." — Brad Leithauser, *Hence*

tutelary ("TOO-tə-ler-ee") serving in the role of protector or guardian—especially one who teaches or influences

> "Charles Dickens, whose novels are mentioned several times by narrators, hovers as a kind of tutelary spirit over the book." — from a review on *BostonGlobe.com*, 2021

hermetic ("hər-MEH-tik") air-tight; or immune to outside influence; or pertaining to alchemy or the occult

> "And with few exceptions classical [music] announcers exist in hermetic bubbles, known only to their flocks, ignored by their peers." — from a *New York Times* article, 2012

gnomic ("NOH-mik") pithy; or expressed in the form of aphorisms, which may be hard to interpret

> "…her single-mindedness is offset by the lure of her fractured forms, her gnomic sentences, and her fairy-tale settings." — from a review of a collection of stories by Cristina Rivera Garza, in the *New Yorker*, 2022

eidetic ("eye-DET-ik") vivid and detailed, as if physically visible (refers to images in the mind)

> "She let all of that go from her mind and allowed herself only the chessboard of her imagination… this eidetic image was her proper domain." — Walter Tevis, *The Queen's Gambit*

commensal ("kə-MEN-səl") eating at the same table; or, in biology, living in close connection with another organism and benefiting from the relationship, without detriment to the other organism (as distinct from symbiotic or parasitic relationships)

> "Commensal bacteria are part of the normal flora in the mouth." — from the website medicinenet.com

minatory ("MIN-ə-tore-ee") menacing, threatening

"We… start circling each other in deep kung-fu stances, making threatening movements—dog-paddle punches, minatory half-kicks—that look like an angry, disco-style hokey-pokey." — Adam Davies, *Mine All Mine*

banausic ("bə-NAW-zik") pertaining to earning a living (used contemptuously); or mundane; or merely practical

"… a sensitive, self-conscious creature… in sad revolt against uncongenially banausic employment." — from an article in *London* magazine, 1957

holophrastic ("hah-lə-FRASS-tik") expressing more than one simple idea with one word

Holophrastic also refers to a stage in the development in a child's language: "Toddlers pass through a holophrastic stage early in life, during which they are able to communicate complex ideas using only single words and simple fixed expressions. As an example, the word 'food' might be used to mean 'Give me food'…" — from Wikipedia, "Holophrasis"

"To Be Is to Do" "To Do Is to Be" "Do Be Do Be Do": Verbs

You wouldn't believe some of the things people do. And this is just a partial list.

Don't talk like that!

prate/prattle to talk on and on, foolishly or trivially

> "You prate, he said, instead of answering." — Plato, *Euthydemus,* translated by Benjamin Jowett

twaddle to talk or write foolishly or trivially (as a noun, *twaddle* means foolish, trivial chatter or nonsense)

> "I am afraid I am twaddling." — Sir Walter Scott, in his *Journal,* 1831

maunder to talk in a rambling, aimless way

> "While he was maundering on in this way I was… returning to my senses." — Wilkie Collins, *The Woman in White*

thrum to recite in a monotonous, tiresome way; or to make a monotonous humming sound

> "…beautifully printed and illustrated text-books invite the young student's attention and stimulate his interest; attractive maps and globes illustrate to his eye lessons that formerly were only got by tedious thrumming…" — James Maitland, *The Golden Northwest* (1879)

When you have a strong opinion

asseverate ("ə-SEV-ər-ate") to state emphatically or solemnly

> "The tramp of their boots upon the dry road seemed to asseverate nothing, nothing, nothing.'" — Virginia Woolf, *Night and Day*

confute ("kən-FYOOT") to prove conclusively that something is wrong or invalid

> "If you wish to win a man's heart, allow him to confute you." — Benjamin Disraeli, *Vivian Grey*

remonstrate (American, "rə-MON-strate"; British, "REH-mən-strate") to speak in protest, giving reasons for objection

"My mother remonstrated, opined I would be a great unwomanly tomboy." — Miles Franklin, *My Brilliant Career*

inveigh ("in-VAY") to protest strongly or bitterly (usually *against* something)

"How could America have convincingly inveighed against the Iron Curtain while an equally oppressive Cotton Curtain remained draped across the South?" — from an article about Martin Luther King, Jr., in *Time* magazine, 1998

Mr. Stickles inveighed against pending legislation that would tax broad-brimmed hats such as his own.

fulminate ("FULL-mə-nate") to issue thunderous verbal attacks or protests

"...though you could not actually hear what the man was saying, you could not be in any doubt about its general nature. He might be... demanding sterner measures against thought-criminals and saboteurs, he might be fulminating against the atrocities of the Eurasian army, he might be praising Big Brother...—it made no difference." — George Orwell, *1984*

gainsay ("gain-SAY" or "GAIN-say") to contradict or oppose

"And no one dared gainsay him, for he was a strong-willed, direct man…" — D.H. Lawrence, *The Rainbow*

derogate ("DEH-rə-gate") to disparage, or detract from

"'In Jones Day's fraternity culture,' the complaint says, 'male brotherhood is affirmed and strengthened by comments and conduct that derogate women…'" — from an article in the *New York Times* about a suit accusing a prominent law firm of gender discrimination, 2020

Hold on, just a minute

temporize ("TEM-pə-rise") to evade making a decision or declaring an opinion, in order to gain time

"On the first day when his father formally gave him the hint that he was to place his affections at Miss Swartz's feet, George temporized with the old gentleman. 'You should have thought of that sooner, sir,' he said. 'It can't be done now, when we're expecting every day to go on foreign service…'" — William Makepeace Thackeray, *Vanity Fair*

hang fire to delay making a decision or taking action

The phrase originally referred to a delay between pulling a trigger and the gun firing. The Rolling Stones used "Hang Fire" as the title of a song (on *Tattoo You*, in 1981) but the lyrics have more to do with idleness (as a result of England's economic decline) than with delay or hesitation.

Deceit! Trickery! Fraud!

cozen (pronounced like "cousin") to deceive by trickery or fraud

"You might say the same of a man who was cozened into leaving every shilling away from his own children." — Anthony Trollope, *He Knew He Was Right*

inveigle ("in-VAY-ghəl") to entice or trick someone into doing something; to lead on or deceive; to obtain something through cleverness or flattery

"The two cell-surface proteins that SARS-CoV-2 uses to make contact with its target cells and inveigle its way into them…" — from an article in *The Economist*, 2020

dissemble ("dih-SEM-bəl") to conceal one's true beliefs or feelings, deceitfully

> "The doctors attending him are public servants and shouldn't dissemble or strategize when answering questions that citizens are entitled to ask." — from an article in the *Star Tribune* (Minneapolis) about President Trump's case of coronavirus, 2020

"No dissemblin' 'ere, Sir. All our victuals are organic, cage-free, gluten-free, hormone-free, ek cetera, ek cetera."

euchre ("YOO-kər") to cheat or outwit (someone, out of something)

> This word comes from a card game of the same name, in which a player can be blocked from winning by deceit.

> "The stockholders... have been euchered out of their investments in Vermont railroads." — from an article in the *Concord* (New Hampshire) *Monitor*, 1887

palter ("PAWL-tər") to talk or act insincerely; to deal crookedly

> "If you palter or double in your answers, I will have thee hung alive in an iron-chain." — Sir Walter Scott, *Quentin Durward*

Good grief!

keen to lament (the dead, usually) with a long, loud wail or wordless cry

> This was a long-standing Irish tradition, practiced by women during funeral processions and at the site of burial. The tradition had faded out by the middle of the 20th century.

> "It is the wild Irish women, keening over their dead." — George A. Lawrence, *Guy Livingstone*

ululate ("ULL-yə-late" or "YOO-yə-late") to make a loud, prolonged, high-pitched trilling sound, expressing grief or sometimes joy

> You may have seen women ululating in movies about the Middle East, e.g., *Lawrence of Arabia* or *The Battle of Algiers*.

> "Women ululated as [Pope] Francis and the king walked along the promenade of the Hassan Tower complex under umbrellas." — from an article in the *Seattle Times*, 2019

Thinking, studying, deducing, proving

excogitate ("ex-KAHJ-ə-tait") to think out in great detail

> "But now all was nebulous and dark, a murk of irritation from which no spark could be excogitated." — Samuel Beckett, *Murphy*

adduce ("ə-DOOSE") to cite as an example, or as a means of proof in an argument

> "Divine providence is often adduced when a few faithful people survive a disaster, but all the religious folks who died and atheists who lived are expediently ignored." — from an article in *Scientific American*, 2018

educe ("ee-DOOSE" or "ee-DYOOSE") to draw out, elicit; to deduce based on evidence

> "In most subjects, few attempts are made to educe principles from ever larger masses of facts." — Jacques Barzun, *The House of Intellect*

vet to examine carefully; to evaluate (especially, candidates for a position)

> This word (the verb, not the shortened form of *veteran* or *veterinarian*) entered popular usage because of political candidates who were "insufficiently vetted," notably Sarah Palin: "...the team assigned to vet Ms. Palin in Alaska had not arrived

there until Thursday, a day before Mr. McCain stunned the political world with his vice-presidential choice." — from an article in the *New York Times, 2008*

con to study, or carefully examine; or to direct the course of a vessel (from the conning tower, for example)

"Clare regarded her attentively, conned the characters of her face as if they had been hieroglyphics." — Thomas Hardy, *Tess of the D'Urbervilles*

Writing, analyzing, censoring

indite ("in-DITE") to put into writing; to compose

"He crossed swiftly to the dressing table... and discovered a message, neatly indited on scented note paper, for him..." — Thomas Pynchon, *V.*

parse to break (a sentence) down into its parts, explaining its grammatical structure; or to analyze something carefully, part by part

"The Free Press spoke with advocates and critics of the amendment and legal experts to parse the language of the amendment and evaluate what its passage would mean for Michiganders seeking abortions." — from an article in the *Detroit Free Press, 2022*

redact ("rə-DAKT") to edit (a document) for publication; or to censor part of a document

"In a heavily redacted section of the special counsel's report, Mueller writes, 'The Trump Campaign showed interest in Wikileaks' releases of hacked materials throughout the summer and fall of 2016.'" — from an article in the *Washington Post*, 2019

Please, no more pleas!

importune ("im-por-TUNE" or "-pər-") to request or demand urgently and persistently

"Some officers... after vainly importuning the government during many years, had died for want of a morsel of bread." — Thomas Macaulay, *The History of England*

blandish ("BLAN-dish") to gently coax someone using flattery

"...when politicians, in their zeal to win the backing of noisy single-issue partisans on the issue of, say, abortion, manage to blandish either the pro-lifers or the pro-choicers... into loud endorsement of their candidacies, they simultaneously persuade the vast majority of citizens to stay away from the polls." — from a book review in the *Washington Post,* 1991

Another dissatisfied customer

repine ("rə-PINE") to complain, or grumble; or to be discontented
> "She had left him everything but her pictures, and here their tastes differed and he didn't repine." — P.D. James, *Original Sin*

No, no, no

interdict ("in-tər-DIKT") to prohibit; or to intercept and block
> "...a RAND Corporation study concluded that interdiction—seizing drugs in transit—was unlikely ever to make much difference in U.S. cocaine consumption." — from an article in the *New Yorker,* 2013

With kid gloves

coddle ("KAH-dl") to treat someone with an overabundance of protective care and indulgence; or to cook gently by heating in water that isn't quite boiling (e.g., an egg)
> "You were a coddled and petted child, a pampered and spoiled youth." — Charles Horton, *Bred of the Desert*

cosset ("KAH-sət") to pamper, make a pet of
> "For most of his youth, he was cosseted by his family." — from an article about Andy Warhol in the *New Yorker,* 2020

mollify ("MAHL-ə-fy") to placate, soothe, or appease
> "He wants to mollify me, so that I'll give up the idea of parting with him." — Samuel Beckett, *Waiting for Godot*

Mockery

guy (rhymes with "eye") to make fun of (someone or something)

"...happy the Roman street-boy who ate his peanuts and guyed the gladiators from the dizzy gallery." — Mark Twain, *The Innocents Abroad*

Legalese

remand ("rə-MAND") to send back: especially, a prisoner, into custody, to await a next appearance in court

> "They rendered their opinion, which reversed the order of the Court of Appeals... and remanded the record to the Circuit Court..." — John Barth, *The Floating Opera*

suborn ("səb-ORN") to induce (someone) to commit an unlawful act

> When you see this word, it's often followed by *perjury,* as here: "Brindley also made national legal headlines for beating his own indictment for suborning perjury in 2015." — from an article in the *Milwaukee Journal Sentinel,* 2020

amerce ("ə-MƏRSS") to punish by fine

> "The freeman is not to be amerced in a way that will ruin him." — William Stubbs, *The Constitutional History of England*

Shady business

defalcate ("də-FAL-kate," the middle syllable rhyming with *pal*) to take or misuse money or property you've been entrusted with; to embezzle

> "Defalcation and the Hazards of Board Membership" — headline of an article on the website Weil Restructuring, 2016

Waxing and waning

wizen ("WIZZ-ən") to dry up, wither, wrinkle, usually due to old age

> You've probably encountered the past participle of this word, functioning as an adjective, as it does here: "On that sliver of rock are a cottage and a lighthouse... that are defended by a wizened old man who prefers the roar of the tide to the ring of the phone." — from an article in the *New York Times,* 2002.

> I would guess that at least three out of four occurrences of the word *wizened* are followed by *old man* or *old woman.* If you don't like to use clichés, try finding some other word or phrase to

place after *wizened*—perhaps *youngster,* for the element of surprise.

etiolate ("EE-tee-ə-late") to become pale and weak, especially from lack of sunlight; or to make something pale

> "She went on... taking care of her looks, remembering how drink hardens the skin and how drugs etiolate it." — Jean Stafford, *Bad Characters*

deliquesce ("dell-ə-KWESS") to melt away, dissolve; when referring to once-living matter, to liquefy when decomposing

> "I have known several very genteel idiots whose whole vocabulary had deliquesced into some half dozen expressions." — Oliver Wendell Holmes, *The Autocrat of the Breakfast-Table*

batten ("BATT-n") to thrive, or grow fat, especially at someone else's expense

> "There, in these Dens of Satan... do Sieur Motier's *mouchards* consort... battening vampire-like on a People next-door to starvation." — Thomas Carlyle, *The French Revolution*

> (A *mouchard* is a snitch, or informer.)

> This meaning of *batten* has nothing to do with *batten down the hatches,* which means to secure doorways and other openings on a ship to prepare for a storm, by placing *battens* (strips of lumber) over the canvas.

Looking a bit shaky there

yaw to move unsteadily; or to deviate from course

> *Roll, pitch,* and *yaw* refer to an aircraft's movement around three different axes: to *yaw* is to turn on the vertical axis, which means that the nose of the plane veers right or left. When pitching, the plane's nose moves up or down. If the plane rolls, then the nose rotates like a drill bit.

> Ships yaw as well, when they move from side to side and therefore deviate from their course.

> Figuratively: "The rider yawed in his saddle as a boat... yaws on a cross-sea swell." — from an article in *Pall Mall Magazine,* 1896

wamble ("WAHM-bəl") to stagger, or move unsteadily

> "...there was not an evening for two weeks when he did not return home late and shaky... He came wambling into the house." — Sinclair Lewis, *Babbitt*

Insertions and entanglements

intercalate ("in-TƏR-kə-late") to insert between other things

"Northward melted the green, gray, bluish mountains... separated by narrow dim valleys with intercalated cotton-wool bits of cloud..." — Vladimir Nabokov, *Pale Fire*

intromit ("in-trə-MIT") to insert; or to allow to enter

Searching for a sentence to offer as an example, I was surprised to find the word—in its noun form—used this way: "Finally [the spotted hyena] mounted her and began to achieve intromission." — from an article in the *New York Times*, 2011

embrangle ("em-BRANG-əl") to entangle or confuse

This seems to be a more fun way to say *embroil*.

From the *London Herald*, 1861, referring to an incident involving two ships, one from the Confederacy, one from the Union: "But we are as a neutral nation somewhat affected by the course taken by a war-ship of either of the belligerents, when she is coming into our ports on a mission to our Government, because that course may have a tendency to embrangle us with one or the other party."

Things one rarely does

jacklight to hunt or fish at night, using a light to attract and illuminate prey (also a noun: the light itself)

"It was Avery who always found the time to take the kids out in the middle of the night frog-gigging or jacklighting deer." — John Varley, *Red Thunder*

flense ("FLENSS") to strip the skin/fat/blubber from a carcass (especially a whale's)

"But in very many cases, circumstances require that the harpooneer shall remain on the whale till the whole flensing or stripping operation is concluded." — Herman Melville, *Moby-Dick*

Things you don't want done to yourself

hector ("HECK-tər") to bully or browbeat

"We are... not to be hectored, and bullied, and beat into Compliance." — Henry Fielding, *Tom Jones*

lapidate ("LAP-ih-date") to stone (as in *to death*)

"Let him who's in a sinless state / Be the first to lapidate."

frog march to force someone forward roughly, with arms pinned behind the back

But what's frog-like about that? The phrase comes from the original, more aggressive maneuver, in which police would carry away a downward-facing prisoner by the arms and legs.

"I failed to wait behind the yellow line, as instructed, and was promptly frog-marched... to a welcoming interrogation room." — Stephen Brown, *Free Gift Inside!*

chevy/chivy/chivvy ("TCHEH-vee/ TCHIH-vee") to hunt or chase; or to harass/annoy

"For smaller losses... policyholders often have to be chivvied into claiming." — from an article in *The Economist,* 2019

Making your mark and shaping things

scarify ("SKAIR-ə-fye") to make small, superficial punctures (in skin); or to criticize sharply (with "cutting" remarks)

"The ... word means 'writing,' but also stands for the practice of scarification that's common to West Africa. Followers of the custom place superficial incisions on their skin... amounting to permanent body decoration that communicates a myriad of cultural expressions." — from an article in the *Huffington Post,* 2014

obtund ("ahb-TUND") to make blunt or dull; to deaden; to take the edge off (literally or figuratively)

"Madeira did not seem to be unconscious, but his senses were obtunded, and it was some minutes before he could sit up." — Rose E. Young, *Sally of Missouri*

chamfer ("TCHAM-fər") to bevel (an edge), i.e., to cut along a right-angled edge, producing a 45° angle

I first heard this word from my Wood Shop teacher in 7th grade and had no idea what he was talking about. We chamfered the edges of the bookends we were making, using a Stanley plane. I can't remember hearing the word since.

"You clumsy fool!"

foozle ("FOOZ-əl") to do something awkwardly; to bungle—
especially a stroke in golf

> "Should we look at the back of the ball and think of driving a tack
> into it...or should we mark out a line on a blade of grass an inch
> or two in front of the ball and roll the stroke through that
> point...? The former thought produces an infallibly crisp hit, but
> in a variable direction, and the latter gives excellent aim to a
> sometimes foozled stroke." — from an article by John Updike in
> *Golf World* magazine, 1983

"Hellfire and damnation!"
"Yes, my Lord, but it was less frightfully foozled than the last three."

"Brilliant!"

scintillate ("SIN-tə-late") to throw off sparks, or to flash; to be
animated or brilliant

Cliché alert: If you refer to *scintillating wit*, you'll join a long line of writers who have already done so.

"A tall and very dignified old woman clothed from head to foot in snow white... and scintillating with jewels." — Elizabeth Goudge, *City of Bells*

fulgurate ("FULL-ghə-rate") to give off flashes like lightning

This somewhat literary word also refers to a procedure in which diseased tissue is destroyed with electricity: "*THINKS CURE FOR CANCER IS FOUND; Dr. Hart Has Used His Fulguration Treatment for 18 Months. SURGEONS ARE IMPRESSED...*" — headline in the *New York Times*, 1907

Grinding, breaking, softening

comminute ("KAHM-ə-noot" or "-yoot") to pulverize, reduce to powder

Only a brute would comminute a common newt. They're so cute!

triturate ("TRIT-yə-rate") to comminute, i.e, grind into powder

"Worms swallow many little stones... it is probable that they serve, like mill-stones, to triturate their food." — Charles Darwin, *The Formation of Vegetable Mould, Through the Action of Worms*

(I'm imagining Darwin's publisher here: "Mightn't we aim for a more engaging title, Charles? Perhaps something like *Worms! Worms! Worms!*")

levigate ("LEV-ə-gate") to grind to a fine, smooth powder; or, to turn something into paste by grinding and adding liquid

"The mud in the harbor where we lay was of a fine white... it is probable, that it is no more than shells, and other calcareous matter, levigated by the friction of the particles, produced by the constant motion of the water." — Andrew Ellicott, *Journal* (1802)

spall ("SPAWL") to break something into smaller pieces, especially stones; or used as a noun, a rock chip

"She looked at the huge chip of stone spalled off by a bullet." — Mary Napier, *Blind Chance*

macerate ("MASS-ə-rate") to soften something (especially food) by soaking it in liquid

"The fruit is macerated for a time in alcohol, usually a clear, unaged grape brandy." — from an article in *Bon Appétit* magazine, 1984

Crazy -ates

vitiate ("VIH-shee-ate") to spoil; or to lessen the quality or value of something

"The climate effects of such wanton deforestation will partially vitiate any environmental gains from the collapse in ground and air transport this spring." — from an article in *The New Republic,* 2020

obviate ("AHB-vee-ate") to render something unnecessary

"This anti-parasitic drug has been championed in right wing circles, presumably as a way to obviate the need for a coronavirus vaccine." — from an article in *Forbes,* 2021

abrogate ("AB-rə-gate") to formally annul or abolish; or to fail to do something one is supposed to do

"The sanctions imposed by the United States in 2018, after President Trump abrogated the nuclear agreement between the two countries, have aggravated those failures and intensified the corruption of the governing élite." — from an article about Iran in the *New Yorker,* 2020

adumbrate ("ADD-əm-brate") to sketch or outline in a partial or vague way

You can't help noticing the word *dumb* in the middle. But that has nothing to do with its etymology. In other words, it's irrelevant—just like this comment.

"There is no room in these pages to do more than adumbrate the scope of such arguments." — from an article in *New York* magazine, 1975

arrogate ("ARR-ə-gate") to take or claim something without right

"He went so far as to arrogate to himself the right of harming her." — Thomas Hardy, *Tess of the D'Urbervilles*

immolate ("IMM-ə-late") to kill as a sacrifice, usually by burning

"A former Tibetan Buddhist monk protested Chinese rule by killing himself through self-immolation this month, becoming the 100th person to do so inside Chinese-governed Tibet..." — from an article in the *New York Times,* 2013

expostulate ("eks-PAHS-tchə-late") to reason earnestly with someone, in an attempt to dissuade or correct

"My old pal would shout, scream, cackle, laugh, giggle, holler, preach his rule today, just as he used to expound, expostulate, rap it in the middle of campus parties, street crowds, into a mike, into your ear, into a garbage can while he was barfing." — John Edgar Wideman, "Arizona"

titivate ("TIH-tə-vate") (informal) to put on decorative touches; to dress up (can be used as a transitive or intransitive verb)

"She was a friendly girl, happy to titivate the thinning locks of old-age pensioners as well as the sticky pungent beehives of her contemporaries." — Margaret Drabble, *The Ice Age*

crepitate ("KRƏP-ə-tate") to crackle

Yes, but hundreds of years ago, this word meant *to fart*. And some young scholars brought that meaning back in the 1970s, when I was in college. My friend Kenny Shulman wrote and described to me the annual Crepitation Contest held at his college, SUNY at Stony Brook. Each competitor gave himself a bold, proud name, e.g., the Farting Dutchman. It seemed so witty at the time!

decrepitate ("dee-KRƏP-ə-tate") to crackle when heated, in the process of disintegrating (refers to salts and minerals)

The *Oxford English Dictionary* quotes the *Dictionary of Chemistry*: "This is owing to the sudden conversion into steam of the water enclosed within the substance, or, as in some natural minerals, to the unequal expansion of the laminæ which compose them." The things you learn by reading the dictionary!

hebetate ("HƏB-ə-tate") to make dull; or to become dull

"Men's souls were blinded, hebetated; and sunk under the influence of Atheism and Materialism, and Hume and Voltaire: the world for the present was as an extinct world, deserted of God, and incapable of welldoing till it changed its heart and spirit." — Thomas Carlyle, *The Life of John Sterling*

colligate ("KAHL-ə-gate") to bind together, or group together; to connect (isolated facts) with an overarching explanation or theory

"We can observe and colligate the facts of emotion and volition, as we can observe the position of the stars and the laws of heat." — Leslie Stephen (father of Virginia Woolf), *Social Rights and Duties*

stridulate to make a shrill, grating, or chirping sound, like some insects (the sound itself is called *stridulation*)

"A window was open, and the crickets were stridulating at an ominous speed in the black motionless foliage." — Vladimir Nabokov, *Ada*

nictate ("NIK-tate") to wink or blink

> This word has a synonymous variant, *nictitate,* which often appears as part of the phrase *nictitating membrane*: a thin membrane, beneath the eyelid, that helps moisten and clean the eyes of certain birds and fishes.
>
> "The lid of her left eye began, inexplicably, to nictate." — Salman Rushdie, *Shame*

exuviate ("eg-ZOO-vee-ate" or "ig-") to cast off (a skin or shell); to molt

> "The young crayfish exuviate two or three times in the course of the first year." — Thomas Huxley, *The Crayfish*
>
> By the way, *exuviae* are the cast-off coverings of animals. You needed to know that.

estivate ("ESS-tə-vate") to spend the summer—especially in a dormant state

> When used in zoology, this is the summer equivalent of *hibernate*. But its use is not limited to drowsy non-humans: "Too soon we will be forced to estivate, to draw the shades against the sun… and live our days in gloom; we will go out only when it's cool, in the early morning or after sunset. Pandemic claustrophobia will arrive." — from an article in the *New York Review of Books,* March 2020

A few more things you can do

degust ("dih-GUST") to taste attentively, in order to appreciate or discern flavor

> Wine: "a deity to be invoked by two or three, all fervent, hushing their talk, degusting tenderly." — Robert Louis Stevenson, *Silverado Squatters*

scotch to crush, stifle, or put an end to

> "Fanaticism which constitutes a danger to mankind should be scotched." — from an article in the *Expositor* magazine, 1908

absterge ("ab-STƏRDJ") (archaic) to cleanse, or to wipe clean; or purge

"He made the sign of the cross three times over Fortnight's head… and then suddenly cried out 'My God, I have forgotten to absterge the podex!'" — Roger Scruton, *Fortnight's Anger* (The *podex* is the rump, or anal area.)

Etc.

pique ("PEEK") to stimulate (interest in something); or to injure the feelings or pride of (someone)

A confusing word, because of its various meanings and homonyms. "Now you've piqued my interest." "I see you peeked into the beauty contestants' dressing room." "The press conference is over. I am leaving in a fit of pique." "He was looking a bit peaked,* don't you think?" "His popularity peaked years ago."

"The posthumous revelation of Cheever's alcoholism, numerous infidelities and bisexuality may have piqued interest precisely because he presented himself so earnestly as the Man in the Brooks Brothers Suit." — from a *New York Times* review of John Cheever's *Journals*, 1991

*This word is pronounced "PEEK-id," and means "pale, sickly-looking."

occlude ("ə-KLOOD") to block or close up

"Feinstein extrapolated that statement to express a fear that Barrett, a textualist who once clerked for Justice Antonin Scalia, would allow her faith to occlude her legal judgment if a challenge to Roe should arise." — from an article in the *Washington Examiner*, 2020

debouch ("də-BOWTCH," the second syllable to rhyme with *couch*, or "də-BOOSH") to emerge, usually from a small area into a larger one

Streets and rivers can *debouch;* so can groups of soldiers.

"Nakidino Creek, into which an important stream debouches." — Henry M. Stanley, *Through the Dark Continent*

Word Play

Which verb doesn't belong with the others?

1. prate, maunder, batten, importune
2. cozen, lapidate, inveigle, euchre
3. fulgurate, wizen, etiolate, deliquesce
4. comminute, triturate, levigate, foozle

Cupidity, Keglers, and Comedos: Uncommon Words for Familiar Objects, Actions, etc.

Why do we need unfamiliar words when we already know common words for the same things? I'll tell you why. Most of these words carry shades of meaning that the more common ones don't. And some of them just sound better. Doesn't *piffle* convey the idea of "foolish, trivial talk or ideas" perfectly?

The many varieties of abuse, mockery, nonsense, and bluster

malediction ("mal-ə-DICK-shən") a curse, intended to bring harm to its target

> "Oaths, curses, maledictions, exploded like the firing of successive mines." — Frank Norris, *The Octopus*

brickbats insulting or critical remarks; literally, pieces of brick, especially when thrown at someone or something

> "That earned brickbats from former Goldman Sachs CEO Lloyd Blankfein, who said in interviews… that Wall Street has too often tried to have it both ways." — from an article in *Fortune* magazine, 2021

billingsgate coarse, abusive speech (as was commonly heard in Billingsgate, a former fish market in London)

> "DEPUTY LUISE ZIETZ DEAD. Stricken at Thursday's Reichstag Session—Noted for Billingsgate." — headline of article in the *New York Times*, 1922 ("…one of the foremost veteran champions of women's rights… notorious or famous, according to the observer's point of view, for her crude and often vulgar remarks… a born baiter of reactionaries, militarists and Nationalists.")

cachinnation ("KAK-ə-nation") loud, convulsive laughter

> "And then she laughed too, a weird, high-pitched laugh, off key, an altogether unexpected piece of cachinnation." — Henry Miller, *Tropic of Cancer*

piffle ("PIFF-əl") foolish or trivial talk or ideas; nonsense

> "Behavioral experts… have been probed for reaction, calling the theory everything from irrelevant piffle to groundbreaking." — from an article in the *Washington Post*, 2000, about an

anthropology paper claiming that rape is a behavior programmed in men by evolution.

"He's quite good. This is the most impressive piffle we've heard tonight."

japery ("JAPE-ə-ree") (archaic) joking, mocking, pranking, clowning

"...and Falstaff is egging Prince Hal on to some japery." — from the description of a mug, for sale at The Literary Gift Company's website (£10.99, as of this writing)

double Dutch unintelligible language, gibberish; or jump-rope played with two long ropes

"Double Dutch apology from royals who went on holiday." — headline in the *Times* (London), 2020, about the king and queen of the Netherlands, who vacationed in Greece with their three daughters during a partial pandemic lockdown

persiflage ("PER-sə-flahzh") light, teasing banter

"Now go away then, and leave me alone. I don't want any more of your meretricious persiflage." — D.H. Lawrence, *Women in Love*

(Remember that *meretricious* means "whore-like.")

blatherskite ("BLA-thər-skite") blustering talk, nonsense; or a person who talks a lot, emptily

"For Nietzsche… there is no such thing as abstract knowledge; there is only useful knowledge and unprofitable blatherskite." — Colin Wilson, *The Outsider*

gasconade ("GAS-kən-aid") boastful, blustering talk
"He recounted his victory with many exaggerations and gasconades." — Tobias Smollett, *Roderick Random*

rodomontade ("rahd-ə-mahn-TAHD" or "rohd-ə-mahn-TAID") arrogant boasting or blustering talk (the word derives from Rodomonte, a character in the Italian epic poems *Orlando Furioso* and *Orlando Innamorato*)

"Between Chester and the capital there was not an inn where [Dick Talbot] had not been in a brawl. Wherever he came he… swore at the cooks and postilions, and almost raised mobs by his insolent rodomontades." — Thomas Macaulay, *The History of England*

fanfaronade ("fan-fair-ən-AID" or "fan-fair-ən-AHD") blustering talk, bravado

"He loves bright colours, he easily becomes audacious, overcrowing, full of fanfaronade." — Matthew Arnold, *Celtic Literature*

calumny ("CAL-um-nee," the A pronounced as in *cat*) slander: a false, malicious statement (or statements) intended to damage someone's reputation

"To spread suspicion, to invent calumnies, to propagate scandal, requires neither labour nor courage." — Samuel Johnson, *The Rambler* (a series of articles Johnson published between 1750 and 1752)

obloquy ("AHB-lə-kwee") public criticism; or disgrace as a result of such criticism

"Of course in order to earn a living (ha ha) it is unavoidable that one exposes oneself to ridicule and obloquy now and then." — Evelyn Waugh, *Letters*

contumely ("kahn-TYOO-mə-lee") (archaic) insolence: rude or contemptuous language or behavior

"This grocer being a bachelor and not a man who looked upon the surface for beauty, had once made honourable offers for the hand of Berry, which Mrs Pipchin [her aunt] had, with contumely and scorn, rejected." — Charles Dickens, *Dombey and Son*

131

Cf. *contumacious:* stubbornly rebellious or resistant to authority.

Two ways to end a discussion

sockdolager ("sahk-DAHL-ə-jər") a statement that decisively finishes an argument; or a knockout blow; or an outstanding person or thing

> The most famous use of this word (or, at least, a derivative) occurred on April 14, 1865, during a performance of *Our American Cousin.* John Wilkes Booth waited for the biggest laugh in the play to fire his shot. Here's the line: "Well, I guess I know enough to turn you inside out, old gal—you sockdologizing old man-trap." (As explained in an article by Rachel Manteuffel in the *Washington Post,* you had to see the whole play to understand why the line is funny: at this moment, the supposed American hick reveals that he's onto the British aristocrat who's after his money, and has been all along. Even so, it's hard to see how the word fits in that sentence!)

eructation ("ee-ruk-TAY-shən" or "ih-") a belch, or the act of belching; or matter belched forth

> "There are some eructations that sound like cheers—at least, mine did." — Vladimir Nabokov, *Lolita*

Words of praise

panegyric ("pan-ə-JY-rik" or "pan-ə-JIH-rik") an elaborate speech or text in praise of a person or thing

> "…all of the above is unbeknownst to Grace, who… delivers a panegyric to her parents for their total fabulosity…" — from a movie review in the *New Yorker,* 2019

plaudit ("PLAW-dit") an expression of praise; or a round of applause

> Usually seen in the plural, as here: "…overall his record won plaudits from industry representatives and consumer advocates alike." — from the obituary of Donald Kennedy, former head of the FDA, in the *Boston Globe,* 2020

eulogy ("YOO-lə-jee") any speech of high praise; or, such a speech delivered at a funeral

> "To be honored by being requested to give the eulogy at the funeral of Dr. Martin Luther King Jr. is like asking one to eulogize his deceased son—so close and so precious was he to

me." — from the eulogy delivered by Benjamin Mays, reprinted in *Time* magazine, 2018

encomium ("en-KOH-mee-əm") a panegyric, characterized by warm enthusiasm

> "He brought in the bread and cheese, and beer, with many high encomiums upon their excellence." — Charles Dickens, *The Old Curiosity Shop*

The inmate carefully unfolded the page, which contained an encomium upon the criminal justice system.

Other speeches, treatises, etc.

screed a long, tiresome speech or written text, usually a rant, often tedious

> "Don't think that this book is a Luddite screed about the evils of the internet." — Charles Seife, *Virtual Unreality*, about the viral spread of falsehood online

philippic ("fə-LIP-ik") a bitter verbal attack or condemnation; a diatribe

Where this word comes from: Greek orator Demosthenes (the one who practiced speaking with pebbles in his mouth) spoke fiercely against Philip II of Macedon, warning his fellow Greeks about that king's dangerous intentions.

> "Mr. Harper and Mr. Pinckney pronounced
> bitter philippics against France." — Thomas Jefferson, *Writings*

enchiridion ("en-kə-RID-ee-ən") a handbook; or a book containing key information on a topic; or, with a capital E, a book of advice written by the Stoic philosopher Epictetus

> "*The Song of Ice and Fire* is not the Westerosi enchiridion any more... The TV universe has eclipsed the books and become the *Game of Thrones* canon." — from an article in *Wired*, 2017

pandect ("PAN-dekt") a complete treatise on a subject; or a country's complete code of laws

> "A Layman's Pandect of Geminology Compended by Henry Burlingame, Cosmophilist" — title of chapter in *The Sot-Weed Factor,* by John Barth

disquisition ("dis-kwə-ZIH-shən") a formal discussion of a topic, often in writing

> "...[Bronx Borough Commander Anthony] Bouza offers a mighty disquisition on poverty and ghettoization that should be inscribed on the walls of every station house in the country." — from an article in the *New Yorker,* 2020, referring to *The Police Tapes,* a 1977 documentary

Beginnings and endings

exordium ("eggs-OR-dee-əm") the beginning or introduction, especially of a speech or text.

> "Alkibiadês started up forthwith—his impatience breaking loose from the formalities of an exordium." — George Grote, *A History of Greece*

prolegomenon ("proh-lə-GAHM-ə-nahn") the introduction to a book; especially a formal prefatory discussion in a scholarly work (plural: *prolegomena*)

> "Prolegomena to Any Future Metaphysics That Will Be Able to Present Itself as a Science" — title of a book by the German philosopher Immanuel Kant (The original German title begins with *Prolegomena*, too.)

peroration ("per-ə-RAY-shən") the concluding section of an oration, often intended to arouse the audience's emotions; the "summing up" part of an argument

> "At turns scornful, hopeful, and angry, Obama delivered an emotional peroration on the issue that has perhaps frustrated him more than any other." — from an article in the *New Yorker,* 2016 (The issue was gun control.)

In his surprising peroration, Senator Shnipps called upon the laboring classes to rise up against their masters.

Comments, changes, digressions

emendation ("ee-mən-DAY-shən") a change that improves something, especially a literary work; or the process of making such changes

> "I should like to see any man's biography with corrections and emendations by his ghost. We don't know each other's secrets quite so well as we flatter ourselves we do." — Oliver Wendell Holmes, *The Poet at the Breakfast Table*

divagation ("dy-və-GAY-shən") a digression; or a deviation from one's course

> "…with that vile lad to head them off on idle divagations… they would have smiled and stumbled through the woods." — Robert Louis Stevenson, *The Silverado Squatters*

scholium ("SKOH-lee-əm") a marginal note, explaining or commenting on a text

> "An illustration, like a funny story, loses its pungency if it requires a scholium." — Paul Klapper, *College Teaching*

"This scholium suggests that an army may win more victories by attacking than by withdrawing."

"Hm!" "Hm!" "Hm!" "Hm!"

Linguistic stuff

schwa ("SHWAH") ə: the symbol used in phonetics to indicate the common vowel sound "uh," e.g., the sound of the *a* in *announce*

> Have you noticed the many schwas in the pronunciation guides in this book? The majority of words in English seem to include this sound.

> "...of all the sounds we use, it demands the least of us. All you have to do to make a schwa is start up the vocal cords. Other sounds require you to raise or lower the tongue, or move it forward or backward... The schwa just is. ... The essence of speech itself." — from an article on the website MentalFloss.com, 2014

amphibology ("am-fə-BAHL-ə-jee") ambiguity resulting from unclear grammatical constructions

> Also known as amphiboly ("am-FIB-ə-lee"). Here are a few comical examples from an article on the website ThoughtCo.com:

> Marijuana Issues Sent to a Joint Committee.
> Dr. Ruth to Talk About Sex With Newspaper Editors
> Burglar Gets Nine Months in Violin Case
> Prostitutes Appeal to Pope
> Juvenile Court to Try Shooting Defendant

patois ("pah-TWAH," the A pronounced as in *cat*) any regional dialect that differs from the standard language of the country; or the jargon of a particular group

> "What about the 'rabble' you talk about? Should they be condemned to speak the patois of their family members, with no education in grammar? That's undemocratic. They can't move up." — from a mock dialogue between Aristophanes and Socrates, by grammarian Bryan Garner, in *National Review*, 2020 (Socrates argues from the opposing point of view.)

Printed matter

recto ("REK-toe") the right-hand page of an open book; or the front of a single sheet of paper (the side that is meant to be read first)

> "...second edition, green cloth, gilt trefoil design, previous owner's name on recto of flyleaf erased." — James Joyce, *Ulysses*

verso ("VƏR-so") the left-hand page of an open book; or the back of a single sheet of paper

> "Thistlewood did not, however, divide his diaries into a recto and a verso side but used both sides of his diary notebooks to write daily entries in which philosophical reflections were mixed with his activities as a slave owner." — from an article in the *New York Review of Books, 2020*

solidus, virgule, separatrix ("SAH-lih-dəs," "VƏR-gyool," "seh-pə-RAY-trix") a slash: /

> "The purpose of language is understanding between person/person, person/animal, person/machine and machine/machine. (I knew I'd find a use for the virgule.)" — from a column by William Safire in the *New York Times,* 1983

Attitude problems

incivism ("in-SIV-iz-əm") lack of loyalty to one's country or government; or bad citizenship

> "National commissions bemoaned the seemingly inexorable increase in youthful apathy and incivism. The National Commission on Civic Renewal said, '...We are in danger of becoming a nation of spectators.'" — from an article in the *Boston Globe, 2008*

temerity ("tə-MER-ə-tee") foolish boldness, reckless audacity, overconfidence

"...he had the temerity to believe that fighting for safety and quality and transparency was a quintessentially American thing to do." — from a review of a documentary about Ralph Nader, in *Entertainment Weekly*, 2007

contumacy ("CON-too-mə-see" or "–tyoo-mə-see") contemptuous disobedience of authority; insolent defiance

"If they refused to answer, they were punished for contumacy; if they complied, they were punished for Nonconformity." — Thomas Coleman, *Memorials of the Independent Churches in Northamptonshire*

Images and phantoms

simulacrum ("sim-yoo-LAY-krəm") an image, imitation, or representation of a thing or person; especially one that resembles the original without possessing any of its substance

"To make a portrait of him at first seemed a matter of small difficulty. There is his coat, his star, his wig, his countenance simpering under it... And yet after reading of him in scores of volumes... you find you have nothing—nothing but a coat and wig and a mask smiling below it—nothing but a great simulacrum." — William Makepeace Thackeray, *The Four Georges* (He's describing King George IV.)

eidolon ("eye-DOH-lən") a phantom; an image without substance; or a representation of an idea or a person

"Humbert, however, is not satisfied... He wants to 'incarnate'... Annabel, representative of the spell of the past, in an actual nymphet. The impossibility and tragic results of such a wish are part of the story of Lolita. The person, Lolita, vies with her eidolon." — from an article in the journal *Twentieth Century Literature*, 1975

Hodgepodges

gallimaufry ("gal-ə-MAH-free") a hodge-podge, a jumbled assortment (especially of social types gathered together)

"As a directing-writing team, the Wachowskis added fashionable academic flavor by referencing cultural theorist

Jean Baudrillard, which made their juvenile gallimaufry...
seem highbrow." — from an article in *National Review*, 2019

congeries ("KAHN-jə-reez") a jumbled collection of things; a heap

"Instead of assuming a dignified critical attitude toward the new administration... [the *New York Times*] has become a raving maniac, and fairly froths at the mouth with every mention of the new tariff bill... [I]t speaks of it as 'this congeries of abominations'..." — from an article in *Gunton's Magazine of Practical Economics and Political Science,* 1897

Big shots and exceptional types

muckamuck ("MUCK-ə-muck") (slang) a person of importance: a bigwig (also written as *muck-a-muck, mucky-muck,* etc.)

"The hotel houses the legendary Capital Bar, which is the prime watering hole for local and visiting muck-a-mucks." — from an article in *Vanity Fair,* 1994

panjandrum ("pan-JAN-drəm") a muckamuck (used scornfully): an official who has great power, or who acts as if he does, pretentiously; or an imaginary figure of great power

"Mr. Greeley has... again risen to power as Chief Editor and Grand Panjandrum of the paper." — from an article in *Vanity Fair,* 1861

phoenix ("FEE-niks") a person or thing of remarkable excellence or beauty; also, of course, the mythical bird that rises from its own ashes

"Here it was; a human being perfect of its kind, a phoenix amongst barnyard fowls." — John Braine, *Room at the Top*

Ordinary people

canaille ("kə-NYE") the masses, the common people: riff-raff, rabble

"I think perhaps if I were to go out now... and mix with the canaille, it might do me good." — Samuel Beckett, *Murphy*

hoi polloi ("HOY pə-LOY") the common people; the masses

"The first Carters were, of course, carters, medieval truck drivers. Yet despite the family's hoi-polloi origins and plain-folks posture, Jimmy Carter's family tree turns out to have some hoity-toity upper limbs. The President is related to, among others, Queen

Elizabeth I, George Washington, three other previous Presidents and the first American millionaire." — from an article in *Time* magazine, 1977

Le "é" français

éclat ("ay-KLAH," the first syllable rhyming with *hay*) dazzling success or renown: usually refers to a performance or an achievement

> "*Lolita* enjoyed an underground éclat." — John Sutherland, *Lives of the Novelists*

élan/elan ("ay-LAHN," the first syllable rhyming with *hay*) enthusiasm, vigor, flair

> "Izzy exuded effortless rogue elan, reminiscent of punk antihero Johnny Thunders and the ultimate junkie-gypsy guitarist, Keef himself." — from an article on the website al.com, 2021

> In 1966, responding to a news story about soldiers eating the animals in former President Kwame Nkrumah's private zoo, *Time* magazine ran a pun-filled piece that began, "Somehow the old eland was missing." (It helps to know that an *eland* is a type of African antelope.) My sixth-grade teacher, Mr. Catania, read this piece to our class, and I never forgot it. You can find the article if you search for it by title: "Ghana: Fangs a Lot."

élan vital ("ay-LAHN vee-TAHL") the life force; in the philosophy of Henri Bergson, the creative force responsible for growth and evolution

> "Beat preceded Pop and Camp as a burp against liberal rhetoric and official culture. Even in the beginning, however, Kerouac's Beatitude sounded as tinny as Henri Bergson's *elan vital*." — from a review of Jack Kerouac's *Satori in Paris,* in the *New York Times,* by Andrew Sarris, 1967

You'll be criticized if you do these things

tergiversation ("tər-jih-vər-SAY-shən") equivocation; or changing one's party or position, either once or repeatedly

> "The scales seemed to fall from his eyes, and the duplicity and tergiversation of which he had been guilty stung him at once with remorse and shame." — Sir Walter Scott, *Kenilworth*

peculation ("pek-yə-LAY-shən") embezzlement or misuse of funds, especially public funds

"Gouverneur Morris, who wrote the Constitution's preamble, and future president James Madison were worried about a leader who would 'pervert his administration into a scheme of peculation… or oppression…'" — from an essay favoring the impeachment of Donald Trump, in the *Washington Post*, 2017

pettifoggery ("PET-ee-fog-ə-ree") petty, deceitful tactics, especially as practiced by a lawyer; or quibbling over unimportant issues

(A lawyer who does this is a *pettifogger.*)

"Mr Byrd represents everything that is worst about the Senate: its invitations to procedural pettifoggery… its unbearable pomposity." — from an article in the *Economist*, 1995

You can be proud if you do this

supererogation ("super-ər-ə-GAY-shən") the act of doing more than is required or expected

"The launching of a conservative weekly journal of opinion in a country widely assumed to be a bastion of conservatism at first glance looks like a work of supererogation, rather like publishing a royalist weekly within the walls of Buckingham Palace." — William F. Buckley, on the launch of *National Review*, 1955

Oops

gaffe ("GAFF") an embarrassing social blunder, or faux pas

"I am a gaffe machine." — Joe Biden, 2018

"Biden Advisers Worry the Gaffes are Becoming a Problem." — headline in *Vanity Fair*, 2019

Some salient traits

cupidity ("kyoo-PID-ə-tee") greed; lust for wealth

"When not fired by cupidity, Miss Carridge's imagination was of the feeblest." — Samuel Beckett, *Murphy*

gulosity ("goo-LAH-sə-tee" or "gyoo-") gluttony; or greed

"The 206th number of his Rambler is a masterly essay against gulosity." — James Boswell, *The Life of Samuel Johnson*

hauteur ("hoh-TƏRR") snobbery, haughtiness, disdainful pride

"Mrs. [Myrtle] Wilson had changed her costume some time before... With the influence of the dress her personality had also undergone a change. The intense vitality that had been so remarkable in the garage was converted into impressive hauteur." — F. Scott Fitzgerald, *The Great Gatsby*

impudicity ("im-pyoo-DISS-ə-tee") lack of modesty; shamelessness

"...to the old gentleman's eyes there was an abiding impudicity about Cissie's very charms." — T.S. Stribling, *Birthright*

Sportin' life

southpaw (slang) a left-handed person, especially a baseball pitcher

"Ah never go to Yankee Stadium! Ah won't even go to the Polo Grounds unless a southpaw's pitchin'." — attributed to Senator Beauregard Claghorn, a fictitious character on Fred Allen's radio show

(You may be more familiar with his animated descendant, Foghorn Leghorn, the Looney Tunes rooster.)

harrier ("HAR-ee-ər," to rhyme with *carrier*) (slang) a cross-country runner

"The Garnet harriers ran ninth at the 2006 NCAA Mid-East Regional Cross Country Championships on Nov. 11." — from the *Swarthmore College Bulletin*, 2006

kegler ("KEG-lər," (slang) a bowler

"But there's one mom-and-pop San Antonio institution, the 44-lane Astro Superbowl, ... catering to a crowd that includes almost 1,000 league keglers a week." — from an article in the *San Antonio Express-News*, 2019

Body parts

poll ("POHL") (archaic) the top of a person's head

"...the doctor... had taken off his powdered wig, and sat there, looking very strange indeed with his own close-cropped, black poll." — Robert Louis Stevenson, *Treasure Island*

costard ("KAHS-tərd") (archaic, humorous) a person's head

"...it's hard I should get raps over the costard, and only pay you back in make-believes." — Sir Walter Scott, *Rob Roy*

lentigo ("len-TY-goh") a freckle; or a small spot on the skin that's darker than the area around it, found most commonly on the face or hands

> "…it seemed to me her face was less pretty than the mental imprint I had cherished for more than a month: her cheeks looked hollowed and too much lentigo camouflaged her rosy rustic features…" — Vladimir Nabokov, *Lolita*

nevus/naevus ("NEE-vəss") a birthmark or mole, especially a raised, pigmented patch: noncancerous

> "*It's not getting lighter,* his mother says, about the red lump of a strawberry naevus on his forehead just above his nose." — Nick Earls, *Perfect Skin*

> (Actually, that sounds more like a hemangioma. But I'm no dermatologist.)

maculation ("mak-yə-LAY-shən") the spotted markings of a plant or animal

> "Nabokov's comparative illustration of maculation, or wing pattern." — caption of a reproduction of a butterfly drawing by Vladimir Nabokov, in the *Guardian*, 2016

cicatrix ("SIK-ə-triks") a scar left by a wound

> In *The Searchers,* John Wayne learns that his niece has been abducted by an Indian chief named "Cicatriz"—also known as "Scar."

> "The bullet that killed Dong killed me. One shot, two souls. I now am a hollow man, empty and alone. My psyche has a cicatrix." — from an essay by Michael Norman in the *New York Times*, 1996

weal ("WEEL") a raised red mark on the skin left by a blow, e.g., from a lash

> "From shoulder to flank, sir, I am one mass of welts and weals." — Samuel Lover, *Handy Andy*

carbuncle ("KAR-bun-kəl") an infected cluster of boils with open lesions: painful and contagious

> "What is proposed is like a monstrous carbuncle on the face of a much-loved and elegant friend." — Prince Charles, commenting on a proposed extension of London's National Gallery, 1984

caruncle ("kə-RUN-kəl") an outgrowth of flesh, e.g., the comb and wattles of a rooster

> "The weirdest of a turkey's 50 or so caruncles is attached to its face. In the male this cone of flesh, drooping over its bill, can

stretch in a trice from one to eight inches." — from an article in the *New York Times,* 1992

wen (pronounced like *when*) a growth on the skin: a boil, a swelling, a benign tumor, etc.; or, specifically, a sebaceous cyst, usually on the scalp

> "This Brass was an attorney of no very good repute…a tall, meagre man, with a nose like a wen…" — Charles Dickens, *The Old Curiosity Shop*

comedo ("KAH-mə-doh") a blackhead

> "…a slight, very slight, sensual satisfaction, not more I would say than what a petty hedonist enjoys at the moment when, retaining his breath, before a magnifying mirror, his thumbnails pressing with deadly accuracy on both sides of a full stop, he expulses totally the eely, semitransparent plug of a comedo—and exhales an Ah of relief." — Vladimir Nabokov, *Pale Fire*

mamilla ("mə-MILL-ə") a nipple; or a nipple-shaped protuberance

papilla ("pə-PILL-ə") any small, nipple-like protuberance, such as a taste bud

> "The earth [in spring] is all alive and covered with papillae." — Henry David Thoreau, *Walden*

Since a *mamilla* is a nipple, I expected that a *papilla* would be something male and protuberant. But the English language isn't organized to satisfy an adolescent male sense of humor.

cerumen ("sə-ROO-mən") earwax

> "Earwax—which is not really wax at all, but a substance called cerumen that binds with dirt, dust and debris—is normally produced by the body as a way to clean and protect the ears." — from an article in *Scientific American,* 2018

nares ("NAIR-eez") the nostrils; or the nasal passages

Oddly enough, the singular of this noun is *naris.*

One night in Paris,
I nuzzled her naris.
She left in a huff,
Hissing, "Zat's not enough!
Ze man zat I marries
Must love *both* my nares!"

tonsure ("TAHN-shər") the shaven crown of a monk's head

> Dictionaries define the word this way, but I thought it referred to the round fringe of hair around the shaved part. So do many others, apparently—including, possibly, this writer:

"His tonsure looked like it had been fashioned by an impostor barber with a toenail clipper." — from an article in the *Washington Post*, 2021, referring to President Andrew Johnson's bad haircut

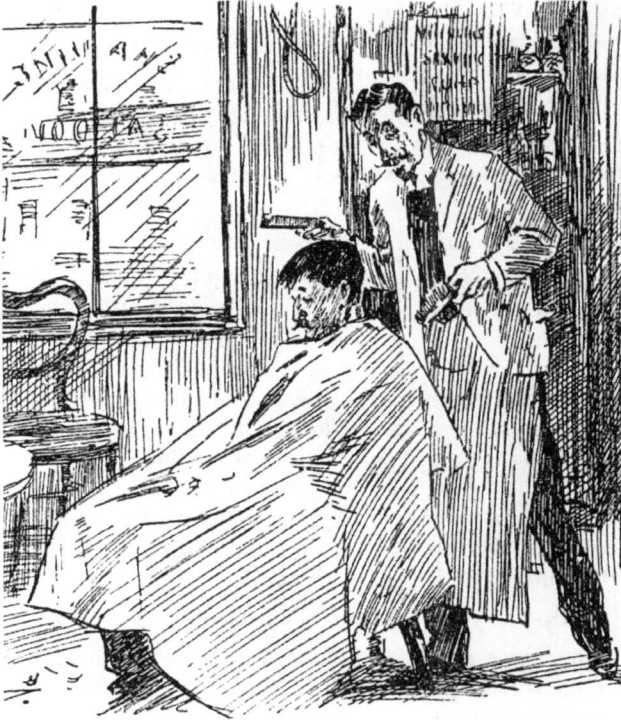

"What'll it be today? The Mohawk? The Braided Side-Part with Reverse Fade? Or the classic Monk's Tonsure?"

lanugo ("lə-NOO-go") fine, downy hair; especially, the soft hair that covers a fetus or newborn

Among the sights seen by Humbert and Lolita out west: "Distant mountains. Near mountains. More mountains; bluish beauties never attainable… early spring mountains with young-elephant lanugo along their spines…" — Vladimir Nabokov, *Lolita*

pelage ("PELL-idj") the hair, fur, or wool of a mammal

"This puppy has all its limbs, pelage—fur, even whiskers." — a Russian scientist commenting on a frozen puppy, 18,000 years old, discovered in the permafrost: in an article in the *New York Post*, 2019

rugae ("ROO-guy," to rhyme with *two pie,* or "ROO-ghee") wrinkles, folds, creases, especially in an internal organ (singular: *ruga*)

"...the vagina is an organ that has deep folds known as rugae enabling it to expand during childbirth or intercourse..." — from an article in *Scientific American,* 2012

scurf ("SKƏRF") small dry flakes shed by the skin, e.g., dandruff

"Thinking of monstrosities, freaks, ogres, and demons, ... God's ugly, punished customers, ... his gargoyle, flyblown hideosities and blemished, poky mutants, all his throwbacks, all his scurf, his doomed, disfigured invalids..." — Stanley Elkin, *The Magic Kingdom*

thews ("THOOZ") muscles; or muscular strength

"Gen. SICKLES, in his speech in Brooklyn, last evening, took occasion to sweep away a fallacy which he finds possessing the minds of laboring men of the North, especially those of foreign birth, and which he regards as one serious obstacle to enlistments. It seems that it is a current belief with them that the war will ultimately end in emancipation, or at least in the liberation of so many blacks that they will crowd our Northern cities, and, by glutting the market with thews and sinews, greatly lower the demand for and value of the labor of our white working population. They are loath to help on such a result." — from an article in the *New York Times,* 1862

oxter ("AHK-stər") (British/Irish/Scottish) the armpit

"...there he was passing the door with his books under his oxter and the wife beside him..." — James Joyce, *Ulysses*

axilla ("ak-SILL-ə") the armpit (*axillary:* pertaining to the armpit)

"I have made a pervaginal examination and, after application of the acid test to 5427 anal, axillary, pectoral and pubic hairs, I declare him to be *virgo intacta.*" — James Joyce, *Ulysses* (from the dreamlike Circe episode)

nates ("NAY-teez") buttocks

"There my beauty lay down on her stomach, showing ... the swellings of her tense narrow nates clothed in black..." — Vladimir Nabokov, *Lolita*

And here's a joke made for eleven-year-old boys with outsized vocabularies:

Q: If a sailor approaches a nude beach, what should he call out?

A: "Ahoy, nates!"

fundament ("FUN-də-mənt") (humorous) the anus, or buttocks; or, more seriously, an underlying principle

> "…just as the legendary bird called Ouida… was reputed to fly in ever-diminishing circles until at the end he disappeared into his own fundament." — John Barth, *The Sot-Weed Factor*

tallywhacker/tallywacker (vulgar slang) penis

> "Five young boys in the nude, a police line-up so that you can identify his tallywhacker." — a line from the movie *Porky's*, 1981

pizzle (archaic) an animal penis—especially a bull's

> In Thomas Hardy's novel *Jude the Obscure*, Jude's first encounter with his future wife comes when she overhears him fantasizing about a lofty career as a clergyman—and throws a pig's pizzle that hits him in the ear.

prepuce ("PREE-pyoos") foreskin; or, a fold of skin covering the clitoris

> "The theft of John Paul II's blood from a church in Abruzzo has been the worst case of relic theft since Jesus's prepuce disappeared from Rome in 1983." — subhead of an article on TheDailyBeast.com, 2017

inguinal ("ING-wə-nəl") relating to the groin

> "The Warriors are hoping that Gary Payton II, working his way back from an inguinal hernia surgery, can play in at least one of the final two preseason games." — from an article in the *San Francisco Chronicle*, 2021

integument ("in-TEG-yə-mənt") a protective outer covering (e.g., the skin of an animal or the coat of a seed)

> "Here's the board that will yield the integument of the pencil…" — Vladimir Nabokov, *Transparent Things*

gristle ("GRIH-səl") cartilage, especially in meat

> "In the American melting pot, gangsters were the indigestible pieces of ethnic gristle…" — from an article in *Time* magazine, 2001

Things your body can do

nictation ("nik-TAY-shən") blinking, especially rapidly (also known as *nictitation*)

> "Look at their eyes—no nictation." — James Blish, *Star Trek 4*

micturition ("mik-tchər-IH-shən") urination

> "The rich foaming sound of a proud man at his micturition." — E.L. Doctorow, *Billy Bathgate*

"Silence! I want to hear this lad's micturition!"

moue ("MOO") a pout or mild grimace, expressing annoyance, etc.; sometimes used flirtatiously

> "'Why, George... it was you who arranged the deal!' With a quaint moue of professional vanity, Smiley conceded that it might well have been." — John LeCarré, *Tinker, Tailor, Soldier, Spy*

deglutition ("dee-gloo-TIH-shən") swallowing

> "Feeling without judgment is a washy draught indeed; but judgment untempered by feeling is too bitter and husky a morsel for human deglutition." — Charlotte Bronte, *Jane Eyre*

suspiration ("suss-pə-RAY-shən") breathing, sighing; or a long deep sigh

"With brief suspiration he reassumed the candle, reascended the stairs, reapproached the door of the front room… and reentered."
— James Joyce, *Ulysses*

fillip ("FILL-əp," like the name) (archaic) a small blow made by flicking the finger; or anything that stirs up or arouses

"…to be broke in upon by [a pun], in a serious discourse, was as bad, he would say, as a fillip upon the nose;—he saw no difference." — Laurence Sterne, *Tristram Shandy*

borborygmus ("bor-bə-RIG-məss") the noise made by gas moving through the intestines: a rumbling or gurgling sound

"All the toilets and waterpipes in the house had been suddenly seized with borborygmic convulsions." — Vladimir Nabokov, *Ada*

Things you can do to your body

depilation ("deh-pə-LAY-shən") the removal of hair, whether by shaving or with chemicals

Depilatory—the more commonly seen form—can serve as an adjective ("for the purpose of removing hair") or as a noun ("a product that does this").

"During the 1950s, hair removal became more publicly accepted. Since many depilatory creams were still irritating to the skin, women relied on razors to shave their legs and underarms…" — from an article in *Elle* magazine, 2013

abstersion ("ab-STƏR-zhən" or "-shən") (archaic) the act of cleansing, especially by wiping or scouring

"I am awakened by the alarm and perform such duties as must be performed to begin the day (defecation, abstersion, depilation)." — André Alexis, *Childhood*

Love, sex, etc.

syngenesis ("sin-JEN-ə-səss") sexual reproduction, i.e., with the male contributing a sperm cell and the female contributing an egg

"Theories of Generation—Of the Spermatists—The Ovists—Evolution—Syngenesis, Epigenesis, and the Neuro Spermatic Theory…" — from a poster advertising a lecture by Dr. Hollick, "For Gentlemen Only," 1844, in the collection of the Library of Congress

venery ("VEN-ə-ree") (archaic) sexual intercourse, or the pursuit of it; or the sport of hunting (the chase)

> "As spread thighs are to the libertine, flights of migratory birds to the ornithologist... so was the letter V to young Stencil... V. ambiguously a beast of venery, chased like the hart, hind or hare, chased like an obsolete, or bizarre, or forbidden form of sexual delight." — Thomas Pynchon, *V.*

houghmagandy/ie ("HOHCCH mə-GAHN-dee," the CCH pronounced as if clearing the throat) (Scottish, humorous) fornication

> "...as if, paradoxically, she would have preferred him to have gone through a bit of wholesome hough-magandy with the wench." — Vladimir Nabokov, *Pale Fire*

exogamy ("eks-AH-gə-mee") the custom of marrying outside one's tribe, clan, etc.: enforced by law or tradition

> "In some cases, the stratagem seems necessary to maintain a healthy degree of exogamy, or outbreeding." — from an article about gorillas by Dian Fossey, in *National Geographic,* 1981

philter/philtre ("FILL-tər") a love potion: meant to arouse desire (for a specific person) in the one who drinks it

> "Good Gods, what Charms! Her very Frowns are Philtres." — Francis Fane, *The Sacrifice* (1686)

parturition ("par-tchə-RIH-shən") childbirth

> "Parturition takes place in secret, without friends or relatives to assist..." — from Horace Miner's article "Body Ritual Among the Nacirema," in *American Anthropologist,* 1956: a satirical piece examining the peculiar customs of the Nacirema, i.e., the Americans

Handy items

grapnel ("GRAP-nəl") a grappling iron: a small anchor with at least four hooks—used, among other purposes, for seizing an enemy ship

> "Don't let reformers of any sort think that they are going really to lay hold of the working boys and young men of England by any educational grapnel whatever, which isn't... something to try the muscles of men's bodies, and the endurance of their hearts, and to make them rejoice in their strength." — Thomas Hughes, *Tom Brown's School Days*

bumbershoot (slang) an umbrella

"Will it come to pipe and dog and bumbershoot? Am I to play at wiving even to the point of—" — John Barth, *Letters*

"A man who fails to keep his bumbershoot neatly furled is a slovenly wretch, I say, a filthy beast! What say you to that, eh? Eh?"

besom ("BEE-zəm") a traditional broom made by tying twigs around a pole

> "…I will sweep it with the besom of destruction, saith the LORD of hosts." — *Isaiah* 14:23 (King James version)

Two pipes and a torch

calumet ("KAL-yə-met") a peace pipe, ornamented, used ceremonially by North American Indians

> "Wash the war-paint from your faces… Smoke the calumet together, / And as brothers live henceforward!" — Henry Wadsworth Longfellow, *The Song of Hiawatha*

narghile/nargileh ("NAR-ghə-lee," the first syllable rhyming with *car*, or "NAR-ghə-leh") a hookah: i.e., a water pipe

> "Beside me was a man puffing away at a nargileh; he seemed to be in a stony trance." — Henry Miller, *The Colossus of Maroussi*

flambeau ("FLAM-boh") a lighted torch

"...the devil carry me away... if I did not see the dead man...
with eyes as big and as fiery as two large flambeaux." — Henry
Fielding, *Tom Jones*

Victuals (that's vittles to you)

viand ("VY-ənd") an item of food, especially a tasty one (*viands:*
provisions)

> "'Using very temperately of the most delicate viands and the
> finest wines and eschewing all incontinence,' Boccaccio writes...
> 'they abode with music and such other diversions as they might
> have...'" — from an article in the *New York Times,* 2020, about
> how diets change during a plague, or a pandemic

provender ("PRAH-vən-dər") dry food for livestock, e.g., hay; or,
humorously, food

> "As to clothing, food, provender, and household necessities—
> they were as usual down to their last stitch, ounce, grain, and bar
> of soap." — Christina Stead, *The Man Who Loved Children*

refection ("rih-FECK-shən" or "ree-") (archaic, literary) a light meal;
or nourishing food or drink taken after a time of hunger or fatigue

> "And then I had to walk to Morningside in a cutting east wind;
> and then... a miserable refection of weak tea and tough toast by
> way of dinner, when I needed to have stimulants 'thrown into the
> system'..." — Jane Carlyle, *Letters* (Jane Carlyle was married to
> Thomas Carlyle, the historian and essayist.)

confiture ("KAHN-fə-tchər") preserved or candied fruit

> "Like fruitcake in a jar, the confiture is jam-packed with
> quince, fig, pear, date, prune, apricot, raisin, citrus, nuts and
> spices..." — from an article in the *Star Tribune* (Minneapolis),
> 2021

tiffin ("TIFF-ən") (Anglo-Indian) midday lunch: a light meal

> "One time Tondelayo think she like to make tiffin for *you.*" —
> Hedy Lamarr to Walter Pidgeon, flirtatiously, in *White Cargo,*
> 1942

vitellus ("və-TELL-əss") the yolk of an egg

> "The first step in the development of the [fish] egg is the
> formation of innumerable cells on the surface of the vitellus..."
> — from an article in *Scientific American,* 1869, with the
> memorable title "Monstrosities Among Trout"

Down the hatch!

potation ("po-TAY-shən") (archaic, humorous) the act of drinking; or a drink, especially an alcoholic one

> "...the Squire retired to his Evening Potation... and as he was of a social Disposition... the Beer was ordered to flow very liberally... so that before Eleven in the Evening, there was not a single Person sober in the House..." — Henry Fielding, *Tom Jones*

stingo (British slang) strong beer; or vigor

> "Host Barnes had tapped a barrel of double stingo for the occasion." — Nathaniel Gould, *The Double Event* (1891)

> "A gorgeous book... full of sheer stingo." — John Galsworthy, Foreword to the memoir *Trader Horn*

gout ("GOWT," rhyming with *out*) (literary) a drop of liquid; or a large splotch

> "I see thee still; / And on thy Blade... Gouts of Blood, / Which was not so before." — William Shakespeare, *Macbeth*

Moolah-related

emolument ("ə-MAHL-yə-mənt") payment, profits, or perks obtained through one's job

> "[T]here is no definitive answer after years of legal wrangling over the Constitution's emoluments clauses, which prohibit presidents and others from accepting gifts or payments from foreign governments without congressional approval." — from an article in the *Washington Post*, 2021

simoleon ("sə-MOH-lee-ən") (slang) a dollar

> "That's one-hundred fifteeen simoleons. For [a pair of] the worst seats in the house." — from an article in the *New York Post*, 2008, about a price hike for N.Y. Rangers tickets

Too much or not enough

nimiety ("nih-MY-ə-tee") excess; an undesirable overabundance

> "A climate conspicuous for a nimiety of rain." — from an article in the *New Statesman*, 1937

penury ("PEN-yə-ree") an oppressive degree of poverty

> "By the World Bank's estimate, some 800m people in China have escaped penury in the past four decades." — from an article in the *Economist*, 2020

exiguity ("eggs-ə-GYOO-ə-tee") scantiness, meagerness (adjective: *exiguous*)

> "…my own exiguous earnings did not even permit me to visit the nightclub where Melissa danced." — Lawrence Durrell, *Justine*

Abs

abnegation ("ab-nə-GAY-shən") self-denial; renunciation; giving up something

> "He, with an abnegation rare in these our times… expressed the dying wish… that the meal should be divided in aliquot parts." — James Joyce, *Ulysses* (*Aliquot*, which you'll encounter later, means "leaving no remainder after division.")

abscission ("ab-SIH-zhən") removal: the act of cutting something off; or the normal separation of plant parts (e.g., dead leaves, ripe fruit) from the living plant

> "There must be a resolute abscission of what is corrupt in church and state." — from an article in the *Anti-Jacobin Review and Magazine*, 1809

The criminal element

Black Maria ("mə-RYE-ə") (slang) a police vehicle, especially one used to transport prisoners

> "I felt what it was like to be handcuffed and taken off in the Black Maria." — Cecil Beaton (photographer and costume designer), *Self-Portrait with Friends*

> Trivia: At Thomas Edison's laboratory and workshop, three miles from my home, you can see a recreation of the inventor's rotating film studio. It's known as the Black Maria, because of its supposed resemblance to a police van.

durance (pronounced like *endurance,* minus the first syllable) imprisonment; restraint by force

> "A Workhouse!... In durance vile here must I wake and weep…" — Robert Burns, "Epistle from Esopus to Maria"

gyves ("JIVES") shackles or fetters, especially for the legs

"In 'The House of Eld' you read of a youth brought up in a country where all the world wore a gyve on the right leg, except only when they cast it off in secret and danced." — from an article about Robert Louis Stevenson, in the *Quarterly Review*, 1900

roscoe ("RAHS-koh") (dated slang) a pistol

"The thump of the blackjack, the bark of the roscoe... — the hardboiled revolution was in full force in print—with Raymond Chandler's Philip Marlowe leading the charge." — from an article on the website RadioSpirits.com

Mood and manner

torpor ("TOR-pər") lethargy, apathy; or a state of inactivity and reduced metabolism and consciousness

"He slept on his back with an old-fashioned nightcap coming down on his forehead... and one could readily suppose that his quilted torpor was entirely devoid of visions..." — Vladimir Nabokov, "The Aurelian"

woolgathering absentminded daydreaming

"It was the following confusion... that Weed Atman... came woolgathering and innocent into the midst of." — Thomas Pynchon, *Vineland*

swivet ("SWIH-vət") (colloquial, U.S.) a state of agitation or panic

"...I've worked myself up into a swivet over unpaid pie bills..." — *Ducks, Newburyport,* by Lucy Ellmann

phrenitis ("fren-EYE-tiss") (archaic) wild delirium, frenzy; or inflammation of the brain

"Galen gives an account of a time he himself was stricken by phrenitis... He writes, 'Stricken by a burning fever... I thought that little sticks of dark straw were protruding from my mattress...'" — from an unpublished Master's Thesis by K.E. Murphy, University of Calgary, 2013

high dudgeon ("DUH-djən") an angry, sullen, or indignant mood

"Friends of high art were in high dudgeon when Mayor Rudolph Giuliani opposed a museum exhibition that included a portrait of the Virgin Mary splattered with elephant dung. Would the dudgeon have been as high if Giuliani had acted, as surely he would have, against similar treatment of a portrait of Martin

Luther King?" — from a *Newsweek* column by George Will,
1999

Asked to remove his cap before entering the chapel,
the young scholar flew into high dudgeon.

Horses and other creatures

cob ("KAHB") a small, stout, strong horse, of calm temperament, often
ridden by a heavy person

"I was never much of a walker, or a rider either. What I like is a
smart vehicle and a spirited cob. I was always a little heavy in the
saddle." — George Eliot, *Middlemarch*

palfrey ("PAWL-free") (archaic) a calm, easy-to-manage saddle-
horse, especially for a woman

"But Rebecca… making her way through the attendants to the
palfrey of the Saxon lady, knelt down, and, after the Oriental
fashion in addressing superiors, kissed the hem of Rowena's
garment." — Sir Walter Scott, *Ivanhoe*

cockerel ("KAHK-ə-rəl") a young rooster

"…he heard the ringing crow of a cockerel in the distance…" —
D.H. Lawrence, *The Rainbow*

bullock ("BULL-ək") a castrated bull, i.e., a steer; or (archaic) a
young bull

"The six bulls, accompanied by tame bullocks, ran together in a pack for most of the 850-meter (930-yard) course to the city's bullring." — from an article in the *Washington Post*, 2019, about that year's Pamplona festival, at which two runners were gored

leveret ("LEV-ə-rət") a young hare, less than one year old

"...the footman... had come in to say that the keeper had found one of Dagley's boys with a leveret in his hand just killed." — George Eliot, *Middlemarch*

pilchard ("PILL-chərd") a small fish of the herring family, found along the coasts of Europe (the term is nearly synonymous with *sardine*)

"...they... began hauling the cargo topside: a few live goats, some sacks of sugar, dried tarragon from Sicily, salted pilchards in barrels, from Greece." — Thomas Pynchon, *V.*

"Semolina Pilchard / Climbing up the Eiffel Tower." — The Beatles, "I Am the Walrus" (What, you find that confusing?)

minikin ("MIN-ih-kin") a small, delicate, or insignificant creature

"...he, in his laboratory, has to place her on a slide under a powerful microscope in order to make out the tiny, though otherwise perfect, shape of his minikin sweetheart, a graceful microorganism extending transparent appendages toward his huge humid eye." — Vladimir Nabokov, *Ada*

loup-garou ("LOO gah-ROO": it's French, so the R comes from the throat) werewolf

"When the show began, patrons viewed a cinema which showed the cheetah, by this time almost as legendary as a loup-garou, retrieving duck and pheasant." — from an article in *Time* magazine, 1935, about a cheetah that was trained to retrieve: the film was shown at that year's Westminster Kennel Club Show

More zoology

biota ("by-OH-tə") the plant and animal life of a region

"The world's biota—its combined plant and animal life—is being homogenized." — from an article in the *New York Review of Books*, 2007

spawn the small eggs of fish, frogs, or other aquatic animals, usually produced in large numbers; or the offspring of something

"USA Today has dropped plans to have conservative author Ann Coulter write a daily column from the Democratic convention. The newspaper dropped Coulter in a dispute over the first column she had written about the Democrats... Here's how Coulter opened the column: 'Here at the Spawn of Satan convention in Boston...'" — from an article on CBSNews.com, 2004

vibrissae ("vy-BRISS-ee") whiskers: i.e., stiff hairs that grow around the mouths of some mammals (singular: *vibrissa,* "vy-BRISS-ə")

"Since whiskers stick so far out, they extend an animal's sense of touch... Many mammals, including seals and cats, can sweep their vibrissae back and forth." — from an article on the website ScienceNewsForStudents.org, 2012

ala ("AY-lə," the first A pronounced as in *hay*) a wing, or winglike anatomical part

The plural is *alae* ("AY-lee"), not *alas,* which would have confused poor Yorick.

ecdysis ("EK-də-səss") shedding, molting, e.g., by snakes, insects, or arthropods

The creative efforts of H.L. Mencken gave us the term *ecdysiast,* a winking name for a stripper: "It might be a good idea to relate strip-teasing in some way... to the associated zoölogical phenomenon of molting... A resort to the scientific name for molting, which is *ecdysis,* produces both *ecdysist* and *ecdysiast.*" — from his book *The American Language,* 1940

Knowing and not knowing

prescience ("PREH-shənss") foreknowledge

"The Tech Seer: Steve Jobs's Uncanny Prescience" — headline of an article in *Newsweek,* 2011. (Subtitle: *An Internet World. When he called it: 1985.*)

vaticination ("və-TIH-sə-nay-shən") a prophecy; or the act of prophesying

"Reading entrails is most likely an older form of vaticination than reading stars." — from an article in the *New York Times,* January 1, 2000

nescience ("NEH-shənss" or "NEH-see-ənss") lack of knowledge; ignorance

"[Science]... pronounces only on whatever, at the time, appears to have been scientifically ascertained, which is a small island in an ocean of nescience." — Bertrand Russell, *A History of Western Philosophy*

You may find yourself in a...

faubourg ("FOH-bərg"; or "FOH-boor," if you want to sound French) a suburb: usually refers to places in France, or in French-speaking places

> Faubourg Marigny, a neighborhood in New Orleans, had very specific associations for Walker Percy, as evidenced by this passage from *The Moviegoer:* "A sharp character... a Faubourg Marigny type, Mediterranean, big-nosed, lumpy-jawed... a great pompadour of wiry bronze hair... He has no use for me at all."

pothouse ("POT-house") (British, archaic) a tavern

> "Where have you been?" "Where! why in the paragon of all pot houses; snug little bar with red curtains; ... barmaid an houri; and for malt the most touching tap in Oxford, wasn't it, Brown?" — Thomas Hughes, *Tom Brown at Oxford*

natatorium ("nate-ə-TOR-ee-əm" or "nat-") a swimming pool, especially one that's indoors

> "In an era of private grandeur, New York City has built a temple for the public in Queens: the Flushing Meadows-Corona Park Natatorium and Ice Rink..." — from an article in the *New York Times*, 2008

carrefour ("kar-ə-FOOR," the A pronounced as in *cat*) a crossroads; or a square or plaza, especially where many roads intersect

> "The farmers as a rule preferred the open *carrefour* for their transactions, despite its inconvenient jostlings and the danger from crossing vehicles, to the gloomy sheltered market-room provided for them." — Thomas Hardy, *The Mayor of Casterbridge*

Less appealing places

fen a marsh or bog; a low-lying area, frequently flooded

> "The fens" refers to a region in eastern England. Most of it has long been drained and used for agriculture.

warren ("WAR-ən," like *worn* with an extra syllable) an overcrowded group of buildings, inhabited by the poor; or any space with small rooms and connecting passageways

This word originally referred to the interconnected burrows where rabbits live.

"A plate crashes: a woman screams: a child wails. Oaths of a man roar, mutter, cease. Figures wander, lurk, peer from warrens." — James Joyce, *Ulysses*

midden ("MID-ən") a dump for household garbage, and/or human waste: archaeologists study middens for clues about ancient societies

"They led the horses up through a midden of old truckdoors and transmissions and castoff motorparts behind the café..." — Cormac McCarthy, *All the Pretty Horses*

jakes (archaic) a toilet; or an outhouse

"His book [Roger L'Estrange's translation of Aesop's Fables] is nauseously vulgar, and fit only for the jakes." — Vicesimus Knox, *Winter Evenings* (1788)

cloaca ("kloh-AY-kə," the middle syllable rhyming with *hay*) (archaic) a sewer or latrine

"Along with the rest of the city's effluvia the river sweeps the victims out to sea. Thus for centuries it has fulfilled the functions of road and, as rivers will, cloaca." — Timothy Mo, *Insular Possession*

Pole-ish

bole ("BOHL") a tree trunk

"The boat had been hidden from them by the bole of a great tree which rose from the grass at the water's edge." — Henry James, *The Tragic Muse*

stanchion ("STAN-shən") an upright pole, post, or support

"...Dylan Windler raced up the floor for a transition dunk and got clubbed in the head and shoved into the stanchion by Kyle Kuzma." — from an article on the website Cleveland.com, 2021 (The stanchion referred to here supported a basketball backboard.)

palisade ("PAL-ə-sayd," the final syllable rhyming with *made*) a fence of stakes or tree trunks, forming a barrier of defense; or a line of vertical cliffs

The Palisades—the dark cliffs that line the west shore of the Hudson River for several miles—supposedly got their name from their resemblance to a palisade of closely spaced tree trunks.

Garments and accessories

vesture (rhymes with *gesture*) clothing; or anything that covers like clothing

> "Her graceful vesture swept the ground." — Sir Walter Scott, *The Bridal of Triermain*

décolletage ("day-kahl-ə-TAZH") a low neckline

> "...[Eve] Babitz had often been written off as an insubstantial party girl—as famous for her decolletage (legendary) and her conquests (also legendary) as her work." — from an article in the *Los Angeles Times*, 2019

peignoir ("pain-WAHRR") a negligee or light dressing gown

> "His wife was putting on a peignoir, kimono, housecoat, or negligee. He didn't know the difference..." — Thomas Pynchon, *V.*

tippet a scarf, usually made of fur or wool, worn either over the shoulders or only around the neck, with the ends hanging in front; or a ceremonial scarf worn by clergy

> "Mrs. Weston begs you to put on your tippet. She says she is afraid there will be draughts in the passage..." — Jane Austen, *Emma*

galluses ("GAL-əss-əzz") suspenders

> "...I used to hang around the courthouse for free entertainment, and watch these guys trying cases holler and jump up and down and... snap their galluses and throw their coats on the floor. That's what got me interested in the law." — from the obituary of former Circuit Judge Paul William Ottinger, in the *Baltimore Sun,* 1993

gaiters ("GATE-ərz") coverings worn over shoes and the lower legs, for protection (from snow, etc.)

> *Spats* are similar, but worn for fashion's sake, not for protection.

> "Snow, water, dirt and pebbles have a way of sneaking into even the most waterproof of boots. To prevent this, put on some gaiters." — from the website REI.com

panoply ("PAN-ə-plee") the complete arms and armor of a warrior; or any complete or impressive collection

> "Despite the panoply of challenges, security officials point to the fact that the queen's funeral—dubbed Operation London Bridge—has been decades in the planning." — from an article in the *Los Angeles Times*, 2022

Half or nothing

moiety ("MOY-ə-tee") half; or one of two parts into which a thing is (or can be) divided

> "…inasmuch as Katy had brought him his first joy in years, he had altered the terms of his will and testament: one moiety of his estate was to pass to Kate, and the other to be divided between the boys." — John Barth, *The Sot-Weed Factor*

lacuna ("lə-KOO-nə") a gap, or a missing part (plural: *lacunae*)

> "Then you get into this very interesting question which is a lacuna in the Geneva Convention. The Geneva Convention says you get combatant/P.O.W. status if you obey the four rules… The Geneva Conventions are silent on 'what if you don't,' and people have accused us of making up the term 'unlawful combatant'…" — from a transcript of an interview with Douglas Feith, considered one of the architects of George W. Bush's Iraq War, on *Vanity Fair's* website, 2008

Big business

consortium ("kən-SORE-shəm" or "kən-SORE-shee-əm" or "kən-SORE-tee-əm") a partnership or association, usually including more than two companies

> "The sophisticated computing systems available through this consortium can process massive numbers of calculations… helping scientists develop answers to complex scientific questions about COVID-19 in hours or days versus weeks or months." — from an article in *Fortune* magazine, 2020

Geography

meridian ("mə-RIH-dee-ən") a line of longitude, from pole to pole; or, in acupuncture and Chinese medicine, one of the pathways in the body along which energy flows (each of the 12 meridians is associated with a different organ)

> "Our logical thoughts dominate experience only as the parallels and meridians make a checker-board of the sea. They guide our voyage without controlling the waves, which toss forever in spite of our ability to ride over them…" — George Santayana, *Interpretations of Poetry and Religion*

bight ("BITE") a curve in a coastline between two points of land, forming a small bay; or a loop in a rope

> If you were a Boy Scout, then the word *bight* will remind you of a *bowline on a bight,* a type of knot. You may also suddenly be thinking of a sheepshank, a sheet bend, and a clove hitch.

freshet ("FRESH-ət") a rush of fresh water in a river, resulting from a spring thaw or heavy rain; or any fresh water running into the sea

> "Annual spring freshets and ice jams frequently washed out mill dams, destroyed equipment, and flooded buildings." — Jennifer L. Bonnell, *Reclaiming the Don* (a book about the river that flows through Toronto, not Russia)

Can you find a category that includes all of these? I couldn't.

vagaries ("VAY-ghə-reez") unexpected, erratic changes, actions, occurrences, or ideas

> "…its message points to memory as mutable, prone to the passage of time and the vagaries of imagination." — from an essay in *Humanities* magazine, 2016, about Nabokov's memoir, *Speak, Memory*

comity ("KAH-mə-tee") politeness, civility, courtesy

> "…American courts have sometimes declined to hear cases against other nations for fear that doing so would interfere with international comity." — from an article in the *New York Times*, 2020 (Note: The phrase *comity of nations* refers to mutual respect for each other's laws and institutions.)

> I was going to propose a title for an article about misplaced courtesy—*The Errors of Comity*—but I see that at least one person got there first. And several did it the opposite way, titling their pieces *A Comity of Errors.*

punctilio ("punk-TILL-ee-oh") precise observance of formalities; or a fine point of etiquette or procedure

> "People of birth stood a little too much upon punctilio." — Samuel Richardson, *Clarissa*

desuetude ("DESS-wə-tood") disuse

> "…*swive* was a fine old verb whose desuetude… was much to be deplored, as it left the language with no term for *service* that was not obscene, clinical, legalistic, ironic, euphemistic, or periphrastic…" — John Barth, *Giles Goat-Boy*

> (*Swive* means, um, *to copulate with.*)

praxis ("PRAK-səss") the practice of a science or an art, as opposed to its theory; or, in Marxist thought, the application of theory in the form of real-world action

> "Barbara Katz Rothman… led the sessions with her talk titled 'Midwifery as feminist praxis.'" — from an article in the journal, *International Midwifery*, 2003

ambit ("AM-bit") the limits or scope of something; or the area within which a person or thing is active; or a circumference

> "…a sign of the ever-increasing ideological radicalism of Trump's opposition and of the ever-diminishing ambit for free and open debate…" — from an article in *National Review,* 2020

bailiwick ("BAY-lə-wik" or "BAY-lee-wik") one's specific area of authority or expertise

> I'm surprised that people don't use this word every day, because it's so much fun to say. "Feng shui? Sorry, that's out of my bailiwick." (It seems to have been superseded by the annoying, faddish *wheelhouse.*)

> "The Scripture says to feed the widows and the orphans and take care of those who can't take care themselves, and that is Skip Rutherford's bailiwick." — from an article on *Arkansas Online*, 2021

cognomen ("cog-NOH-mən") the name by which one is known: either a surname or a nickname

> In ancient Rome, the cognomen was usually the third of three names: e.g., *Caesar* for *Gaius Julius Caesar.*

> "Mr. and Mrs. Gelb Would Drop 'Embarrassing' Cognomen" — headline of article in the *Baltimore Sun*, 1918, about a couple who petitioned to change their surname "because the name Gelb is of German derivation and is a source of personal embarrassment to them." The article was published one month after the end of World War I.

suzerainty ("SOO-zə-ren-tee" or "-rain-tee") the power of a suzerain, i.e., an overlord or sovereign; often refers to the power of a ruler or state over another state with its own government

> "Complete self-government, subject to the suzerainty of Her Majesty… will be accorded to the inhabitants of the Transvaal territory." — from an article in the *Times* (of London), quoting the Convention of Pretoria, 1881

superficies ("super-FISH-eez") the outward form or appearance of something, especially as distinct from its true inner nature (Note the resemblance to *superficial.*)

I'm tempted to say something here about small aquatic creatures with extraordinary powers, but I will restrain myself.

"He who has seen only the superficies of life believes every thing to be what it appears." — Samuel Johnson, from a piece in *The Rambler*, 1752

percipience ("per-SIP-ee-ənss") perceptiveness; or the act of perceiving

"More recent events sent me back to the novel itself, and to a new respect for [Sinclair] Lewis' percipience about Americans' vulnerability to the blandishments of political charlatans, and about… how a fascist takeover would unfold." — from an article about the novel *It Can't Happen Here*, in the *Los Angeles Times*, 2021

perlustration ("pər-lə-STRAY-shən") the act of thoroughly inspecting a place, a document, or a set of records; especially refers to the reviewing of correspondence for the purpose of surveillance

"Mr. Hugh Fraser [a conservative Member of Parliament]… asked the Prime Minister whether cables and radio telegrams sent by M.P.s were privileged from perlustration by the security services." — from an article in the *Times* (London), 1967

historicity ("his-tə-RISS-ə-tee") authenticity; historical actuality (as opposed to existence only in myth, legend, or fiction)

"Numerous countries in Western Europe have made it a serious crime to question the historicity of the Holocaust." — from an article on TheDailyBeast.com, 2012

trope a word or expression used in a figurative way; or, more commonly now, a theme or character type that has become a cliché

"Rabin defined the Manic Pixie Dream Girl as a muse whose primary role is to teach and transform a young man. As contemporary a trope as it feels, it's as old as Dante with his vision of being guided through paradise by his saintly Beatrice." — from an article in the *Atlantic*, 2013

(But Beatrice wasn't a manic pixie. Or *was* she?)

exigency ("EGGS-ə-jen-see" or "EKS-ə-jen-see") a pressing need (usually plural, *exigencies*)

"The idea of leisure, after all, is a hard-won achievement; it presupposes that we have overcome the exigencies of brute survival." — from an essay by Tim Wu in the *New York Times*, 2018

celerity ("sə-LER-ih-tee") swiftness

Etymology: Celery is noted for the swiftness of its growth. Thus, *celerity*. (Okay, okay, I made it up. Tried to put one over on you. Sorry.)

"…Gurth defended himself against the attack… covering himself by shifting his weapon with great celerity, so as to protect his head and body." — Sir Walter Scott, *Ivanhoe*

coverture ("KUV-ər-tchoor" or "-tchər") refuge; concealment or disguise; or, formerly, in law, a married woman's status

Considered to be under her husband's protection and authority, a wife had no right to own property in her own name.
"Coverture also meant that a man had largely unrestrained access to his wife's body." — from an article in the *Atlantic*, 2017

Though American women now possess most of the rights they were formerly denied, coverture has not been abolished by law in the U.S.

gloaming ("GLOW-ming") twilight, or dusk

"Roamin' in the gloamin' by the bonnie banks o' Clyde,
Roamin' in the gloamin' wi' ma lassie by ma side,
When the sun has gone to rest,
That's the time that we love best,
Oh, it's lovely roamin' in the gloamin'." — Harry Lauder, "Roamin' in the Gloamin'," 1911 (a popular song)

brume ("BROOM") mist, fog, vapor (*brumous:* foggy, misty)

"The sublime glassy Radnor Lake pulls in photographers from around mid-Tennessee who often arrive early enough to shoot the morning brume that rises from the lake." — from an article in the *New York Times*, 2020

redolence ("RED-ə-lənss") a strong odor, usually pleasant

"Over all New Orleans there hung the pungent redolence that was the very flavor of the bewitching city." — Edna Ferber, *Saratoga Trunk*

bagatelle ("bag-ə-TELL") a trifle; something unimportant or of little value; or a light piece of writing or music

"Umberto Eco's *Nonita* is an amusing bagatelle that spoofs *Lolita* by inverting it: here it is a case of an adolescent boy obsessed with elderly ladies." — from an article on the website of Penn State's libraries

berceuse ("bair-SOOZ" or "bair-SUHHZ") a lullaby; or a musical piece that resembles a lullaby

"In the Barcarolle, the Berceuse, and the Ballades... Chopin discovered a form of expression peculiar to himself." — Edward Dannreuther, *The Oxford History of Music*

congé/congee ("KAHN-zhay" or "koh(n)-ZHAY") a curt dismissal or rejection; or formal permission to leave; or (archaic) a bow at leave-taking

"'It is an honour for me,' says my lord, with a profound congée." — William Makepeace Thackeray, *Henry Esmond*

tellurian ("tə-LOOR-ee-ən") an inhabitant of the earth (used mainly in science fiction)

"It happens... that tellurians of learning and advanced years, such as myself, grow disenchanted with all things martian." — A.B. West, *Wakenight Emporium*

(The word is also an adjective. It means *relating to the earth.*)

blazon ("BLAY-zən") a coat of arms; or a description of a coat of arms; or, as a verb, to proclaim publicly, especially in a boastful way

"...fans sought to buy a copy of the day's paper celebrating the win and a 12-page commemorative edition with a single-word headline blazoned across the top of the front page: CHAMPS!" — from an article in the *Washington Post*, following the World Series victory of the Washington Nationals in 2019

wormwood and gall bitterness, resentment, and/or grief

"I... proposed he should pawn my sword of steel inlaid with gold... This expedient was wormwood and gall to poor Strap, who... still retained notions of economy and expense suitable to the narrowness of his education..." — Tobias Smollett, *Roderick Random*

scotoma ("skə-TOH-mə") a blind spot; or a partial loss of vision, limited to part of the visual field

"There are a zillion things I don't know. And I know that I don't know them. But what about the unknown unknowns? Are they like a scotoma, a blind spot in our field of vision that we are unaware of?" — from an article by Errol Morris, director of *The Unknown Known* (about Donald Rumsfeld), in the *New York Times,* 2010

argosy ("AR-ghə-see," the first syllable rhyming with *car*) (poetic) a large ship, especially one full of precious cargo; or a fleet of such ships; or a rich collection

If you visit Dubrovnik, in Croatia, you may learn that the city (where much of *Game of Thrones* was shot) was once a wealthy

167

port known as Ragusa... and that the word *argosy* derives from that name.

"...you shall find three of your argosies / Are richly come to harbour suddenly." — William Shakespeare, *The Merchant of Venice*

scantling ("SCANT-ling") a piece of lumber that's relatively small in cross-section; or a small amount of something

"About two hundred yards off... we built a pen of scantlings." — Mark Twain, *A Connecticut Yankee in King Arthur's Court*

"You shall get back your Lombardy—all but a scantling which we fling to the Sardinian Majesty." — Thomas Carlyle, *The History of Friedrich II of Prussia*

brannigan ("BRAN-ə-gən") (slang) a brawl, argument, or drinking spree

"It hadn't exactly been a brawl to rank with the most homeric barroom brannigans in which Simon had ever participated." — from an article in the *Star Weekly* (Toronto), 1955

"I said, 'I'd like some *bran again*.'"
"Ohhhhhh!"

succedaneum ("suck-sə-DAY-nee-əm") a substitute; often refers to a less effective drug used in place of another

"...his expense for medicines was not great, he being the most expert man at a succedaneum of any apothecary in London, so that I have been sometimes amazed to see him, without the least hesitation, make up a physician's prescription though he had not in his shop one medicine mentioned in it." — Tobias Smollett, *Roderick Random*

funicular ("few-NIK-yə-lər") (adjective, but often used as a noun) usually refers to a railway on a steep incline, operating by cable, with the ascending car balanced by the descending one; or relating to ropes or cord

> An article on the website CKTravels.com lists some of the world's most spectacular funicular railways, including Australia's Blue Mountains Scenic Railway, Hong Kong's Peak Tram, and the Ljubljana Castle Funicular in Slovenia (which my wife and I rode in a downpour in 2019), among others. The article fails to mention the Duquesne Incline in Pittsburgh, however: a glaring omission, I'd say.

shunpike ("SHUN-pike") a side road, taken to avoid a highway's toll or traffic

> The word can also be used as a verb. When you take one of these roads for this purpose, you're *shunpiking.*

> "For those who would savor the texture of the land and recover their sense of place, there are the shunpike and the minor road...: tortuous drives that skirt oceans below and wind around mountains, cross plains and valleys, run after rivers..." — from an article in *Time* magazine, 1964

parterre ("par-TAIR," the A pronounced as in *car*) a formal garden, with its beds arranged in a (usually symmetrical) pattern and paths between the beds

> "Tir'd of the scene parterres and fountains yield, / He finds at last he better likes a field." — Alexander Pope, "Epistles to Several Persons"

withe ("WITH," the TH pronounced as in *with*, or "WYTH," the TH pronounced as in *there*) a tough, flexible twig, especially a willow twig, used for binding things

> "We lay on the front porch... One of us lay on the rear seat of a chevrolet sedan, the other on a piece of thin cotton-filled quilting taken from the seat of a divan made of withes." — James Agee, *Let Us Now Praise Famous Men*

Word Play

Challenge: Write a rhyming couplet for each of the following word pairs.

1. calumny, obloquy
2. cachinnation, eructation
3. schwa, patois
4. historicity, impudicity
5. tergiversation, supererogation (bonus: add a third line, ending in *peculation*)

"I'll Have Nepenthe on the Rocks": Interesting Concepts and Unusual Practices

Here you'll find ways to understand the world and ourselves... phobias and -philias... experiences you'll hope you never have... outdated theories and foreign customs... and assorted quirky concepts, all worth noting, some quite useful.

Concepts

Life's ups, downs, and interruptions

vicissitudes ("vih-SISS-ə-toods" or "-tyoods") unpredictable changes in fortune, especially for the worse; ups and downs

> "...this vast work, describing vicissitudes of revolution and exile, reveals a masterpiece of historical narrative and tumultuous self-portraiture." — from a review of Chateaubriand's *Memoirs from Beyond the Grave,* in the *New York Review of Books*

the grand climacteric ("kly-MAK-tə-rik" or "kly-mak-TƏR-ik") the 63rd year of life, when major changes are supposed to occur and the risk of death increases

> The ancient Greeks believed that certain years, starting at age seven and recurring every seven years thereafter, marked critical turning points in a person's life. The grand climacteric would be the ninth of these.

> "Such superannuated old geese, as those who had passed their grand climacteric, ought not to meddle with affairs of which they must have lost even the memory." — Fanny Burney, *The Wanderer, or Female Difficulties*

anabiosis ("anna-bye-OH-siss") suspended animation; or coming back to life after a period of apparent death or greatly reduced metabolism

> "John Hunter, supported by his experiments on anabiosis, hoped to prolong the life of man indefinitely by alternate freezing and thawing." — James G. Frazer, *Belief in Immortality and the Worship of the Dead*

Ways to be born, or reborn

parthenogenesis ("par-thə-noh-JEN-ə-səss") a form of asexual reproduction, through the development of an unfertilized egg

> "…the go-to scientific explanation for the virgin birth has long been that Mary somehow achieved human parthenogenesis, a process by which some animals reproduce without mates." — from an article on Vice.com, 2015

abiogenesis ("AY-bye-oh-JEN-ə-səss," the first syllable rhyming with *hay*) the development of living organisms from lifeless matter, also known as spontaneous generation; or the theory that life originated from inorganic matter

> "There was a widespread persistence of the old belief that living creatures could arise from appropriate non-living matter, insects from a carcass… and internal parasites in man from nothing in particular. This was the theory of present-day spontaneous generation (abiogenesis)—a false view that has died hard." — J.A. Thomson and E.J. Holmyard, *Biology for Everyman* (1934)

palingenesis ("pal-in-JEN-ə-səss") rebirth, regeneration; or the doctrine of reincarnation

> "Death is worthy of homage, as the cradle of life, as the womb of palingenesis." — Thomas Mann, *The Magic Mountain*, translated by H.T. Lowe-Porter

All in your head

engram ("EN-gram") a permanent alteration or trace in brain cells, resulting from temporary stimulus, thought to be key to memory: a hypothetical concept, and the subject of long-standing neuropsychological research

> "Although the concept of memory engrams has been recognized for about a century, the molecular mechanisms that drive memory formation and recall… have remained a neuroscientific mystery, until today. This morning, MIT neuroscientists published a potentially groundbreaking paper…" — from an article in *Psychology Today*, 2020

ataraxy/ataraxia ("AT-ə-rack-see," the first A pronounced as in *cat*; "at-ə-RACK-see-ə,") peace of mind; emotional tranquility; stoical dispassion

"…ataraxy, together with freedom from physical pain, is one way of specifying the goal of life, for Epicurus." — from an article on the *Stanford Encyclopedia of Philosophy* website

eudemonia/eudaimonia ("yoo-də-MOH-nee-ə") in Aristotle's philosophy, happiness, well-being: attained through an active life governed by reason

"Where Aristotle diverged from Plato… is in his belief about what is 'enough' … for eudaimonia. For the latter, virtue was enough for the ultimate good that is eudaimonia. For Aristotle, virtue was required, but not sufficient…" — from an article on the website PositivePsychology.com, 2020

acedia/accidie ("ə-SEE-dee-ə"/ ("AK-sə-dee") apathy, ennui, listlessness

"Vacation accidie is upon me. I'm supposed to be writing this perishing film-script—haven't touched it yet." — Kingsley Amis, *Letters*, 1961

abulia ("ə-BOO-lee-ə") an abnormal inability to act or make decisions; a pathological lack of willpower or motivation

"This reading deepens Hamlet's motives… Now, Hamlet's angst has justification in his repressed feelings toward his parents. It explains his deep abulia and indecision." — from a post on an online forum about Hamlet's Oedipus Complex, 2016

mythomania ("mith-ə-MAY-nee-ə") in psychology, an abnormal tendency to lie or exaggerate

"His singular magnetism was originally built on impudent lies, then further enriched by a permanent and compulsive mythomania." — from a review of biography of André Malraux, in the *New York Review of Books*, 1997

titubation ("titch-ə-BAY-shən") a stumbling, staggering gait, or tremors of the head, characteristic of certain diseases of the cerebellum

"…as ingenious and hilarious as taking a bunch of drunks and constructing out of their meanderings and titubations a precisely honed piece of choreography." — from a theater review in *Hudson Review*, 1974

floccillation ("flock-sə-LAY-shən") a delirious patient's random plucking at his/her bedclothes

"And when I see my hands, on the sheet, which they love to floccillate already, they are not mine, less than ever mine, I have no arms, they are a couple, they play with the sheet, love-play perhaps…" — Samuel Beckett, *Molloy*

ideomotor ("id-ee-oh-MOH-tər" or "IDE-") in psychology, denotes an involuntary, unconscious movement

> "Ouija board cups and dowsing wands—just two examples of mystical items that seem to move of their own accord, when they are really being moved by the people holding them. The only mystery is… why we can make movements and yet not realise that we're making them. The phenomenon is called the ideomotor effect…" — from an article on the website BBC.com, 2013

agoraphobia ("AG-ə-rə-FOH-bee-ə") fear of leaving home, or of going out into open spaces, or of being in a crowd—i.e., of places where you might feel trapped or embarrassed

> "The distance between London and myself was really caused by agoraphobia and anxiety, which forced me to spend most of my first six months in London holed up in one room…" — from an article on the website ElectricLiterature.com, 2017

ailuraphobia ("eye-loor-ə-FOH-bee-ə" or "AY-") extreme fear or dislike of cats

> "I do not quite understand ailurophobia, but then I am an ailurophile." — from an article in the *New York Times*, 1992

arachnophobia ("ə-rack-nə-FOH-bee-ə") extreme fear of spiders

> *Arachnophobia* is the title of a 1990 horror-comedy starring Jeff Daniels and John Goodman as a doctor and an exterminator, respectively.

trypanophobia ("TRY-pən-oh-FOH-bee-ə") extreme fear of injections or needles, in the context of medical treatment: more commonly referred to as *needle phobia*

> "…trypanophobia has the added danger of potentially altering behavior. People may avoid visiting the doctor or dentist so they don't have to have any injections." — from an article on the website VeryWellMind.com, 2019

nyctophobia ("NICK-tə-FOH-bee-ə") an excessive fear of darkness or night

> "In most cases, nyctophobia is simply a collateral phobia; in the rest, it is not a fear of darkness, but of that which the darkness may conceal." — from an article in the journal *Mind,* 1905

> Bonus info: according to an article in *Esquire,* those who have suffered from this condition include Augustus Caesar, Muhammad Ali, and Keanu Reeves.

coprophilia ("kahp-rə-FILL-ee-ə") a preoccupation with or fondness for obscenity or pornography; or an abnormal interest in feces, including for sexual arousal

"[Jonathan Swift's] coprophilia is explained along the lines suggested by Freud." — from an article in the *Times Literary Supplement*, 1934

vagal response ("VAY-ghəl") **AKA vasovagal syncope** ("vay-zoh-VAY-ghəl SIN-kə-pee") a sudden drop in blood flow to the brain, leading to fainting or severe weakness, triggered by a distressing sight or experience, e.g., the sight of blood, or a hypodermic injection

> I experienced this a handful of times before I knew it had a name: at the Smithsonian medical museum, where a brain floated in formaldehyde in a display case; at my nephew's circumcision; and during movies as diverse as *The Toxic Avenger* and *Born on the Fourth of July*. My daughter experienced it when she had her ears pierced.

synesthesia/synaesthesia ("sin-əss-THEE-zhə") a phenomenon in which the stimulation of one sense results in a perception by a different sense: e.g., seeing a color as a result of hearing music

> "[David] Verdesi is so sensory-fluid that in his meditations... he experiences synesthesia in which sounds become colorful forms with textures or he can sense the temperature of trees and flowers." — from an article in *Psychology Today*, 2018

cathexis ("kə-THEK-sis," the TH pronounced as in *with*) in psychoanalysis, concentrating one's mental or emotional energy on a person, thing, or idea, especially to an unhealthy degree (a concept first defined by Freud)

> "Dependency and cathexis are also incredibly painful and difficult to extricate yourself from." — from an article on the website Refinery29.com, 2020

Desire

estrus ("ESS-trəss") in many female mammals, *heat* (a periodically recurring state of sexual excitement and fertility)

> "'Synchronized estrus is thought to increase reproductive success in the pride,' says Mweetwa... Having cubs at the same time means that mother lions can rely on each other to nurse, babysit, and protect the youngsters." — from an article in *National Geographic*, 2016

rut in some male mammals (especially those with hooves), the equivalent of estrus: a periodically recurring state of sexual excitement

"The bugling or whistling of the bull elk in the early autumn is the signal… that the rut is starting." — Austin Loomer Rand, *Mammals of the Eastern Rockies and Western Plains of Canada*

algolagnia ("al-go-LAG-nee-ə," the first A pronounced as in *cat*) a sexual predilection in which pleasure is derived from inflicting or receiving pain

"The Theatre-of-Cruelty boys argue that they're performing a liberating service by exploring the roots of algolagnia in all of us." — from an article in *The Listener*, 1969

nympholepsy ("NIM-fə-LEP-see") a frenzied emotional state, especially resulting from desire for an unattainable thing or ideal; or a sexual desire for beautiful young girls

"The Cinematic Art of Nympholepsy: Movie Star Culture as Loser Culture in Nabokov's *Lolita*" — title of article in the journal *Criticism*, 1999

satyriasis ("sat-ə-RYE-ə-sis") abnormally strong sexual desire in a male: the equivalent of nymphomania; or a prolonged, painful erection

"The attempts to recognize such states as nymphomania and satyriasis as discrete entities, can, in any objective analysis, refer to nothing more than a position on a curve which is continuous." — Alfred C. Kinsey, *Sexual Behavior in the Human Male*

Your body

coenesthesia ("see-nəss-THEE-zhə") the many sensory impressions that collectively create an awareness of one's body or one's existence

"In the nineteenth century, neurological thinking about the means by which the body communicates with the brain emphasized the importance of the concept of coenesthesia, a mainly unconscious sense of the normal functioning of the body and its organs which emerges to full consciousness only when one is unwell." — from a journal article posted on the website OvercomingHatePortal.org, 2009

inanition ("in-ə-NIH-shən") exhaustion caused by lack of food and water; or a feeling of emptiness

"Dr. Black says, I shall not die of a dropsy, as I imagined, but of inanition and weakness." — John Hill Burton, *Life and Correspondence of David Hume*

Who rules?

hagiarchy ("HAG-ee-ar-kee") government by saints or holy men

> "When the People's Liberation Army struck in 1950, Tibet, having metamorphosed over a millennium into a reclusive hagiarchy, possessed neither the vocabulary to parley with the communists nor the strength to resist them." — from a book review in *The Spectator*, 2017

ochlocracy ("ahk-LOCK-rə-see") mob rule; or government by the masses

> "The commonest of the old charges against democracy was that it passed into ochlocracy." — James Bryce, *The American Commonwealth* (1888)

timocracy ("tim-AH-krə-see") in Plato, government in which the rulers are motivated by a love of honor or glory; in Aristotle, government in which only property owners can hold office

> Or, in Monty Python, government led by the flame-throwing enchanter who says, "There are some who call me... Tim."

plebiscite ("PLEB-ə-site") a vote on an important public question, especially relating to the government's structure or leader, in which all registered voters may participate; or a nonbinding expression of public sentiment on an important issue

> "If people by a plebiscite elect a man despot over them, do they remain free because the despotism was of their own making?" — Herbert Spencer, *The Man Versus the State* (1884)

Knowledge: broad, shallow, or false

pantology ("pan-TAHL-ə-jee") a system encompassing all areas of human knowledge

> "Pantology, or, A systematic survey of human knowledge : proposing a classification of all its branches, and illustrating their history, relations, uses, and objects : with a synopsis of their leading facts and principles; and a select catalogue of books on all subjects, suitable for a cabinet library : the whole designed as a guide to study for advanced students, in colleges, academies, and schools; and as a popular directory in literature, science, and the arts" — title of book by Roswell Park, 1841

sciolism ("SY-ə-liz-əm") a superficial display of knowledge; or charlatanism

"What could have been an exercise in sciolism becomes a path to enlightenment." — from an Amazon reader review of *Prisoner of Trebekistan,* a *Jeopardy!* contestant's memoir, 2006

pansophism ("pan-SOH-fiz-əm") pretended possession of universal knowledge or wisdom

> Before it acquired its derogatory connotation, the word referred to a 17th-century educational philosophy with lofty aims: "[Jan Amos Komensky] came to develop a philosophy, called Pansophism, which emphasized political unity, religious reconciliation, and cooperation in education..." – from an article on the website TresBohemes.com, 2016

Fine points and quirks

quiddity ("KWIH-də-tee") in philosophy, the essence of a thing: that which makes it unique; or in law, a fine distinction; or a hairsplitting quibble (Another word that means nearly opposite things!)

> "*No Island of Sanity* is not your usual pussyfooting exercise in polite quibbles and quiddities; it is boisterous, Menckenesque pamphleteering." — from a book review in the *Washington Post,* 1998

quodlibet ("KWAHD-lə-bet") a point suitable for philosophical or theological debate; or such a debate

> The Dominican student brothers at Blackfriars, Oxford, have a webpage called *Godzdogz.* They invite readers: "Quodlibets: Send us your questions!" Example: "Why couldn't the damned simply have never been created?"

crotchet ("KROTCH-ət") an eccentric, whimsical or perverse belief, whim, or preference

> "But airy whims and crotchets lead / To certain loss, and ne'er succeed." — William Wilkie, "The Ape, the Parrot, and the Jackdaw" in *One Hundred Fables in Verse,* 1825

Unusual types

lunarian ("loo-NAIR-ee-ən") an imagined inhabitant of the moon; or an astronomer who studies the moon

> In the Wallace and Gromit short "A Grand Day Out," the adventurous Englishman and his dog run out of cheese and travel to the moon for more. There they encounter a hostile robot who looks like a combination oven and radio; this lunarian terrified

my daughter when she was a toddler. From the day she saw the video, the Wallace and Gromit theme song alone was enough to make her run out of the room.

relict ("RƏL-ikt") a widow; or something left unchanged; or a surviving remnant of an otherwise extinct species

> "She had also been the relict of the late P. Homer Horlick, the Cheese King, and he had left her several million dollars." — P.G. Wodehouse, *The Small Bachelor*

Philosophically speaking

antinomy ("an-TIN-ə-mee") a paradox: a contradiction between two ideas that seem equally valid or reasonable

> "[Gödel's incompleteness] theorem is a variation on the only well-remembered line of the Cretan poet Epimenides, who said, 'All Cretans are liars.' Another version of the same antinomy... reads, 'This sentence is false.'" — from a review of the book *Gödel, Escher, Bach* in the *New York Times,* 1979

noumenon ("NOO-mə-nahn") in Kant's philosophy, "the thing-in-itself" (*das Ding an sich*): an object as it is, not as it is perceived by an observer

> "Ask any (philosophy) person on the street, and you'll no doubt hear how Kant divided the world into the phenomenon and noumenon, and that we can't know anything about the noumenon, but have to resign ourselves to dealing with phenomenon... etc. etc." — from an article in *Epoché* magazine, 2017

probabilism ("PRAHB-ə-bəl-izm") a doctrine introduced by the ancient Greek Skeptics, asserting that certainty is impossible, and that we may therefore form judgments based on what is most probable

> "Probabilism mostly replaced logicism as the dominant form of rationalism in the mid-twentieth century. Unfortunately... [p]robabilism's defects are not just theoretical; they regularly produce large practical catastrophes." — from an article on the website Metarationality.com

tertium quid ("TER-shee-əm KWID") an unknown or undefined thing that's related to but distinct from two other things; or something that belongs to neither category when a dichotomy is made

> During Thomas Jefferson's presidency, dissident members of his party broke away and were called "Tertium Quids," because they sided neither with the Federalists nor with Jefferson's Democratic-Republican party.

Tertium Quid is also the name of a New Jersey camp "for transgender and gender creative children."

reify ("REE-ə-fie") to treat an abstraction or idea as if it were a real thing; to give solid form to a concept

> Marxism leans heavily on the concept of *reification*: "Marx's early writings are the first explicit statement of the process of reification (*Verdinglichung*)…" — Herbert Marcuse, *Reason and Revolution*

> Note that *Verdinglichung* literally means "making into a thing." In Marx's theory, workers come to believe that the status quo is fixed and natural, and thus unchangeable.

Drink this, you'll feel better

nepenthe ("nə-PEN-thee," the TH pronounced as in *with*) a mythical drug that induces forgetfulness, and thereby removes pain or suffering

> Nepenthe is also the name of a restaurant in Big Sur, California, with a panoramic view of the coast. Opened in 1949, it was built around a cabin formerly owned by Orson Welles and his wife, Rita Hayworth. Presumably, the view will make you forget your troubles—especially at sunset.

Songs of woe, etc.

threnody ("THREN-ə-dee") a song or poem of lamentation, especially for the dead

> "The most powerful eloquence is the threnody of a broken heart." — Anthony Farindon, *Sermons Lately Preached* (1657)

jeremiad ("jer-ə-MY-ad") a long lamentation; a catalogue of complaints; a tale of woe; or an angry harangue

> "Though Trump ultimately failed in his quest to steal the election, his weeks-long jeremiad succeeded in undermining faith in elections and the legitimacy of Biden's victory." — from an article in the *Anchorage Daily News*, 2020

epithalamium ("ep-ih-thə-LAY-mee-əm," the TH pronounced as in *with*) a song or poem written in honor of a bride and groom, often sung or read at their wedding

> "…there was something peculiarly novel… in the idea of a wedding taking place amid the clouds, with all mundane

witnesses shut out by fleecy vapors, and the epithalamium sung by the rattling cordage of the aerial ship." — from an article about a wedding performed in the wicker basket of a balloon, in the *New York Times,* 1865

Avoid these

euphuism ("YOO-few-izm") an affectedly lofty style of speech or writing; specifically, a style popular in Elizabethan England, characterized by excessive use of alliteration and other literary devices

> "As soon as men begin to write on nature, they fall into euphuism." — Ralph Waldo Emerson, "Nature"

bombast ("BAHM-bast") cotton batting used to stuff garments in order to make them appear baggy; or, figuratively, inflated language meant to impress, but without substance

> "Their eloquence is all bombast." — Charles Kingsley, *Alton Locke*

Texts of various types

holograph ("HAHL-ə-graff") a manuscript (or other document) written entirely in the author's own hand

> My copy of Joyce's *A Portrait of the Artist As a Young Man* has the subtitle "The Definitive Text Corrected from the Dublin Holograph," which awed and mystified me, until now.

chrestomathy ("kress-TAH-mə-thee," the TH pronounced as in *with*) a collection of passages written by one author or more, especially for instruction in a foreign language

> H.L. Mencken's vocabulary must have baffled most of his readers. He casually tossed off many words defined in this book—e.g., *usufruct, punctilio, haruspices, and Mariolatry*—as well as others so obscure that I haven't included them. It seems appropriate that, when he published a collection of his favorite pieces, he titled it *A Mencken Chrestomathy.*

palimpsest ("PAL-imp-sest") a piece of writing on which earlier writing has been erased, but which shows traces of that earlier writing; or anything reused, on which signs of its earlier form remain

> "All history was a palimpsest, scraped clean and re-inscribed exactly as often as was necessary." — George Orwell, *1984*

rune ("ROON") (poetic) a poem, verse, or song; or any of the characters in the alphabets used by early Germanic peoples; or something written in this alphabet; or any similar character with a mysterious meaning or a supposed magical power

> "Look at the map... and you will see there the runes in red." — J.R.R. Tolkien, *The Hobbit*

boustrophedon ("bow-strə-FEE-dən," the first syllable rhyming with *cow*, or "boo-") an ancient form of writing in which the lines run, as in plowing, alternately left to right and right to left (the word means *ox turn*)

> A clever use of the word: "Big Apple Boustrophedon" is the title of a blog post on the website CharlesMcNamara.com, about a *New York Times* crossword puzzle which has as its theme Manhattan's alternating-direction one-way streets. When solved, the puzzle reads boustrophedon style.

analects ("AN-ə-lekts") collected literary excerpts or fragments

> If you encounter this word, it's likely to be in the title *The Analects:* a collection of teachings attributed to Confucius, supposedly gathered by his students shortly after his death in 479 B.C.

recension ("rə-SEN-shən") a text that has been edited based on critical study of the manuscript and its sources; or the act of editing a text this way

> Figuratively: "...the Islamic State sought to recast political Islam in its recension as entirely continuous with premodern classical Islamic political governance." — Noah Feldman, *The Arab Winter: A Tragedy*

incunabula ("in-kyoo-NAB-yə-lə") (plural of *incunabulum*) early printed books, especially from before 1501; or any product or artwork made during an early period

> "The core of this sale is an extensive collection of incunabula, mostly from Italian workshops and some with fine illumination and contemporary bindings..." — from an announcement of a sale of antiquarian books, on the website of Sotheby's

corrigendum ("kor-ə-JEN-dəm") something that needs to be corrected; as a plural, *corrigenda,* the word refers to errors in a printed work, listed on a separate sheet with corrections

> If this book requires an insert listing corrigenda, I'll be dammed!

Words about words

logodaedaly ("lohg-ə-DEE-də-lee") clever playing with words; or the coining of new words

> "He mimed and mocked me. His allusions were definitely highbrow. He was well-read. He knew French. He was versed in logodaedaly…" — Vladimir Nabokov, *Lolita*

logomachy ("low-GAHM-ə-kee") an argument about words; or a controversy marked by profuse verbiage

> "Dispute over proper usage did not begin 30 years ago with John Simon and Edwin Newman. There is even a word for it, *logomachy*, which Samuel Johnson defined in 1755 as 'a contention in words; a contention about words.'" — from an article in the *Baltimore Sun*, 2006

mondegreen ("MAHN-də-green") a misheard word or phrase, especially in a song

> We all have our favorites. (Mine are Elton John singing, "Rocket Man—burnin' off the shoes of everyone," Carly Simon singing, "I had some dreams, there were clowns in my coffee," and Bob Dylan singing, "I once loved a woman, a child, and a toad.") But why on earth are they called mondegreens?

> Here's the origin story: in 1957, Sylvia Wright published an essay in *Harper's*, in which she described the phenomenon and gave an example from her own past. Her mother was reading aloud to her, and she misheard a line from a Scottish ballad. Here's what she thought she heard: "They hae slain the Earl o' Moray and Lady Mondegreen." The actual line: "They hae slain the Earl o' Moray and laid him on the green."

Military men and strategy

poilu ("pwah-LOO") (informal) a French infantry soldier, especially during World War I

> "Swaying, her hands clasped in the small of his back in a new conjugal way, like a French girl saying farewell to her *poilu*, she squeezed him close and leaned away from him." — Walker Percy, *The Last Gentleman*

perdu ("pər-DOO") (obsolete) a soldier sent on an extremely dangerous mission

The word means *lost* in French. You may know it from the title of Proust's multivolume novel, *À la Recherche du Temps Perdu*, known in English as *Remembrance of Things Past*, but literally meaning, *In Search of Lost Time*.

Maquis ("mah-KEEZ") groups of rural resistance fighters in Nazi-occupied France during World War II

"… these disparate elements all came together, albeit sometimes uncomfortably. The young men became hardened maquisards, committed to the cause, and the groups largely set aside their differences to take on the Germans." — from an interview with Matt Elton, author of a book on the French resistance, on the website HistoryExtra.com, 2018

phalanx ("FAY-lanks") a group of soldiers or police in close formation; originally, an infantry formation used by Alexander the Great, in which soldiers' shields overlapped, with long spears protruding

"After eight months of frustrating searches, false leads and mounting doubts about the chance of finding the deposed Iraqi president, a phalanx of heavily armed U.S. troops made their historic discovery." — from an article in the *Chicago Tribune*, 2003, about the capture of Saddam Hussein

Parthian delivered while in retreat: Parthian horsemen shot arrows at their enemies while feigning retreat (At the time when Jesus Christ lived, the kingdom of Parthia occupied more or less the same territory as today's Iran.)

"Mrs. Gilbert Jones Lets Fly a Parthian Shot at Mrs. Harper." — headline of a letter to the editor of the *New York Times,* 1910, disputing a point about women's suffrage

Turnabouts and reappearances

volte-face ("vahlt-FAHSS" or "vole-tə FAHSS") an about-face; an abrupt reversal in policy or opinion

"…the catastrophe which caused a reversal so complete in Miss Rosa as to permit her to agree to marry the man whom she had grown up to look upon as an ogre. It was not a volte-face of character: that did not change." — William Faulkner, *Absalom, Absalom*

recrudescence ("ree-kroo-DESS-əns") a reappearance after a period of absence or dormancy, especially of something unwanted, such as a disease

"He was her past, a whimsical recrudescence, trapped in her bedroom." — Leonard Michaels, "Reflections of a Wild Kid" (The protagonist has come to visit his ex, but her current lover has just arrived, so now he's in hiding.)

The natural world

anemochore ("ə-NEM-ə-kor") any plant whose seeds are distributed by the wind

Etymology time: *Anemo-* means "related to wind" (think *anemometer*) and *-chore* refers to the method by which a plant's seeds are dispersed.

epiphyte ("EP-ə-fyte") a plant that grows on another plant but doesn't take nourishment from it

Examples include orchids, lichens, and ferns. "The 15-acre garden, on Sarasota Bay, was established in 1971 as the only botanical garden in the world focused solely on the study of epiphytes…" — from an article in the *New York Times,* 2018 (This passage refers to the Marie Selby Botanical Gardens.)

cordate ("KOR-date") heart-shaped (used mainly in botany and zoology, e.g., to describe leaves)

My mother had philodendrons growing in pots all over our living room. The leaves were cordate.

graminivorous ("gram-ə-NIV-ə-rəss") feeding on grass

Can you think of any graminivores? Let's see: geese, horses, cattle—even giant pandas, though they've also been known to munch on a carcass now and then.

shrike a bird that impales its prey (insects and smaller birds) on thorns or on wire barbs

"For nature is one with rapine, a harm no preacher can heal; / The Mayfly is torn by the swallow, the sparrow spear'd by the shrike, / And the whole little wood where I sit is a world of plunder and prey." — Alfred, Lord Tennyson, *Maud*

titman ("TIT-mən") the smallest pig in a litter: the runt; a puny, weak person, or the smallest in a group

"We are a race of tit-men, and soar but little higher in our intellectual flights than the columns of the daily paper." — Henry David Thoreau, *Walden*

Don't confuse these

cachet ("ka-SHAY") prestige; a quality that earns someone or something respect; originally, an official seal, as on a letter or document

> "They found an impresario for the thing, Bill Graham, a New Yorker who had a lot of cachet in the hip world of San Francisco as a member of the San Francisco Mime Troupe…" — Tom Wolfe, *The Electric Kool-Aid Acid Test*

cache ("kash") a hiding place, used for storing valuables or provisions

> As you may have noticed, this word is often followed by *of weapons*.

> "Police in Denver arrested four people after a cache of guns, ammo, and body armor was discovered in a hotel near the upcoming MLB All-Star Game." — from an article in the *Salt Lake Tribune*, 2021

Ill-gotten gains

pelf wealth or money, especially when dishonestly acquired

> "And though many [New Wave musicians], especially in America, proudly proclaimed their passion for pelf, they didn't suck up musically, and they proved again and again that a rock and roll album didn't have to be financed by Krupp." — from an article by Robert Christgau in the *Village Voice*, 1979

swag goods gotten by force or illicit means

> However, you're more likely to hear this word used with a newer meaning: free things given to attendees at a convention, etc.

> "Actors and directors nominated for an Academy Award receive an eclectic swag bag… The gifts—which in total are worth more than $200K—range from quirky wellness items to all-expenses-paid trips." — from an article in *USA Today*, 2020

Aye, there's the rub

frottage ("fraw-TAZH" or "FRAH-tidj") the technique of rubbing (as with a pencil on a paper covering something with a raised surface) to transfer an image; or the act of rubbing against a clothed stranger in public for sexual pleasure

> The link between the two meanings is obvious—i.e., rubbing. Here's a frottage anecdote that combines the innocuous with the sexual: in 1978, while visiting London, I made a brass rubbing at St. Martin-in-the-Fields. Visitors from many lands chatted congenially as we worked. A young German tourist asked if the eraser in his hand was called a *rubber* in English, and a British woman replied, "Yes." The other American and I looked at each other, and kept our mouths shut.

Landforms

polder ("POHL-dər") an area of land reclaimed from the sea by dikes

> I took a German literature class during my freshman year of college. The textbook included a novella called *Der Schimmelreiter* (*The Rider of the White Horse*), first published in 1888. I struggled through it in a fog of half-comprehension, looking up multiple words in each sentence. One particular word baffled me: in this novella, the protagonist becomes dikemaster, responsible for the maintenance of the dikes that protect the *polder*. But what, I wondered, is a polder? My dictionary didn't say.

glacis ("GLAY-sis") a slope; or a manmade slope running down from a fort, enabling soldiers to fire at approaching enemies; or a buffer zone separating enemy armies

> "Construction of Fort McHenry almost certainly entailed removal of soil in the areas of its parade ground and ditch, to provide the fill used to create its rampart and portions of its glacis." — from an archeological overview of Fort McHenry, published by the National Park Service, 2000

These are not words of praise

postiche ("pah-STEESH" or "PAH-steesh") a pretense, sham; or an imitation, an artificial substitute

> "It was the private opinion, publicly expressed, of some leading 'floor managers' that the gems were paste. Other connoisseurs pronounced the stones real, but the lady *postiche*." — from an article in *Harper's* magazine, 1866

Note: Don't confuse *postiche* with *pastiche*, which usually means a work of art created in a mixture of styles, or with parts drawn from multiple sources. (However, *pastiche* can also mean a work that imitates or parodies a certain style. Are you confused yet?)

fallal/fal-lal ("fal-LAL," both syllables rhyming with *pal,* or "fə-LAL") a showy trimming on an article of clothing; a fancy ornament; or a useless bit of finery

> "Look how she goes in her Farthingale and her rich Trimmings and Fallals, no less than a whole Tradesman's Shop about her mangy back." — Miguel de Cervantes, *Don Quixote* (translated by Pierre Motteux, et al.)

frippery ("FRIP-ə-ree") showy, frivolous, or excessive ornamentation in dress, speech, etc.; or cheap, gaudy clothes

> "She is as fond of gauze, and French frippery, as the best of them." — Oliver Goldsmith, *She Stoops to Conquer*

Sister Leonora held a low opinion of young Constance's fallals, which paled in comparison to the fripperies of her own youth.

Round and round

rondure ("RAHN-jər") (poetic) roundness, especially graceful roundness

> "There was some rondure, but nothing undue at his age or out of reach of the lash of diet and situps." — Norman Rush, *Mating*

embonpoint ("ahm-boh(n)-PWAHN": pretend you're French) stoutness, corpulence

> "He's less a victim of fashion than of the new middle-class esthetic of moderation, which frowns upon any sign of embonpoint. The days when a bulging waistline was an expression of European joie de vivre… are over." — from an article about Umberto Eco in the *New York Times,* 1989

Jumbly wumbly

olla podrida ("AH-lə pə-DREE-də") (literally "rotten pot") a stew; or any assortment or medley

> "'That big dish that is smoking farther off,' said Sancho, 'seems to me to be an olla podrida, and out of the diversity of things in such ollas, I can't fail to light upon something tasty and good for me.'" — Miguel de Cervantes, *Don Quixote* (translated by John Ormsby)

salmagundi ("sal-mə-GUN-dee," the U pronounced like the OO in *book*) a salad-like dish that combines meats, seafoods, eggs, and vegetables, arranged separately on a plate; or any medley or mixture

> *Salmagundi* was the title of a satirical periodical published in 1807-8 by Washington Irving and others, poking fun at New York City's politics and culture. It's also the name of a literary quarterly founded in 1965.

gallimatia/galimatias ("gal-ə-MAY-shə"/"-shəss") meaningless talk; gibberish; confused nonsense

> "Now it seemed to me that Mr. C— had no opinions, only words, for his assertions seemed a mere *galimatias*." — Henry Crabb Robinson, *Diary* (entry dated 1824)

farrago ("fə-RAH-go") a confused jumble, a hodgepodge

> "…significant new evidence has appeared from the news media. It demonstrates beyond a doubt that [Brett] Kavanaugh's emotional testimony was a farrago of evasions and outright lies." — from an article in *New York* magazine, 2018

buncombe/bunkum ("BUNG-kəm") talk that is empty, insincere, or foolish, nonsensical

> Origin story: Congressman Felix Walker, representing Buncombe County, North Carolina (1817-1823), made frequent speeches "for Buncombe," usually unrelated to whatever matter was under discussion.

> "…Lenehan's version of the business was all pure buncombe."
> — James Joyce, *Ulysses*

> "Almost no records survived… so the history of the Pony Express is littered with impostors, inaccuracies, and plain bunkum." — from an article in *National Geographic*, 2018

A Farrago of Bunkum, thought the Ambassador. But nicely deployed.

Remainders

aliquot ("AL-ə-kwaht") in mathematics: contained in a larger number so that there is no remainder after division, e.g., 8 is an aliquot part of 24

> "...the central figure of the tragedy... rose nobly to the occasion and expressed the dying wish (immediately acceded to) that the meal should be divided in aliquot parts among the members of the sick and indigent roomkeeper's association..." — James Joyce, *Ulysses*

aliquant ("AL-ə-kwant") the opposite of aliquot: 7 is an aliquant part of 24

Science, new and old

albedo ("al-BEE-doh") an index of reflectiveness, calculated by dividing the amount of light a surface reflects by the amount of light that hits it

> A hypothetical pure black surface, reflecting none of the light that hits it, would have an albedo of 0, while a pure white surface, reflecting all light that hits it, would have an albedo of 1. In astronomy, this is a feature used to describe planets and other bodies in space.

> "Venus' enormous albedo of 0.76 is accounted for by the permanent veil of cloud surrounding the planet." — from an article in *Popular Science* magazine, 1964

phlogiston ("flow-JISS-tən") a hypothetical substance believed by chemists of the 1700s to be present in all combustible materials: the essence of fire, released during combustion

> "Lavoisier didn't think that Priestley was right about phlogiston, prompting a long-running battle." — from an article in *Smithsonian* magazine, 2017

Group behavior

fifth column people in a country at war who collaborate with the enemy by spying or by sabotage (originally said of Franco supporters in Madrid during his coup against the democratic Spanish government)

"Parliament has given us the powers to put down Fifth Column activities with a strong hand." — Winston Churchill, *Into Battle* (a collection of speeches, published in 1941)

syndicalism ("SIN-də-kəl-izm") a trade union movement that seeks (by direct action, especially strikes) to bring all means of production and distribution under the control of federations of unions

When I've encountered this word, it has usually been part of the hyphenate *anarcho-syndicalism*, a political movement that adds the goal of decentralized, egalitarian control.

"The full list of anarchist schools of thought is long, but includes anarcho-syndicalism, anarcha-feminism, green anarchism, Black anarchism, and individualist anarchism, which is similar to libertarianism." — from an article on *refinery29.com*, 2020

shibboleth ("SHIB-ə-ləth") a slogan used by a group for recognizing fellow members; or a belief held by a group of people, especially one that is viewed with disdain by others

In Judges 12:5-6, the Ephraimites tried to escape after a military defeat by crossing the Jordan River, into territory held by their enemy, the Gileadites. When they denied that they were Ephraimites, they were forced to say *shibboleth* ("stream" in Hebrew). The Ephraimites pronounced the word *sibboleth*, giving themselves away, and were summarily executed: 42,000 of them, according to the Bible. (In New Jersey, we ask, "What do you call this, pork roll or Taylor ham?")

"The Republican shibboleth of voter fraud deserves to be put to rest once and for all." — from an editorial in the *Star Tribune* (Minneapolis), 2020

That which did not fit elsewhere

synergy ("SIN-ər-jee") the action of two or more organisms, substances, or organizations, resulting in an effect greater than the sum of their individual effects

"So there's this kind of happy sort of synergy between technology progress and our great ability to tell stories." — PlayStation CEO Jim Ryan, quoted in the *Washington Post*, 2020

duende ("doo-EN-day") passion, or an inspired spirit (especially in a flamenco performance); or an elf-like creature that hides inside the walls of a home, in Hispanic folklore

"Antonio radiated '*duende*,' that stage magnetism that smacks you in the face even at the back of the stalls." — from the obituary of Antonio Ruiz Soler, a famous Spanish dancer, in the *Independent*, 1996

When it comes to duende, few can match our pal, Vladimir Peebles.

imprimatur ("im-prih-MAH-tər") a guarantee that something is of high quality; an official authorization, especially to publish

> (Originally this word referred to a license to publish a religious book, issued by the Roman Catholic Church.)

> "The gambit appeared to be a rogue effort to put the imprimatur of the federal government on research that aims to undermine the established science of climate change." — from an article in the *New York Times*, 2021

hamartia ("hah-mar-TEE-ə") in Aristotle's *Poetics*, a tragic hero's guilt, error, or "fatal flaw," which causes his downfall

> "[Robert F.] Kennedy's ruthlessness and ambition, which are treated as the family's hamartia in [the film] *Chappaquiddick,* are swept under the rug of his compassion." — from a movie review in *The New Republic*, 2018

teratology ("ter-ə-TAHL-ə-jee") the study of congenital deformities; or mythology as it relates to monsters and fantastic creatures

> The word comes from the Greek: the root means *monster.*

> "One may say, then, that a being possessing both arms and wings is a monster and belongs to the department of Teratology." — Anatole France, *The Revolt of the Angels*

antipodes ("an-TIP-ə-deez") any two places at opposite points on the Earth; or two exact opposites

> "I live in [New Zealand,] a faraway island nation of five million. I sometimes sign my emails… 'Yours from the antipodes,' because that's how it feels to be so distant from the centers of American and European influence." — from an article in *National Geographic*, 2021

bricolage ("brih-kə-LAZH") the creation of something using whatever is available; or a piece made this way

> *Bricolage* often refers to works of literature or art: "Magnificent Bricolage" is the title of an article about the artist Joseph Cornell, on the website of Indiana University's Cinema Department, 2020

tare ("TAIR") the weight of a container when empty: to calculate the weight of the contents, subtract the tare from the combined weight of contents and container

> Have you noticed the word TARE on the side of tractor-trailer trucks, followed by a weight in LBS or KG? Now you know what it means.

shebeen ("shə-BEEN") (Irish) an unlicensed or illegal drinking establishment

> "Blind to the world up in a shebeen in Bride street after closing time, fornicating with two shawls and a bully on guard, drinking porter out of teacups." — James Joyce, *Ulysses*

lagniappe ("lan-YAP") an extra or unexpected gift; a small gift given to a customer with a purchase

> "The Kaufmans specialized in architectural lagniappe: one downtown building has a sculptured rendering of a Sopwith Camel on the roof, along with a lighted AstroTurf runway." — from an article in the *New Yorker,* 1981

spindrift/spoondrift sea spray, blown from waves by strong winds; *spindrift* can also refer to fine, wind-blown snow or sand

> "Man, whose young passion sets the spindrift flying, / Is soon too lame to march, too cold for loving." — John Masefield, "On Growing Old"

stochastic ("stə-KASS-tik" or "stoh-") random; involving chance or probability, especially because of a random variable

> "This Week's Mail Bombs Are No Surprise: They are examples of stochastic terrorism—individually random, but these days, statistically predictable." — headline of an article in the *New York Times,* 2018

caducous ("kə-DOO-kəss") fleeting; or, in botany, dropping off once it has served its purpose (refers to a plant's organs or parts)

> Searching for a good example of this word's use, I found only a review of John Banville's novel, *Ancient Light,* which pointed out the author's challenging vocabulary: "You can be both charmed and baffled by a beautiful description of falling snow as 'great flocks of whiteness hosting haphazard in the brumous air,' [and] 'caducous leaves' lying in the road..." — from the *Toronto Star,* 2012

excipient ("ek-SIP-ee-ənt") an inert substance that serves as a vehicle for a medication: sometimes referred to as a "bulking agent"

> "Between 2015 to 2019, health-care professionals, patients, and manufacturers filed nearly 2,500 reports to the FDA about an adverse reaction to an excipient." — from an article in *Popular Science,* 2020

anachorism ("ə-NAK-ə-rizm") an incongruity regarding place (in the same way that *anachronism* refers to time)

> "From its mouth* echoes the anachoristic sound of an Andean band, piping and thumping love songs of the Bolivian highlands." — from an article in the *New York Times,* 2002

> *That is, the mouth of a street in Budapest.

posthaste ("POST HAYST") with great haste (as a postal courier would ride when delivering an urgent letter)

> "When the House passed... the HEROES Act designed to bring billions to cash-strapped New York, Governor Andrew Cuomo urged the Senate to pass it posthaste..." — from the website AMNY.com, 2020

Hobson's choice a situation in which you can take what's offered or nothing; or a situation in which neither alternative is acceptable

> Around the time when Shakespeare was writing his plays, Thomas Hobson rented out horses to students. To avoid overworking the more popular horses, he imposed a strict rule: he rotated the horses in the stable, and renters could only take the horse closest to the door.

> "The Bruins-Maple Leafs series, recently completed, presented a brutal Hobson's choice for fans of the Montreal Canadiens. Seeing our two most hated rivals face off against each other, and with the Habs already defeated and out of the playoffs, Montrealers... felt rather like Poles caught between Germany and Russia. You want no one to win, and everybody to suffer." — from an article in the *New Yorker,* 2013

emprise ("em-PRIZE") an undertaking, especially one that is chivalrous or adventurous

> "Even if he were recognized who would suspect a poor fool of being sent on so important an emprise?" — from a story in *Boys' Life*, 1924

cartel ("KAR-təl") (archaic) a letter expressing defiance; a written challenge; or, currently, a group of businesses that collude to keep prices high rather than competing (with that meaning, it's pronounced "kar-TELL")

> "He instantly sent back the herald with a 'cartel' of defiance, in which he... challenged [the emperor] to single combat, requiring him to name the time and place for the encounter, and the weapons with which he chose to fight." — William Robertson, *The History of the Reign of the Emperor Charles V*

oriflamme ("OR-ə-flam") the red banner of the Abbey of St. Denis, which served as the battle standard of the French kings during the Middle Ages; or a knight's standard; or any inspiring symbol or ideal that rallies followers

> "I bought a copy of 'Ulysses,' whose light-blue-and-white cover was then an oriflamme for such as me." — from a piece in the *New Yorker,* 1959

Unusual Practices

Rites

maundy ("MAWN-dee") the religious ceremony of washing the feet of the poor, on Maundy Thursday, i.e., the Thursday before Easter: commemorating Jesus's washing of the disciples' feet at the Last Supper

> "My wife... had been today at White-hall to the Maundy... but the King did not wash the poor people's feet himself, but the Bishop of London did it for him." — Samuel Pepys, *Diary* (1667)

potlatch a ceremonial feast among the indigenous people of the Pacific Northwest, at the end of which the host gives valuable goods to his guests or destroys his own, to show his wealth

> "The game has become secondary to a potlatch ceremony called tailgate picknicking... [which] requires that the host participants outdo their neighbours in the quality and variety of food and

drink and the elegance of serving accessories." — from an article in Toronto's *Globe & Mail*, 1970

Worship and sacrifice

ophiolatry ("oh-fee-AHL-ə-tree" or "ah-fee...") worship of snakes

"The Greeks... have... greatly obscured the real symbolism of the ophiolatry of Egypt..." — W.R. Cooper, *The Serpent Myths of Ancient Egypt* (1873)

heliolatry ("hee-lee-AHL-ə-tree") sun-worship

"I can understand why heliolatry was so widespread in the ancient world. I think it's hard for most people now to comprehend just how dark and foreboding the night used to be." — comment on a discussion board on the website Fark.com, 2011, about new sun-worshipping sites found near Stonehenge

hecatomb ("HEK-ə-tohm") a slaughter or sacrifice of many

In ancient Greece or Rome, *hecatomb* meant the slaughter of one hundred cattle at a time, as an offering to the gods. (The prefix *heca*, from Greek, means a hundred.)

"ANOTHER ARMENIAN HECATOMB: Nine Hundred Persons Killed at Biridjik, Near Aintab" — headline in the *New York Times,* 1896

Justice, law, censorship

talion ("TAL-ee-ən," the A pronounced as in *cat*) the principle of punishing offenders by subjecting them to the same harms they are guilty of inflicting (e.g., for murderers, capital punishment)

"In the primitive code of the talion nothing was more simple—an eye for an eye, a tooth for a tooth—thou hast killed; I kill thee." — Georges Clemenceau, *South America To-Day* (1911)

attainder ("ə-TAIN-dər") loss of civil rights, including the right to hand down land to one's heirs, by a person convicted of treason or a felony and outlawed or sentenced to death

"By the constitution of the United States, no bill of attainder shall be passed; and no attainder of treason... shall work corruption of blood or forfeiture, except during the life of the person attainted." — Noah Webster, *An American Dictionary of the English Language* (1864)

moulage ("moo-LAZH") the technique of making a mold of a mark, e.g., a footprint, for the purpose of identification in a criminal investigation; or a mold made this way

> "Sheriff tells me you decided not to make a moulage," an investigator says to Deputy Barney Fife on the *Andy Griffith Show*. Barney answers, "Yeah, that's right. We decided not to make a moulage, hee-hee. Oh, we told a few people, but we decided it didn't make sense upsettin' folks runnin' around blabbin', makin' a big moulage out of it." (from the episode *The Cow Thief*, 1962 — cited on IMDB.com)

comstockery ("KAHM-stock-ə-ree") zealous, prudish suppression of plays, books, etc., that are considered dangerous to public morals

> The word derives from Anthony Comstock, U.S. Postal Inspector and secretary of the New York Society for the Suppression of Vice: a dedicated upholder of Victorian morality.

> George Bernard Shaw used the word in a letter to the *New York Times* in 1905, written because Comstock had alerted police to the subject of Shaw's play, *Mrs. Warren's Profession*: "Comstockery is the world's standing joke at the expense of the United States. Europe likes to hear of such things. It confirms the deep-seated conviction of the Old World that America is a provincial place, a second-rate country-town civilization after all."

Things you can do with vegetation

topiary ("TOH-pee-err-ee") the art of training and trimming shrubs and trees to create ornamental shapes

> "The good Doctor... was as sturdy and square-shaped as ever with his well-padded shoulders, square chin, square nostrils... and rectangular brush of grizzled hair that had something topiary about it." — Vladimir Nabokov, *Pnin*

> In the movie *Edward Scissorhands,* Edward turns suburban shrubs into a dancer, a dinosaur, and a family of four: topiary *a la* Tim Burton.

espalier ("eh-SPAL-yər," the A pronounced as in *cat*) a tree or shrub that has been trained to grow flat along a wall, supported by a trellis; or the framework that supports such a plant; also, as a verb, to train a plant this way

"Almost any fruit or citrus tree can be espaliered, but some are better suited." — from an article in the *Mercury News* (San Jose), 2019

When you eat things that aren't food

geophagy ("jee-AHF-ə-jee") the practice of eating earthy substances, such as clay: most common during times of famine

"The practice of dirt-eating, or geophagy, is common, perhaps because 'clean' dirt appears to impart some protection against parasites and pathogens." — from an article in *Scientific American*, 2011

pica ("PY-kə") a craving for unnatural food, e.g., chalk, paper, or ashes: usually found in people or animals suffering from nutritional deficiencies; most common in children and pregnant women

"…when you have a compulsive urge to ingest substances that aren't food, like paint chips from the hardware store, cotton balls from the medicine cabinet or even something as seemingly innocuous as crunching on ice from the freezer, that's actually a condition known as pica, and it could signal a health issue that needs your doctor's attention." — from an article in *Today's Parent,* 2019

The sports section

skijoring ("skee-JOR-ing") a sport in which a skier is drawn over ice or snow by a horse, dog, or motor vehicle; it originated as a way to travel in winter

"As skijoring made its way to other countries, including the United States, dogs replaced horses." — from an article on DigitalJournal.com, 2012

bye (pronounced as in *goodbye*) an automatic advance to the next round of competition, without playing a match

"The obvious beneficiaries are the top four seeds. They get free passes into the second round, eliminating the chance they'll be handed a first-round exit… First-round byes are such a feature of the ATP tour, at least in part, because they help smaller tournaments convince big-name players to sign up." — from an article on the website TennisAbstract.com

harvest home the last part of a year's harvest; formerly, the festival celebrating this; or the song sung by harvesters as they bring in the last load

> In 1973 Thomas Tryon published a horror novel called *Harvest Home*. Ever since, the phrase has evoked mild dread in me, rather than sentimental nostalgia for a long-gone way of life. (I just read the plot summary and am more disturbed than ever.)

charivari/shivaree ("shah-rə-VAR-ee"/"shiv-ə-REE") a noisy mock-serenade to newlyweds, by a group of people (from *caribaria*, Latin for "headache")

> In *It's a Wonderful Life*, when Bert and Ernie serenade George Bailey and Mary, singing "I Love You Truly" in the rain, does that count as a shivaree? Maybe not—but it's close.

couvade ("koo-VAHD") a custom of some cultures in which the husband fasts or goes to bed as if in childbirth while his wife is bearing their child

> The custom goes back to ancient Egypt, and has been observed in Papua New Guinea and among indigenous people of the Americas, among others.

> "Research has shown that a number of expectant fathers join expectant mothers in experiencing signs of pregnancy... Couvade symptoms generally include morning sickness, fatigue, backache, insomnia, irritability, depression, increased stress, weight gain and cravings for particular foods." — from an article in the *New York Times*, 1985

suttee/sati ("sə-TEE") the practice of Hindu widows in India, now banned, in which they threw themselves on their husbands' funeral pyres

> "He had become resigned to her perpetual lamentation and living Suttee for his defunct rival." — George Meredith, *The Ordeal of Richard Feverell*

flyting ("FLY-ting) an impromptu folk contest in which opponents insult each other

> The word comes from Scotland, where, in the 15th and 16th centuries, poets performed an early version of rap battles... which had a more recent ancestor in "the dozens," an African American tradition of bantering insults exchanged in front of friends.

"In the 'flytings' between Katherine and Petruchio the exchanges wear the guise of wit." — G.K. Hunter, *John Lyly: The Humanist as Courtier*

Etc.

corvée ("KOR-vay" or "kor-VAY") unpaid labor, either a) for a day, by a vassal for a feudal lord, or b) required of local residents, often in place of unpaid taxes, e.g., for repairing roads

"International diplomacy has facilitated the partnering of foreign business and Chinese Communism, and the German government has done especially well in that role. We need to remember that extraction of profit from slave labor is not new to Germany. The Nazis used corvée labor… [Today] VW builds its cars in China…"— from an essay in the *New York Times,* 2020, by the artist Ai Weiwei

martingale ("MAR-tn-gale") a system of trying to recoup one's gambling losses by doubling the amount of the next bet, or by increasing it by enough to cover the losses; or a device made of straps, which keep a horse from throwing its head back

On a TripAdvisor.com forum, someone asked whether anyone had had success with the martingale system. Here's a helpful reply: "No system works. If one did Vegas would not exist. There's no way to win just lose more slowly."

kedging pulling a ship forward by means of a rope tied to an anchor and thrown a distance ahead of the ship

"Normally when kedging off of a shoal, it does not much matter which direction you go, so long as it is generally the right one." — from an article in *Sail* magazine, 2017

When English Lacks That *Je Ne Sais Quoi:* Foreign Words and Phrases

I've heard Latin in Manhattan
And French in train and trench.
Ethel Merman spoke some German;
While deeper souls gush in Russian.
Learn some foreign phrases!
You'll impress and win high praises.

Latin

ad hoc ("add HOCK") created as necessary, for a special purpose, e.g., an ad hoc committee

> This quotation won't help you use the phrase correctly, but it may amuse you: "Ad hoc, ad loc, and quid pro quo, so little time, so much to know." — Jeremy Hillary Boob, Ph.D. (better known as the Nowhere Man), in the movie *Yellow Submarine*

The ad hoc committee convened for its study of women's conjugal needs.

quid pro quo ("KWID PROH KWOH") "something for something": a thing given with the expectation of getting something in return

> "'No quid pro quo': Trump's defenses in the impeachment investigation" — headline of article on Reuters.com, 2019

> (The article begins: "U.S. President Donald Trump has maintained… that he did nothing improper in his dealings with

Ukraine, even as witnesses have detailed efforts by his White House to get Ukraine to take actions that could help him politically.")

sine qua non ("SIH-nə kwah NOHN") something that is absolutely necessary

"One can live without friends, as one can live without love, or even without money, that supposed *sine qua non*. One can live in Paris—I discovered that!—on just grief and anguish." — Henry Miller, *Tropic of Cancer*

ne plus ultra ("nee plus ULL-trə") the ultimate; the highest point or achievement attainable; the most perfect example

"In the fascination of young Russians for Western things, jeans are the *ne plus ultra* of the modish, cult and modern." — Colin Thubron, *Among the Russians* (1985)

qua ("KWAH") as; in the capacity of

"Philip Larkin was unquestionably… better loved, qua poet, than John Betjeman, who was loved also for his charm." — from an article in the *Guardian,* 1993

infra dig (from *infra dignitatem*) ("IN-frə DIG") (informal, British) beneath (one's) dignity

"Few will consent to sing; it is *infra dig*." — Charles James Wills, *In the Land of the Lion and Sun: Or, Modern Persia* (1891)

ipso facto because of that very fact; as an inevitable result of that fact

"Democrats insist with great simplemindedness that making voting easier is, ipso facto, good." — from an article in the *Wall Street Journal,* 2021

conferatur, or cf. ("kohn-ferr-AH-toor") compare (a signal to the reader to compare a related but contrasting text)

quod vide, or q.v. ("kwahd WIH-deh") "which see": directs readers to a cross-reference, where more information or documentation can be found

videlicet, or viz. ("və-DEH-lə-set") "namely," or "that is"

floruit, or fl. or flor. ("FLOR-yə-wit") "s/he flourished": the approximate period when a person lived, if dates of birth or death are unknown

quod erat demonstrandum, or Q.E.D. "what was to be shown": the abbreviation is commonly placed at the end of a mathematical proof or philosophical argument, meaning that the point has now been proven

"If… people can walk about and do their business without brains—then certes the soul does not inhabit there. Q.E.D." — Laurence Sterne, *Tristram Shandy*

a posteriori ("Ā poh-steer-ee-OR-eye" or "AH poss-TEE-ree-or-ee") derived from observed facts; inductive; moving from specific examples to a general principle

a priori ("Ā pry-OR-eye" or "AH pree-OR-ee") derived by reasoning, not by observation; deductive

"I think arguments *a posteriori* are unnecessary for confirming what has been… sufficiently demonstrated *a priori*." — George Berkeley, *A Treatise Concerning the Principles of Human Knowledge*

You may remember Berkeley as the guy who supposedly asked whether a tree falling in the forest makes a sound if no one is there to hear it. According to Wikipedia, however, Berkeley never actually posed that question—though he did write about whether things truly exist if they are unperceived.

a fortiori ("Ā for-she-OR-eye" or "AH for-she-OR-ee") for an even stronger reason: refers to a conclusion backed by stronger evidence or arguments than one reached previously

"…*a fortiori*, there is no excuse for gratuitously embarrassing someone who is suspected of no wrongdoing." — from an essay in the *Wall Street Journal*, 2018

"If intelligence is pluralistic, so, *a fortiori*, is creativity." — Howard Gardner, *Creating Minds*

vade mecum ("VAY-dee MEE-kəm" or "VAH-day MAY-kəm") "go with me": a useful thing that a person carries constantly; a guidebook or ready-reference book

"…*The Annotated Lolita*, a text that has served for decades as a *vade mecum* for students interested in Nabokov's most famous novel." — David Rampton, *Vladimir Nabokov: A Literary Life*

lusus naturae ("LOO-səss nah-TOO-ree") a sport of nature: a freak, monster, or deformed person or animal

"The New-York *Observer*… contains a letter from its correspondent… at Larnaca, in the Island of Cyprus… describing a most remarkable lusus naturae recently discovered there. It is nothing less than a woman with horns growing out of her head." — from an article in the *New York Times*, 1864

per aspera ad astra ("PƏR ASS-pə-rə ADD ASS-trə") "Through hardship to the stars"

Transposed—"Ad astra per aspera"—this serves as the state motto of Kansas.

sub specie aeternitatis ("SUB SPEE-shee ee-tər-nih-TAH-tis") viewed from the perspective of eternity; from a universal perspective

> "…the recognition that, *sub specie aeternitatis*, there was no more reason to commit suicide than not to." — John Barth, *Letters*

Sic Transit Gloria Mundi ("seek TRAHN-sit GLOR-ee-ah MOON-dee") Thus Passes Earthly Glory: a reminder that fame and honor are temporary, like life itself

> For years, I have waited for a prolonged subway strike to be resolved late on a Sunday night, so the *Daily News* could print the headline, **SICK TRANSIT'S GLORIOUS MONDAY.**

In hoc signo vinces ("in hohk SIG-noh WEEN-case") By this sign (i.e., the Cross) you will conquer

> Constantine, the first Christian Roman emperor, had a vision of a cross of light in the sky with these words, in Greek. He then had a dream in which Jesus explained its meaning: that he should go into battle with the sign of the cross. The phrase is the motto of many schools and organizations—but is familiar to many Americans mainly because it appeared for a long time on Pall Mall cigarette packs.

peccavi ("pə-KAH-vee") "I have sinned": a confession of guilt or sin

> "He roared out *peccavi* most frankly when charged with his sins." — William Makepeace Thackeray, *The Adventures of Philip*

> There's also a famous bit of wit attached to this word: Sir Charles Napier, after winning battles in the Indian province of Sind, supposedly sent a dispatch that read, simply, *Peccavi.* Those who knew Latin understood: "I have sinned," i.e., *I have Sind.* (According to Britannica.com, this probably never happened; it was invented by *Punch* magazine.)

in extremis ("in ek-STREE-məss") at the point of death; or in an exceptionally difficult situation

> "'…where did I leave the women?' 'At the ship's rail, with their virtue in extremis.'" — John Barth, *The Sot-Weed Factor*

Semper Fidelis ("SEM-pər fə-DAY-ləss") "Always Faithful"

The motto of the U.S. Marine Corps, it's also the title of the official Marines' march, composed by John Philip Sousa. (You've definitely heard it. It goes like this: duh-duh-duh RAH-dah, da da da da da Duh-de-da-de-duh-de-da-dah, etc.)

casus belli ("KAH-səss BELL-ee" or "KAY-səss BELL-eye") an act or event that justifies a declaration of war

"Is the Trump administration deliberately searching for a casus belli for direct military confrontation with Iran?" — from an opinion essay in the *Washington Post*, 2019

Quo vadis? ("KWO VAH-dəss" or "WAH-dəss") Where are you going?

The quote is attributed to St. Peter, addressing Jesus, whom he meets on the road—*after* the crucifixion. It served as the title of a novel by the Polish author Henryk Sienkiewicz, about a Roman tribune who falls in love with a Christian girl. The 1951 film starred Robert Taylor and Deborah Kerr, and featured Peter Ustinov as Nero.

Siste, viator ("SIS-teh wee-AH-tor") "Stop, traveler"

This inscription was carved on roadside tombs in ancient Rome— usually followed by words meaning, "As you are now, so once was I, / As I am now, soon you must be."

Sic semper tyrannis ("sik SEM-pər tih-RAN-əss") "Thus always to tyrants"

This is what John Wilkes Booth shouted after shooting Abraham Lincoln; the phrase is attributed to Brutus, one of Caesar's assassins.

Here's how satirist Alexandra Petri used the quote, in an essay mocking a realtor who promoted her business on social media just before entering the Capitol on January 6, 2021: "Sic semper tyrannis! Hi, Ford's Theatregoers! If you liked what you just saw right now, please remember: My name is John Wilkes Booth, and I am an actor!" — from the *Washington Post*, 2021

ad hominem ("add HAH-mə-nəm") "to the man": referring to an argument that attacks an opponent's character rather than the idea or policy the opponent is propounding

"In politics… and in the media the ad hominem argument and personal attack has become the first and last refuge… for many angry but misguided critics." — from an opinion essay in the *Seattle Post-Intelligencer*, 2004

mirabile dictu ("mə-RAH-bə-lay DIK-too") "wonderful to tell"

"I donated to his campaign and mirabile dictu, he won!" — from a short feature on the website of *National Review,* 2010

vox populi ("vahks PAHP-yə-lye") "voice of the people": the beliefs of the majority

"In this age of technology, social media has become the vox populi." — from an essay in the *Chicago Tribune*, 2018

rara avis ("RAH-rə AY-vəss," the second word pronounced like the rent-a-car company) "rare bird": an unusual person or thing— especially, unusual in a good way

"Finding that rara avis of product design that combines pretty with practical is thrilling, and porcelain tile is both." — from an article in *Good Housekeeping*, 2020

mutatis mutandis ("myoo-TAH-təss myoo-TAHN-dəss") the needed changes having been made (used when comparing two generally similar things, some specifics having been altered)

"Roderick made an admirable bust of her... and a dozen women came rushing to him to be done, mutatis mutandis, in the same style." — Henry James, *Roderick Hudson*

pari passu ("PAH-ree PAH-soo") at an equal rate; proportionally, without preference

The term is used most often in bankruptcy law, to indicate that creditors will be paid proportionally, depending on the amount of their investment.

vale ("VAY-lee") "be in good health," i.e., farewell

"Latin has gone at present out of fashion;
still, to tell you the truth,
he had enough knowledge of Latin
to... put at the bottom of a letter *vale...* " — Aleksandr Pushkin, *Eugene Onegin* (translated by Vladimir Nabokov)

misericordia ("mih-seh-rə-KOR-dee-ə") pity, compassion, mercy

"[The Christian soldier] was reminded that he had to serve with *humilitas* and *misericordia...*" — Aldo Scaglione, *Knights at Court*

ad captandum vulgus ("ahd kahp-TAHN-dəm VUL-ghəss," or "WOOL-guss," the final syllable rhyming with *puss*) "for catching (i.e., pleasing) the crowd": refers to an emotional argument that catches the attention and appeals to the emotions of ordinary people

"Without speaking ad captandum vulgus, he captured them all the same." — from an article in the *Times* (of London), 1993

ignis fatuus ("IG-nəss FA-chew-əss," the A pronounced as in *cat*) a hope or goal that is illusory

> "What an ignis fatuus this ambition is!" — John Adams, *Letters*, 1777

> The phrase also refers to a light that may appear over marshes at night, thought to be produced by the combustion of gas from decomposing plants, a phenomenon also known as *Will-o'-the-wisp*.

nemo ("NAY-moh") nobody

> The name of Captain Nemo, Jules Verne's mysterious inventor and submarine commander, comes from this word. Verne may also have been alluding to *The Odyssey*, in which Odysseus outwits the Cyclops by telling him his name is Nobody.

French

(Be aware that the suggested pronunciations are only preposterous approximations. French is a whole different language!)

chacun à son goût ("shah-KUHH(N) ah sun GOO") "each to his own taste" (implying that there's no accounting for taste)

> "Chacun à son goût, or, why we eat turkey" — headline of essay in the *New York Times,* by Art Buchwald, November, 2004 (The essay originally appeared in the International Herald Tribune, many years earlier.)

plus ça change, plus c'est la même chose ("ploo sah shahnzh, ploo say lah memm shohz") the more things change, the more they stay the same

> Among the most common of French phrases, this one actually has an author: Jean-Baptiste Alphonse Karr, writing in his journal *Les Guêpes* (The Wasps), in 1849.

entre nous ("AHN-trə NOO") "between us": i.e., confidentially

> "I proposed to keep the matter *entre nous*—"
> "*Entre nous?* Marry, thou'rt learning to scheme in French!"
> — John Barth, *The Sot-Weed Factor*

mot juste ("MOH ZHOOST") the right word or expression; the perfect word for the occasion

"My head is a squeezed rag, so don't expect le mot juste in this letter." — Ezra Pound, in a letter to James Joyce, 1915 (from *Letters of James Joyce*)

sangfroid ("sahng FRWAH") "cold blood": imperturbable coolness under stress

> "He's projected a sort of white-collar attitude of cheery competence and sangfroid." — David Foster Wallace, *Infinite Jest*

comme il faut ("KUM eel FOH") as it should be; proper; in keeping with accepted etiquette or convention

> "... it never can have been *comme il faut* in any age or nation for a man of note... to be constantly asking for money." — Thomas Macaulay, *Journal* (1857)

épater le bourgeois ("ay-pah-TAY leuh boor-ZHWAH") to shock the (respectable) middle class

> "...aging punk rockers have two options, real-estate-wise: a rat-infested hovel decorated with clumps of black tar heroin or a terrifying megamansion filled with baroque horrors designed to *épater le bourgeois*." — from an article on the Curbed Los Angeles website, 2013

l'esprit de l'escalier ("less-PREE də less-kah-LYAY," the final syllable rhyming with *day*) "staircase wit": the perfect retort that comes to you only after you've left someone else's apartment, when you're going down the stairs

> According to Wikipedia, the phrase originated with philosopher Denis Diderot, who describes a moment when, at a formal dinner, someone addressed a remark to him that left him speechless. He explains: "A sensitive man, such as myself, overwhelmed by the argument leveled against him, becomes confused and doesn't come to himself again until at the bottom of the stairs."

aperçu ("ah-pər-SOO," the A pronounced as in *cat*) a brief, insightful comment, especially an entertaining one

> "Each book feels both surprising and inevitable ... proceeding with her hallmark disdain for conventional wisdom and with a flair for the beautifully tossed-off aperçu." — referring to biographer Stacy Schiff, from the introduction to an interview in the *Paris Review*, 2017

mise en scène ("MEEZ awhn SENN") the staging of a play, film, etc.: everything the audience sees, including the actors, scenery, costumes, lighting, composition, etc.

"The premise and mise-en-scène are dark and sad: an alcoholic, middle-age, working-class loser caring for his elderly, demanding, bedridden de facto father in the desolate Texas-Mexico borderlands." — from a review in *Variety*, 2017

dernier cri ("DAIRN-yay KREE") the latest fashion; the newest thing

"The style is playful, … bumptiously Fieldingesque, and yet as pumped-up and heightened and chock-full of late-20th-century references as the dernier cri from the street." — from a review by T.C. Boyle of Thomas Pynchon's *Mason & Dixon,* in the *New York Times,* 1997

soupçon ("soop-SAW(N)") a small amount of something; a trace

"…a pastiche of styles and musical-theater in-jokes—a little music hall, a little Kander-and-Ebb with a soupçon of Mozart for the especially quick-eared." — from a review of the musical *The Sneetches* on the website TwinCities.com, 2017

amour-propre ("ah-MOOR PROH-pr(ə)") self-respect; a sense of one's own ability or worth

As I typed the definition above, I thought that by now someone must have written a book with the title *Amour Impropre*. And yes, someone has: John McKeown, in 2005.

"Hugh had never seen such a vile temper, such morbid *amour-propre*, so self-centered a nature." — Vladimir Nabokov, *Transparent Things*

contretemps ("kahn-trə-TAHHM" or "kohn-") an unexpected, embarrassing occurrence or disagreement

"Elsewhere in Cannes, the ongoing contretemps between the festival and Netflix… may have cooled a little in recent years." — from an article in *Los Angeles Times*, 2022

demimonde ("DEM-ee-mahnd") the class of women kept by wealthy lovers; or prostitutes as a class; or any group on the margins of respectability (A woman who moves in this circle is a *demimondaine.*)

"Zola's innocent blonde Venus rises from dire streetwalker's poverty to soar like a mythic amoral angel through the corrupt society of the second empire… Zola's descriptions of the Parisian demi-monde… are unequalled." — referring to the novel *Nana,* from an article in the *Guardian*, 2013

demi-vierge ("DEM-ee-vee-AIRZH") a girl or woman whose sexual activities stop just short of intercourse

"She knew that he didn't mind whether she were demi-vierge or demi-monde, so long as he didn't absolutely know, and wasn't made to see." — D.H. Lawrence, *Lady Chatterley's Lover*

parvenu ("PAR-və-noo") someone who has risen suddenly or recently and hasn't yet acquired the manner appropriate to his or her new position

"In 1952, backed by little more than his reputation as a war hero and a fortune staked by his parvenu father, 35-year-old John F. Kennedy swiped a Senate seat from Republican Henry Cabot Lodge, himself a wealthy combat veteran." — from an article in *The New Republic*, 2020

déclassé ("DAY-klah-SAY") fallen in social class or status

"If she had been a generation younger and a bit more déclassé, she would have been saying 'like.'" — from an article by Christopher Hitchens in *Vanity Fair,* 2010, referring to Caroline Kennedy's repeated use of the phrase "you know"

soi-disant ("SWAH dee-ZOH(N)") self-styled; self-proclaimed; would-be

"Which is more amusing, the number of Marxists who have never cracked a volume of *Das Kapital,* or the number of today's *soi-disant* conservatives who have been so busy praising Burke they have not taken time to read, or at least comprehend, him?" — George Will, *Statecraft as Soulcraft*

recherché ("reh-shair-SHAY") rare, exotic; or overly refined, pretentious

"The smell... was fresh and bitter and at the same time nauseating. Hilda wondered if it were not caused by some extremely recherché form of dry rot." — Iris Murdoch, *A Fairly Honorable Defeat*

frisson ("free-SOH(N)") a shiver or shudder; a brief, sudden feeling of excitement or fear

"Driving under the proper conditions—the right kind of car, small, light, and responsive to the slightest touch—made driving a sport and a pleasure, with a frisson of underlying danger to penalize a lack of skill." — from an article by Bruce McCall in the *New Yorker*, 2020

faute de mieux ("FOHT də MYƎ") for lack of a better alternative

"When a state severely limits access to safe and legal procedures, women in desperate circumstances may resort to unlicensed rogue practitioners, faute de mieux, at great risk to their health and safety." — Ruth Bader Ginsburg, in a concurring opinion, *Whole Woman's Health v. Hellerstedt*, 2016

au fond ("oh FAHN") "at the bottom": basically, essentially

"*Au fond* every man is a hunter, a cave-man." — Mary Lutyens, *Forthcoming Marriages*

tant pis ("tahn PEE") "so much the worse": too bad (said when there's nothing to be done)

"…she saw the awful lone longing in my lowered eyes… and with one beat of her lashes: 'Tant pis' she said, and made as if to move away." — Vladimir Nabokov, *Lolita*

lese majesty ("LAYZ MA-jəss-tee," the second word rhyming with *travesty*) (in actual French: *lèse majesté*) a crime against the reigning monarch, or against a monarch's dignity

"Thailand's lèse majesté law is the toughest in the world, and those judged guilty of breaking it face up to 15 years in jail for each count of offending the king, queen, heir or regent." — from an article on the website Yahoo!Style, 2018

passe partout (rhymes with *pass far too*) something that enables a person to go anywhere; or a master key

In the Jules Verne novel *Around the World in 80 Days,* the English hero has a likable French valet, aptly named Passepartout, who accompanies him on his adventures and serves as a sort of Sancho Panza to Phileas Fogg's Don Quixote.

l'enfer c'est les autres ("lawhn-FAIR say layz OHT(R)") "hell is other people"

This is a quote from Sartre's play *Huis Clos (No Exit).*

One might retort: "Okay, but what would you call the permanent absence of all other people?" (If he says, "*Paradis,*" he's guilty of bad faith.)

pot-au-feu ("PAH-toh-FEUHH") a thick soup with meats, vegetables, etc.

"…peasant stews like *pot-au-feu*… are hearty enough to make up an entire meal." — Joanne Harris and Fran Warde, *The French Kitchen*

réchauffé ("ray-shoh-FAY") warmed leftovers; or old material reworked or rehashed

One of my long-ago college roommates loves French cuisine but hates leftovers. Perhaps he would tolerate réchauffé.

"A *réchauffé* of one's own stale speeches is not an appetising dish." — Rhoda Broughton, *Red as a Rose Is She*

dégagé ("day-gah-ZHAY") relaxed, unconcerned; easy and free in manner

> "He was handsome, *dégagé*, extremely gallant, and in his dress exceeded most others." — Henry Fielding, *Tom Jones*

roturier ("roh-TOOR-ee-ay") a commoner; a person of low rank

> "If my uncle behaves like a *roturier*, it is because his mind has gone." — Arthur Quiller-Couch, *Fort Amity*

bibelot ("BEE-bə-loh") a small, decorative object, especially a rare or beautiful one; a trinket or curio

> "Oh, if only Trump had a crystal ball among those Bedminster bibelots! Maybe he would have done everything differently, hanging onto old Comey…" — from an article in *Vogue*, 2017

Grand Guignol ("GRAHND geen-YOHL") theatrical entertainment that features violently gruesome spectacle

> The phrase comes from the name of a theater in Paris that operated from 1897 until 1962, specializing in realistic horror shows. It is also applied to gory horror films. The theater's last director attributed its decline to the Holocaust: "Before the war, everyone felt that what was happening onstage was impossible. Now we know that these things, and worse, are possible in reality."

> "Tim Burton's adaptation of Steven Sondheim's quasi-operatic exercise in Dickensian-Brechtian Grand Guignol is a movie of bombastic, impossible camera moves and rhapsodic yuckiness." — from a review of the movie *Sweeney Todd* in the *Village Voice*, 2009

longueur ("long-ƏRR") a long, dull passage (e.g., in a novel or a piece of music); or a period of boredom

> "The book is full of wonderful things (as well as some longueurs and some hair-tugging complexifications of intrigue and plot)." — from a review of John Barth's novel *Letters*, in the *Washington Post*, 1979

> "The longueurs of the middle-class Sunday, the deadly frustrations of office routine." — from an article in the *Times Literary Supplement*, 1963

retroussé ("reh-troo-SAY") turned up at the end (said of noses)

> "Schoenmaker [a plastic surgeon] was a craftsman… and had two assistants, one a secretary/receptionist/nurse with an impossibly coy retroussé nose and thousands of freckles, all of which Schoenmaker had done himself." — Thomas Pynchon, *V*. (Notice that the doctor's semi-German name means "beautiful-maker.")

blague ("BLAHG") a joke or prank; or nonsense, empty talk (*sans blague:* no kidding)

> "What he's saying in his characteristically ironic way is… that any fiction that imparts to us a sense of orderliness in life… is lying to us. These traditional techniques, this 'realism,' Barthelme calls blague." — from an article about the author Donald Barthelme in the *New York Times*, 1970

German

Weltschmerz ("VELT-shmairts") "world-pain": sorrow caused by contemplating the nature of the world, especially as contrasted with one's ideals; or a world-weary, pessimistic feeling

> "'What's the matter?' I asked. 'Things in general… The state of this wicked world. A touch of Weltschmerz, that's all.'" — Christopher Isherwood, *Mr. Norris Changes Trains*

Weltanschauung ("VELT-ahn-shao-oong," the third syllable rhyming with *Mao*) worldview: one's conception of life

> "The main reason why evolutionism… made such slow progress is that it was the replacement of one entire *weltanschauung* by a different one." — from an article in *Science* magazine, 1972

Schadenfreude ("SHAH-den-FROY-də") pleasure taken in someone else's misfortune (often an antagonist or rival)

> "There is no English word for Schadenfreude, because there is no such feeling here." — from an article in the *Spectator*, 1926 (This quote reliably elicits chuckles.)

Zeitgeist ("TSITE-geyst," to rhyme with *kite heist*) "the spirit of the time": the beliefs and general spirit that define an era

> "My business is to incarnate the Zeitgeist." — from a letter written by George Bernard Shaw, 1889

> "A clear mark of the Zeitgeist of the late 1960's and the 1970's is the increased demand for participation in decision-making by those affected by it." — from an article in *Science* magazine, 1972

Fernweh ("FAIRN-vay") "far-pain": a longing to leave home and travel to distant places; the opposite of homesickness

> Novelist Teju Cole titled his book of photographs taken in Switzerland *Fernweh*.

Waldeinsamkeit ("VAHLT-EYN-zahm-kite," the second syllable rhyming with *mine*) "forest loneliness": the spiritual feeling one sometimes gets when alone in the woods: serene, connected to nature, either blissful or wistful

The German Romantic writer Ludwig Tieck coined this word in his novella *Der Blonde Eckbert,* published in 1797. In the story, a magical bird sings songs that begin and end with the word.

A *Schmeck* of *Waldeinsamkeit.*

Ohne Wurst und ohne Speck hat das Leben keinen Zweck ("OH-neh VOORST oont OH-neh SHPECK haht dahss LAY-bn KY-nən TSVEK") "Without sausage and without bacon, life has no point."

I saw this rhyming maxim on a sign outside a pork store in Germany. It's also the title of a 1930 movie.

From other languages

¿Quien sabe? (Spanish) ("kee-EN SAH-bay") Who knows?

> "We have to choose between the quick and the dead... In the room where I write, there is a little table that is dead... And there is a sleeping cat, very quick... What makes the difference? *Quien sabe!*" — D.H. Lawrence, *Reflections on the Death of a Porcupine*

risorgimento (Italian) ("ree-ZAWR-jih-MEN-toh") renaissance, resurgence

> With an upper-case R, the word refers to the movement to free the Italian states from foreign domination and unite them as one country: a goal achieved in 1861.

> "For Little Italy... is flirting with a renaissance. South of Houston Street they call it 'risorgimento.'" — from an article in the *New York Times*, 1977

pococurante (Italian) ("POH-koh-koo-RAHN-tay") "caring little": nonchalant; or indifferent

> In Voltaire's *Candide*, the hero visits a Venetian nobleman named Signor Pococurante, who "cares little" for the art and music that give others so much pleasure. In response, Candide murmurs, "What a great genius is this Pococurante! Nothing can please him."

samizdat (Russian) ("SAH-meez-daht") "self-published": literature written and distributed in secret under Soviet rule; or the system of printing and distributing this forbidden literature

> "Those lines [of Solzhenitsyn] have not been published in the Soviet Union. But they are nonetheless read and passed from hand to hand in *samizdat*, the readers' answer to Soviet censorship." — from an article in *Time* magazine, 1968

tovarich (Russian) ("toh-VAH-ritch" or "-ish") comrade: the common form of address in Soviet Russia, and also the title of a 1930s play and movie about a Russian émigré couple working as servants in Paris

> "Samizdat? Da, Tovarich" — headline of article in the *New York Times*, 1970

sputnik (Russian) ("SPUT-nik": the first syllable can rhyme with either *but* or *put*) traveling companion ("fellow traveler")

That's a cute name for the first man-made satellite to achieve stable Earth orbit (1957)—an event that lit a fire under the U.S. space program and inspired both the phrase *space race* and JFK's promise that the U.S. would put a man on the moon before the end of the decade.

ochone (Irish, Scottish) ("ə-KHOHN," the CH pronounced as if hawking phlegm) "alas": an expression of sorrow or regret

> "OLD GUMMY GRANNY: *(Rocking to and fro.)* … Strangers in my house, bad manners to them! *(She keens with banshee woe.)* Ochone! Ochone!" — James Joyce, *Ulysses*

Sláinte (Irish) ("SLAHN-tchə" or "-dzhə") Cheers (literally: *health*): a traditional toast

> "'*Slainte mhor*, Rory!' cried Kurt, who knew what was necessary in every language." — Elizabeth Coxhead, *A Wind in the West* (*Slainte mhor* means "great health.")

mavourneen (Irish) ("mə-VOOR-neen") my darling

> *Mavourneen* was the title of a romantic Irish drama presented in New York in 1891.

Shanah Tovah (Hebrew) ("shə-NAH toh-VAH") "good year": the traditional greeting at Rosh Hashonah, the Jewish New Year

> This is actually shorthand for a longer Hebrew phrase, which means "May you be inscribed and sealed (in the Book of Life) for a good year."

Chag Sameach (Hebrew) ("KHAG sah-MAY-akh," again, both CHs are pronounced as if hawking phlegm) "happy holiday": a greeting commonly used at Passover, Hanukkah, and other Jewish holidays

hygge ("HYOO-gheh") coziness: a Danish/Norwegian word that denotes a feeling of comfort and contentment, especially with friends or family; as an adjective, the word can describe a setting that creates this feeling

> "There may also be deeper reasons why hygge is having a moment, these Nordic authors say. 'I think it's because a lot of people in different countries are having the experience of growing richer but not necessarily happier,' Wiking says." — from an article in *Time* magazine, 2016

lagom ("LAH-GAWM") a Swedish word that refers to the ideal of living a balanced life, with moderation in all things and without fuss or ostentation; the word implies a rejection of bustle, fads, and artifice

> "Lagom is: laidback, unplugging, connecting with others in real life and disengaging from social media. It's about taking time for yourself, doing something with your own hands and also about giving back." — from an article in New York's *Daily News*, 2017

mulligatawny ("MULL-ih-ghə-TAW-nee") a spicy soup, originally from India, flavored with curry, described in one recipe as "a melting pot of different spicy and rich taste profiles"

> "Dr. [Philip] Rieff often dazzled and occasionally puzzled students with multilayered but always authoritative lectures that blended philosophy, theology, economics, history, literature, psychology and dashes of poetry and Plato-like ingredients in a sociological mulligatawny." — from an obituary in the *New York Times,* 2006 (Rieff was married to Susan Sontag for eight years in the 1950s.)

Word Play

International Relations: Sometimes the solution to your problem lies outside your nation's borders. See if you can find relief from the emotional states on the left among the options on the right:

If You're Feeling...	*Why Not Try...*
Weltschmerz	Schadenfreude
in extremis	misericordia
déclassé	pot-au-feu
Waldeinsamkeit	épater le bourgeois
Fernweh	Grand Guignol
pococurante	amour-propre

Afflictions and Anodynes: Medical Terminology

A complete dictionary of medical terminology would fill a volume as thick as the Manhattan phone book. (That's roughly four inches, for those who have never seen one.) What you'll find here are words from novels, mainly. It's amazing how many medical problems fictional characters have!

Diseases, Conditions, Disorders

sclerosis ("sklə-ROH-səss") the hardening of a body part, usually resulting from tissue growth or disease; or, figuratively, a hardening of one's attitudes and resistance to new ideas

> "Whether visionary or naïve, Suarez is offering an escape from the sclerosis of America's big cities." — from an article in *National Review*, 2020

edema ("ə-DEE-mə") swelling caused by accumulation of fluid in the body's tissues: most common in the feet, ankles, and legs (also known as *dropsy*)

> "For the last 30 years of his life, his legs had to be kept tightly wrapped in bandages and compression stockings because of chronic edema and varicose veins." — from an article in the *New York Times* about chef James Beard, 2020

hypertrophy ("hy-PER-trə-fee") growth of an organ or part beyond what is normal, as a result of the cells' growth in size; or any excessive growth

> "Financial sector hypertrophy and financial transaction tax" — headline of a post on the blog Naked Keynesianism, 2016

hypotrophy ("hy-PAH-trə-fee") degeneration of an organ; or less than normal growth

> "Because his mother chain-smoked throughout her pregnancy, her son was afflicted with fetal hypotrophy, a condition that limited his height to 4 feet 11 inches." — from a review of *Irène*, a novel by Pierre LeMaitre, in the *New York Times,* 2014

phlogosis ("flə-GO-siss") inflammation of external body parts; or, specifically, inflammation due to erysipelas, a bacterial skin infection

> "That 'fyrie red hue' sounds like phlogosis." — John Barth, *The Sot-Weed Factor*

analgesia ("an-əl-JEE-zhə" or "-JEE-zee-ə") loss of the ability to feel pain; or freedom from pain

"A special case of this phenomenon is placebo analgesia, in which the mere belief that one is receiving an effective analgesic treatment can reduce pain." — from an article in *Science*, 2004

aphasia ("ə-FAY-zhə" or "-zhee-ə") partial or total loss of the ability to articulate ideas or understand language, resulting from brain damage (most commonly from stroke)

"The researchers realized a change needed to be made after administering the test to people suffering from primary-progressive aphasia..." — from an article in *Smithsonian* magazine, 2013 (Patients were failing to correctly identify noted figures, e.g., Jawaharlal Nehru and Emperor Hirohito, not because of cognitive impairment, but because they were too young to recognize these once-famous faces.)

alexia ("ə-LEX-ee-ə") loss of the ability to read written language: a neurological disorder

"In a world filled with traffic signs, printed labels, and directions on everything from a prescription bottle to the television, ordinary life is a continuing, daily struggle for anyone with alexia." — from an article by Oliver Sacks in the *New Yorker*, 2010

Afflicted as he was with alexia, Mr. Jones did not take kindly
to interruptions in his daughter's readings from the
Hammacher Schlemmer catalogue.

anarthria ("an-AR-three-ə") loss of the ability to speak, due to impaired muscular function

"The characteristics of [Locked-In] syndrome are quadriplegia and anarthria with preservation of consciousness. Patients retain vertical eye movement, facilitating non-verbal communication." — from an article in the *BMJ* (British Medical Journal), 2005

anosmia ("an-OZ-mee-ə") loss of the sense of smell, or the absence of this sense.

I never encountered this word until Covid-19 entered the news. (Freudian slip: instead of *entered the news*, I just typed *entered the nose.*)

"Large surveys from Iran and the United Kingdom suggest that 50–60 percent of people infected with the virus have experienced anosmia." — from an article in *Harper's* magazine, 2021

strabismus ("strə-BIZ-məss") a defect in which the eyes can't look in the same direction at the same time

"[Jean-Paul Sartre] certainly has strabismus (with his distinctive lazy eye, so he appears to be looking in two directions at once)… and he considers his ugliness to count as a kind of disability." — from an essay in the *New York Times,* 2010

diplopia ("dih-PLOH-pee-ə") double-vision

"Understandably, strabismus is frequently accompanied by diplopia, or double vision." — from an article in the *San Francisco Chronicle*, 2017

nystagmus ("nə-STAG-məss" or "ny-") spasmodic, involuntary movement of the eye(s)

"[Richard Osman's] love of TV partly resulted from having nystagmus… 'I'd sit right next to the screen and see everything,' Osman said, describing TV as his 'constant companion' at the time." — from an article in the *New York Times,* 2021

amblyopia ("am-blee-OH-pee-ə") impaired vision, usually in one eye, which wanders either inward or outward: also known as "lazy eye"

"Vivid Vision uses VR [virtual reality] to treat amblyopia and other vision disorders." — from an article in *Smithsonian* magazine, 2017

presbyopia ("prez-bee-OH-pee-ə") farsightedness resulting from hardening of the eye's lens, usually beginning in middle age

"I need friendly font sizes that don't cause premature use of unattractive, presbyopic eyewear." — from an article on the website Bookslut.com, 2005

(Note, however: "Although extensive or prolonged reading of fine print can cause eye strain, there is no evidence to suggest that it will damage or wear out your eyes." — from a web page entitled, "Common Eye Myths," on PreventBlindness.org.)

nyctalopia ("nik-tə-LOH-pee-ə") inability to see well in dim light: night blindness

dementia praecox ("də-MEN-shə PREE-kahks") (a term no longer used) schizophrenia

"Diagnosed with dementia praecox (schizophrenia), [Jack] Kerouac was sent to the Naval Hospital in Bethesda, Maryland... for further examination." — from an article on the website of the National Archives, 2011

hebephrenia ("hee-bə-FREE-nee-ə") a form of schizophrenia characterized by childish behavior, delusions, erratic speech, and inappropriate emotions

"There were not many patients about as Murphy followed Bom through the wards... Melancholics, motionless and brooding... A hebephrenic playing the piano intently." — Samuel Beckett, *Murphy*

asthenia ("ass-THEE-nee-ə," the TH pronounced as in *with*) loss or lack of bodily strength or energy; abnormal weakness

"Did anyone ever witness such an exhibition of ineptitude and spiritual asthenia?" — John S. Vaughan, *The Purpose of the Papacy* (1910) (Vaughan is criticizing an Archbishop of the Church of England for failing to adequately respond to a doctrinal inquiry.)

neurasthenia ("noor-əss-THEE-nee-ə") nervous exhaustion, characterized by fatigue, loss of energy, irritability, headache, and/or feelings of inadequacy: a dated term for a condition considered to be similar to (or synonymous with) chronic fatigue syndrome

"Some of the caddies were poor as sin and lived in one-room houses with a neurasthenic cow in the front yard..." — F. Scott Fitzgerald, "Winter Dreams"

strangury ("STRANG-yə-ree") a blockage of the bladder causing painful urination in small, spasmodic discharges

It's not easy to find nonmedical occurrences of this word. Here's one—which should serve as a warning to those who tempted to overload their writing with words from this book: "Max talks like someone with a thesaurus permanently implanted in his brain: his monologue is studded with words like 'leporine,' 'strangury,' 'perpetuance,' 'finical,' 'flocculent,' 'anthropic,' 'Avrilaceous,' 'anaglypta' and 'assegais.'" — from an unfavorable review of *The Sea*, by John Banville (winner of that year's Man Booker Prize), written by Michiko Kakutani, in the *New York Times*, 2005

enuresis ("en-yə-REE-siss") involuntary urination: especially, nighttime bed-wetting by children

"About 15 percent of children with nocturnal enuresis grow out of the condition without any specific treatment." — from an article on *Philly.com*, 2017

hematuria ("hee-mə-TOOR-ee-ə") the presence of blood or blood cells in the urine

tenesmus ("tə-NEZZ-məss") the frequent, urgent need to urinate or defecate, followed by straining, ineffectual attempts

"Tenesmus is commonly associated with inflammatory bowel disease (IBD) but may also be caused by hemorrhoids, infections, and even cancer." — from an article on the website VeryWellHealth.com

lues ("LOO-eez") (archaic) a contagious disease; especially, syphilis

"~~Many of the kings of France were~~…"

chancre ("KANG-kər" or "SHANG-kər") a sore or ulcer, especially on the genitals, resulting from venereal disease; a primary lesion in syphilis

Though it's sometimes pronounced the same way, a *chancre* is not the same as a *canker* (sore), which usually refers to a small ulcer on the mouth or lips. (Both derive from the Latin word *cancer*, meaning "crab.")

"The old, Hearst-style journalists had a privileged relationship with power—and they paid for that privilege by keeping a lot of warts and chancres off the public record." — Hunter S. Thompson, *Fear and Loathing in America*

paresis ("pə-REE-siss") muscular weakness or partial paralysis; or inflammation of the brain in the later stages of syphilis, causing worsening dementia and paralysis

"PARESIS MAY SAVE THAW FROM DEATH PENALTY; One Report Is That He Has the Disease in Its First Stage." — headline in the *New York Times,* 1907, referring to Harry K. Thaw (Thaw was the husband of Evelyn Nesbit and the killer of architect Stanford White, which you already knew if you read the novel *Ragtime.*)

marasmus ("mə-RAZZ-məss") severe undernourishment: usually in children, usually in developing countries, resulting in wasting away

"…the starvation disease called marasmus… is increasing in many developing countries because mothers are giving up prolonged breast-feeding and their infants are not receiving an adequate substitute diet during a critical time in development." — from an article in *Scientific American,* 1971

necrosis ("nə-KROH-səss") the death or decay of body tissue as a result of burns, radiation, loss of blood supply, or severe injuries

Gangrene means necrosis of an extensive area due to the lack of blood supply.

"Andrea had… that Edvard Munch look of the terminally cancerous, together with the complications of inanition: she was shrunk and waxy, nearly hairless, bedsore, foul-odoured from necrosis, all I.V. and air pipes going in and catheters coming out…" — John Barth, *Letters*

buboes ("BYOO-bohz") (singular: *bubo*) swollen lymph glands, especially at the groin or armpit: a symptom of bubonic plague

"The nightmare began for Europe one October day in 1347 as 12 ships from the Black Sea arrived in Sicily. Porters greeting the ships found a grisly sight: a few ill sailors, their bodies ravaged with black, oozing buboes, standing on deck among their dead crewmates." — from an article on FoxNews.com, 2020, about history's worst pandemics

quinsy ("KWIN-zee") an inflammation in the throat, especially in the tonsils and surrounding tissue, leading to an abscess: usually caused by a bacterial infection and accompanied by pain and fever

"As a little boy, I showed an abnormal aptitude for mathematics… This gift played a horrible part in tussles with quinsy or scarlet fever, when I felt enormous spheres and huge numbers swell relentlessly in my aching brain." — Vladimir Nabokov, *Speak, Memory*

podagra ("pə-DAG-rə") gout of the foot, especially the big toe

"It is but too evident that Podagra has left its thrilling tenderness in his great toe." — Nathaniel Hawthorne, "Sights from a Steeple" in *Twice-Told Tales*

hematoma/haematoma ("hee-mə-TOH-mə") a pool of blood that has escaped a broken blood vessel and caused part of the body to swell

"...Oliverson was believed to have fractured his skull and suffered an epidural hematoma, which sees blood build between the skull and dura mater, the outermost layer protecting the brain." — from an article on the NBC News website, 2022

cyanosis ("sy-ə-NOH-səss") bluish discoloration of the skin: a result of inadequate oxygen in the blood

"...she claws at her throat and gurgles and slumps over to starboard with a fatal cardiac, her cyanotic mouth still open in surprise." — David Foster Wallace, *Infinite Jest*

apnea ("AP-nee-ə") a temporary cessation of breathing (for at least ten seconds), usually while asleep

"...some disorders, such as sleep apnea and restless leg syndrome, often worsen in old age." — from an article on *Smithsonian* magazine's website, 2017

enteritis ("en-tər-I-təss") inflammation of the intestine (usually the small intestine)

nephritis ("nə-FRY-təss") an inflammation of the kidneys

rhinitis ("ry-NY-təss") inflammation of the mucous membrane inside the nose

"Sexually induced sneezing... may happen at any stage during sex. One term to describe the phenomenon is 'honeymoon rhinitis'... the situation where sexual activity leads to nasal symptoms, including sneezing..." — from an article in the journal *Challenges in Rhinology*, 2020 (This is not a joke, though it sounds like one.)

prurigo ("pru-RYE-go" or "-EE-go") a chronic inflammatory skin disease, with severe itching

ictus ("IK-təss") a stroke, or seizure

eclampsia ("ə-KLAMP-see-ə") an attack of convulsions, occurring especially in the later stages of pregnancy and in childbirth: high blood pressure is the main risk factor

On *Downton Abbey,* Lady Sybil Branson dies from eclampsia after giving birth to her daughter Sybbie.

preeclampsia ("pree-ə-KLAMP-see-ə") a complication during pregnancy, characterized by high blood pressure, often with retention of fluids and liver or kidney damage

"For pregnant women who develop… preeclampsia, the risk for cardiovascular disease at a later date is nearly three times greater than it is for women who do not develop preeclampsia." — from an article in the *Washington Post,* 2021

acromegaly ("ak-roh-MEG-ə-lee") a pituitary dysfunction characterized by overlarge head, hands, and feet

"Goliath, who the Bible indicates was about 10 feet tall, suffered from a pituitary gland disease called acromegaly, the doctor concluded. 'This is the only disease where sufferers can grow to such a height,' he said." — from an article in the *New York Times,* 2000

microcephaly ("my-kroh-SEFF-ə-lee") a birth defect in which the baby has an abnormally small head (Intelligence may or may not be normal, but the head will remain small.)

"Pregnant women who become infected with the Zika virus are at risk of having babies with the severe birth defect known as microcephaly, regardless of whether they have symptoms…" — from an article in the *Washington Post,* 2016

Sources of Relief

palliative ("PAL-ee-ə-tiv") anything that makes pain less severe, without curing its cause (also used as an adjective, as in *palliative care*)

"I see nothing for the treatment of my misery but the melancholy and very local palliative of articulate art." — Vladimir Nabokov, *Lolita* (This is Humbert Humbert speaking, near the end of the book.)

emollient ("ə-MAHL-yənt") a medicine or salve that has a softening or soothing effect on the skin; or, as an adjective, soothing

"…parents who applied an emollient moisturizer to their infants' skin each day for the first 6 to 7 months had babies who were less likely to develop eczema than parents who didn't." — from an article in the *New York Times,* 2020

analgesic ("an-əl-JEEZ-ik") a painkiller: a drug that relieves pain (or, as an adjective, having this property)

> "Incidence of emergency-room visits related to overdose on narcotic analgesics (such as Vicodin, Oxycontin, or Percocet) more than doubled between 1994 and 2001." — from an article in *Teen Vogue*, 2003

anodyne ("AN-ə-dine") a medication that soothes, relieves pain, comforts (also used as an adjective, describing anything that does this, or that avoids causing offense)

> "Fortunately, the overly protective Austen family deemed 160 of Jane's letters sufficiently anodyne, and spared them the flame. These tell us much of what we know of Austen's life." — from an article in the *Houston Chronicle*, 2007

poultice ("POHL-təss") a moist, soft mass—usually flour, clay, or plant material, often medicated—heated, spread on a cloth, and applied to part of the body to relieve pain and inflammation and to promote healing

> "I offered another cited bush cure, a poultice of warm manure, but he declined." — from an article in the *Gold Coast Bulletin* (Australia), 2002

cataplasm (archaic) a poultice

> "Curumilla, after having washed the wounds with clean cold water, applied a cataplasm to them of bruised oregano leaves." — Gustave Aimard, *The Adventurers*

balsam ("BALL-səm") anything that heals or soothes (balsam also refers to a specific plant, and to an aromatic substance produced by some trees and shrubs)

> "'Then thou hast been thrashed too?' said Don Quixote... 'Be not distressed, friend... for I will now make the precious balsam with which we shall cure ourselves in the twinkling of an eye.'" Miguel de Cervantes, *Don Quixote* (translated by John Ormsby)

lenitive ("LEN-ə-tiv") a substance that eases pain or discomfort (also an adjective, meaning "soothing")

> "It's beautiful to have a smoking jacket, a good cigar and a wife who plays the piano. So relaxing. So lenitive." — Henry Miller, *Tropic of Cancer*

paregoric ("per-ə-GORE-ik," or "par-," the A pronounced as in *cat*) opium flavored with camphor, formerly used as a pain-reliever, or to treat diarrhea

"Evenings he sat in his little log shack back of the hotel drinking paregoric and mumbling about God." — John Dos Passos, *The 42nd Parallel*

"Parents have always been overwhelmed by babies crying from teething and have used some truly awful, dangerous methods to stop the pain such as… paregoric (a strong opioid), and now benzocaine." — from an article on the website Philly.com, 2018

clyster ("KLIH-stər") (archaic) an enema; or the medicine injected via the enema

"I must purge and clyster after this…" — Jonathan Swift, *The Journal to Stella*

aperient ("ə-PIR-ee-ənt") a laxative; or, as an adjective, "relieving constipation"

"…he relished a glass of choice old wine in season as both nourishing and bloodmaking and possessing aperient virtues…" — James Joyce, *Ulysses*

carminative ("kar-MIN-ə-tiv") something that induces the expulsion of gas from the stomach; or, as an adjective, inducing the expulsion of gas

"[Marjoram]… was traditionally used in potpourri, in garlands for newlyweds, in funeral bouquets, in love potions and in folk remedies as a tonic and a carminative." — from an article in the *New York Times,* 2000

sternutatory ("stər-NYOO-tə-tor-ee") a substance that induces sneezing; or, as an adjective, "inducing sneezing"

"The odor of the spice [capsicum, AKA pepper] is characteristic, sternutatory but agreeable, and mildly to intensely pungent." — from an article on the website ScienceDirect.com, 2017

analeptic ("an-ə-LEP-tik") (archaic) a restorative: a drug that restores health or strength; or, as an adjective, "tending to restore health or strength"

"I don't as a rule drink at lunch, but right at the moment I feel the need of what Auden calls an 'analeptic swig.'" — Amanda Cross, *Poetic Justice*

But the word now refers mainly to drugs that stimulate the central nervous system: "At many colleges across the country, the ingredients for academic success now include a steady flow of analeptics, the class of prescription amphetamines that is used to treat attention deficit hyperactivity disorder." — from an article in the *New York Times*, 2005

paraldehyde ("pər-AL-də-hide") a colorless liquid used as a sedative and anticonvulsant: $C_6H_{12}O_3$

> "The whole place was overheated and stank of paraldehyde and truant sphincters." — Samuel Beckett, *Murphy*

antipyretic ("an-tee-py-RET-ik" or "an-ty-") a medicine that reduces fever (also used as an adjective)

> "By the early 1900s an expanding array of antipyretic compounds had been discovered and incorporated into the clinical pharmacopoeia." — from an article in the journal *Clinical Infectious Diseases*, 2000

nostrum ("NAH-strəm") a remedy without proof of effectiveness, the contents of which are kept secret; or a questionable plan for solving a problem

> *Nostrum* means "our own," i.e., invented and made by the seller.
>
> "She was… open to every new nostrum, a lightning-rod for herbalista, homeopaths, karma culture, aura photography." — Alexander Theroux, *Laura Warholic*
>
> "Yet whatever your nostrum of choice—stiffer sentences, more police, gun control…—it is up against powerful trends." — from an article in the *Rocky Mountain News* (Denver), 1993

sanatory ("SAN-ə-tor-ee") curative; healing

> This word should remind you of another one: *sanatorium*, a medical facility where convalescent or chronically ill patients are treated.

Bones in the human body, oft-mentioned

maxilla ("mak-SILL-ə") the upper part of the jaw

mandible ("MAN-də-bəl") the lower jawbone

> A store called Maxilla and Mandible opened in 1983 on Columbus Avenue, near the American Museum of Natural History. It sold fossils, animal skulls, and skeletons. (The store closed in 2011.)

clavicle ("KLAV-ə-kəl") the collarbone

> If someone tells you that a clavicle is a small keyboard instrument, don't believe it.

scapula ("SKAP-yoo-lə") the shoulder blade (one of a pair)

"Aim at the shoulder, halfway up the body or a shade more, to hit the scapula, which will aid bullet expansion." — from an article in *Field & Stream,* 2019 (presumably referring to nonhuman targets)

sternum ("STERN-əm") the breastbone: the vertical bone (composed of three fused segments) in the middle of the chest

humerus ("(h)YOO-mə-rəss") the bone of the upper arm, from shoulder to elbow

> Your humerus, sadly, is not your funny bone. That alleged bone isn't even a bone: it's a nerve that gets pinched against the humerus when you bang your arm, which sends that funny (as in *strange*) twinge all the way to your hand.

radius ("RAY-dee-əss") one of the two bones of the forearm: the one on the thumb side

ulna ("ULL-nə") the other bone of the forearm: the one on the pinky side, slightly longer than the radius

carpus ("KAR-pəss") the wrist, or wrist bones: eight small bones connecting the hand to the forearm

sacrum ("SAH-krəm," the A pronounced as in *cat,* or "SAY-krəm") the bony structure at the base of the spinal column, just above the tailbone; it consists of fused vertebrae

> You may have seen characters on old TV shows holding their lower backs and complaining about their *sacroiliac*. This is a rigid joint between the sacrum and the *ilium*. But what's the ilium? It's a large bone that forms part of each half of your pelvis.

femur ("FEE-mər") the thigh bone: the longest and strongest bone in the human body

> At the beginning of *2001: A Space Odyssey,* when the ape-men discover that they can use a bone to bludgeon an enemy to death, and one of them flings a bone into the sky in murderous ecstasy, and then we cut from bone to spaceship (from tool to tool), that lethal bone seems to be a femur.

patella ("pə-TELL-ə") the kneecap: a moveable bone that protects the front of the joint

> "He murmured 'molto bella' / When I sat on his patella, / But he never said he loved me." — Cole Porter, "The Physician"

fibula ("FIB-yə-lə") the narrower of the two bones that connect the knee and the ankle: the calf bone

tibia ("TIB-ee-ə") the thicker of the two bones that connect the knee and the ankle: the shin bone

> "While recovering from that operation… [Tiger] Woods sustained a double stress fracture of his left tibia." — from an article in the *New York Times,* 2008

> Note: If you search for sentences referring to the fibula and tibia, you'll find plenty of examples, most of them about athletes who have broken or fractured the bones.

metatarsal ("met-ə-TAR-səl") one of the five thin bones of the foot, connecting to the toes; also an adjective: relating to these bones

> "She… sat on the footstool in front of the log fire…
> the metatarsals bulging after a lifetime spent in too-high heels."
> — Shirley Conran, *Lace*

Medical Etceteras

etiology ("ee-tee-AHL-ə-jee") the cause or origin of something; in medicine, the study of the causes of disease

> "Chronic kidney disease has swept Central America; again, the etiology of the epidemic has been described as mysterious." — from an article in the *Atlantic*, 2020

metastasis ("mə-TAH-stə-səss") the spread of a disease (usually cancer) from its original site to other parts of the body

> "The word 'metastasized' was the one in the report that first caught my eye, and ear. The alien had colonized a bit of my lung as well as quite a bit of my lymph node." — from an article by Christopher Hitchens in *Vanity Fair,* 2010

prodrome ("PROH-drome") an early symptom suggesting the onset of a disease

> "Migraines can progress through four stages—prodrome, aura, attack, and post-drome—though not everyone feels symptoms at each stage." — from an article in *Self* magazine, 2020

auscultation ("awss-kəl-TAY-shən") listening to sounds made by internal organs (especially the heart and lungs), usually with a stethoscope

anamnesis ("an-əm-NEE-siss") reminiscence; or the ability to remember the past; or the remembering of a supposed previous existence

> "A longer piece called 'Anamnesis: Pt. 1 & Pt. 2'—dedicated to Tamir Rice and Sandra Bland—gradually shifts from elegy to

outrage…" — from an article about jazz bassist Eric Revis in the *New York Times,* 2016

conation ("koh-NAY-shən") in psychology, the drive or wish to act

"Today, we typically divide the mind into two categories: affect (feeling) and cognition (thinking). Conation was once taken seriously as a third part of the mind. It should have remained there as a category." — from an article in *Psychology Today,* 2014

orexis ("or-EK-səss") desire, appetite: feeling and striving, as opposed to mere intellectual desire (The adjective form is *orectic.*)

Not a joke: one of the many pills promising to deliver a larger, harder erection and longer-lasting sex is called *Orexis.*

sequela ("sih-KWEL-ə") a pathological effect resulting from a disease or injury (plural: *sequelae,* "sih-KWEL-ee")

"…a New York State teen's death from MRSA pneumonia as a sequela of flu…" — from an article in *Wired* magazine, 2009

collagen ("KAHL-ə-jən") a protein found in bone, muscle, skin, and tendons, used in cosmetic surgery

"The evidence… suggested that… collagen supplements improve skin moisture, elasticity, and hydration when orally administered. Additionally, collagen reduces the wrinkling and roughness of the skin…." — from an article in the journal *Dermatology Practical & Conceptual, 2022*

galactagogue ("gə-LAK-tə-gahg") a drug, food, or herb that promotes secretion of breast milk

"Although many women worry about making enough breast milk, most women will not need to use a galactagogue." — from an article on the website VeryWellFamily.com, 2020

enteron ("EN-tə-rahn") the digestive tract, or alimentary canal, especially of an embryo or an invertebrate

"Mr. Lay wanted to call it* Enteron, until they realized that was a biology term for the digestive tract. In hindsight, Enteron seems right for a company of such ungoverned appetites." — from an article in the *New York Times,* 2002

* I.e., Enron.

emunctory ("ih-MUNK-tə-ree") any organ or body part involved in excretion, e.g., kidneys, skin (As an adjective, the word means "serving to dispose of waste.")

"Blow your noses—cleanse your emunctories—sneeze, my good people!" — Laurence Sterne, *Tristram Shandy*

eyestrings (archaic) the muscles or tendons of the eyes, supposed to break when one went blind or died

> "I would have broke mine eye-strings; crack'd them, but
> To look upon him..." — William Shakespeare, *Cymbeline*

catheter ("KATH-ə-tər") a slender, flexible tube inserted into a body cavity (the bladder, usually) for draining fluid or distending the passage

> "One in five hospital patients in the UK and the USA has a catheter in place at any given time..." — from an article on the website Vice.com, 2018 (which also states that about a third of catheterized patients develop bacteria in their urine)

curette ("KYOO-rit" or "kyoo-RET") a medical instrument with a scoop or hook at the end, used to scrape parts of the body, especially the uterus, in order to remove tissue

> The process of scraping with a curette is called *curettage*. The term *D&C*, a gynecological procedure, is short for *dilation and curettage*.

> "...I would guess that the Doctor had applied his curette to begin scraping the uterus, but I wasn't looking to find out..." — John Barth, *The End of the Road*

lancet ("LAN-sət") a surgical knife with a short, wide, double-edged blade and a sharp point

> *The Lancet* is the name of a well-known British medical journal, published since 1823.

syrette ("sih-RET") a collapsible syringe that contains one dose of a drug

> The Syrette is a patented device and is therefore often spelled with an uppercase S; however, the word has passed into common use, so you'll also see the S in lowercase.

> "Morphine-containing Syrettes, used by the armed forces during the war to relieve wounded men, are finding their way into illegal narcotic channels." — from an article in the *Baltimore Sun*, 1947

> "He shot another syrette." — William S. Burroughs, *Junkie* (1953)

bolus ("BOHL-əss") a small round mass; or a large pill or tablet

> "Mr. Peacock... had administered a series of boluses which were not otherwise definable than by their remarkable effect in bringing Mrs. Powderell round before Michaelmas from an illness which had begun in a remarkably hot August." — George Eliot, *Middlemarch*

embolus ("ƏM-bə-ləss") an air bubble, detached blood clot, etc. that moves through a blood vessel and then blocks it

> "Former President Nixon's latest medical complication, namely an embolus in the right lung, is responding satisfactorily to a combined therapy of oral and intravenous anticoagulants." — from an article in the *New York Times*, 1974

embolism ("ƏM-bə-lizm") the blockage of a blood vessel by an embolus

> "Her death would be soon and sudden. Ski tumble; embolism." — Lauren Groff, *Fates and Furies* (Here we have a nod to Nabokov's famous two-word account of a death in *Lolita*: "picnic; lightning.")

excrescence ("ək-SKREH-sənss") an abnormal or disfiguring outgrowth or enlargement, on a human or animal body or a plant

> "… a red-faced gentleman with a pendulous excrescence on the end of his nose, that shook like the gills of a turkey-cock." — Charles Dickens, *A Christmas Carol*

cauterize ("KAW-tə-rize") to burn so as to seal a wound or destroy dead tissue and prevent the spread of infection; or, figuratively, to deaden

> "…Humbert's manuscript confession is more a record of the frustration and cauterization of his desires than a chronicle of their satisfaction." — from an article about *Lolita* in *Numero Cinq* magazine, 2013

palpate ("PAL-pate") to examine by touch (usually for the purpose of diagnosis)

> "Learn to trust your fingertips by palpating skin with your eyes closed. Even hidden under an inch of fat tissue, a vein will have a distinctly bouncy feel that Olton likens to pressing on a water bed." — from an article about learning to draw blood, in the *New York Times*, 2017

embrocate ("EM-brə-kate") to moisten and rub (part of the body) with a lotion, as a treatment for disease (The noun form, *embrocation*, can refer either to the act of embrocating or to the lotion itself.)

> "…the dressings on my wound and the embrocation on my sprained wrist steadily subdue the pains which I have felt so far." — Wilkie Collins, *The Two Destinies*

trepan ("trə-PAN") (archaic) to cut a hole in the skull, using a hole saw known as a trepan, or trephine, which resembled a carpenter's brace and bit; or, to deceive, ensnare

Surgeons now perform craniotomies (to relieve pressure resulting from a subdural hematoma, for example) with more precise tools.

"In 2016, I read six different books that mentioned trepanation. So far in 2017, I have read none. So, I am looking back on 2016 as my Year of Literary Trepanations." — from the blog Lindy Reads, 2017

iatrogenic ("eye-ah-troh-JEN-ik, the A pronounced as in *cat*") caused unintentionally by medical treatment

"Doctors' families… seem a normal, generally healthy lot, with a remarkably low incidence of iatrogenic illness." — Lewis Thomas, *The Lives of a Cell*

vulnerary ("VUL-nər-err-ee") (archaic) effective in healing wounds (refers to plants and medicines)

"Rebecca examined the wound, and having applied to it such vulnery remedies as her art prescribed, informed her father that if fever could be averted… there was nothing to fear for his guest's life…" — Sir Walter Scott, *Ivanhoe*

astringent ("ə-STRIN-jənt") tending to constrict or contract tissue; harsh, bitter

"Wylie's first care… was to kiss Miss Counihan's tears away. He had a special kiss for this purpose, an astringent kiss, with a movement like a barber's clippers." — Samuel Beckett, *Murphy*

hypnagogic ("hip-nə-GAHJ-ik") inducing sleep; or relating to the drowsy state preceding sleep

"Many of us, as we lie in bed with closed eyes, awaiting sleep, have so-called hypnagogic hallucinations — geometric patterns, or faces, sometimes landscapes." — from an essay by Oliver Sacks in the *New York Times,* 2012

chirurgical ("ky-RƏR-ji-kəl") (archaic) surgical

"I carry about a very troublesome and dangerous complaint, which admits no cure but by the chirurgical knife." — James Boswell, *The Life of Samuel Johnson* (According to Boswell, the complaint Johnson refers to here was a *sarcocele,* a tumor-like swelling of the testicle.)

zoonotic ("zoo-ə-not-ik" or "zoh-ə-not-ik") caused by germs that spread from animals to humans (The term refers to diseases, e.g., bird flu.)

A zoonotic disease is also known as a zoonosis. "About 60 percent of human infectious diseases are zoonoses." — from an article in *Popular Science* magazine, 2012

catamenial ("kat-ə-MEE-nee-əl") menstrual (*Catamenia* means menstruation)

> "Gilbreth determined that 'catamenial bandages,' as the products were then known, were not selling well because they did not address women's needs." — from an article on the website TheBaffler.com, 2014, about the origins of the sanitary napkin industry

> ("Gilbreth" is Lillian Gilbreth, wife of Frank. The Gilbreths were the efficiency experts portrayed in *Cheaper by the Dozen*.)

suppurating ("SUP-yə-rayt-ing") festering; forming pus

> "...he saw her eyes go red and dull, her teeth rot in the gums, her flesh go raw with suppurating lesions..." — John Barth, *The Sot-Weed Factor*

purulent ("PYOOR-ə-lənt" or "PYOOR-yə-lənt") containing pus, or secreting it

> "No lover ever found a cure for love / ... His wound was nine long years in healing, / Purulent with dead hope..." — Robert Graves, "The Cure"

stertorous ("STƏR-tə-rəss") loud and strained (said of breathing); making a heavy snoring sound

> "...at his feet reposed a savage animal of the canine tribe whose stertorous gasps announced that he was sunk in uneasy slumber..." — James Joyce, *Ulysses*

intercostal ("in-tər-KAHS-təl") between the ribs: often refers to the muscles located there

> "Garver missed 27 games because of an intercostal strain..." — from an article in the *Star Tribune* (Minneapolis), 2020

murrain ("MURR-ən") (archaic) the plague; or any of several infectious cattle diseases

> "'A murrain take thee,' rejoined the swine-herd." — Sir Walter Scott, *Ivanhoe*

ich ("IHK") a contagious disease of tropical fish, especially in aquariums: its main symptom is small white pustules

> This word has absolutely nothing to do with JFK's pronouncement, "Ich bin ein Berliner," which means (according to some) "I am a jelly doughnut." Go look it up.

Word Play

Anatomically Correct: Draw lines connecting the affliction to the
affected part of the body.

quinsy

strabismus

anarthria

podagra

strangury

rhinitis

Prating Coxcombs and Bestraught Bezonians: Shakespearean Vocabulary

Chances are you won't be calling your archenemy a *white-livered runagate* or a *thrasonical whoreson* anytime soon. But it's entertaining to see how Shakespeare used these and other words that disappeared from common use long ago. You'll also run into a few that will sound familiar: *arrant, varlet, motley,* and *maw,* for instance.

And the next time you read *Hamlet,* you'll know your *fardels* from your *bare bodkins.*

Men: Be not like these wretches

coxcomb ("KAHKS-kohm") a conceited, pretentious, affected, or foolish man; or (archaic) the cap worn by a jester

> "If the enemy is an ass and a fool and a prating coxcomb, is it meet, think you, that we should also... be an ass and a fool and a prating coxcomb...?" — *Henry V*

princox ("PRIN-kahks") a conceited boy or young man

> "You are a princox; go: Be quiet, or... I'll make you quiet." — *Romeo and Juliet*

cullion ("KULL-yən") a contemptible fellow or rascal; or, formerly, a testicle

> "Up to the breach, you dogs! avaunt, you cullions!" —*Henry V*

varlet a youth serving as a knight's page; or a knave, scoundrel

> "...I am the veriest varlet that ever chewed with a tooth." — Falstaff, in *Henry IV, Part 1*

whoreson ("HOR-sən") a bastard; the son of a whore; or a general insult for a man

> "Thou whoreson, senseless villain!" — *The Comedy of Errors*

pickthank a person who curries favor by flattering or by informing on others

> "...many tales devised... by smiling pickthanks and base newsmongers..." — *Henry IV, Part 1*

bezonian ("bih-ZOH-nee-ən") a beggar; or a low person or rascal

> "Great men oft die by vile bezonians: ... Brutus' bastard hand stabb'd Julius Caesar..." — *Henry VI, Part II*

> (The word derives from the Italian, *bisogno*, meaning "need.")

jackanapes ("JACK-ə-napes") a conceited, insolent, presumptuous fellow; or an impudent, mischievous child (A *jackanapes* was a pet monkey.)

> "...a whoreson jackanapes must take me up for swearing; as if I borrowed mine oaths of him and might not spend them at my pleasure." — *Cymbeline*

Taunted by the diminutive jackanapes, Vittorio vowed revenge.

cotquean ("KAHT-kween") a man who meddles in women's affairs, or who does women's work

> "Capulet: Look to your baked meats, good Angelica.
> "Nurse: Go, get you to bed, you cotquean." — *Romeo and Juliet*

wittol ("WIT-əl") a willing cuckold: a man who doesn't mind that his wife is unfaithful

> "Cuckold! Wittol!—Cuckold! the devil himself hath not such a name." — *The Merry Wives of Windsor*

mome a blockhead, or fool

> "Mome, malt-horse, capon, coxcomb, idiot, patch!" — *The Comedy of Errors*

white-livered runagate ("RUN-ə-gayt") a cowardly traitor

> "There let him sink, and be the seas on him! White-livered runagate, what doth he there? Let him sink there so the sea will cover him!" — *Richard III*

tosspot a drunkard, or heavy drinker

"But when I came unto my beds... toss-pots still had drunken heads..." — *Twelfth Night*

"The monthly meeting of the Twickenham Tosspot Society will come to odor—I mean, order!"

Disreputable women

trull a prostitute

"How ill-beseeming is it in thy sex to triumph like an Amazonian trull upon their woes whom Fortune captivates." — *Henry VI, Part 3*

flirtgill a loose woman

"If he stand to anything against me, I'll take him down... I am none of his flirt-gills, I am none of his skains-mates." — *Romeo and Juliet*

A few divers types

pander/bawd the pander brings the clients to the brothel; the bawd manages the establishment

"A knave; a rascal; an eater of broken meats; a base, proud, shallow, beggarly, three-suited, hundred-pound, filthy, worsted-stocking knave; a lily-liver'd, action-taking, whoreson, glass-gazing, superserviceable, finical rogue; one-trunk-inheriting slave; one that wouldst be a bawd in way of good service, and art nothing but the composition of a knave, beggar, coward, pander, and the son and heir of a mongrel bitch; one whom I will beat into clamorous whining…" – *King Lear*

collier a coal dealer (often with the connotation of "tending to cheat")

"Sampson: Gregory, on my word, we'll not carry coals.*
Gregory: No, for then we should be colliers."** — *Romeo and Juliet*

* In other words, we won't let the Montagues humiliate us.

** I.e., people of low station.

underskinker an assistant (or apprentice) bartender

"…to sweeten which name of Ned, I give thee this pennyworth of sugar, clapped even now into my hand by an under-skinker…" — *Henry IV, Part 1*

bairn a child

"…what have we here? Mercy on 's, a bairn! A very pretty bairn." — *A Winter's Tale*

With these, thou mayest modify

arrant notorious, complete, out-and-out (used to intensify a pejorative)

"Fortune, that arrant whore, Ne'er turns the key to th' poor." — *King Lear*

bootless futile: without profit, benefit, or chance of success

"When, in disgrace with fortune and men's eyes,
I all alone beweep my outcast state,
And trouble deaf heaven with my bootless cries,
And look upon myself and curse my fate…" — Sonnet 29

puisny (pronounced like *puny*) inexperienced, ineffectual, weak; or small, insignificant

"O, that's a brave man! he writes brave verses, speaks brave words, swears brave oaths and breaks them bravely, quite traverse, athwart the heart of his lover; as a puisny tilter, that spurs his horse but on one side, breaks his staff like a noble goose." — *As You Like It*

bestraught distraught, or distracted, or insane

> "What, would you make me mad? ... What! I am not bestraught!"
> — *The Taming of the Shrew*

mickle large, much; or mighty

> "O, mickle is the powerful grace that lies / In plants, herbs,
> stones, and their true qualities." — *Romeo and Juliet*

thrasonical ("thrə-SAHN-ih-kəl") boastful

> "...his humour is lofty, his discourse peremptory, his tongue
> filed, his eye ambitious, his gait majestical, and his general
> behaviour vain, ridiculous, and thrasonical." — *Love's Labour's
> Lost*

A single word suffices

Soho! ("so-HO") the hunter's cry (to the dogs and other hunters) when
the hare is sighted; or a call upon discovering any hidden person or
thing

> "Mercutio: So ho.
> Romeo: What hast thou found?
> Mercutio: No hare sir." — *Romeo and Juliet*

sirrah ("SEER-ə") a term of address to an inferior (as opposed to
"Sir"): often expressing disdain or reprimand

> "Come hither, sirrah." — *Julius Caesar*

Hoy-day! a playful exclamation of surprise

> "Hoy-day!
> What a sweep of vanity comes this way!" — *Timon of Athens*

avaunt ("ə-VAWNT") a command to go away

> "Macbeth (seeing the Ghost): Avaunt, and quit my sight! Let the
> earth hide thee." — *Macbeth*

exeunt ("EK-see-unt") a stage direction meaning, *they exit:* i.e., two or
more actors leave the stage

> "Exeunt Iago and Attendants." — *Othello*

Other succinct terms

certes ("SƏR-teez") certainly: "it is certain that"

> "'For 'Certes,' says he, 'I have already chose my officer.'" —
> *Othello*

Beshrew ___! A curse: "May evil befall ___!"

> "Beshrew me, if I would do such a wrong..." — *Othello*

paucas pallabris what one says to urge others to be quiet, or at least succinct (from the Spanish, *pocas palabras*: "few words")

> "Hostess: A pair of stocks, you rogue!
>
> Sly: ... the Slys are no rogues; look in the chronicles; we came in with Richard Conqueror. Therefore *paucas pallabris*; let the world slide." — *The Taming of the Shrew*

Artifacts of yore

bodkin a dagger

> "For who would bear the whips and scorns of time,
> The oppressor's wrong, the proud man's contumely,
> The pangs of despised love, the law's delay,
> The insolence of office and the spurns
> That patient merit of the unworthy takes,
> When he himself might his quietus make
> With a bare bodkin?" — *Hamlet* (As you may know, this comes shortly after "To be or not to be.")

poniard ("PAHN-yərd") a small dagger

> "She speaks poniards, and every word stabs." — *Much Ado About Nothing*

hornbook a first reading book, containing the alphabet and a few other basics, printed on a single sheet, mounted on a wooden tablet with a handle, and protected by a thin layer of horn

> "Armado (to Holofernes): Monsieur, are you not lett'red?
> Moth: Yes, he teaches boys the hornbook." — *Love's Labour's Lost*

motley the colorful costume worn by a jester or harlequin

> "O that I were a fool! I am ambitious for a motley coat." — *As You Like It*

jordan a chamber pot

> "Why, they will allow us ne'er a jordan, and then we leak in your chimney..." — *Henry IV, Part 1*

arras ("ARR-əss," the first A pronounced as in *cat*) a wall hanging made of tapestry, usually with colorful woven images

> "Be you and I behind an arras then." — Polonius, in *Hamlet*

(He'll be killed there, when Hamlet mistakes him for a spy and plunges his sword through the arras.)

sennet a trumpet call to announce a procession: for ceremonial stage entrances and exits

> "Sennet sounded. Enter Macbeth, as king, Lady Macbeth, as queen..." — *Macbeth*

How they said it then

anon ("ə-NAHN") at once

> "Nurse: (from within) Madam!
> Juliet: I come, anon." — *Romeo and Juliet*

pennyworth a bargain (in Britain, pronounced "PEN-əth")

> "Pirates may make cheap pennyworths of their pillage,
> And purchase friends and give to courtesans, ...
> While as the silly owner of the goods
> Weeps over them and wrings his hapless hands..." — *Henry VI, Part 2*

meed reward, or recompense

> "I will most thankful be, and thanks, to men of noble minds, is honorable meed." — *Titus Andronicus*

welkin the sky; the vault of heaven above

> "The sun of heaven... made the western welkin blush..." — *King John*

purlieus ("PƏR-lyooz") the surroundings of a place; or the outer parts of a forest; or (singular) a place one visits frequently, without restriction

> "...pray you, if you know, where in the purlieus of this forest stands a sheep-cote fenc'd about with olive trees?" — *As You Like It*

pia mater ("PEE-ə MAH-tər") the brain

> "...one of thy kin has a most weak pia mater." — *Twelfth Night*

lineaments ("LIN-ee-ə-mənts") distinctive features—especially facial

> "Tell them, when that my mother went with child
> ...My princely father then had wars in France
> And, by just computation of the time,
> Found that the issue was not his begot;

Which well appeared in his lineaments,
Being nothing like the noble duke my father..." — *Richard III*

maw stomach; or the mouth or throat of a hungry animal

"Scale of dragon, tooth of wolf,
Witches' mummy, maw and gulf
Of the ravin'd salt-sea shark..." — The Third Witch, in *Macbeth*

fleer to grin or laugh coarsely or scornfully

"What dares the slave come hither, cover'd with an antic face, to
fleer and scorn at our solemnity?" — *Romeo and Juliet*

ames-ace in dice, double-ones (snake-eyes)

"I had rather be in this choice than throw ames-ace for my life."
— *All's Well That Ends Well*

fardel ("FAR-dəl") bundle, piece of baggage, burden

"Who would these fardels bear,
To grunt and sweat under a weary life,
But that the dread of something after death—
The undiscover'd country, from whose bourn
No traveller returns—puzzles the will..." — *Hamlet* (These lines
immediately follow the "bare bodkin" in Hamlet's soliloquy.)

tremor cordis palpitation of the heart

"Too hot, too hot!
...I have tremor cordis on me: my heart dances;
But not for joy; not joy." — *A Winter's Tale*

Neapolitan bone-ache syphilis

"After this, the vengeance on the whole camp! or, rather, the
Neapolitan bone-ache!" — *Troilus and Cressida*

green-sickness a form of anemia believed to occur only among
virginal teenage girls

"... thin drink doth so over-cool their blood... that they fall into a
kind of male green-sickness..." — Henry IV, Part 2

The animal kingdom

eyas ("EYE-əss") a young hawk taken from its nest and trained in
falconry

"...there is, sir, an eyrie of children, little eyases, that cry out..."
— *Hamlet*

kite among birds of prey, the lowest: used metaphorically, it means a
vile person who preys on others

248

"...ravens, crows and kites fly o'er our heads and downward look on us, as we were sickly prey..." — *Julius Caesar*

Graymalkin a common name for a gray cat

In *Macbeth,* this is the first Witch's familiar. She addresses it just before the three say, in unison, "Fair is foul, and foul is fair."

jade an inferior, worn-out, or ill-tempered horse

"...bending forward, [Harry Percy] struck his armed heels against the panting sides of his poor jade up to the rowel-head..." — *Henry IV, Part 2*

cry havoc to give soldiers the command to pillage and seize spoils, or to wreak devastation

"Caesar's spirit, ranging for revenge... shall in these confines with a monarch's voice cry 'Havoc,' and let slip the dogs of war..." — Antony, after Caesar's assassination, in *Julius Caesar*

We still say this today

quintessence ("kwin-TESS-ənss") the most essential aspect of something: its purest form; or the perfect example of a certain type (Originally, the word referred to a "fifth essence": in alchemy, that which remained when the four elements had been distilled away.)

"What a piece of work is a man! how noble in reason! how infinite in faculties! in form and moving how express and admirable! in action how like an angel! in apprehension how like a god! the beauty of the world, the paragon of animals! And yet to me what is this quintessence of dust? Man delights not me." — *Hamlet*

Word Play

Shakespeare or Don Rickles?

Which master of insult was responsible for each of the following?
Can you detect the subtle differences?

1. Thou whoreson senseless villain!

2. We kid about great stars such as you, Bob [Hope]. Why?
   Because you're old and washed up.

3. A knave, a rascal; an eater of broken meats... one that wouldst
   be a bawd in way of good service, and art nothing but the
   composition of a knave, beggar, coward, pander, and the son
   and heir of a mongrel bitch...

4. Make yourself at home, Frank [Sinatra]. Hit somebody.

5. Go, get you to bed, you cotquean.

6. It's so good to see you. I didn't know you were still on. [To
   Johnny Carson, on *The Tonight Show.*]

7. Mome, malt-horse, capon, coxcomb, idiot, patch!

8. I'm delighted that you have a show because you're fresh,
   you're funny, you're great. And I want you to know something,
   from my heart: I never liked you. [To Jimmy Fallon, on *The
   Tonight Show.*]

These Are a Few of My Favorite Things

We're surrounded by things, and most of them have names—but we don't always know those names. Learning them can be useful. For example, if you want to build an indoor racetrack for cycling, it's important to know and understand the word *camber*. And very soon, you will.

Then there are the things you hardly ever see, because they come from other places or times, or because they're rare. If I hadn't read about *corium*, I wouldn't have known or suspected that such a thing existed.

Finally, every field has its terminology. Even if you never study architecture, it's satisfying to know the difference between the *pediment* and the *entablature*.

All of these things—*apses, gesso, battlements, slivovitz, shakos*—pop up in books when you least expect them. The next time you encounter a *simoom* in a novel, you'll know that a *burnoose* can't be far behind.

Things You Don't Run Into Every Day

When traveling by elephant, camel, or horse

howdah ("HOW-də") a canopied seat for riding on the back of an elephant or camel

> "...two of the guests had missed the train, and consequently he could ride on the howdah instead of following in a cart..."
> — E.M. Forster, *A Passage to India*

caravansary/caravanserai ("kar-ə-VAN-sə-ree," the first A pronounced as in *cat* / "-sə-rye") an inn with a large central courtyard, where caravans stopped for the night

> "So the whole caravansary had fallen in like a card house at the disapproval in her eyes." — F. Scott Fitzgerald, *The Great Gatsby*

yurt ("YƏRT") a round tent on a collapsible frame, used by nomads, especially in Mongolia

> You might not think this word would come up often in the United States these days, but when my kids went to sleepaway camp—at Frost Valley Farm Camp, in the Catskills—they slept in yurts.

caparison ("kə-PAR-ih-sən," the second A pronounced as in *cat*) an ornamented covering for a horse (also, as a verb, to cover with fancy, decorative material)

"How is the horse on the left different from the horse on the right?

"Are you kidding? There's no caparison!"

Ingenious devices

lorgnette ("lorn-YET") eyeglasses or opera glasses with a handle on one side

> "Anna Sergeyevna looked through her lorgnette at the steamer and the passengers as though looking for acquaintances..." — Anton Chekhov, "The Lady with the Lapdog"

> Also note: "As a rule, monocles were a male accessory: If in need of an aid to vision, a woman would use spectacles or a lorgnette..." — from an article in the *Atlantic*, 2019

clepsydra ("KLEP-sə-drə") a device that measures time based on the flow of water through a small opening

> "... the clepsydra was used to time lawyers' arguments in court." —*Encyclopedia of American Poetry: The Twentieth Century* (Eric L. Haralson, editor, commenting on a poem entitled "Clepsydra," by John Ashbery)

orrery ("OR-err-ee") a model of the solar system, or of the sun, earth, and moon, which demonstrates the relative movements of these bodies

> "These tabletop devices became known as orreries, after the Earl of Cork and Orrery, for whom the first one was built, and once were a popular fixture in the libraries of the wealthy." — from an article in the *New York Times*, 2000

dibble ("DIB-əl") a pointed tool used to make holes in soil for seeds

> "This dibble, inspired by the one Martha saw in her friend David Rockefeller's greenhouse, is used in the garden beds to make evenly spaced holes for crops such as lettuce and Asian greens." — from an article on MarthaStewart.com, 2011 (The pictured

dibble had 88 pegs in an 8x11 grid, and was designed by Martha herself, according to the article.)

reamer ("REEM-ər") any tool used to enlarge holes; or a kitchen device for extracting juice from a citrus fruit

"Just hold the citrus in one hand, press the reamer into the flesh with the other, and presto." — from an article in *USA Today,* 2019

Pornographic performers often adopt pseudonyms with sexual meanings. One of the subtler examples was Harry Reems.

portmanteau ("port-man-TOE") a large suitcase, usually leather, that opens like a book into two equal-sized compartments

Lewis Carroll coined the phrase *portmanteau word,* to mean a word composed of two parts, combined, e.g., *smog,* smoke + fog; and *spork,* spoon + fork. "Well, 'slithy' means 'lithe and slimy'... You see it's like a portmanteau—there are two meanings packed up into one word." — Lewis Carroll, *Through the Looking-Glass*

bobeche ("boh-BESH") a collar on a candlestick that catches dripping wax

"The candelabra used were of clear crystal, the *bobèche* of ruby glass, and the red wax candles had each one a little jaunty cap, or shade, of scarlet silk." — from an article in *Scribner's Monthly,* 1879

fescue ("FESS-kyoo") a pointer used by teachers to point out letters when small children are learning to read; or a type of grass, often used in lawns

"How could he do other... / Than rush... to the rescue, / Play schoolmaster, point as with fescue / To each and all slips in Man's spelling / The law of the land?" — Robert Browning, "Of Pacciarotto, and How He Worked in Distemper"

ferule ("FERR-əl") a flat stick or ruler used to punish children, usually with a blow on the hand

"Though he be given to play, it is a sign of spirit and liveliness... [F]rom the rod or ferule I would have them free, as from the menace of them; for it is both deformed and servile." — Ben Jonson, *Discoveries Made Upon Men and Matter*

ferrule ("FERR-əl") a metal band that either reinforces the end of a wooden stick or joins two different parts, e.g., the pencil and the eraser

"With the introduction of the Eberhard Faber Van Dyke pencil... many other pencil manufacturers in the US follow[ed] suit and began getting really creative with their ferrule designs." — from an article on CWPencils.com, 2017

punkah ("PUNK-ə") in India, a fan made of a large palm frond or cloth, hung from the ceiling and moved (usually by a servant) by pulling on a cord

> "The hand-pulled punkahs, for in those days there were no electric fans, flapped vigorously to and fro… and agitated the hot food-smelling air." — Winston Churchill, *My Early Life*

runcible spoon a combination spoon, fork, and knife, with a spoon-like bowl, fork-like teeth, and one serrated edge

> Edward Lear coined this term in one of his nonsense poems: "The Dolomphious Duck, who caught Spotted Frogs for her dinner with a Runcible Spoon." But the drawing that went with the poem didn't resemble the utensil described above; that meaning came later.

gambrel ("GAM-brəl") a hook used for hanging slaughtered animals

> "I helped hoist the carcass on a gambrel and make the eviscerating cut from breastbone to belly." — Kristin Kimball, *The Dirty Life*

> A *gambrel roof*, on the other hand, is one with two sides, each of which has a steep slope below a shallower slope.

bilboes ("BILL-boze") shackles, connected with a bar, for fettering a prisoner's feet

> "The Puritans eventually replaced bilboes with wooden stocks." — from the New England Historical Society's web page about Puritan punishments

thills (in the U.S., "THEELZ"; in the U.K., "THILLZ," which makes more sense) the two long wooden poles by which a horse or other animal is hitched to a wagon

> "…the wheels were just as strong as the thills, / And the floor was just as strong as the sills…" — Oliver Wendell Holmes, "The Deacon's Masterpiece"

Arts and crafts

scrimshaw whale ivory, bones, or shells decorated with intricate carvings or designs; or the art of making these pieces

> "The age of word-processor technology is upon us, about to make *writing*… as quaint a handicraft as fletching or scrimshaw." — John Barth, *Tidewater Tales* (1988)

lithophane ("LITH-ə-fane") thin, translucent porcelain molded with an image that can only be seen when light shines through it

Lithophanes were popular in Europe in the early 19th century.

> "Today, the most common way to create a lithophane is by 3D printing [it] from plastic or resin." — from an article on the website LithophaneMaker.com

ormolu ("OR-mə-loo") a technique for gilding bronze; or, an object finished by this method

> "These grand but monstrous apartments... with their oceans of Savonnerie carpets and mountains of ormolu and boule." — Cecil Beaton, *Diary*, 1944

majolica ("mə-JAH-lə-kə") a type of glazed pottery on which designs have been painted in metallic colors

> "Fields and roads, all golden and floating like atmospheric majolica." — D.H. Lawrence, *The Lost Girl*

faience ("FY-ahnss" or "fy-AHNSS") a type of ceramic ware decorated with opaque glazes

> "The breakfast set was of taffy-like peasant faïence from Normandy." — Sinclair Lewis, *Dodsworth*

Antiquated apparel

farthingale ("FAR-thing-gale," the TH pronounced as in *the*) a pad or hoop worn around the hips, under a woman's skirt, to give it an enlarged shape (most common in the 16th and 17th centuries)

> "Whatever he was saying or doing, he stopped short at the sight of a farthingale." — Charles Reade, *The Cloister and the Hearth*

plus fours ("PLUS FORZ") baggy knickers that extend four inches below the knee (i.e., four inches longer than standard knickers) — commonly worn when playing golf, until the 1930s

> "...he cheerfully accepted a game of chess proposed by the former editor of a Frankfurt newspaper, a melancholy baggy-eyed patriarch in a turtle-neck sweater and plus fours." — Vladimir Nabokov, *Pnin*

galligaskins ("gal-ə-GAS-kinz") loose, long breeches of the 1500s and 1600s: used humorously to denote any loose breeches

> "...his whole thoughts... were taken up with a transaction which was going forwards at that very instant within the precincts of his own Galligaskins." — Laurence Sterne, *Tristram Shandy*

crinoline ("KRIN-ə-lin") a petticoat with hoops or stiffened fabric, worn to give a bell shape to a long skirt; or the fabric used for this purpose

> "The story of the old lady whose crinoline acted as a parachute when she fell from Clifton Suspension Bridge was 'pure bunkum'." — from an article in the *Times* (of London), 1921

Having concealed her three lovers from the Reverend Mr. Bonzo,
Miss Wigglesworth thanked the inventor of the crinoline
from the deepest depths of her heart.

chiton ("KY-tin") a long, loose tunic worn in ancient Greece and Rome, by both men and women (Men wore it to the knees, women full length.)

> Do not confuse this with *chitin*, pronounced the same way: the substance that is the main component in the exoskeleton of an arthropod. (See? I *knew* you were mixing them up.)

chlamys ("KLA-məss") a short cloak worn by men in ancient Greece, clasped at the shoulder

> "She found him… a red chlamys for his shoulder and a big gold pin." — Mary Renault, *Fire from Heaven*

> "I'd sooner cloak a Titan in a chiton / Than drape a chlamys 'cross my frammis." — Anonymous

himation ("hə-MAT-ee-ən") an ancient Greek garment: a rectangular cloth draped over the left shoulder and around the body

"It was the usual practice among the Greeks to wear an Himation, or outer garment, over the Chiton." — William Smith, *A Dictionary of Greek and Roman Antiquities*

Distinctive designs

quincunx ("KWIN-kunks") an arrangement with four objects at each corner of a square or rectangle and a fifth in the center, as on dice

> "Mr M'Coy had tried unsuccessfully to find a place in the bench with the others, and, when the party had settled down in the form of a quincunx, he had tried unsuccessfully to make comic remarks." — James Joyce, "Grace," in *Dubliners*

gammadion (pronounced variously, but here's one: "ghə-MAD-ee-ən") the Greek letter gamma (Γ) drawn four times from a center point, especially in the form of a swastika

> According to Wikipedia, the gammadion, or swastika, "became a popular symbol of luck in the Western world in the early 20th century… [I]ts use in Western countries faded after the Nazi association became dominant in the 1930s."

triskelion ("try-SKƏLL-yən") a symbolic figure with three legs (either human or stylized, often as spirals) radiating from the center

> "…the image is a heraldic shield, with… two triskelion-like symbols that, rather grotesquely, combine eight bent legs in place of the usual three." — from an article in *Art in America,* 2015

bend sinister in heraldry, a diagonal bar crossing a coat-of-arms from top right to bottom left, indicating bastardy (sometimes erroneously called a *bar sinister*)

> "…it so fell out, however, to our reproach, that instead of the bend-dexter, which since Harry the Eighth's reign was honestly our due—a bend-sinister… had been drawn quite across the field of the Shandy arms." — Laurence Sterne, *Tristram Shandy*

broad arrow the symbol the British government puts on its property and on prisoners' uniforms:

> "A man is sent to prison because he has proved himself unfit to be at liberty… He is given a uniform coarse in texture clumsy and grotesque in appearance and branded over with the broad-arrow

and with his prison number. In this garb it is impossible for a man to preserve his sense of self-respect." — J.L.A. Kayll, *A Plea for the Criminal* (1905)

ankh ("ANK," to rhyme with *spank*) a cross with a loop in place of the upper vertical piece: a symbol of life, especially in ancient Egypt:

"This incarnation of Death was not a scythe-wielding Grim Reaper but rather a cute goth girl with a spunky attitude and a pretty ankh symbol." — from an article on EW.com, 2020, about Neil Gaiman's *Sandman* graphic novels

The natural world

macaque ("mə-KAHK" or "mə-KAK," to rhyme with *crack*) a kind of monkey found in Asia and North Africa

"At this, the frightened macaque exploded forward like a racehorse leaving the gate." — Mark Helprin, *A Soldier of the Great War*

loris ("LORE-əss") a small, nocturnal, arboreal primate found in tropical Asia, with a cute face

"…Nekaris and her colleagues built up local pride and interest in slow lorises by teaching children about the animals and assigning each family an individual slow loris mascot." — from an article in *Scientific American,* 2020

terrapin ("TERR-ə-pin") a small turtle living in either freshwater or coastal marshes

"Once river terrapins meet and mate, plenty can still go wrong. If nests full of eggs get too hot or too cold, the sexes may be out of sync." — from an article in *National Geographic*, 2015

chaffinch ("CHAFF-fintch") a common finch native to Europe, North Africa, and Asia, with a light-brown breast and dark wings and tail

"'As with any star athlete… what separates a champion bird from a loser is natural talent,' said Filip Santens, … who prepares his five-time champion chaffinch for matches by pumping heavy-metal Guns N' Roses music into his cage and feeding him high-protein birdseed." — from an article about a Belgian tweeting competition in the *New York Times*, 2007 (The winner is the bird that tweets the most times in an hour. You may insert your own Twitter-related joke here.)

chiropteran ("ky-RAHP-tə-rən") a member of the only order of flying mammals, *chiroptera*: i.e., a bat

"While the tube-nosed bats may be the first chiropterans found to cozy up in a snowbank, plenty of small mammals have been known to hibernate just under the snow…" — from an article in *National Geographic*, 2018

bandicoot ("BAN-dih-koot") a large rat in India and Sri Lanka that destroys gardens and rice fields; or a marsupial native to Australia and nearby islands

There is a video game franchise called Crash Bandicoot. From Wikipedia: "Crash was intended to be a mascot character for Sony to use to compete against Nintendo's Mario and Sega's Sonic the Hedgehog." But he's really a scion of the whirling Tasmanian Devil from Looney Tunes.

aerie/eyrie ("AIR-ee"/"EYE-ree") the nest of an eagle or other large bird of prey, in a high place; or any house or stronghold in a high place, especially if secluded

"You ought not to be rude to an eagle, when you are only the size of a hobbit, and are up in his eyrie at night!" — J.R.R. Tolkien, *The Hobbit*

"Up in the rarefied aerie of the 102nd floor observatory, new floor-to-ceiling windows reveal the panorama of the possibilities below." — from an article about the Empire State Building, in the *Wall Street Journal*, 2020

spinneret ("SPIN-ər-et" or "spin-ər-ƏT") an organ that produces silk or thread in spiders and silkworms

"She climbed back up, moved over about an inch to the left, touched her spinnerets to the web, and then carried a line across to the right, forming the top of the T." — E.B. White, *Charlotte's Web*

rime (pronounced like *rhyme*) hoarfrost: the white, icy coating that forms on grass or leaves; or frost formed when mist contacts something cold

"Freezing fog over the weekend created more beautiful displays of rime ice." — from an article in the *Star Tribune* (Minneapolis), 2021

duff decaying organic matter on the forest floor

"The forest floor consisted of a soft duff of rotting redwood foliage…" — from an article in the *New Yorker,* 2005

ambergris ("AM-bər-griss" or "AM-bər-grease" or "AM-bər-gree") a waxy, grayish substance used as an ingredient in perfumes, secreted by sperm whales and found floating on the sea's surface or washed up on the shore

"…until a comparatively late day, the precise origin of ambergris remained, like amber itself, a problem to the learned." — Herman Melville, *Moby-Dick*

calipash ("KAL-ih-pash," the first syllable rhyming with *pal*) the edible jellylike material inside the upper shell of a turtle

"The London Tavern, Bishopsgate Street, was famous for serving turtle… Turtles were kept in massive tanks and, at various times, some two tons of turtle could be seen swimming in one vat. It was a skillful and time-consuming exercise to prepare a turtle dinner in the shape of calipash (upper part, green meat) and calipee (under part, yellow meat)." — from the website NewYorkAlmanack.com, 2020

nux vomica ("NUKS VAHM-ə-kə") a tree with poisonous seeds: the source of strychnine; or the seeds themselves

Nux vomica is used in drugs that treat many medical disorders.

"Regulators have issued five warning letters this year to companies selling [homeopathic] products with nightshade or nux vomica." — from an article on ChicagoTribune.com, 2017

curare ("kyoo-RAH-ree") a substance prepared from the bark of certain South American plants, used to poison the tips of arrows and blowpipe darts (It induces paralysis in victims.)

"A moral curare… paralysing will and emotion…" — from an article in *The Contemporary Review*, 1883

Things we do with the natural world

pollard ("PAHL-ərd") a tree whose upper branches have been cut off, to promote new growth at the top

"'I do not often walk this way *now*,' said Emma as they proceeded, 'but… I shall gradually get intimately acquainted with all the hedges, gates, pools, and pollards of this part of Highbury.'" — Jane Austen, *Emma*

stannary ("STAN-ə-ree") a region of tin mines, especially in Cornwall and Devon, England (usually plural)

> "He came as the captain of a gang from one of the Cornish stannaries." — R.D. Blackmore, *Lorna Doone*

tantivy ("tan-TIV-ee") (archaic) a gallop; or a hunting cry, used to signal a faster chase

> In *Gravity's Rainbow,* a British character is named Tantivy Mucker-Maffick.

> "The tantivy of wild pigeons, flying by twos and threes athwart my view… gives a voice to the air." — Henry David Thoreau, *Walden*

corium ("CORE-ee-əm") a molten substance created in the core of a nuclear reactor during a meltdown; or the layer of skin beneath the epidermis

> Corium is also known as fuel-containing material (FCM). "Man-made lava is a real thing and it is created in one of the most dangerous situations known: during the reactor core meltdown of a nuclear power plant. This rare variety of lava, named corium, has incredible properties…" — from an article in *Wired* magazine, 2013

Stones that don't roll

dolmen ("DOHL-mən") a prehistoric structure: two or more upright monoliths with a capstone, used as a tomb in some cases

> "He started telling her about Vheissu. How it was reached, on camel-back over a vast tundra, past the dolmens and temples of dead cities…" — Thomas Pynchon, *V.*

cromlech ("KRAHM-lək") an ancient stone monument: according to one definition, it consists of monoliths arranged in a circle; according to another, the word is another name for a dolmen

menhir ("MEN-heer") an upright prehistoric monolith

> "[He] was wholly responsible for such footnotes as: 'The cromlech (associated with mleko, milch, milk) is obviously a symbol of the Great Mother, just as the menhir ("mein Herr") is as obviously masculine.'" — Vladimir Nabokov, *Transparent Things*

hoodoo – a column of rock, shaped by weathering, as seen in Bryce Canyon and the Badlands; or another name for voodoo

In *The Bachelor and the Bobby-Soxer* (1947, with an Oscar-winning script by Sidney Sheldon, who later wrote for *The Patty Duke Show* and *I Dream of Jeannie,* and still later wrote best-sellers like *The Other Side of Midnight*), Cary Grant engages a teenage Shirley Temple in this exchange: "You remind me of a man." "What man?" "A man with a power." "What power." "The power of Hoodoo." "Hoodoo?" "You do." "Do what?" "You remind me of a man"... and so on, to infinity.

The food of love

Aeolian harp ("ee-OHL-yən" or "ay-OHL-yən," the A pronounced as in *make*) a box with an opening and strings that make music when air passes through them

ocarina ("AHK-ə-ree-nə") a small wind instrument with a mouthpiece and fingerholes, traditionally made of terra cotta

> After first encountering this word in a book, I was pleased to recognize an ocarina in Bernardo Bertolucci's movie *1900.* (It looked like a sweet potato.) Many years later, the popular Ocarina app enabled users to produce similar sounds by blowing into an iPhone.

flageolet ("flaj-ə-LET" or "-LAY," the A pronounced as in *cat*) a wind instrument like a recorder but smaller

> "...vagabond groups assembled round the doors to see the stroller woman dance, add their uproar to the shrill flageolet and deafening drum." — Charles Dickens, *The Old Curiosity Shop*

psaltery ("SAWL-tər-ee") a musical instrument from the medieval era and before, similar to a dulcimer or zither

> "I will sing a new song unto thee, O God: upon a psaltery and an instrument of ten strings will I sing praises unto thee." — Psalms 144:9 (King James version)

rebec, shawm, theorbo, sackbut, tabor these are musical instruments from the medieval and Renaissance eras:

> The *rebec* was a stringed instrument, played with a bow.
>
> The *shawm* was a woodwind instrument with a reed.
>
> The *theorbo* was a lute-like instrument, played by plucking.
>
> The *sackbut* was an early trombone.
>
> The *tabor* was a small drum that accompanied a pipe.

oud ("OOD") a musical instrument like a lute, played mainly in Arab countries

"As he passed over into the unlighted district he heard a few languid notes being strummed on an oud." — Joseph Wambaugh, *The Blue Knight*

koto ("KOH-toh") a long Japanese instrument with 13 strings, similar to a zither

"Head outside of the American Art museum in Chinatown for taiko drumming and koto performances and Les the DJ spinning Japanese pop and soul records…" — from an article in the *Washington Post,* 2022

charango ("tchə-RANG-goh") a small guitar-like instrument used in Andean music, traditionally made from an armadillo shell

Do not confuse the *charango* with a *charanga*—a type of Cuban ensemble that plays dance music with European instruments— OR with a *churinga,* which is a sacred object made of wood or stone with designs carved into it, kept in a secret place by aboriginal tribes of central Australia and believed to represent a person's soul.

"As she prepared to make her forthcoming album… Sofía Rei embarked upon a trek through Chile's mountainous Elqui Province. She brought a charango and two backpacks full of recording gear…" — from an article in the *New York Times*, 2021

"There we were expecting the chief to bring us a churinga, and he shows up with a Sears catalog!" — Walker Percy, *The Message in the Bottle*

Whip it!

quirt ("KWERT") a riding whip with a short handle and a lash made of leather, most commonly used in the American Southwest

"The sedate throwing of flowers erupted into a fistfight, a ministampede and people lashed with whips and riding quirts." — from an article in the *San Antonio Express-News,* 2018.

(This reminds me of something a woman-friend from Texas used to say: "Why are we talkin'? We could be fightin'!")

knout ("NOWT") a whip with multiple leather thongs, used in czarist Russia for flogging criminals

"'Iván Dmítritch, forgive me!' he cried. 'When they flogged me with the knout it was not so hard to bear as it is to see you now . . . yet you had pity on me, and did not tell. For Christ's sake forgive me, wretch that I am!'" — Leo Tolstoy, "God Sees the Truth, But Waits" (translated by Aylmer and Louise Maude)

FYI, according to Wikipedia, "A sentence of 100 or 120 lashes was equivalent to a death sentence."

kurbash ("KOOR-bahsh") a whip for punishing criminals, made from the hide of a rhinoceros or hippopotamus, formerly used in the Ottoman Empire, especially in Turkey and Egypt

"It is the peculiar mission of the hippopotamus to supply Kurbashes for the backs of the natives." — John Colborne, *With Hicks Pasha in Soudan* (1884)

cat-o'-nine-tails ("CAT-ə-nine-tailz") a whip with a handle and nine cords, each knotted, used to flog offenders, especially in the British navy and army, until 1881

"Police records discovered in the 20th century reveal that [the Marquis de Sade] stomped on a Crucifix and screamed blasphemies while abusing himself with a cat-o'-nine-tails." — from an article in *Smithsonian* magazine, 2015

Food, drink, etc.

kipper a herring (or other fish) that's been split, salted, dried, and smoked

"Avoid eating goulash with ice cream and kippers / Remember these things, you obnoxious young nippers…"— from "Things to Remember," a song in the musical *The Roar of the Greasepaint, the Smell of the Crowd*

haggis ("HAG-əss," the A pronounced as in *cat*) a Scottish dish consisting of calf's or sheep's heart, liver, and lungs mixed with suet, oatmeal, onions, and spices, and boiled in the animal's stomach

Yum!

"…a large haggis is paraded into the room, preceded by bagpipers. A reader then recites [Robert Burns's] 'Address to a Haggis,' almost certainly the most passionate dialect poem ever composed by a man to a meat product." — from an article in the *New York Times*, 2007

tripe (rhymes with "ripe") the stomach lining of a cow, sheep, or goat, prepared as a food

In Nicaragua, our hostess served a dish of rubbery off-white meat with cells like a honeycomb. She called it *mondongo*; my dictionary informed me that this was tripe. I tried to take a bite, but couldn't get my teeth through it. Clowning for my friends, I pulled at the meat with my fork until it stretched many inches from my mouth. At that moment, our hostess walked by and saw what I was doing. I regretted my tomfoolery.

poteen ("pah-TEEN" or "poh-TEEN") Irish whiskey distilled unlawfully, in a private still, usually from potatoes

"...Frank O'Connor has a nice way of making his people look, feel and sound like anyone else. Any reader might find himself saying: there but for lack of poteen, a certain uneasiness about sex and a wary relationship with the parish priest, go I." — from a review of a collection of O'Connor's stories, in *Time* magazine, 1954

scuppernong ("SKUP-ər-nahng") a grape variety to the South in the U.S.; or wine made from this grape (the name comes from the Scuppernong River, where the grape was originally found)

"...the old dead Sunday afternoons of monotonous peace which they spent beneath the scuppernong arbor in the back yard..." — William Faulkner, *Absalom, Absalom!*

chicle ("TCHIK-əl") a gum obtained from the sapodilla tree: the main ingredient in chewing gum

When I was traveling in Central America, small children in many places held out their hands and asked for *chicle* ("CHICK-leh"). I thought they wanted Chiclets: not Juicy Fruit, not Bazooka Joe Bubble Gum, only Chiclets. It turns out that *chicle* is the Spanish word for "chewing gum."

Sen-Sen a chewable breath freshener, tasting like black licorice, popular especially in the 1930s and 1940s.

"Hildy had brassy blond hair, wore a garnet-colored chiffon bow around her neck, chewed sen-sen, knew all the latest songs and was a good dancer." — Betty Smith, *A Tree Grows in Brooklyn*

Fragrance vs. odor

attar ("A-tər," the A pronounced as in *cat*) a perfume or essential oil made from the petals of flowers, especially roses

"Debs... expressed a common attitude: working in the AFL was as 'wasteful of time as to spray a cesspool with attar of roses.'" — Michael Harrington, *Socialism*

effluvium ("ə-FLOO-vee-əm") an outflow of foul-smelling fumes, often from decaying matter

"At the distance of half a mile... I have perceived the whole air tainted with the effluvium." — Charles Darwin, *Journal*

Here's a little something for you

baksheesh ("back-SHEESH") a small amount of money given as a tip, a gift, or a bribe—usually in exchange for faster or better service (in Asia and North Africa)

> "... those who participated in the game did so for the same reason they haggled at shops or gave baksheesh to beggars: it was in the unwritten laws of Baedeker land." — Thomas Pynchon, *V.*

stiver ("STY-vər") an extremely small amount of money, or of anything; originally, a Dutch coin worth 1/20 of a guilder, or five Dutch cents

> "As for that lady's fortune, Sir, you shall never touch a single stiver of it." — Oliver Goldsmith, *The Vicar of Wakefield*

doit ("DOYT") (archaic) an old Dutch coin worth very little; or a small amount of money; or anything of small value

> "When they will not give a doit to relieve a lame beggar, they will lay out ten to see a dead Indian." — William Shakespeare, *The Tempest*

Art and architecture

caryatid ("carry-A-tid," the stressed A pronounced as in *cat*) in architecture, a supporting pillar carved in the shape of a woman

> "...caryatids were so called after the women of Caryae, a city that rebelled against the Greeks in the Persian Wars and was defeated. When the menfolk had been slaughtered, their widows were led away as captives... 'To ensure that they exhibited a permanent picture of slavery... the architects of those times designed images of them specially placed to uphold a load.'" — from an article in the *New York Times*, 1986

telamon ("TELL-ə-mahn") a male caryatid

> "A reconstituted Atlas statue, or telamon, from the Valley of Temples [in Sicily] greets the museum's visitors." — from the caption of a photo in the *New York Times,* 2020

cartouche ("kar-TOOSH") in architecture, a scroll-like tablet used for inscriptions; or a rounded surface bearing a low-relief decoration

> "A romantic 6-story masterpiece. Note the dragon and crown cartouche set up high into the brickwork." — from the *AIA Guide to New York City*, in its entry on the Red House, the building I lived in for many years on the Upper West Side of Manhattan. (A

fact that will amaze current Manhattanites: in 1977, when I moved in, the rent was $225 per month.)

acanthus ("ə-KAN-thəss") a flowering Mediterranean plant; or an architectural ornament in the shape of the plant's leaves, used in the capitals of Corinthian columns

> "Hillsides of unruly acanthus—nature's template for Corinthian columns—precede the Domus Augustana." — from a travel article about the seven hills of Rome, in the *Washington Post*, 2019

anaglyph ("AN-ə-glif," the first A pronounced as in *cat*) an architectural ornament, carved in low relief

> This is the word with which I lost the district spelling bee in 1966, when I was in sixth grade. It now has an additional meaning: a 3-D photo produced by superimposing two different images printed in different colors and viewing them through two filters of different colors.

maquette ("ma-KET," the A pronounced as in *cat*) a small model or prototype, usually of a building or sculpture

> "A Picasso maquette for the public sculpture in Chicago's Daley Plaza could go for as much as $35 million at Christie's on Nov. 4." — from an article in *Art in America*, 2013

Home goods

antimacassar ("an-tee-mə-KASS-ər," the stressed A pronounced as in *cat*) a small cover placed over the back or arms of a chair or sofa, to protect it from soiling (as by *macassar* hair oil)

> On *The Big, Comfy Couch*, a children's TV show (1992-2007), the main character often referred to her Auntie Macassar—a joke that must have been lost on all but a few parents and grandparents.

salver ("SAL-vər") a serving tray, often made of silver, on which drinks, food, or visiting cards are presented

> "A ubiquitous mess-waiter, in a clean linen jacket, ... presently appeared with the visitor's card on a salver." — George Whyte-Melville, *Uncle John*

pier glass a tall mirror, such as the kind formerly set in a *pier*, the section of a wall between two windows

"He stood before the pier-glass, viewing his trim dinner-coat, his beautiful triple-braided trousers; and murmured in lyric beatitude, 'By golly, I don't look so bad...'" — Sinclair Lewis, *Babbitt*

cheval glass ("shə-VAL") a tall, framed mirror that can be tilted

"...the stranger surveyed himself with great complacency in a cheval glass..." — Charles Dickens, *The Pickwick Papers*

Mr. Gormley practiced making faces in the cheval glass
before trying them in company.

jeroboam ("jer-ə-BOH-əm") an oversized wine bottle that holds about a gallon; also, in England, a chamber pot

"There had been a little party for me here in my brother's house, my wife's contribution to which was a jeroboam of Piper-Heidsieck..." — John Barth, *Letters*

demijohn ("DEM-ee-jahn") a large bottle, usually encased in wicker, with a narrow neck

"We have at present 500 demijohns filled with vinegar going by one of our steamers to the West Indies." — from a letter from Messrs. Scrutton, Sons, & Co., a British shipping company, 1894

ewer ("YOO-ər") a large pitcher with a wide mouth and a handle, used to pour water for washing; often paired with a basin

"The [S]mithsonian offers free downloads of 3D scans of objects in their collection and that's why I now have a Lidded Ewer from 1050 BCE to put my weed in." — from a Tweet, 2019

firkin ("FƏR-kən") a small wooden barrel or keg, used especially for storing butter

> "She had no figure and no vanity about her appearance. 'Alas!' she said. 'I look like one butter firkin on another.'" — Henry Roth, *Call It Sleep*

Easy to confuse

hob ("HAHB") a shelf inside a fireplace, used to heat pans or keep things warm

> "If he comes to you riding a cob... / If he puts up his feet on the hob... / If his brow or his breeding is low... / My own Araminta, say 'No!'" — W. Mackworth Praed, "A Letter of Advice" (1839)

hod ("HAHD") a V-shaped tray with a long handle, carried on the shoulder, used to transport bricks or mortar

> "A reporter found Sir Winston [*sic*] acting the part of a bricklayer to perfection on the home of one of his servants on his estate at Westerham. His young daughter, Sarah, was 'hod carrier' for him, carrying the bricks while her father set them in place and tapped them with a trowel." — from an article on the website WinstonChurchill.org

Ornamentals

rosette an ornament or badge of ribbon or silk, made to resemble a rose, presented especially to the winner of a competition, or worn as a symbol of an honor; or an architectural ornament representing a rose

> "Lady Bullingdon supposes that where there is a village there must be a village idiot, and... the fact of his having appeared upon election day wearing the rosette of both the two opposing parties appears to Lady Bullingdon to put the matter quite beyond doubt." — G.K. Chesterton, *Manalive*

cockade ("kah-KADE") a rosette or knot of ribbon worn on a hat, usually as part of a uniform

> "In revolutionary France, the Marquis de Lafayette, the same French aristocrat who fought in the American revolutionary war, is said to have designed the red, blue and white cockade." — from an article in the *Economist,* 2020

parure ("pə-ROOR") a set of jewelry pieces meant to be worn together

"Among the highlights: A Patek Philippe's parure in diamonds, onyx and coral, circa 1970s, composed of a watch, necklace and bracelet…" — from an article in *Forbes*, 2022

frisette ("frih-ZƏT") ("little curl") a curled or frizzed fringe of hair, often artificial, worn by women on the forehead

"… a somewhat more than middle-aged female, with a parchment forehead and a dry little 'frisette' shingling it… left the table prematurely…" — Oliver Wendell Holmes, *The Autocrat of the Breakfast-Table*

uraeus ("you-REE-əss") the figure of a sacred asp or cobra on the headdress of ancient Egyptian rulers, symbolizing royal power

"'Take the Uraeus crown from my head,' he continued aloud, as he seated himself at the feast. 'Today I will wear a wreath of flowers.'" — Georg Ebers, *A Romance of Ancient Egypt* (translated by Clara Bell)

You realize, of course, this means war

petard ("pə-TARD") a small gunpowder bomb used to breach a wall, blow up a gate, or break down a door

From the French word *péter*, to break wind.

You're not likely to encounter many petards these days—except in the phrase, *hoist by his own petard*, meaning, tripped up by his own foul scheme (or, literally, blown sky-high by the bomb he himself planted). The phrase was invented by Shakespeare: he puts it in Hamlet's mouth, as the melancholy Dane plans to undo Rosencrantz and Guildenstern, who have been assigned to undo him.

onager ("AHN-ə-jər") a heavy catapult used during the fourth and fifth centuries in the Roman Empire; or a wild ass of the Middle East and Asia

The military device supposedly takes its name from its powerful kick, or recoil—like the wild ass's.

trebuchet ("TREB-yoo-shet") a long-armed medieval catapult used during sieges

"Since 1986, Delaware was known for hosting the annual Punkin Chunkin in Sussex County the first weekend after Halloween, a competition consisting of hurling gourds as far as possible by human muscle, catapult, centrifuge, trebuchet or air cannon." — from an article in the *Washington Post*, 2020

cordite ("CORD-ite") a smokeless explosive powder, formerly used in bullets, etc., as a replacement for gunpowder

> Cordite gets its name from its form: it was pressed into thin, short cords that looked like spaghetti.

> If you read military or crime fiction, you're likely to have come across the phrase *the smell of cordite*. But if you google the phrase, you'll find a flock of aficionados annoyed by the anachronism: because cordite hasn't been used in ammo since World War II.

gelignite ("JEL-ig-nite") an explosive gel invented by Alfred Nobel, used for blasting rocks

> "Her aunt Bridie Dolan... had been horribly disfigured at twenty-seven, after accidentally dropping a cache of gelignite in an I.R.A. explosives dump. The blast blew off both of her hands, and permanently blinded her." — from an article in the *New Yorker*, 2015

claymore mine a land mine with steel fragments

> "American arms designers have produced a mine called a 'Claymore,' which has found wide use here [*i.e.* in Vietnam]. The Claymore... has an optical sighting device and hurls a blast of shrapnel directionally at the point toward which it has been pre-aimed." — Malcolm W. Browne, *The New Face of War* (1965)

vesicant ("VESS-ə-kənt") any substance that blisters the flesh: used in chemical warfare and in medicine

> Mustard gas is the most widely known vesicant.

It came from outer space

bolide ("BOH-lide," the second syllable rhyming with *tide*) a large, bright meteor: usually one that explodes in the atmosphere

> "Bolides have peppered Earth as well in the past—a particularly big one probably finished off the dinosaurs 65 million years ago—and today they pose an unknown risk to human civilization." — from an article in *Discover*, 1996

tektite ("TECK-tight") a small, black, glass-like object, thought to have originated as a bit of meteorite

> Tektites are found in abundance in certain parts of the world. It's believed that the molten bits scattered on impact. "Scientists have largely been able to determine the source crater for tektites, with the exception of one—the Australasian field." — from an article on CNN.com, 2020

Gems, stones, and charms

cabochon ("KAH-bə-shahn," the first A pronounced as in *cat,* or "kah-bə-SHOHn," ending with a French N) a precious stone that has been rounded and polished but not faceted

"An iconic necklace that Cartier made for María Félix in 1975 gets an upgrade: 46.45 carats of rare cabochon-cut emeralds." — from an article in *Town & Country,* 2020

porphyry ("POR-fə-ree") a hard, reddish rock with large crystals

"Verrocchio constructed monumental bronze sculptures, carved delicate marble and terra-cotta portrait busts, designed porphyry tombs and marble fountains, as well as painting exquisite panel paintings." — from an article in the *Wall Street Journal,* 2018

carnelian ("kar-NEE-lee-ən") a red semiprecious stone used in jewelry

"There are 88 gems in total in what is officially known as the Devonshire Parure, including carnelian, amethyst, garnets, emeralds, sapphires, and diamonds." — from an article about a tiara designed to be worn at a Romanov Coronation, in *Town & Country,* 2019

breloque ("brə-LOHK") a charm, key, etc. worn on a watch chain

"…the Duke of St. James showered a sack of whimsical breloques among a scrambling crowd of laughing beauties." — Benjamin Disraeli, *The Young Duke*

periapt ("PEH-ree-apt") (archaic) a charm worn on a necklace, or an amulet, worn as protection against evil or bad luck

"Drape your amulets, periapts, talismans… and other various charms over this mystical mitt in order to keep them visible and organized…" — from the description of a "Palm Reader Jewelry Stand," part of a holiday gift guide on *Flood* magazine's website, 2017

A few odds and ends

ullage ("ULL-ij," the U pronounced as in *dull*) the amount of liquid lost, as by leakage or evaporation, during shipment, storage, etc.; or the difference between the amount of liquid in a container and the amount it can hold (formerly, the amount that had to be replaced).

"I held the bottle up to the candle to ascertain the ullage." — Frederick Marryat, *Olla Podrida*

tanka ("TAHNG-kə") a non-rhyming Japanese poem with five lines, portraying an event or a feeling; the first and third lines have five syllables, the others have seven.

"[Lafcadio Hearn's] haiku and tanka translations influenced Pound, Rexroth, and others." — from an article in the *New Yorker*, 2019

raree-show ("RAIR-ee") (archaic) a peep show, with puppets or pictures, carried in a box and exhibited on the street; figuratively, any show or spectacle considered vulgar

"Neither a loaded pistol pointed at my head nor a bribe of lottery-jackpot proportions could have persuaded me to watch Martin Bashir's raree-show about Michael Jackson." — from an article in the *Herald* (Glasgow), 2003

palestra/palaestra ("pə-LESS-trə") in ancient Greece or Rome, a public place for training in wrestling or athletics; a gymnasium

"But when we leave the child 'free as a man' in the palestra of his own intelligence, his type changes entirely." — Maria Montessori, *Spontaneous Activity in Education*

bezel ("BEZZ-əl") the grooved rim that holds a watch crystal or a clock's cover; or the sloping facets below and surrounding the flat top of a cut gem, visible above its setting

The bezel of a smartphone is the border around the display screen. Manufacturers have steadily shrunk the bezel to offer larger displays; some phones are now bezel-less.

vuvuzela ("voo-voo-ZAY-lə") a long plastic horn used as a noisemaker at sporting events

If you watched any of the 2010 World Cup soccer matches, held in South Africa, you must remember this word, which is so much fun to say, you'll have to control yourself. (My copy editor, however, comments, "Horrid to listen to.")

"South African fan attempts to hit referee with vuvuzela" — headline in *Sports Illustrated*, 2013

meconium ("mih-KOH-nee-əm") the dark green excrement in a fetus's intestinal tract, discharged just after birth: i.e., baby's first poop

"Occasionally meconium stools will be passed while your baby is still in utero." — from an article on the website VeryWellFamily.com, 2020

(Too much information? Sorry.)

fleshpot a place that offers plentiful luxuries and pleasures, especially food, drink, and sex

> Exodus 16:3 refers famously to the *fleshpots of Egypt*. More recently, the term has been applied closer to home: "Sex is for sale seemingly everywhere in Las Vegas… But for those who want their Sin City experience at a safe distance, the city offers its many fleshpot revues." — from an article in the *New York Times*, 2006

Word Play

Though these words refer to things most of us don't encounter daily, the objects are all out there, waiting to be seen. Challenge: Invent a story in which a person uses or sees each of the following:

1. howdah
2. clepsydra
3. quincunx
4. hoodoo
5. charango
6. haggis
7. caryatid
8. demijohn
9. triskelion
10. yurt

Things You Probably Didn't Know the Names For

From A to Z

No such list would be complete without these two popular favorites:

aglet ("AG-lət") the small sheath that protects each end of a shoelace and makes it easier to lace the shoes.

> "AGLET is the word that always comes up in bar bets: 'Drinks are on me if you know the word for that plastic tip at the end of a shoelace...'" — from an article in the *New York Times*, 2018

zarf ("ZARF") a holder, often ornamental, for a handleless cup or glass that contains hot coffee or tea

> Zarfs were typically metal. (You may have seen a picture of a Russian drinking tea from a glass in a zarf, with a sugar cube held between the teeth.) But the same word also refers to the plastic holders for conical paper cups in which fountain treats were served at Woolworth's counters in the 1950s and 1960s.

Useful objects

gnomon ("NOH-mən") the upright part of a sundial, which casts a shadow

> "... the sense of [Time's] motion is derived from many natural, or at least familiar, sources—the body's innate awareness of its own bloodstream... and, of course, our methods of measurement, such as the creeping shadow line of a gnomon, the trickle of an hourglass, the trot of a second hand..." — Vladimir Nabokov, *Ada*

nock the notch at the end of an arrow, into which the bowstring fits; or the groove at either end of the bow, which holds the string

> "Every Thursday afternoon, after the last serious arrow had been fired, they were allowed to fit one more nock to their strings and to discharge the arrow straight up into the air." — T.H. White, *The Sword in the Stone*

rowel ("RAO-əl") the small wheel with sharp points mounted at the end of a spur

> "Rowels quickly became popular as they did not pierce a horse's sides yet still got the animal's attention." — from an article on AmericanCowboy.com, 2017

tang the part of a knife that projects back from the blade and is covered by the handle

> "The full-tang blade (meaning, it runs the full length of the handle), in a Santoku shape, is made from tempered American high-carbon stainless steel." — from an article on BonAppetit.com, 2020

pannier ("PAN-yər") a basket or pack, especially one of a pair, carried on an animal's back or a person's shoulder; or one of a pair hung over the back wheel of a bicycle or motorcycle

> "The women… had wicker panniers on their shoulders, supported by a band across the forehead." — Evelyn Waugh, *A Handful of Dust*

planchette ("plan-SHƏT") the moving indicator on a Ouija board, which spells out messages from the spirit world when fingers are placed lightly on it; or one that is fitted with a pencil, to produce automatic writing

> "This convinces people that something truly sinister is at play when the planchette moves. 'You hoodwink yourself into thinking that something mystical is happening,' McAndrew said." — from an article on Today.com, 2019

felloes (pronounced like *fellows*) the round outer rim of a wheel, connected to the hub by the spokes (One felloe is a curved segment of the rim; put together, the felloes form the rim. A variant spelling is *felly/fellies*.)

> "A closed carriage was ordered from a roadside inn… It had stout wheel-spokes and heavy felloes…" — Thomas Hardy, *Tess of the D'Urbervilles*

Bits of nature

samara ("sə-MAR-ə" or "SAM-ə-rə") the winged fruit containing a maple or ash seed

> They twirl as they fall, like little helicopters. That's for seed dispersal. Sometimes kids split them open and stick them on their noses. Did you?

lamella ("lə-MEL-ə") one of the gills on the underside of a mushroom (plural: *lamellae*)

> The word *lamella* can refer to various structures, in botany, physiology, ophthalmology, and even in construction.

chalaza ("kə-LAY-zə") one of the two white spiral bands connecting an egg yolk to the opposite ends of the shell

"At each end of this are two ligaments, called chalazoæ...
which... keep the white and the yolk in their places." — Oliver
Goldsmith, *A History of the Earth and Animated Nature*

So you see, when it comes to the class system in England, not
even an egg is exempt.

Myth and magic

talaria ("tə-LAIR-ee-ə") in myth, the wings (or winged sandals) on
certain figures' feet (usually Mercury, A.K.A. Hermes)

"In his job as messenger, he wears a broad-rimmed traveler's
hat... and talaria, or winged sandals, made 'of imperishable gold
which bore him swift as a breath of air over sea and earth'..." —
from the website Hermograph.com

pentacle (rhymes with *tentacle*) a five-pointed star, also known as a
pentagram, used as a magical talisman

"To settle a lawsuit, the Department of Veterans Affairs has
agreed to add the Wiccan pentacle to a list of approved religious
symbols that it will engrave on veterans' headstones... There are
1,800 Wiccans in the Air Force, according to a Pentagon survey
cited in the suit..." — from an article in the *New York Times*,
2007

(Wait—*Pentagon*? *Pentacle*? Is there more here than meets the
eye?)

Working with fabrics

selvage/selvedge ("SEL-vidj") a woven edge that prevents fabric
from unraveling or fraying; or a narrow strip of unfinished cloth,
meant to be cut off or covered by a seam

"...denim done the right way... featuring a tighter weave, more
interesting textures and of course, the de rigueur selvage stitching
on the inside seam that jeans lovers proudly reveal by rolling
their cuffs." — from an article about the closing of the last major
selvage denim factory in the U.S., in the *New York Times*, 2017

galloon/galoon ("gə-LOON") a decorative band of fabric, usually
with scalloped edges, used especially as trim on military and police
uniforms.

Galloon usually consists of gold or silver thread, lace, or
embroidery. "... and Four scarlet Footmen, grand as galoon and

silver fringe could make them, did the due magnificence in dress." — Thomas Carlyle, *The History of Friedrich II of Prussia*

rickrack a flat braid in a zigzag pattern, used as trimming

"She kept her eyes to the band of black asphalt... gunning the engine through every curve on highways that zigzagged like rickrack." — Nell Zink, *Doxology*

A versatile word

papillote ("PAP-ə-loht" or "pah-pə-YUT") I defer to the *Chicago Tribune*:

"The word papillote in French is an interesting one because it means several things, not all having to do with cooking and eating. First, if something is cooked in paper, it is called papillote. But the little frills that some restaurants place on the exposed bone of a lamb chop are also papillotes. And the end papers used with hair curlers have the same name." — from an article in the *Chicago Tribune*, 1987

Woodworking

shim a thin piece of wood, metal, or stone, often tapered, inserted between things as a leveler or support

"Set two or three cardboard shims in the hinge mortises on the door and jamb, then replace the hinge." — from instructions for repairing a skewed door, on ThisOldHouse.com

kerf ("KƏRF") the slit made when cutting with a saw; or the width of the cut

"The thin-kerf chain (its teeth are 3/32-inch wide) zips through each cut with smoothness and precision." — from an article in *Popular Mechanics*, 2020

purfling ("PER-fəl-ing") an inlaid ornamental border, especially on a violin

"A team of scientists in Italy has completed an investigation into the purfling and decoration techniques used by Antonio Stradivari in his early period." — from an article on the website TheStrad.com, 2013

Dogs and people: a similarity

hackles ("HACK-əlz") the hairs on the back of a dog or other animal: they rise when the animal is surprised or angry

> "The ways young children play can also raise animals' hackles." — from an article in the *New York Times,* entitled, "How to Stop Your Child from Tormenting Your Pet," 2020

> This word is often used figuratively, to describe a human reaction: "His voice was… tinged with enough condescension to make my hackles rise." — Sybil Marshall, *A Nest of Magpies*

horripilation ("haw-rip-ə-LAY-shən") the bristling of hair (on the head or the body) as a result of fear or cold

> "Adrenaline stimulates tiny muscles to pull on the roots of our hairs, making them stand out from our skin. That distorts the skin, causing bumps to form. Call it horripilation, and you'll be right—bristling from cold or fear." — from an article on NPR.org ("The Science of Goose Bumps"), 2015

Also about dogs

dog days the hottest weeks of the year (in the Northern hemisphere), occurring in July and August—so called because Sirius, the Dog Star, rises and sets with the sun during this period

> And you thought *Dog Day Afternoon* got its title from the poster, in which Al Pacino peers over the title like a forlorn pup.

Geography and earth science

Mercator projection ("mər-KAY-tər") in maps, a representation of the Earth as a rectangle, with lines of latitude and longitude crossing at right angles; on these maps, the farther you get from the equator, the larger bodies of land appear

> (Did you know that, in reality, Greenland is smaller than Manhattan?)

talus ("TAY-ləss" or "TA-ləss," the A pronounced as in *cat*) the slope formed by rock fragments at the base of a cliff or steep slope; or the rocks themselves (The rocks are also called *scree.*)

"From there, proceed along talus slopes to Morning Star Campground." — from a description of a hike in Glacier National Park, on NationalGeographic.com, 2010

Body parts

lunula ("LOON-yə-lə"): the pale, half-moon-shaped area at the base of a fingernail

"The word is so handy: Alone or in a pair, lunulae resemble the moon." — from an undated essay by JoAnna Novak, on the website *Catapult*

canthus ("KAN-thəss") either corner of the eye, where the upper and lower eyelids meet

epicanthus ("eh-pih-KAN-thəss") a small fold of skin covering the inner corner of the eye, common among East Asian people

tragus ("TRAY-ghəss") the cartilaginous protrusion at the front of the ear, which partially blocks the opening

"Celebrities led the trend, with the likes of Zoë Kravitz, Rihanna and Scarlett Johansson all sporting a tragus piercing." — from an article in *Elle* magazine, 2020

Body parts, part 2

carapace ("KAR-ə-pace," the first A pronounced as in *cat*) the upper shell of a turtle

"While all other sea turtles have hard, bony shells, the inky-blue carapace of the leatherback is somewhat flexible and almost rubbery to the touch." — from a page on *National Geographic*'s website

plastron ("PLA-strən," the A pronounced as in *cat*) the bottom plate of a turtle's shell; or a covering worn by a fencer to protect the chest

"I spent my first weekend of college in the hospital because I didn't wear a plastron. Now, I always wear a plastron." — from a Reddit thread about fencing injuries and the efficacy of plastrons

wattle/wattles the skin hanging from the throat of certain birds (e.g., the turkey) or other animals, often bright-colored; humorously, refers to the loose hanging skin on an older person's neck

"Just as a double chin is usually an unwelcome sign of fatness, wattles—used mainly in the plural, like wrinkles—mean that time's winged chariot is catching up." — William Safire, in the *New York Times,* 1983

Child's play

jackstraws the game of pick-up sticks: in which players try to remove a long, thin piece of wood, etc., from a pile without causing the other pieces to shift

"...Anna was still the quicker and better coordinated, and therefore usually the winner in the games they played: shuttlecock, fives, or paille maille; squalls, Meg Merrilies, jackstraws, or shove ha'penny." — John Barth, *The Sot-Weed Factor*

spillikins ("SPILL-ih-kinz") another name for jackstraws; or the long, thin pieces themselves

"Our little visitor has just left us, & left us highly pleased with her; she is a nice, natural, openhearted, affectionate girl, with all the ready civility which one sees in the best Children of the present day;... Half her time here was spent at Spillikins; which I consider as a very valuable part of our Household furniture..." — Jane Austen, *Letters*, 1807

Evelyn never failed to defeat her younger brother at Invisible Spillikins.

ducks and drakes the game of skipping flat stones across the surface of water

> "Ye poorest ship Boy might on ye Thames make duckes & drakes wth pieces of Eight, fetchd out of Spayne." — Anonymous, *Dick of Devonshire* (1626)

pips the dots on dice or dominos, indicating numerical value; or the small seeds of a fruit, such as an apple or orange

> "Big Jule... is mock-scary as he insists on shooting craps on credit, with his own invisible dice, whose special pips only he can see." — from a review of *Guys & Dolls* in the *Mail Tribune* (Medford, Oregon), 2015

mumblety-peg (spelled various ways; originally, "mumble the peg") a game in which players try to flip a knife from a series of positions so that it sticks in the ground, point-down

> "Jody and Fodder-wing... went into a corner to play mumbledepeg. Ma Baxter would never have allowed pocket knives to be flipped into her clean smooth floors." — Marjorie Kinnan Rawlings, *The Yearling*

> On *4 Way Street*, the Crosby, Stills, Nash & Young live album, after a false start to a new song, Crosby says of Nash, "He's very quick. You don't want to play mumbly-peg with him, he'll steal your leg." It didn't make sense to me when I heard it in the Seventies, and it still doesn't. But it's funny in context.

Printed matter

rubric ("ROO-brick") a heading in a book or manuscript, in a different color from the rest of the text; or, more commonly in recent years, a set of guidelines for evaluating student work

> The word comes from the root *rub-,* meaning red, because that was the most common color for rubrics.

> "Jacquet and his team map out what skills are required to be successful in each role and create a rubric based on that." — from an article in *Fortune*, 2022

colophon ("KOLL-ə-fon") a publisher's logo, on the title page or spine of a book; or a statement at the end of a book, giving information about its production

> "The volume was uninjured and entire from title-page to colophon." — Sir Walter Scott, *The Antiquary*

paraph ("PAR-əf" or "pə-RAFF") a flourish at the end of a signature

Did you assume those flourishes were purely ornamental? I did. In fact, though, the paraph's original purpose was to help make a signature unique, and thus harder to forge.

palindrome ("PAL-in-drome") a word, phrase, or sentence that's spelled the same backwards and forwards: famous examples include *Able was I ere I saw Elba* (Napoleon's complaint), and *Madam I'm Adam* (on meeting Eve)

The book *So Many Dynamos!*, written and illustrated by Jon Agee, contains dozens of original palindromes—including the title.

Used as an adjective: "We've closed out the palindrome year of 2002." — from an article in the *Green Bay Press-Gazette* (Wisconsin), 2003

Handy to have around

hamsa ("HAHM-sə") an amulet shaped like a stylized hand, commonly used in jewelry and decorations in the Middle East, believed to defend against the evil eye

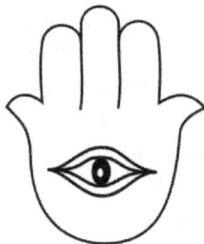

"Another age-old Silk Road amulet: hand-shaped *hamsas*, plentiful in markets from Morocco to Israel. The graceful palms—which Jews call Hands of Miriam and Muslims know as Hands of Fatima—are… available to go on necklaces, wall hangings, door knockers, coffee mugs, and what are surely meant to be protective candles." — from an article on NationalGeographic.com, 2020

Wooden structures

pergola ("PURR-ghə-lə") a framework in a park or garden on which plants can climb, resulting in a shaded area or walkway

What's the difference between a pergola and an arbor? The sides of a pergola are left open, while an arbor is usually enclosed by lattice-work.

"'Let's have cheese and white wine under that pergola,' suggested Van." — Vladimir Nabokov, *Ada*

burladero ("boor-lə-DAIR-oh") a wooden barrier in a bullring, behind which bullfighters can hide when chased

Have you ever seen a bullfight in a movie? Then you've seen a burladero—because there's always a moment when someone leaps behind it.

"Ernest Hemingway, standing next to me behind the burladero, couldn't help beaming. 'This bull's got all the defects in the world,' said Papa, 'and this boy just owns him now.'" — from an article in *Sports Illustrated*, 1959

Medievalia

oubliette ("oo-blee-ETT") a concealed dungeon, with a trap door in the ceiling as its only entrance

This word comes from the French word *oublier*, to forget. Once you're in the oubliette, you're forgotten.

"I found my arms swathed down—my feet tied so fast that mine ankles ache at the very remembrance—the place was utterly dark—the oubliette, as I suppose, of their accursed convent..." — Sir Walter Scott, *Ivanhoe*

portcullis ("port-KULL-əss") the heavy grating at the entrance to a castle, which can be lowered to prevent entry

How did medieval soldiers penetrate a portcullis? This question was posted on the website Quora, and answered by David Cartwright, in 2017, as follows: "Very often, they didn't. Castles were extremely hard to take down, and almost always survived the siege. The portcullis was actually perfect for the defender... The ideal thing was that the defender could shoot through it, harming the enemy as they approached the gate."

pennon ("PEN-ən") a long, narrow banner or streamer, formerly mounted at the top of a lance, now seen flying from the masts of yachts

Used figuratively: "There were little factory villages... with their tall chimneys, and their pennons of black smoke..." — Nathaniel Hawthorne, *Our Old Home* (an account of his travels in Britain)

cuirass ("kwih-RASS," to rhyme with *pass*) the piece of armor that protects the chest and back

> "My favourite application of bronze has always been the cuirass (breastplate), shield, spear, sword and greaves of the Spartan soldiers." — from an article in *Vanity Fair*, 2018

You slay me

uxoricide ("uck-ZORE-ə-side" or "-SORE-") the killing of a wife by a husband; or a husband who has killed his wife

> "This… may seem at first to be on the nutcake fringes of paranoia. But English history is studded with regicide and uxoricide." — from an article in the *Washington Post*, 1997, about speculation after the death of Princess Diana

mariticide ("MAR-it-ə-side," the A pronounced as in *cat*) the killing of a husband by a wife; or a wife who has killed her husband; or the killing of one's spouse, of any gender

> "The fashion of poisoning husbands… is a mania susceptible of… radical cure... We fear that these victims of mariticidal mania must be sacrificed to save surviving husbands." — from an article in the *Brooklyn Daily Eagle,* 1882

Things you can wear

burnoose ("bər-NOOSE") a hooded cloak worn by Arabs

> "Out of a 70-mm desert rides 'Lawrence of Arabia,' a thundering restoration of the 27-year-old legend… Arabs sway along with the wind in their burnooses. Lawrence… smiles philosophically from atop his camel." — from an article in the *Washington Post,* 1989

djellaba ("jə-LAH-bə") a long, loose outer garment commonly worn in North Africa

> Because this is an Arabic word, written in a different alphabet, it has more spellings in English than Hanukkah, including: jellaba, galabiya, and many more.

> "The [Egyptian] working man in the towns… rustles a few more notes in his trouser (no longer, let us note in passing, his galabiya) pocket." — from an article in the *Economist,* 1965

chaplet ("CHAP-lət") a wreath or garland for the head, such as those worn by ancient Romans on festive occasions or as a symbol of victory or authority

> "Around the leader's brow was a chaplet which marked him master of the feast, if not the giver." — Lew Wallace, *Ben-Hur*

peruke/periwig ("pə-ROOK," to rhyme with *duke;* "PER-ə-wig") a wig, especially the stylized kind worn in the 17th and 18th centuries (*Peruke* is the older term for *periwig*, which is also archaic.)

> British judges and barristers still wear periwigs.

> "I dined with Mrs. Vanhomrigh, where I keep my best gown and periwig, to put on when I come to town and be a spark." — Jonathan Swift, *The Journal to Stella*

"What have we here? A peruke upon a stand,
or the mummified remains of Lord Blathersby?"

snood a bag, made of netting or fabric, worn at the back of a woman's head and holding her the hair

> "Sheitels, Snoods, Tichels And Shpitzels: A Visual Guide To Orthodox Jewish Women's Head-Coverings" — headline of an article on the website JewInTheCity.com, 2020

barm the yeasty foam that rises to the top of fermenting malt liquors
"The sea was working like barm." — Sir Walter Scott, *The Antiquary*

creel a wicker basket used for holding and transporting just-caught fish.
"It is not every fish you hook that comes to the creel." — W.C. Smith, *Kildrostan* (1884)

camber the slight convexity of a road or other surface, usually created for the purpose of drainage; or the tilt at the curve of a track, enabling racing vehicles to maintain their speed (The word has other meanings when applied to the tires of a car or the wings of an airplane.)
"The corners [of the switchbacks] are built thoughtfully, with a camber favoring the biker." — from an article on a mountain-bike trail in Mexico, in the *Robb Report*, 2021

tachycardia ("ta-kih-KAR-dee-ə," the first A pronounced as in *cat*) an abnormally rapid heart rate
"...and Sandy's heart racing at a constant tachycardia and his brain racing and reeling out and so essential to... *keep moving, Cassady!*" — Tom Wolfe, *The Electric Kool-Aid Acid Test*

excelsior ("ek-SELL-see-ər" or "-or") wood shavings used to pack fragile items for shipping, or to stuff furniture; or a Latin word meaning *ever higher,* used as the motto of the State of New York
"When the bud vases came she unpacked the barrel herself, tearing her dress on a nail and getting excelsior all over the place." — John Cheever, *The Wapshot Chronicle*

Come to think of it, *Excelsior* could also have served as the motto of Ken Kesey's Merry Pranksters.

trifecta ("try-FEK-tə") a bet that correctly predicts the first three finishers in a race, in order
"A lucky OTB player on Staten Island is sitting on the windfall of a lifetime after hitting the boxcars trifecta in last Saturday's Kentucky Derby." — from an article in the *New York Post,* 2005

(The phrase *boxcar odds* refers to a longshot: because in craps, rolling "boxcars" can only be done with one possible combination, a six and a six.)

potter's field a place for the burial of unknown or indigent persons
"As coffins have stacked up... city officials wouldn't attribute the increase in burials in the city's longtime potter's field to the

coronavirus crisis." — from an article in New York's *Daily News*, April 2020

On a lighter note: In *It's a Wonderful Life,* if Lionel Barrymore had used his wealth to build a ballpark, he could have called it "Potter's Field."

phosphenes the lights you seem to see when you close your eyes hard or press on your eyeball

"His reward had been a nightmare display of images, always just beyond his ability to grasp properly—like the phosphenes that result from pressure on the eyeballs, but far more brilliant." — Arthur C. Clarke, *The Hammer of God*

Word Play

Murphy's Law & Disorder

Pinky Pensington has been found dead in his garden, skewered by a gnomon, mouth stuffed with excelsior, periwig tied about his wattles, with a papillote wrapped around his ankle. His lorgnette, found amid the folds of his burnoose, was missing one lens.

Challenge: Solve the mystery! Whodunit, and why?

(Confession: Not even the author knows the answer.)

A Few Lists

Architecture: parts of buildings, etc.

pediment ("PED-ə-mənt") the triangular part of a classical building's façade, above the columns and the entablature (see next entry)

"The West Pediment, the sculptural group of nine figures above the entrance to the Supreme Court Building, is the work of artist Robert I. Aitken..." — from the website of the U.S. Supreme Court

entablature ("en-TAB-lə-tchər" or "-tchoor") the upper part of a classical building: the part that is supported by columns; it consists of an architrave, frieze, and cornice, but does not include the triangular pediment

"The luxurious Breakfast Room's fireplace ensemble, including Roman Doric columns supporting an exquisite entablature, is as brilliantly designed, if not as eye-catching, as the Banquet Hall's triple fireplace." — from an article in the *Wall Street Journal*, 2022

architrave ("AR-kə-trave") the long beam that rests atop the columns

"Atop massive half-columns, 38 Atlases, each 25 feet tall and carved from limestone, seemingly held up the architrave... with their bent arms." — from an article in the *New York Times*, 2020

frieze ("FREEZ") a decorative band, sculpted or painted, occupying the space between architrave and cornice

Ancient Greek cop to bas-relief carvings: "Frieze!"

cornice ("KOR-niss") the crown of a building: its edge against the sky; or, on a classical building, the element above the frieze and below the pediment; or, indoors, the ornamental moulding just below the ceiling

capital the topmost part of a column, upon which the architrave rests

You may be familiar with the most famous styles of Greek capitals: Doric, Ionic, and Corinthian. Doric: flat, square, simple. Ionic: curved in two *volutes,* resembling ram's horns. Corinthian: ornate, modeled on acanthus leaves.

plinth a square slab that serves as a base for a column; or a pedestal

"What Should Be Done With All the Empty Confederate Monument Plinths?" — title of article in *Architectural Digest*, 2017

bollard ("BAHL-ərd") a short, sturdy post, usually one of a series: on a wharf, they're used to moor ships with ropes; on a street, they prevent cars from passing while allowing pedestrian access

> "The City Council passed legislation that will require the city to install bollards on sidewalks to ensure pedestrians' safety in the aftermath of a vehicle terror attack in Lower Manhattan..." — from an article in the *Observer*, 2017

cantilever ("KANT-ə-lee-vər," the first syllable rhyming with *ant*) a long, horizontal beam or girder, securely mounted at one end, with the other end projecting outward

> "...they are vista-grabbing, profit-generating cantilevers the likes of which Frank Lloyd Wright probably did not contemplate in 1935 when he designed a rural residence known as Fallingwater, which levitated, with assistance from cantilevers, above a 30-foot waterfall in Mill Run, Pa." — from an article about new cantilevered buildings in NYC, in the *New York Times,* 2014

mansard ("MAN-sard") a steep, four-sided roof, used commonly in France in the 1800s

> "It was a craze, a fad, just like Art Deco... The mansard mania of 1868 to 1873 swept over New York with a peculiar incandescence, but then went out like a guttering candle." — from an article in the *New York Times,* 2011

widow's walk a platform on the roof of a house, with a railing; this architectural feature originated in New England, and usually commanded a view of the ocean

> "Many older houses along the coast have what are usually described as a 'widow's walk.' But, contrary to popular belief, these may have been built as much for fighting chimney fires as they were for catching a first glimpse of returning seafarers." — from a story on NPR.org, 2006

lintel ("LIN-təl") a horizontal piece of wood, stone, steel, or concrete that spans the top of a door or window and supports the materials above it

> When you're feeling low on inspiration: "You say to a brick, 'What do you want, brick?' And brick says to you, 'I like an arch.' And you say to brick, 'Look... arches are expensive and I can use a concrete lintel... What do you think of that, brick?'

Brick says: 'I like an arch.'" — architect Louis I. Kahn, quoted in an article on the website ArchitecturalDigest.com, 2015

casement a window that opens like a door, on side hinges

"Long, narrow-shaped casement windows are a versatile choice for Tudor homes." — from an article on the website Milgard.com

lunette ("loo-NET") a window or opening shaped like a crescent or half-moon; or anything in this shape

"…Colonial American elements, including the lunette window and beadboard walls and ceiling, are complemented by furnishings such as the four-poster bed and the Windsor chair." — from an article in *Architectural Digest,* 2009

corbel ("KORE-bəl") a piece of stone, wood, or metal that projects outward from a wall and supports something above it

"…the grim, grotesque human heads for corbels, every one differing from the other, where the mason seems to have indulged his humorous fancy without regard to the sacred character of the house…" — William Howitt, describing a typical village church, in *Rural Life of England* (1838)

mullion ("MULL-yən") a vertical member that supports a glass wall, or that separates adjoining windows

"Wrapped in a glass curtain wall with steel mullions that catch the Arabian sun, the building tapers gradually from its Y-shaped base, with setbacks culminating in a 700-foot spire." — from a description of the Burj Khalifa in Dubai, in *Architectural Digest,* 2018

muntin ("MUN-tən") a narrow piece of wood or metal that separates the panes of a window

Some sources define *mullion* this way, too; but others make the distinction I've made here.

oculus ("AHK-yə-ləss") a round, eye-like window or opening, especially in the center of a dome

The transit hub formerly located under the old World Trade Center has reopened a block away, beneath a spectacular structure called the Oculus, designed by Santiago Calatrava. The building—which suggests a bird's skeleton, or an angel's wings—doesn't feature a traditional oculus, but it lets plenty of light in from above.

fanlight a small window above a door or another window, in the shape of a semicircle or a rectangle

> "Nothing—nothing! Just the scent of camphor, and dust-motes in a sunbeam through the fanlight over the door. The little old house! A mausoleum!" — John Galsworthy, *To Let*

pilaster ("pə-LASS-tər") a flat, decorative, non-weight-bearing element on a wall, resembling a column

> "...our taste in building rejects paint... and shows the original grain of the wood: refuses pilasters and columns that support nothing, and allows the real supporters of the house honestly to show themselves." — Ralph Waldo Emerson, "Beauty"

porte cochère ("PORT koh-SHAIR") a covered entrance to a house or public building, designed to shelter passengers exiting a carriage or car

> "Under the glass porte-cochère of a theatre Amory stood, watching the first great drops of rain splatter down and flatten to dark stains on the sidewalk." — F. Scott Fitzgerald, *This Side of Paradise*

quoin ("KOIN") an exterior corner of a building; or a cornerstone; or any of the stones or bricks at the outer corners of a building

> "The architectural detail we call the quoin... is often used as decoration, defining space by visually outlining the geometry of a building." — from an article on the website ThoughtCo.com

> To avoid possible confusion: Shakespeare coined the phrase *coign of vantage* in *Macbeth*. (The first word is pronounced the same way as *coin* and *quoin*.) It means "a position from which one can easily observe what's going on." A famous painting with the title *"Coign of Vantage,"* by Sir Laurence Alma-Tadema, shows three lovely women in classical garb watching a ship return on a pale azure sea, far below.

spandrel ("SPAN-drəl") one of the two roughly triangular spaces formed by the top of an arch and the rectangle that encloses it: often filled with ornament; or, in a multistory building, the space above the top of one window and below the windowsill above it.

> "In the curved spandrels of the [Washington Square] arch, [Stanford] White placed allegorical winged figures carrying war and peace themed symbols such as banners, horns, and laurel wreaths." — from an article on the website CreatingDigitalHistory.wikidot.com

pont-levis/pontlevis ("PAHNT LEV-ee" or "LEV-iss") a drawbridge, especially at the entrance to a castle

rafter one of the sloping beams that support a roof, running from the eaves to the roof's peak

> "A yellow bulb hangs from the rafters but the service door is open and the areaway is filled with the darkness of the evening." — Walker Percy, *The Moviegoer*

joist a timber or piece of steel, one of a parallel series, which supports a floor or ceiling

> "This project is heavy, so attach it to a heavy-duty hook in a ceiling joist for hanging." — from an article in *Better Homes & Gardens*, 2021

balustrade ("BAL-əss-traid," the first A pronounced as in *cat*) a railing and the vertical balusters that support it, forming a barrier around the edge of a terrace, etc.

> "The priest's figure now stood upright in the pulpit… crowned by a massive red face, appearing above the balustrade." — James Joyce, "Grace"

baluster ("BAL-əss-tər," the first A pronounced as in *cat*) one of several upright legs or columns supporting a railing: often shaped like a vase

banister ("BAN-əss-tər," the first A pronounced as in *cat*) the handrail at the side of a staircase; or, the handrail and its vertical supports

> "Banisters! … The most exciting part of any staircase! The elderly cling to them. The young and sprightly slide down them. Mary Poppins slides up them." — from Ken Jennings's blog, *The Debunker*

newel post ("NOO-əl" or, if you're British, "NYOO-əl") the upright post at the top or bottom of a staircase, where the handrail ends (a *newel cap* rests on top)

> "The part where Clark 'fixes' the newel post by sawing it off with a chainsaw is an homage to *It's a Wonderful Life*." — from an article about *National Lampoon's Christmas Vacation* on the website MentalFloss.com, 2008

vernacular architecture the common architecture of a culture, seen in buildings erected without an architect's involvement

> "Frank Lloyd Wright described vernacular architecture as 'Folk building growing in response to actual needs, fitted into the environment by people who knew no better than to fit them with native feeling.'" — from an article on the website StructuresInsider.com

Googie architecture a style common in the U.S. in the 1950s, featuring vivid colors and striking shapes reminiscent of cars, jets, and rockets

> "This style wasn't just about futurism or expressiveness; it was strategic. Googie architecture was designed to get drivers to stop and patronize roadside businesses." — from an article on the website Curbed.com

> According to the same article, the name comes from a coffee shop named Googie's in West Hollywood. An architecture critic named the style after the restaurant.

Inside a church

narthex ("NAR-thex," the TH pronounced as in *with*) a lobby or vestibule that leads to the nave of a church

> "Most of the congregation that had gathered in little groups on the steps and in the narthex fell back from them as they entered." — Sue Miller, *Family Pictures*

nave ("NAYV") the central part of a church, where most of the congregation sits

> "The candles on the high altar had been extinguished but the fragrance of incense still floated down the dim nave." — James Joyce, *A Portrait of the Artist as a Young Man*

chancel ("CHAN-səl") the part of a church that contains the altar and seats for the choir

> "…he followed the others in, blinking in the screened light. The coffin lay on its bier before the chancel, four tall yellow candles at its corners… Mr Bloom… fitted his black hat gently on his left knee and, holding its brim, bent over piously." — James Joyce, *Ulysses*

rood screen an ornate screen, usually of carved wood or stone, that separates the nave from the chancel in a church

> "Harriet sat dreamily beside her, with eyes fixed on the softly-tinted saints in the rood-screen." — Dorothy L. Sayers, *Gaudy Night*

transept ("TRAN-sept") in a cross-shaped church, either of the arms of the cross, intersecting the nave at right angles

> "The transept of the Jesuit Church in Gardiner Street was almost full; and still at every moment gentlemen entered from the side door and, directed by the lay-brother, walked on tiptoe along the

aisles until they found seating accommodation." — James Joyce, "Grace"

crossing the place in a cross-shaped church where the four arms of the cross meet; in many churches, a tower or dome covers the crossing

apse ("APPS") a recess at one end of a church, behind the chancel, often beneath a dome

> "But another priest, Don Mario Carminati at the church of San Giuseppe... refused such rites, instead piling up coffins in his aisles and apse." — from an article about Covid-19 in Italy, in the *New York Review of Books,* 2020

sacristy ("SAK-rəss-tee," the A pronounced as in *cat*) a room in a church where a priest's vestments and other ritual objects are kept, and where the priest prepares for a service

> "He thought of the dark silent sacristy. There were dark wooden presses there where the crimped surplices lay quietly folded. It was not the chapel but still you had to speak under your breath. It was a holy place." — James Joyce, *A Portrait of the Artist as a Young Man*

Clerical garments

wimple a cloth that covers the head, the sides of the face, and the neck: common in the Middle Ages, still worn by some nuns

> "She drew the wimple well over her head, so that in its shadows her face might lie concealed..." — Rafael Sabatini, *Mistress Wilding*

guimpe ("GIMP") a blouse or undergarment that is visible beneath a low-necked dress; or the white cloth worn by some nuns around neck, shoulders, and bust

> "Behind the grating... one perceived... a head, of which only the mouth and the chin were visible; the rest was covered with a black veil. One caught a glimpse of a black guimpe, and a form that was barely defined, covered with a black shroud. That head spoke with you, but did not look at you and never smiled at you." — Victor Hugo, *Les Miserables* (translated by Isabel F. Hapgood)

cassock ("KASS-ək," the A pronounced as in *has*) the coat worn by a clergyman, usually ankle-length and dark (the French word for the same garment is *soutane*)

The shortest chapter in *Moby-Dick* is entitled "The Cassock," and describes a whaler playfully donning a whale's penis as if it were a priest's cassock.

surplice ("SƏR-pləss") a loose white vestment worn over the cassock

"Why does the judge don his robe, the priest his surplice, the scholar his gown, the barrister his wig, the queen her crown?" — from an article in *National Review*, 2020

chasuble ("CHAZZ-ə-bəl") a sleeveless outer vestment worn by priests when celebrating Mass

"… his chasuble had swung open… as he turned to the altar again after having blessed the people." — James Joyce, *A Portrait of the Artist as a Young Man*

alb (the A pronounced as in *pal*) a white linen vestment worn during church services: ankle-length, usually belted

"I hadn't a clean alb left and I'm not much of a hand at laundering." — Barbara Pym, *Less Than Angels*

biretta ("BƏ-rət-ə") a square cap worn by some Roman Catholic clergy

Not to be confused with a Beretta: a brand of pistol commonly used by police and soldiers.

miter/mitre ("MY-tər") the tall headdress worn by bishops, tapering to a point at the top

"PRELATE'S MITRE FALLS OFF: Bishop of Salford Finds That It Is Too Small for His Head." —headline in the *New York Times,* 1925

And two more things: i) the bishop in chess is topped with a stylized miter; ii) the word also refers to the joint between two pieces of wood, each ending in a 45° angle.

Art and art history

chiaroscuro ("kee-ah-rə-SKOO-roh") (literally, "light-dark") the juxtaposition of strongly contrasting lights and darks in a painting

"Artists who are famed for the use of chiaroscuro include Leonardo da Vinci and Caravaggio. Leonardo employed it to give a vivid impression of the three-dimensionality of his figures, while Caravaggio used such contrasts for the sake of drama." — from the website of the National Gallery in London

contrapposto ("kon-trə-PAHS-toh") a position in which most of the weight rests on one leg: a relaxed, natural pose, used by sculptors in ancient Greece and revived in the Italian Renaissance

> The most famous example of contrapposto is Michelangelo's *David.*

> "Why Viewers Are Drawn to Renaissance Artists' Go-To Pose: A new study finds that the contrapposto stance reduces the waist-to-hip ratio, an attribute popularly associated with attractiveness" — headline of an article in *Smithsonian Magazine*, 2019

I dreamed I stood naked in a niche, while passing tourists
admired my contrapposto.

sfumato ("sfoo-MAH-toh") a technique in painting or drawing, pioneered by Leonardo da Vinci, in which transitions between colors and shapes are softened so as to become imperceptible

> "In all encounters with Leonardo there is never a definite answer to any of the artistic, aesthetic, historical or psychological questions which he raises. The *sfumato*—the suggestive smoke-like contour—is as much a characteristic of his personality as it is a feature of his drawing." — from an article in the *New Statesman*, 1965

impasto ("im-PAHSS-toh") a technique in painting in which the paint is applied thickly enough to stand out from the surface

"Scientists solve the mystery of Rembrandt's 'impasto' paint recipe" — headline of an article on the website ArsTechnica, 2019

gesso ("JESS-oh") a white mixture used to prepare a surface (such as canvas or wood) for a painting; gesso stiffens the surface, adds texture, and prepares the surface to receive paint

"Leonardo was always striving for something new... For example, he used powdered glass mixed with gesso... in priming a painting to give it, presumably, a kind of radiance." — from an article in the *Atlantic,* 2019

secco ("SEK-oh") (short for *secco fresco*) the art of painting on dry plaster; or such a painting (as opposed to *fresco,* which is done on wet plaster)

"Leonardo da Vinci's *The Last Supper* is one of the most famous *secco* frescos... The *secco* approach allowed him more time to complete the fresco, but it unfortunately contributed to the gradual deterioration of the painting." — from an article on the website DrawPaintAcademy.com, 2020

xylography ("zy-LAHG-rə-fee") the art of printmaking with wood, e.g., woodcuts or wood engravings

Where did this strange word come from? Aha: from the root *xyl-,* which means *wood.* This should help you remember that a xylophone has wooden bars (even though most toy versions use metal).

aquarelle ("ahk-wə-RELL") a painting technique using transparent watercolors; or a painting in this style

"Van immediately recognized Ardis Hall as depicted in the two-hundred-year-old aquarelle that hung in his father's dressing room..." — Vladimir Nabokov, *Ada*

verdigris ("VƏR-də-gree" or "VƏR-də-greese") the green patina that forms on copper or bronze exposed to the elements over time

"Most people know copper reacts with air to form verdigris, but the Statue of Liberty is its own special color because of its unique environmental conditions." — from an article on the website ThoughtCo.com, 2019

pentimento ("pen-tə-MEN-toh") an image that remains (or becomes) visible through a painting that has covered it (The word is Italian for *repentance.*)

"Alabama's flag is a giant crimson X, St. Andrew's cross, that's almost a pentimento of the Confederate flag." — from an article in the *Washington Post,* 2019

"Paul Cezanne was among the first to actually embrace pentimenti as something more than just evidence of a work in progress; he began to deliberately include a lot of pentimenti in his drawings to enhance the expressive nature of a work, as well as the three-dimensional appearance." — from an article on the website PrincipleArtTalk.com, 2015

scumble ("SKUM-bəl") to soften the outlines of a drawing by blurring or rubbing; or to soften the lines or colors of a painting with a thin coat of color

"The confusion of the times… the scumbling of boundary lines." — from an article in the *Times* (London), 1977 (That initial phrase would have made a great headline—especially in the *Times.*)

quattrocento ("KWAH-troh-CHEN-toh") the 15th century in Italian art and architecture

This word literally means *four hundred*, and confused me in Art History class: why is the 15th century called the *four hundred*? Well… another way of saying "15th century" is "the 1400s." That gets us closer.

craquelure ("krak-ə-LOOR") a fine network of cracks on a surface, especially on an old painting

"The team then digitally stitched the scans together to construct a model that would allow them to study the [Mona Lisa's] color, relief, and craquelure." — from an article in *ARTnews* magazine, 2007

trompe l'oeil ("TRAHMP l(e)oy," but with a French accent) (literally, "deceive the eye") a style of painting that deceives the viewer into believing that the image is a real, three-dimensional object

"…Eystein showed himself to be a prodigious master of the trompe l'oeil in the depiction of various objects surrounding his dignified dead models and making them look even deader by contrast to the fallen petal… that he rendered with such love and skill." — Vladimir Nabokov, *Pale Fire*

"…Aristotle's arguments in defense of art do not really challenge Plato's view that all art is an elaborate trompe l'oeil, and therefore a lie. But he does dispute Plato's idea that art is useless." — Susan Sontag, "Against Interpretation"

plein air ("plain AIR") painting outdoors in daylight

"For plein-air… painters, the arrival at each location begins with scoping out a scene to paint. This is a relatively quick exercise, as the light is changing by the minute…" — from an article on the website NJ.com, 2011

painterly in a style that emphasizes color, texture, and brushwork, without sharp outlines

"Botticelli is a linear painter, whilst Rembrandt's work would be considered painterly." — Frederic Taubes, *The Painter's Dictionary of Materials and Methods*

provenance ("PRAHV-ə-nənss") a documented history of an art object's past ownership; or, the source or origin of something

"…though the tool makes seeing lots of information about a painting's provenance in one place easy, tracking down the real history of the artwork can be anything but." — from an article in *Smithsonian Magazine*, 2017

Fortifications

parapet ("PAR-ə-pet," the first A pronounced as in *cat*) a wall, usually along the edge of a roof, that serves to shield soldiers; or a wall along the side of a bridge, meant to protect people from falling

"…she threw open the latticed window… and in an instant after, stood on the very verge of the parapet…" — Sir Walter Scott, *Ivanhoe*

battlement a parapet on top of a castle's outer wall with open spaces (for archers, etc.)

"…I will shave thy crown for thee!—Here, let them tear the scalp from his head, and then pitch him headlong from the battlements…" — Sir Walter Scott, *Ivanhoe*

breastwork a crude temporary wall, chest-high and often made of earth, that soldiers can fire over while standing

"During the fight the whites had thrown up breastworks but they were not very high and we could easily have jumped over them." — from an article in the *Star Tribune* (Minneapolis), reprinting an interview with Chief Big Eagle (a combatant in the U.S.-Dakota War of 1862), which originally appeared in 1894 in the *St. Paul Pioneer Press*

merlons ("MƏR-lənz") the toothlike projections on a battlement behind which soldiers can take shelter

crenels ("KREN-əlz") the open spaces on a battlement, between the merlons, through which soldiers can shoot

crenellation ("kren-ə-LAY-shən") an alternating series of crenels and merlons

embrasure ("em-BRAY-zhər") a narrow opening in a battlement, through which soldiers can shoot while being shielded from return fire

"…every arrow had its individual aim, and flew by scores together against each embrasure and opening in the parapets…" — Sir Walter Scott, *Ivanhoe*

loophole a narrow opening in a wall, through which soldiers can fire

"Ah, the slim castle! dwindled of late years, / But more mysterious; gone to ruin—trails / Of vine through every loophole." — Robert Browning, *Sordello*

rampart a wall built as a defense for a city or a castle, usually with a parapet on top; or the walkway near the top of such a wall

"O say can you see, by the dawn's early light,
What so proudly we hail'd at the twilight's last gleaming,
Whose broad stripes and bright stars through the perilous fight
O'er the ramparts we watch'd were so gallantly streaming?" — Francis Scott Key, "The Star-Spangled Banner"

bulwark ("BULL-wərk") a strong defensive wall

"Madison's early draft discussed more fully the protections for the written word. He wrote, 'The people shall not be deprived or abridged of their right to speak, to write, or to publish their sentiments; and the freedom of the press, as one of the great bulwarks of liberty, shall be inviolable.'" — from an article about the First Amendment, on the American Bar Association's website, 2019

bastion ("BASS-chən") a fortification that projects beyond a wall, enabling soldiers to fire in multiple directions; or a place or institution that strongly defends some principle or way of life

As a paralegal in the 1970s, I found myself at a meeting of the coop board at the Pierre when a resident, protesting a change of policy, memorably referred to the building as "the last bastion of gracious living in New York."

earthwork an embankment made of earth, used as a fortification on an open battlefield

"Although Greene's men were outnumbered more than 2-to-1, the earthworks helped to minimize Union casualties while Confederate blood spilled onto Culp's Hill's rocky slopes." — from an article about the Battle of Gettysburg on History.net

machicolation ("mə-CHICK-ə-LAY-shən") an opening in the underside of a parapet, through which rocks, burning objects, molten lead, etc., could be dropped on attacking enemies

barbican ("BAR-bih-kən") an outer fortification defending a castle or walled city; or a double tower over a gate or bridge, which serves as a watchtower

> "Long before his pursuers had reached the courtyard and alarmed the watch at the barbican, the American had… hastened across the broad clearing…" — Edgar Rice Burroughs, *The Mad King*

Horse-drawn carriages in 19th century fiction

Popular in More Than One Country

barouche ("bə-ROOSH") a luxurious four-wheeled carriage with a folding hood, seats for four passengers, and a raised seat in front for a driver

> "We got into an open barouche at the station and started on a brisk trot for the rendezvous…" — Henry Miller, *Tropic of Cancer*

post-chaise ("post-SHAYZ") a closed fast carriage with four wheels, used for transporting mail and/or passengers; the driver sat on one of the horses

fiacre ("fee-AHK-rə") a small hackney coach, i.e., a carriage for hire, with four wheels

> The name comes from the Hotel St. Fiacre in Paris, where Nicholas Sauvage hired out his horses and carriages for ten sous an hour, starting in 1645. Later, Saint Fiacre became the patron saint of cab drivers.
>
> "…after Cesare had removed two middle-aged ladies and a cab driver, they took possession of a fiacre and clattered off pell-mell for the Ponte San Trinitá." — Thomas Pynchon, *V.*

In England

hackney a carriage (or, much later, a car) for hire

tilbury ("TILL-bə-ree") an open two-wheeled carriage

stanhope an open, one-seated carriage, usually with two wheels, sometimes with four

phaeton ("FAY-ə-tən") an open carriage with four large wheels

gig a light, two-wheeled carriage drawn by a single horse

curricle a light, open, two-wheeled carriage drawn by a pair of horses and capable of moving at a brisk clip

> "In *Northanger Abbey,* Henry Tilney drives a curricle; John Thorpe drives a gig. Could there be any significance to those gentlemen's respective vehicles? ...if you compare the two young men, one can imagine that Jane Austen did not arbitrarily assign them a vehicle... In more modern terms, Thorpe drove a Firebird, but Henry drove a Trans Am." — from an article on the website TilneysAndTrapdoors.com

In Russia

droshky an open carriage with four wheels; passengers sat on a bench in the back

> "...the haphazard way Russian cabs had of turning whenever they liked... so that instead of the straight, self-conscious stream of modern traffic one sees... a dream-wide street with droshkies all awry under incredibly blue skies..." — Vladimir Nabokov, *The Real Life of Sebastian Knight*

britzka ("BRITCH-kə") a long open carriage with a folding hood and room inside for reclining on an overnight journey

Elsewhere

litter a seat for one passenger, usually enclosed (with curtains for privacy), borne by two or more carriers ("litter-bearers")

> "The better people... began moving towards the Circus about the first hour of the morning, the noble and very rich among them distinguished by litters and retinues of liveried servants." — Lew Wallace, *Ben-Hur: A Tale of the Christ*

palanquin ("pal-ən-KEEN") an enclosed litter with one seat, carried by four or more bearers lifting two long poles: formerly common in India and East Asia

> "One of the most captivating items in the show is a palanquin from 1856, which was used to carry a wealthy bride to her groom's home." — from an article in the *Wall Street Journal,* 2019

calèche/calash ("kə-LESH"/"kə-LASH") a light, two-wheeled carriage with a removable folding hood, formerly common in Canada

aquavit ("AHK-wə-veet," the first A pronounced as in *fa-la-la*) a clear liquor produced mainly in Scandinavia, made from potatoes and grain and flavored with caraway seeds or other herbs

> "The idea is as Norwegian as cross-country skis and aquavit."
> — from an article in *National Geographic*, 2020

slivovitz ("SLIVV-ə-vitz") a plum brandy produced mainly in the Balkans and eastern Europe

> "The night is chill, mein Herr, and my master the Count bade me take all care of you. There is a flask of slivovitz... underneath the seat, if you should require it." — Bram Stoker, *Dracula*

rakia/rakija ("RAH-kee-ə") a strong brandy made from various fruits, popular in the Balkans

> "It ends at a series of bunkers where Serb soldiers swig rakia to keep out the frost." — from an article in the *Independent on Sunday* (London), 1994

kvass a slightly alcoholic beverage produced in Central and Eastern Europe, usually made with rye flour and malt

> "And if I do drink some kvass, why is it that there is bound to be something of the most indelicate nature in it, such as a beetle?" — Anton Chekhov, *The Cherry Orchard*

pousse-café ("poose-kah-FAY") an after-dinner drink containing liqueurs of different colors, in separate layers

> "Whether your interest in the drinking habits of New Yorkers is envious, non-committal or purely academic, you really ought to know about George's 32-deck pousse cafe." — from an article in the *Reno Evening Gazette*, 1938

caipirinha ("kai-pə-REEN-yə," the first syllable rhyming with *eye*) a cocktail popular in Brazil: ingredients include cachaça (a liqueur made from sugar cane juice), lime, and sugar.

> "Cocktail geeks aside, if you mention the word 'cachaca' to most people, you'll receive a blank stare. What is surprising, though, is that many of the same people will recognize the most famous drink made with cachaca: the caipirinha." — from an article in the *Washington Post*, 2007

Parts of a boat (and other nautical vocabulary)

bow ("BAO") the front of the ship

> "My pathway led by confusion boats
> Mutiny from stern to bow
> Ah, but I was so much older then
> I'm younger than that now." — Bob Dylan, "My Back Pages"

> Even if this confuses you, at least you can understand "stern to bow."

stern the rear of the ship

> "Called Senses and measuring 193 feet from bow to stern, it... has no fewer than 10 suites for him, his lucky young wife and friends." — from an article in the *Independent*, 2011, about a yacht bought by Larry Page, co-founder of Google

> Superfluous note: When I searched for a quote using the phrase "from bow to stern," the first result was an article about the bow used by violinist Isaac Stern.

fore/forward the front of the ship; or toward the front, especially as compared with an object or location on the ship

aft the rear of the ship; or toward the rear

> "From fore to aft?" "He'll feel a draft." — Alan Jay Lerner, "Then You May Take Me to the Fair," from *Camelot* (Here, Sir Sagramore is boasting to Guinevere that he'll run Lancelot through with his sword: not exactly a nautical quote, but a good one.)

abaft ("ə-BAFT") to the rear of; specifically, toward the stern of a boat

> "His boats were carvel-built, half-decked, smack-rigged, and with an outrigger sail abaft." — W.C. Smith, *A Short History of the Irish Sea Herring Fisheries* (Wouldn't that be a great title for a novel?)

prow ("PRAO") the front of the ship: sometimes used interchangeably with *bow*, sometimes meaning the most forward part of the bow

> "I seized a large Man of War, ty'd a Cable to the Prow, and, lifting up the anchors, I stripped myself... and, drawing it after me, between wading and swimming arrived at the Royal Port of Blefuscu." — Jonathan Swift, *Gulliver's Travels*

poop (deck) an elevated deck at the rear of a ship that also serves as the roof of a cabin

> Is there a child in America who, having heard this phrase, doesn't delight in saying it?

port the left side, when you're on the boat and facing forward (The traditional way to remember this is to think, *The ship left the port.*)

> "That night, she turned north again; and, at dawn the next day, spotted two sails far off her port bow." — from a history of the U.S.S. Saratoga, on the website USS-Saratoga.com

starboard ("STAR-bərd") the right-hand side, when you're on the boat and facing forward

> "The convention worldwide is that a vessel on a starboard tack has right of way." — Craig Collie, *The Reporter and the Warlords*

larboard ("LAR-bərd") the left-hand side: an archaic term for *port*

> You can see why this word fell out of use, can't you? Picture the captain calling out orders in a gale: "Whud he say? Is it starboard or larboard?" "Damn'd if I know!"

> "…yonder off to larboard is Castlehaven Point, and two points farther down is Cooke's." — John Barth, *The Sot-Weed Factor*

gunwale ("GUN-əl") the top edge of either side of a boat's hull

> "Our canoes were not a foot above the water at the gunwales." — David and Charles Livingstone, *Narrative of an Expedition to the Zambesi*

bower (or bower anchor) (rhymes with *flower*) a large anchor carried on the bow of a ship

> "…the thunderbolt had made hay of the best bower anchor, but otherwise all was well…" — Patrick O'Brian, *The Mauritius Command* (The "best bower" is the larger of a pair.)

scuppers the openings in the side of a ship, which allow water to run off the deck

> "…she was *holy* enough before we had done with her, riddled like a sieve … and every scupper of her running blood and water." — Frederick Marryat, *Peter Simple* (1833)

mizzenmast the mast aft of a ship's mainmast

> "Marlow sat cross-legged right aft, leaning against the mizzenmast." — Joseph Conrad, *Heart of Darkness*

cleat ("KLEET") a metal fitting, usually T-shaped, to which a rope can be fastened

> "Since mooring is a crucial part of boating, the Cleat Hitch Knot is an essential knot to learn. And while every good sailor should know it, you'd be surprised at just how many boaters get it wrong." — from an article on the website BoatSafe.com, 2020

draft the depth of water a boat needs in order to float (measured vertically from the waterline to the bottom of the boat, when it's fully loaded with passengers, equipment, cargo, etc.)

> The draft of a Sunfish, a small sailboat, is slightly less than three feet; the draft of the *Titanic* was thirty-four feet, seven inches.

dead reckoning calculating a ship's location based on the distance traveled (speed x time) and course (according to the compass), taking into account the drift due to the current, without using electronics or observations of the stars and planets; the term is also used for aircraft

> "We had drifted too much to allow of our dead reckoning being anywhere near the mark." — Richard Henry Dana, *Two Years Before the Mast*

Boats of different times and places

corsair ("CORE-sair" or "core-SAIR") a pirate ship; or a pirate (especially a French privateer)

> "On a resupply mission to Malta in August 1801, the twelve-gun schooner *Enterprise* under the command of Lieutenant Andrew Sterett encountered a 14-gun Tripolitan corsair." — from an article in *National Review*, 2020

corvette ("core-VET") a small, fast warship

> "HMS *Surprise* was the name the Royal Navy gave to the French Navy's corvette *Unité* after her capture in 1796... Patrick O'Brian set many of his Aubrey–Maturin series aboard HMS *Surprise*..." — from the Wikipedia entry on "HMS *Surprise* (1796)"

coracle ("CORE-ə-kəl") a small, roundish boat with a wicker frame covered by watertight material, used since ancient times in the British Isles

> "Coracles provided an easy way of crossing a river without travelling considerable distances to reach a bridge or paying a toll... In the 19th Century, it was common to see coracles outside people's homes in Ironbridge where nearly every villager had their own coracle, hung in a tree when not in use." — from an article on the BBC's website

dhow ("DAO") a ship used in the Indian Ocean, with one or two masts

> "But before... / Any shape of sailing-craft was known, / The Junk and Dhow had a stern and a bow, / And a mast and a sail of their own.../ As they crashed across the Oceans on their own!" — Rudyard Kipling, "The Junk and the Dhow"

felucca ("fə-LOO-kə") a fast, narrow boat, propelled by sails or oars, formerly used in the Mediterranean and along the Nile

> Note: Both the dhow and the felucca have *lateen sails*. A lateen is a triangular sail set on a long yardarm that's mounted at an angle on the mast.

tender a boat that serves larger ships by transporting people or supplies between ship and shore

pinnace ("PIN-əss") a small boat (usually propelled by oars but able to be rigged with sails), carried aboard warships and merchant vessels during the Age of Sail, serving as a tender

> "A motor-pinnace splashed down heavily into the water from the cruiser, turned, and made for the sinking wreckage." — Nevil Shute, *Landfall*

trireme ("TRY-reem") a warship of ancient Greece or Rome, with three tiers of oars on each side

> "It is our Caesar's will, further, that you cause a hundred triremes… to be despatched without delay against the pirates who have appeared in the Aegean…" — Lew Wallace, *Ben-Hur*

Metrical feet

Note: In poetry, rhythm is measured in *meter*, which means the pattern of stressed and unstressed syllables in each line. A *metrical foot* usually consists of two or three syllables, one or two of them stressed; and a line of poetry consists of one or more metrical feet. Among the many standard metrical patterns, the most famous is *iambic pentameter*, or five *iambs* per line. Shakespeare used it in both his plays and his sonnets. See below for the definition of an iamb.

In the following definitions:
> " / " represents a stressed syllable
> "–" represents an unstressed syllable

iamb ("I-am"): – / ("I wish I had a bowl of mush")

> One of the cleverest cards I've ever received had a drawing of Shakespeare on the front, with the question, "Who's wishing you a happy birthday?" Inside was the answer: "Iamb, iamb, iamb, iamb, iamb." (However, I just noticed that the word *iamb* is actually a *trochee*, with the accent on the first syllable.)

trochee ("TROH-kee"): / – ("lonely cowboys lying naked")

anapest ("AN-ə-pest"): – – / ("what was *that*?" "I don't *know!*")

dactyl ("DAK-tl"): / – – ("solitude shmolitude")

spondee ("SPAHN-dee"): / / ("go, go, big Joe")

amphibrach ("AM-fə-brack"): – / – ("I knew it, she blew it")

amphimacer ("am-FIM-ə-sər"): / – / ("over there… over where?")

pyrrhic ("PIRR-ik"):   – – ("bye bye")

Winds

trade winds winds that reliably blow from east to west near the equator: for centuries, sailing ships used these winds to cross the oceans; they were an important factor in both colonization and trade

> "As warm air rises near the Equator… it flows toward the poles… The consistently circulating patterns of these air masses are known as trade winds." — from the website of *National Geographic* (citing a PBS Learning Media article on the Coriolis effect)

sirocco ("sə-RAHK-oh") a hot wind, originating in North Africa, that crosses the Mediterranean and often brings rain and/or dust to southern Europe, especially Italy

> "The lukewarm air of the sirocco breathed upon him, he leaned back among his cushions and gave himself to the yielding element, closing his eyes for very pleasure in an indolence as unaccustomed as sweet." — Thomas Mann, *Death in Venice* (translated by H.T. Lowe-Porter)

mistral ("MISS-trəl" or "mə-STRAHL") a cold wind that blows through southern France, toward the Mediterranean, in winter

> "Each day as we left with… the threat of the mistral whispering in the trees, our pensioner neighbours made the sign of the cross." — Jamie Ivey, *Extremely Pale Rosé*

williwaw ("WILL-ee-waw") a sudden, powerful, cold gust blowing from a mountainous coast to the sea, especially near the poles

> A gathering place in downtown Anchorage, Alaska, opened in 2015, with a restaurant, a lounge, a coffee bar, and a summer-only rooftop bar. The name of the complex: Williwaw.

libeccio ("lih-BETCH-ee-oh") a wind that blows from the southwest in Italy and often causes violent squalls

> "The Libecchio here howls like a chorus of fiends all day." — Percy Bysshe Shelley, *Letters*

simoom ("sə-MOOM") a strong, hot, sandy desert wind, especially in the Sahara or the Arabian desert

> "Herodotus records that a small nation called the Psylli marched into the desert to declare war on the simoom—and were subsequently buried by it." — from an article in *Harper's* magazine, 2019

haboob ("ha-BOOB") in Sudan, a strong wind that carries sand from the desert

> "...if I hadn't been wearing goggles she might've *blinded* me with that haboob she created." — Lucy Ellmann, *Ducks, Newburyport* (The narrator is describing a traumatic experience with a dental hygienist's abrasive cleaning device.)

A handful of hats

trilby ("TRILL-bee") in England, a soft felt hat with a narrow brim, turned slightly up at the back: like a fedora, except that the brim can't be adjusted

> "Puffing, consulting his wrist watch, and fanning himself with his trilby... he reached at last the transverse continuation of the looping road he had left below." — Vladimir Nabokov, *Pale Fire*

tam-o'-shanter ("tam-ə-SHAN-tər") a traditional Scottish cap with a round, flat top and a pom-pom in the center

> Robert Burns wrote a long poem called "Tam o' Shanter," that being the name of its hero. The name of the hat comes from the character in the poem.

mobcap a woman's full, loose cap, covering all of the hair, worn indoors (during the 18th and 19th centuries)

> "...in the 1860s, the British upper classes required their maids to wear a common uniform: a white mobcap, an apron, and a simple black dress." — from an article in the *Atlantic*, 2017

bicorne ("BY-korn") a hat with the brim turned up in on two sides, worn by European and American military officers in the early 19th century

> "When it came to the battlefield, Napoleon's personal style signifier... was his hat: a black felt bicorne... The convention of the time was to wear such hats with their corners pointing forward and back. In order to ensure he was instantly identifiable on the battlefield, Napoleon wore his sideways." — from an article on Christies.com, 2015

tricorn ("TRY-korn") a hat with the brim turned up on three sides: the three-cornered hat popular at the time of the American Revolution

"Get your tricorn hat on" — headline of an article about a Revolutionary War reenactment, in the *Boston Globe*, 2018

pickelhaube ("PICK-əl-how-beh") the spiked helmet formerly worn by German military men (still worn ceremonially in some countries)

"Germany's *Pickelhaube* helmet, distinguished by a lone spike jutting straight from its top, became a symbol of Prussian militarism in the early 20th century." — from an article on HistoryNet.com, 2020

"I see you are impressed by my pickelhaube.
And how could it be otherwise?"

kepi ("KAPE-ee" or "KEP-ee") a French military cap with a round flat top and a visor (the kind worn by gendarmes, the Foreign Legion, and Charles de Gaulle)

> "Both Vichy and Free French Legionnaires wore the traditional white kepi of the Legion..." — from an article on the website Historynet.com

topi ("TOE-pee") a pith helmet: lightweight, worn as protection from the sun

> "He still wore a topi, despite the darkness, and his face, to which the Ruling Race had contributed little beyond bad teeth, peered out of it pathetically..." — E.M. Forster, *A Passage to India*

shako ("SHA-koh," the A pronounced as in *cat,* or "SHAKE-oh") a tall, stiff military hat with a brim and a plume

> "In black-and-white school photos from the early '60s, Trump can be seen in boots, sash and a plumed shako, like some Austro-Hungarian infantryman." — from an article in the *New York Times*, 2018

busby ("BUZZ-bee") a tall fur hat worn by certain British soldiers

> Note: The guardsmen at Buckingham Palace do *not* wear busbies, though some dictionaries mistakenly say they do. According to the website BritishHeritage.com, the guardsmen wear *bearskin caps.*

Not exactly a hat, but...

havelock ("HAV-lock") a cloth covering for a cap, with a flap for the back of the neck

> "During the war... havelocks proved to be bulky and irritating (as well as a bright target for enemy sharpshooters), so most were quickly abandoned." — John D. Wright, *The Language of the Civil War*

Proper nouns you may encounter in literature

Harlequin and Columbine ("HAR-lih-kwin" or "-kin" and "KAH-ləm-bine," to rhyme with *fine*) traditional characters in comedy and pantomime: Columbine is Harlequin's saucy sweetheart

> These characters, popular in England in the 1700s and 1800s, derived from Italian *Commedia dell'arte*, in which they were known as Arlecchino and Colombina.

"Can we all still become excited over whether Harlequin will win his Columbine and outwit her father, whether Pierrot and Pierrette will reconcile?" — from a review of the Balanchine ballet *Harlequinade* in the *New York Times*, 1984

Xanthippe/Xantippe ("zan-THIP-ee"/"zan-TIP-ee") the wife of Socrates, legendary for shrewishness

"This woman was not very amiable in her person... She was, besides, a profes[sed] follower of that noble sect founded by Xantippe of old; ... for, to confess the truth, [her husband] was never master there, or anywhere else, in her presence." — Henry Fielding, *Tom Jones*

Dr. L.L. Zamenhof the inventor of Esperanto—which, in that language, means *One who hopes*

An ophthalmologist, Zamenhof developed the language as a means of preventing war. "Esperanto was meant to be the alternate language of everywhere, a universal second language... that would 'commit its users to transcend nationalism.'" — from a book review in the *New York Times,* 1984

Saracen ("SAR-ə-sən") an Arab Muslim: a word used by Christians during the Middle Ages; originally, a nomad of the Arabian desert who harassed the frontiers of the Roman Empire

"This reverend brother has been all his life engaged in fighting among the Saracens for the recovery of the Holy Sepulchre; he is of the order of Knights Templars, whom you may have heard of; he is half a monk, half a soldier." — Sir Walter Scott, *Ivanhoe*

Kaffir ("KAF-ər") a black African: an extremely offensive term used by white South Africans, especially during the apartheid era; also, among Muslims, an offensive term denoting a non-Muslim

"The kaffirs here in Joburg are terrible. I'm so sick of it." — part of a tirade by a white South African woman after thieves broke into her car: caught on video and reported in the *New York Times,* 2016 (She was later sentenced to three years in jail for her outburst—the first sentence of its kind.)

Cathay ("ka-THAY," the TH pronounced as in *with*) (poetic/archaic) China

"This is the story of the Jesuit who more than 500 years ago made himself part of Cathay." — from a roundup of books about "Outsiders in China" on the website *Daily Beast,* 2012

Deseret ("dezz-ə-RET") a state proposed by the Mormons in 1849, which would have comprised a large portion of the southwestern U.S.

In the *Book of Mormon,* this word is translated as *honeybee*, and signifies industrious, productive labor.

Bucephalus ("byoo-SEF-ə-ləss") ("bull-head") the war horse of Alexander the Great

> "Plutarch tells the story of how a 12-year-old Alexander won the horse... Since no one could tame the animal, Philip [Alexander's father] wasn't interested, but Alexander was and promised to pay for the horse should he fail to tame it. Alexander was allowed to try and then surprised everyone by subduing it." — from an article on the website ThoughtCo.com, 2018

Bushido ("BOO-shee-doh") the code of honor of the samurai: the word means "the way of the warrior"

> "The preservation of the Bushido code... lives on through promotion by history revisionists, who elevate samurai to a status similar to that of the chivalric knight seen in Western media. They are portrayed as an honor-bound and noble group of people that cared deeply for the peasantry, when that was often not the case." — from an article on the website Polygon.com, 2020

Dutch courage courage gained by drinking liquor; or the liquor itself

> "Grandma's hot chocolate is served with a twist: fortifying shots of bourbon, brandy, whiskey and whatnot—Dutch courage for skittish skaters." — from a review of a pop-up café by a skating rink, in the *New York Times*, 2011

French leave the act of leaving hastily or secretly, or without permission (from the 18th-century French custom of leaving a social event without saying goodbye to the host)

> "But as I was certain I should not be allowed to leave the enclosure, my only plan was to take French leave and slip out when nobody was watching..." — Robert Louis Stevenson, *Treasure Island*

Word Play

Lightning Round!

Quick! Where would you be most likely to see each of the following? (And don't say, *Paris*.)

I've supplied the first answer, to clarify what's wanted.

1. mansard (answer: on top of a building)
2. apse
3. biretta
4. craquelure
5. droshky
6. machicolation
7. slivovitz
8. scuppers
9. trireme
10. trochee
11. simoom
12. kepi

Answers:

2. In a church. 3. On a Roman Catholic clergyman's head. 4. On an old painting. 5. On a Russian road in the 19th century. 6. Near the top of a castle. 7. In a drinking glass in Eastern Europe. 8. On a boat. 9. In the waters near ancient Greece or Rome. 10. In a poem. 11. In the Sahara or Arabian desert. 12. On a gendarme's head.

Etcetera

Whether or not you've ever studied law, music, religion, or rhetoric, you've encountered the vocabulary of those fields, and others. This final section of the lexicon will clear up any uncertainties you may have about what a Manichaean believes, who qualifies as a coloratura, how to be an amicus curiae, what an umlaut does, and the difference between metonymy and synecdoche. You'll also learn some things you didn't know—unless you've memorized a large dictionary.

But first, let's catalogue a few fields of study that may be new to you.

The Study of...

cosmogony ("kahz-MAH-ghə-nee") the origin and evolution of the universe, as a branch of religion and philosophy; the word also means a *theory* about this

> "With such shifting, grotesque and inadequate fables, the cosmogonic myths of the world are necessarily bewildered and perplexed." — Andrew Lang, *Myth, Ritual, and Religion*

cosmology ("kahz-MAHL-ə-jee") the origin and evolution of the universe, as a branch of science

> "…the new data has swiftly sharpened the biggest conundrum in modern cosmology: the unexpectedly fast expansion of the universe, known as the Hubble tension." — from an article in *Quanta* magazine, 2020

geodesy ("jee-AHD-ə-see") the size and shape of the Earth: the branch of mathematics that focuses on measuring the planet, its orientation in space, and its gravitational field

> "The story of why the two countries couldn't agree on the height [of Mount Everest] and resolve the world's highest border dispute is part geopolitics and part geodesy." — from an article in the *Wall Street Journal,* 2020

horology ("hə-RAHL-ə-jee") the measurement of time; or clockmaking

> "…to be fair, many innovations in horology, including the invention of the wristwatch, were initially regarded as frivolous." — from an article in *Forbes, 2022*

dendrology ("den-DRAHL-ə-jee") trees

"While wandering through the woods, take advantage of the free dendrology lessons: Informative signs detail the characteristics of the surrounding linden, beech, maple and oak trees." — from an article about Gothenburg, Sweden, in the *New York Times,* 2018

pomology ("pə-MAHL-ə-jee") fruit, and its cultivation

"If you love a good peach half as much as I do, it's important to know that the fruit suffers sorely if put in the refrigerator before it's ready to eat. It took Carlos Crisosto, a University of California at Davis pomologist, 30 years to find out why." — from an article in *Sunset* magazine, 2004

mycology ("my-KAHL-ə-jee," the first syllable rhyming with *eye*) fungi

"For most of its history, mycology has been overlooked and understudied, relegated to the shadows of botany and microbiology." — from an article in *Wired* magazine, 2021

ethology ("ee-THAHL-ə-jee") animal behavior; or human behavior, as shaped by biology

"Ethologist and conservationist Jane Goodall redefined what it means to be human and set the standard for how behavioral studies are conducted through her work with wild chimpanzees…" — from an article on *National Geographic*'s education website

herpetology ("hər-pə-TAHL-ə-jee") reptiles and amphibians

"For some years now, a prolific amateur herpetologist has published an absolutely extraordinary number of new taxonomic names for snakes, lizards and other reptiles." — from an article in *Scientific American,* 2013 (The article goes on to criticize the unscientific names and their author.)

ophiology ("oh-fee-AHL-ə-jee" or "ah-fee-") snakes

"'The attitude of different races and different classes of people toward snakes is a most interesting subject of study,' said an expert in ophiology, recently…" — from an article in the *New York Times*, 1900

myrmecology ("mər-mə-KAHL-ə-jee") ants

"…what really piqued myrmecologist Erik T. Frank's interest about these ants was that they carry their wounded home after a raid…" — from an article in *National Geographic,* 2018

oncology ("ahn-KAHL-ə-jee") tumors

"If oncologists could not bring themselves to provide care for their terminally ill patients, she would leverage other specialists… to help patients die painlessly and gracefully." — Siddhartha Mukherjee, *The Emperor of All Maladies* (The passage refers to Cicely Saunders, pioneer of the hospice movement.)

nosology ("noh-SAHL-ə-jee") in medicine, the classification of diseases

"Whether the 15,000 maladies which are known… compose the entire definitive and dismal collection of diseases, is not for the layman unlearned in nosology to guess at." — from an article in the *Baltimore Sun*, 1937

hermeneutics ("her-mə-NYOO-tiks") the study of textual interpretation, especially the branch of theology dealing with Biblical interpretation

"Walicki has clearly been schooled in the continental tradition of philosophical hermeneutics, in which every sentence of a text is scoured for tensions, ambiguities and sources of influence." — from an article in *Prospect*, 1998

philology ("fill-AHL-ə-jee") historical linguistics (the evolution of languages), including the study of literary texts

"Philology is a word with a wide range of meaning. I use it here to designate the study of written documents." — E.H. Sturtevant, *An Introduction to Linguistic Science*

"Philology meant, and still ought to mean, the general study of literature." — from an article in the *Yale Review*, 1980

"The bewildering intertextuality that has become the very essence of modern philology." — from an article in *Hispanic Review*, 2004

eschatology ("ess-kə-TAHL-ə-jee") the branch of theology concerned with "last things": death, judgment, heaven, and hell

"Now, I'm sure Lewis would never place himself into any definite categories when it came to eschatology." — from an article on C.S. Lewis on the website TorreyGazette.com

teleology ("tell-ee-AHL-ə-jee" or "teel-ee-AHL-ə-jee") in philosophy, the explanation of things based on their purpose, goal, or function; or the study of evidence of design in nature

"Childish teleology sets us up for religion." — Richard Dawkins, *The God Delusion*

ontology ("ahn-TAHL-ə-jee") the branch of metaphysics concerned with the nature of being or existence

> During the 11th century, St. Anselm of Canterbury "proved" the existence of God by defining him as "a being than which no greater can be conceived," and going on to say that such a being *must* exist. This is an extremely crude summary of what is called Anselm's Ontological Argument.

epistemology ("ə-piss-tə-MAHL-ə-jee") the branch of philosophy that examines the nature, origin, and validity of knowledge

> "Lodge's purpose is not... to question epistemological certainties, which is often the goal of postmodernist writers such as Salman Rushdie, Julian Barnes, Graham Swift or Kazuo Ishiguro." — from a scholarly essay about David Lodge's novel *Author, Author,* in *Études Anglaises,* 2007

The lecture on epistemology sent Johann into spasms of ecstasy.

psephology ("see-FAHL-ə-jee") elections and voting trends

> The word comes from the Greek for *pebble*: because ancient Greeks voted with pebbles.

"In fact, people who have been in psephology for 50 years have never seen a party come from the mid-20s to the high 30s in a space of three weeks." — from an article about the resurgence of the British left after Brexit, in *The New Republic*, 2017

eugenics ("yoo-JEN-iks") the practice of controlling human breeding in order to improve genes; or the advocacy of this strategy

"During the Nazi era in Germany, eugenics prompted the sterilisation of several hundred thousand people then helped lead to antisemitic programmes of euthanasia and ultimately, of course, to the death camps." — from an article in the *BMJ* (British Medical Journal), 1999

euthenics ("yoo-THEN-iks," the TH pronounced as in *with*) the science of enhancing human health and well-being by improving living conditions, especially the quality of education

"Vassar to Give Euthenics Course" — headline in the *New York Times,* 1928

coprology ("kə-PRAHL-ə-jee") pornography (or filth), in art and literature

"All English readers, I trust, will agree with me that Coprology should be left to Frenchmen." — Algernon Charles Swinburne, *A Study of Ben Jonson* (1889)

Rhetoric, Grammar, and Dramaturgy

metonymy ("mə-TAHN-ə-mee") figurative use of the name of one thing when a different, related thing is meant (e.g., *The White House,* when speaking about the president)

"Virginia Woolf uses metonymy more regularly than Amis. She uses Buckingham Palace (over a dozen instances) and the Court (72, 95, etc.) as metonyms for the monarchy." — from an article on the website Narrative And Memory

synecdoche ("sə-NECK-də-kee") a figure of speech in which a part stands for the whole (e.g., *boots on the ground,* when speaking about deployed soldiers)

"He creates a tale of three cities and their interaction... as a synecdoche for the larger patterns of urban policy." — from an article in the *New York Review of Books*, 1991

In Charlie Kaufman's 2008 film, *Synecdoche, New York*, the title refers meaningfully to the plot, but it's also a child's mispronunciation of Schenectady, the upstate city where the protagonist lives (until he leaves).

pleonasm ("PLEE-ə-naz-m") the use of more words than necessary; redundancy (can be evidence of bad writing or an intentional choice)

> "All the comically baroque pleonasms help Humbert shield from himself how repulsively he has acted. They allow Nabokov, meanwhile, to describe a rapine act of frottage without becoming explicitly pornographic." — from an article about *Lolita* on Slate.com, 2015

solecism ("SAHL-ə-siz-əm") a nonstandard grammatical construction or use of words; or a violation of common practice or etiquette

> "The idea of having committed the slightest solecism in politeness, whether real or imaginary, was agony to him." — Sir Walter Scott, *Waverley*

anaphora ("ə-NAH-fə-rə," the second A pronounced as in *cat*) the repetition of a word or phrase at the beginning of at least two successive clauses.

> The most famous example may be the first sentence of *A Tale of Two Cities:* "It was the best of times, it was the worst of times, it was the age of wisdom, it was the age of foolishness, it was the epoch of belief, it was the epoch of incredulity, it was the season of Light, it was the season of Darkness, it was the spring of hope, it was the winter of despair."
>
> The Police song "Every Breath You Take" also uses this device. Think of the lyrics and you'll see how.

syncope ("SIN-kə-pee") the omission of one or more sounds within a word aloud: for example, in casual speech, "choc-late" for *chocolate*; or, in poetry, "o'er" for *over*; or, in place names, "Gloss-ter" for *Gloucester*

> This word also has a medical meaning: "a temporary loss of consciousness."

litotes ("LY-tə-teez" or LIH-tə-teez") expressing an idea by negating its opposite: for example, *Not bad.* Or *He's not the brightest bulb in the box.* Usually a form of understatement.

paronomasia ("par-ə-noh-MAY-zha," the first A pronounced as in *cat*) a play on words: a pun

> "The Punderful World of Paronomasia" — title of an article on the website Language Trainers, 2013 (The article surveys noted punsters in literature, including Shakespeare, Nabokov, and Joyce, among others.)

zeugma ("ZOOG-mə") a figure of speech in which a word refers to two others in different ways

> It's easier to understand zeugma with examples than with a definition:

> "They tugged and tore at each other's hair and clothes… and covered themselves with dust and glory." — Mark Twain, *The Adventures of Tom Sawyer*

> "Yet time and her aunt moved slowly…" — Jane Austen, *Pride and Prejudice*

antiphrasis ("an-TIH-frə-siss") irony: the use of a term in a sense opposite to its true meaning

> Again, an example to clarify the meaning:

> "I was awakened by the dulcet tones of Frank, the morning doorman, alternately yelling my name, ringing my doorbell, and pounding on my apartment door…" — Dorothy Samuels, *Filthy Rich*

prolepsis ("proh-LEP-siss") treating a future event as if it had already happened; or anticipating and answering an argument before your adversary has a chance to advance it

> "I know it will be said, continued my father (availing himself of the Prolepsis), that in itself, and simply taken…'tis an affair neither good or bad—or shameful or otherwise." — Laurence Sterne, *Tristram Shandy*

prosopopoeia ("proh-soh-pə-PEE-ə") a figure of speech in which an absent, dead, or imaginary person is reported as speaking—or in which an inanimate object or abstract idea is personified

> Example: "The iron tongue of midnight hath told twelve: Lovers, to bed; 'tis almost fairy time." — William Shakespeare, *A Midsummer Night's Dream*

syncrisis ("SIN-krə-siss") a figure of speech formed by comparing opposite persons or things

> Examples:

> "He always feels hot, I always feel cold… He speaks several languages well; I do not speak any well." — Natalia Ginzburg, "He and I"

> "You say goodbye and I say hello." — The Beatles, "Hello, Goodbye"

protasis ("PRAHT-ə-siss") the introductory part of a play; or in a conditional sentence, the subordinate clause (usually beginning with *if*)

> "For a good deal of his new novel one might as well be reading the protasis of a fair-to-middling detective story." — from a review in *The Listener*, 1961

epitasis ("eh-PIT-ə-siss") the central part of a classical drama, in which the plot is developed, and which leads to the catastrophe

> "The epitasis thereof, that is to say, the bustle, comes next." — John Mathers, *The History of Mr. John Decastro and His Brother Bat* (1815)

peripety/peripeteia ("pə-RIP-ə-tee"/"pər-ə-pə-TEE-ə") in Aristotelian poetics, a reversal of fortunes

> "By no means... let us have a peripety caused by the casual overhearing of something in the nick of time." — from an article in the *Saturday Review*, 1904

> "It has its *Protasis, Epistasis, Catastasis*, its *Catastrophe* or *Peripeteia* growing one out of the other in it, in the order Aristotle first planted them." — Laurence Sterne, *Tristram Shandy*

anagnorisis ("an-ag-NOR-ə-siss") in Aristotelian poetics, the disclosure or recognition of one's true identity or core truth (or that of another major character), occurring at the climax of a tragedy

> "One of the greatest expositions of (the idea of) anagnorisis... is when Siegmund and Sieglinde discover each other's identities as brother and sister." — from an article on ChicagoTribune.com, 2017, about a planned performance of Wagner's *Die Walküre*

> (Was that the source of Luke and Leia's story in *Star Wars*? George Lucas, please comment.)

catastrophe ("kə-TA-stroh-fee") the final event of the dramatic action, which resolves any remaining mysteries and brings the story to its close—especially in a tragedy

> In writing his *Poetics*, Aristotle carefully studied the structure of *Oedipus Rex,* by Sophocles, which offers vivid peripeteia, anagnorisis, and catastrophe. When Oedipus finally recognizes the truth (that he has killed his father and married his mother), his mother hangs herself and Oedipus blinds himself. And if that's not catastrophe, then all I've got to say is, God didn't make little green apples and it don't rain in Indianapolis in the summertime.

denouement ("day-noo-MAH(N)," pronounced as in French) the conclusion of a story (or film, or play, etc.), when the plot and any subplots are resolved: the final outcome

"This is a dénouement that can be found in much contemporary academic fiction. David Lodge usually ends his novels on the same, happy note—family reconciliation and the end of financial and occupational problems." — from a dissertation by Eva Lambertsson Björk, 1993

pasquinade ("pass-kwin-AID") a mocking satire (originally, one that was posted in a public place)

How this word came to be: a statue in Rome's Piazza Navona acquired the name Pasquino. For years, people would dress it up on St. Mark's Day and post Latin verses on it. Those verses evolved into satire, often featuring sharp criticism of the powerful, which came to be known as *pasquinades*.

eclogue ("EK-log") a short pastoral poem, usually in the form of a dialogue between two shepherds

Virgil, the Roman poet, wrote a book consisting of ten short poems, called the *Eclogues,* which pioneered this form.

dithyramb ("DITH-ə-ram") any wildly emotional, enthusiastic song, speech, or writing (originally, in ancient Greece, a choral hymn praising Dionysus)

"I will not dwell on Naumann's... dithyrambs about Dorothea's charm..." — George Eliot, *Middlemarch*

proem ("PRO-əm") an introduction or preface: sometimes used figuratively

"The reign of George I was little more than the proem to the history of England under the House of Brunswick." — Horace Walpole, *Letters*

nonce word ("NAHNSS") a word coined for a single occasion

Something is "for the nonce" if it is for a particular occasion, or for the time being. Horace Walpole (coincidentally, the author of the quote just above) coined a nonce word that has survived the passage of time: to name the phenomenon of things being discovered by chance, he referred in a letter to a fairy tale about three princes of Serendip (Sri Lanka), and called that sort of luck *serendipity*.

neologism ("nee-AHL-ə-jiz-əm") a word or phrase that is newly coined

> "The Marshall Project's review of 40 major news outlets in the five years after his *Weekly Standard* article shows the neologism [*superpredator*] popping up nearly 300 times..." — from an article on NBCNews.com, 2020

anacoluthon ("an-ə-kə-LOO-thahn") a change in mid-sentence from one type of grammatical construction to another

> This word derives from the Greek words meaning *not following,* which makes anacoluthon a sort of grammatical non sequitur.

> Example: "Rather than try to define this word, I'll—the author then cheats and merely offers an example."

aposiopesis ("app-ə-SI-ə-PEE-siss," the first I pronounced like *eye*) the sudden breaking off of a thought in mid-sentence, as if the speaker/writer couldn't go on

> "At this aposiopesis I looked inquiringly at the speaker." — Thomas de Quincey, *Autobiographic Sketches*

> Here's an example from Shakespeare. Enraged at his two unscrupulous daughters, King Lear fulminates:

>> "No, you unnatural hags,
>> I will have such revenges on you both,
>> That all the world shall—I will do such things,—
>> What they are, yet I know not: but they shall be
>> The terrors of the earth."

catachresis ("kat-ə-KREE-siss") the use of the wrong word

> In a book review, William Safire gives the nod of approval to Philip Howard, who writes about language in the *Times* of London: "[H]e dissociates himself from... the purist drawn to 'misprint, catachresis, misspelling, solecism, barbarism and other evidence that English ain't what it used to be. It never was.'" — from the *New York Times,* 1981

synaeresis/syneresis ("sin-AIR-ə-səss") the combination of two vowels or syllables usually pronounced separately, so that they form one sound

> Examples: *ne'er* for never; *o'er* for over; and the pronunciation of *Asia* with only two syllables.

diphthong ("DIFF-thong") the sound made by two adjacent vowels that are pronounced as one syllable, as in *join* or *wait*

"…that mishmash of h-dropping Cockney and diphthong-slaying Brooklynese." — from a book review in the *Washington Post*, 2021

Music

obbligato ("AHB-lə-GAH-toh") a distinctive instrumental part, integral to a musical piece, which accompanies the main melody (The word literally means *obligatory*, i.e., *not to be left out*.)

> "My own misty snapshots of coastal New England… are atmospherically augmented by tapes of seagulls crying to an obbligato surf, with time marked by the distant buoy bell at the harbor pier." — from an article in the *New York Times*, 1981, about taking a tape recorder on vacation

antiphony ("an-TIFF-ə-nee") alternating, responsive singing, especially by two groups in a choir; or a sound that echoes or responds to another

> "… what man stirs a finger, breathes a sound,
> But all the multitudinous beings round…
> Thrill, haply, in vibration and rebound,
> Life answering life across the vast profound
> In full antiphony…" — Elizabeth Barrett Browning, "Life"

ostinato ("AHSS-tə-NAH-toh") a phrase that is persistently repeated in a piece of music (The word is Italian for *stubborn*, or *obstinate*.)

> "The sound of buildings going up is the city's ostinato—its thrumming, hammering heartbeat." — from an article in the *New Yorker*, 2020

fermata a musical symbol that tells the performer to hold the note as long as s/he would like—i.e., longer than the written note value

> This is what the symbol looks like:

> Nicholson Baker's novel *The Fermata* tells the story of a man who uses his ability to stop time to act out his sexual fantasies.

cadenza ("kə-DEN-zə") an ornamental solo passage, either for a vocalist or an instrumental player, sometimes improvised, near the end of a movement

> "As for Williams, he was charged with the daunting task of composing a cadenza to play over the opening credits for the violinist Isaac Stern, who would perform the music for the

onscreen fiddler." — from an article about John Williams's score for *Fiddler on the Roof*, on BostonGlobe.com, 2022

Pro Tip: When speaking of music, be careful not to refer to a *credenza*. That is a piece of furniture.

As the Hatter embarked upon the cadenza,
the entire company fled the table.

coloratura ("kə-lə-rə-TOO-rə") a passage of vocal music with trills, leaps, and/or other ornamentation that shows off a virtuoso's skills; or a singer who specializes in opera roles featuring such melodies

> "Known for long phrases with boundless colors, emotions and dynamics, [Brenda] Rae's coloratura soared effortlessly with a glittery vibrato…" — from a music review in the *Washington Post*, 2020

tessitura ("tess-ə-TOO-rə") a singer's comfortable range (the notes that sound best); or the range that includes most of the notes in a vocal part

> "…as an experienced singer, [Placido Domingo] knows how vocally demanding the role of Aeneas is. It demands tremendous stamina and, in singers' talk, the tessitura is high." — from an article in the *New York Times,* 1983

melisma ("mə-LIZ-mə") singing several notes on one syllable

> "In current music, we hear a lot of melisma in the vocal styles of artists like Christina Aguilera and Beyoncé." — from an article on the website Performance High, 2011

> Or think of Whitney Houston singing "I Will Always Love You": count the syllables she squeezes out of *I* and *you.*

descant ("DESS-kant," the second syllable pronounced like the word *can't*) an ornamental melody or counterpoint sung or played above a musical theme

> "Typically, Lennon would sing the structural line, and McCartney the descant above." — Walter Everett, *The Beatles as Musicians*

diapason ("dy-ə-PAY-zən") a swelling burst of sound; or a harmonious combination of organ notes; or the entire range of an instrument or voice

> "I hear... in tones of thunder the diapason of the cannonade." — Henry Wadsworth Longfellow, "The Arsenal at Springfield"

opéra bouffe ("BOOF") a French comic opera, often farcical, with characters taken from ordinary life

> The Italian version is called *opera buffa.*

> "The trial of Dreyfus has now been in progress for some days, and... not a particle of proof has been offered... [T]he whole proceeding has been mere opera bouffe, the absurdity of which nobody but a Frenchman could fail to appreciate." — from a letter to the *New York Times,* 1899

con dolcezza ("kohn dohl-CHAYZ-zah," the last two syllables rhyming with *raise a*) "with sweetness": an instruction to play lightly, with a gentle tempo

> With a C turned into an E, this became the first name of Condoleezza Rice. (Her mother was a pianist and teacher.)

tattoo a bugle or drum signal that calls soldiers back to their quarters in the evening

> "...the monotonous fall of the waves on the beach, which for the most part beat a measured and soothing tattoo to her thoughts... seemed consolingly to repeat over and over again... the words of some old cradle song, murmured by nature..." — Virginia Woolf, *To the Lighthouse*

Religion

gnosis ("NOH-səss") knowledge of spiritual and/or mystical truths: especially in the ancient Gnostic tradition

> Not really relevant here, but... an English design group calling itself Hipgnosis created the cover art for many rock LPs, including Pink Floyd's *Dark Side of the Moon.* (You can instantly

picture it, right? A prism breaks a beam of light into a spectrum, on a black background.)

hagiography ("hag-ee-AHG-rə-fee" or "hayg-") biographical writing about a saint or saints; or (pejoratively) writing that is excessively flattering to its subject

"[Oliver Stone's] hagiographic Snowden is an embarrassing paean to anti-patriotism." — from an article in *National Review*, 2021

theodicy ("thee-AHD-ə-see," the TH pronounced as in *with*) an attempt to defend divine justice against the charge that God allows evil to exist

"While Alyosha and Zosima express the positive religious consciousness of Dostoevsky, it is in Ivan that the problems of evil are elucidated and shaped, and theodicy rejected." — Michael Stoeber, "Dostoevsky's Critique of Theodicy," in *Evil and the Mystics' God* (He's writing about *The Brothers Karamazov*.)

theophany ("thee-AH-fə-nee," the TH pronounced as in *with*) an appearance of God (or a god) to a person or people: a divine manifestation

"Sinai was the setting for three theophanies that shaped the history of Israel." — from an essay on the website of Brigham Young University's Religious Studies Center

theosophy ("thee-AHSS-ə-fee," the TH pronounced as in *with*) any philosophical teaching that seeks to establish a direct relationship between God and the individual by contemplation or speculation

Helena Blatavsky led a religious movement with this name, which brought together elements of Christianity, Buddhism, and Hinduism, including reincarnation.

"What is the essence of Theosophy? It is the fact that man being himself divine, can know the Divinity whose life he shares." — from an article in *The Theosophist*, 1910

theocracy ("thee-AHK-rə-see," the TH pronounced as in *with*) a form of government in which religious leaders (presumed to be interpreting God's will) hold the ultimate power

"Upon ascension to the post of de facto ruler of Iran, the Ayatollah Khomeini called for other countries in the region to adopt the Iranian model of theocracy, which would entail overthrowing their existing governments." — from an article in *Forbes*, 2021

theogony ("thee-AHG-ə-nee," the TH pronounced as in *with*) a history of the gods: their origins and genealogy

> "...the 12 major deities of ancient Greece uneasily cohabit in a dilapidated town house in 21st-century London, dwelling just above the city's 'greasy tide' of human flesh. It's like Hesiod's 'Theogony' meets MTV's 'Real World.'" — from a review of *Gods Behaving Badly*, a novel by Marie Phillips, in the *New York Times*, 2008

syncretism ("SIN-krə-tizm") an attempt to reconcile various religious or philosophical systems, or cultures

> "The lines between syncretism and appropriation were often fuzzy." — from an article in the *New Yorker*, 2021

henotheism ("hen-oh-THEE-iz-əm" or "HEE-nə-thee-iz-əm") worship of a single dominant god, while recognizing the possible existence of lesser gods

> "It seems quite apparent that the Hebrew people were for long in the stage of henotheism when they recognized that Yahweh was the only God for them, but that other nations had other gods who were real and to be feared." — Laura H. Wild, *The Evolution of the Hebrew People and Their Influence on Civilization* (1917)

nomism ("NOH-miz-əm") legalism in religion; basing one's conduct on strict adherence to law or scripture

> "Brauer shows the complex and fluid nature of... Puritan piety; nomism, evangelism, rationalism and mysticism were principal threads." — from an article in *Economic History Review*, 1989

antinomianism ("an-tih-NOHM-ee-ən-iz-əm") the belief that, because of Christian grace, moral laws need not be obeyed, since faith alone is enough to guarantee salvation

> "No society and no religious faith can live without moral rules. Jesus wasn't an antinomian, one who believes that Christians, because they are saved by grace, are not bound to religious laws. But he understood that what ultimately changes people's lives are relationships rather than rule books, mercy rather than moral demands." — from an essay by Peter Wehner in the *New York Times*, 2020

anagoge/anagogy ("AN-ə-goh-jee") a mystical interpretation of a word or passage, especially one that detects spiritual allusions to heaven or the afterlife

> "This essay explores [Flannery] O'Connor's sense of the art of fiction as an art of anagogical vision, which sees all things as

instances of participation in God." — from the abstract of an essay in the journal *Christianity and Literature*, 2010

ablution(s) ("ə-BLOO-shən(z)") cleansing of the body, especially as a ceremonial religious act (sometimes used humorously, for its formality)

"The Rajah desired leave to perform his ablutions." — Edmund Burke, *Articles of Charge Against Warren Hastings*

"Casual Ablutions" — title of a *New Yorker* article about the cleaning of the Woolworth Building, 1932

oblation ("ə-BLAY-shən" or "oh-BLAY-shən") the offering of a sacrifice to God/the gods, especially in thanksgiving (The word can also refer to the things offered— especially the bread and wine of the Eucharist.)

"Do you think God will be satisfied with half an oblation? Will He accept a mutilated sacrifice?" — Charlotte Brontë, *Jane Eyre*

catechumen ("kat-ə-KYOO-mən") one who is learning the catechism, i.e., the principles of Christianity: either a young person preparing for confirmation or a convert preparing for baptism

"...the baptismal font stood immediately to my left, and just beyond it, the three catechumens minutes away from being Catholics. They wore clothes they didn't mind getting wet, and no shoes..." — from an article in *Commonweal*, 2010

heresiarch ("hə-REE-zee-ark") the founder or leader of a heretical sect, or its chief exponent

"'Their impatience,' was the answer once given by Cardinal Newman to the question, What is the chief fault of heresiarchs?" — from an article in the *New York Times*, 1906

whited sepulcher/sepulchre ("SEP-əl-kər") a hypocrite; a corrupt or evil person who pretends to be virtuous or pious (the phrase comes from the New Testament, Matthew 23:27)

A sepulcher is a stone tomb. If you paint a sepulcher white, you're concealing the putrescence within.

"Part of [Mark Twain's] satisfaction in wearing the white suit was knowing that it was a joke against himself, a 'whited sepulchre' that concealed a heart with darker moods and a character that was far from spotless." — Michael Shelden, *Mark Twain: Man in White*

sodality ("soh-DAL-ə-tee") an association, especially for the purpose of charitable works or devotion within the Roman Catholic Church

"Something going on: some sodality. Pity so empty. Nice discreet place to be next some girl." — James Joyce, *Ulysses*

synod ("SIN-əd") a governing or advisory council of clergy and sometimes lay leaders

"Meanwhile in Germany, bishops and leading lay Catholics are engaged in a national synod considering major changes to church life, including the possibility of women clergy, married priests and changes to church teaching on sexuality." — from an article in the *Wall Street Journal*, 2021

encyclical ("en-SICK-lə-kəl") a letter from the Pope to bishops of the Roman Catholic Church

"Leaders of every major religion have published declarations similar to Pope Francis' encyclical, calling on their followers to be better stewards of Earth." — from an article on the website TheConversation.com, 2022

simony ("SY-mə-nee" or "SIH-mə-nee") the buying or selling of a church office, an ecclesiastical benefit, or a pardon

"Pierre… became impassioned,… indignant with all that had subsequently sprouted up—the barbarous fetishism, the painful superstitions, and the triumphant simony." — Emile Zola, *The Three Cities: Lourdes, Rome, Paris*

paternoster ("PA-tər-NAHS-tər," the A pronounced as in *cat*) the Lord's Prayer; or any words repeated as a prayer or magical invocation

"…over the flask he repeated more than eighty paternosters and as many more ave-marias, salves, and credos, accompanying each word with a cross by way of benediction…" — Miguel de Cervantes, *Don Quixote* (translated by John Ormsby)

viaticum ("vy-AT-ə-kəm") the Eucharist, if given to a person near death; or supplies or funds for a journey

"No absolution, no viaticum, nor anything! I die like a dog!" — Charles Kingsley, *Westward Ho!*

misericord/misericorde ("mə-ZER-ə-kord") mercy; or the dagger used to kill a seriously wounded medieval knight; or (archaic) in a monastery, the relaxing of a rule (e.g., a dispensation from fasting)

"'It certainly looks like a misericord,' remarked Reeves, drawing the rusty steel from its mouldy sheath." — Percy F. Westerman, *Captured at Tripoli*

Confiteor ("kahn-FIT-ee-or") in Roman Catholicism, a prayer in which sins are confessed and God's mercy is entreated

"He made the sign of the cross and prayed of the priest to bless him for he had sinned. Then, bowing his head, he repeated the Confiteor in fright. At the words my most grievous fault he ceased, breathless." — James Joyce, *A Portrait of the Artist as a Young Man*

latria ("lə-TRY-ə") in Roman Catholicism, the worship that is due to God alone

In Catholic theology, a distinction is made between latria and *dulia,* the veneration due to saints and angels; and also between latria and *hyperdulia,* the veneration due to the Virgin Mary

Mariolatry ("mer-ee-AHL-ə-tree") excessive reverence for the Virgin Mary, akin to idolatry

"Mariolatry in Montreal" — headline of article in the *New York Times,* 1888, about a proposal to erect a statue of the Virgin Mary on Mount Royal

Pelagianism ("pə-LAY-jee-ən-izm") the doctrine that people have free will and are innately good (as distinguished from the doctrines of Original Sin and predestination): the name comes from the 5th-century British philosopher Pelagius

"There are also theological conflicts, since the free-will doctrines of Pelagius are condemned as heretical by the Church." — from a review of *The Eagle's Brood,* part of the series *A Dream of Eagles* (about King Arthur) in *Kirkus Reviews,* 1997

Manichaean ("man-ə-KEE-ən") one who believes in Manichaeism, the dualistic philosophy that views all of history as a struggle between light and dark, good and evil; or, pejoratively, one who sees everything as black or white, good or bad; or, as an adjective, adhering to this worldview

"'Look at Me' is a movie of biting social observation. And it masterfully avoids Manichaean simplicity." — from a review in the *Washington Post,* 2005

Carthusians ("kar-THOO-zhəns") a strict, austere order of monks and nuns, founded at Chartreuse, France, by St. Bruno in 1086

A Carthusian monastery is called a *charterhouse.* The title *The Charterhouse of Parma* refers to such a monastery—which isn't mentioned until the last page of the book.

Bogomil ("BOH-ghə-mill") a member of a heretical medieval sect in Bulgaria; adherents believed that the visible world was created by Satan, one of God's two sons (the other was Jesus); they rejected marriage, meat-eating, and wine-drinking

"To recover the purity of the early church, Bogomils abjured elaborate rites, costly clerical raiments and the corrupting sale of indulgences. Their doctrines... anticipated the Protestantism of Luther." — from an essay in the *New York Times*, 1993, commenting on the deep roots of the conflict in Bosnia

chalice ("TCHA-ləss," the A pronounced as in *cat*) a large cup with a foot and a stem, used for drinking wine: especially the ceremonial goblet used in the Eucharist

"Life is God's chalice filled with tears." — William Bell Scott, *A Poet's Harvest Home*

ciborium ("sə-BORE-ee-əm") a large covered cup that holds the host (i.e., the wafers) for the Eucharist

"His hands were trembling, and his soul trembled as he heard the priest pass with the ciborium from communicant to communicant." — James Joyce, *A Portrait of the Artist as a Young Man*

offertory ("AW-fər-tor-ee" or "AH-") the collection of money at a church service, or the money collected; or the placing of bread and wine on the altar for the Eucharist

"About 60% of the parish's offertory transactions come electronically, and 52% of its members give online..." — from an article on BaltimoreSun.com, 2019

pyx ("PIKS") a container for the consecrated host, used to bring the Eucharist to those too sick to attend church

"She lied and stole, / And spat into my love's pure pyx / The rank saliva of her soul." — Elizabeth Barrett Browning, "Bianca Among the Nightingales"

censer ("SEN-sər") a container for burning incense: especially one that is swung on chains during religious ceremonies

"Recall the Dior fall 2000 show by Galliano, which opened with a model swinging a censer while dressed as the Pope." — from an article in *The New Republic*, 2018

thurible ("THOO-rə-bəl," the TH pronounced as in *with*) a censer

"...Father Conroy handed the thurible to Canon O'Hanlon and he put in the incense and censed the Blessed Sacrament and Cissy Caffrey caught the two twins and she was itching to give them a ringing good clip on the ear but she didn't because she thought he might be watching..." — James Joyce, *Ulysses*

capuche ("kə-POOSH" or "-POOCH") the long pointed hood worn by Capuchin, Franciscan, and other monks

> "A jolly friar, clothed in grey, with his capuche thrown back." — G.P.R. James, *Forest Days*

discalced ("diss-KALST") barefoot, or without shoes (said mainly of religious orders)

> "They were discalced to a man like pilgrims of some common order for all their shoes were long since stolen." — Cormac McCarthy, *The Road*

benison ("BEN-ə-sən") a blessing

> Long ago, this word meant a prayer of grace, said before eating meat. You realize what this means, don't you? There was a benison for venison! (I know what you're thinking. *Deer Lord.*)

orison ("OR-ə-sən") a prayer

> "The fair Ophelia!—Nymph, in thy orisons be all my sins remembered." — William Shakespeare, *Hamlet*

aureole/aureola ("OR-ee-ohl"/"aw-REE-oh-lə") a light or radiance in a circle around the head or body of a holy one; a halo (also, an alternate spelling of *areola,* the round pigmented area around a nipple)

> "Fair shines the gilded aureole / In which our highest painters place / Some living woman's simple face." — Dante Gabriel Rossetti, "Jenny"

perdition ("pər-DIH-shən") in Christian theology, eternal damnation after death, as punishment for unrepented sin; or hell itself; or complete ruin

> "It's really easier to face bereavement, dishonour, and the perdition of one's soul—than this kind of prolonged hunger." — Joseph Conrad, *Heart of Darkness*

> "I'll chase him... round perdition's flames before I give him up." — Herman Melville, *Moby-Dick*

crèche ("KRESH") a representation of the Nativity (i.e., those manger scenes on people's lawns); or, in England, a day care center for infants and young children

> "After decades of personal oversight in the arrangement of the 18th-century Neapolitan crèche figures that were donated to the Met by the painter Loretta Hines Howard, her daughter and

granddaughter were told… that they would have to keep their hands off in the future." — from an article in the *New York Times,* 2014

rood a crucifix, especially one positioned above the entrance to a church's chancel

"To the Rose upon the Rood of Time." — title of poem by William Butler Yeats

matins ("MAT-ənz") morning prayer, especially in the Anglican Church

"Failure to be seen at church, both at matins and at evensong, on Sunday was tantamount to proof of the worst moral laxity." — John Fowles, *The French Lieutenant's Woman*

doxology ("dahk-SAHL-ə-jee") a formula of praise to God

For example:
"Praise God from whom all blessings flow;
Praise Him, all creatures here below;
Praise Him above, ye heavenly host;
Praise Father, Son, and Holy Ghost. Amen." — Thomas Ken, 1674

"At the funeral in the Cathedral of Saint John the Divine, he clapped his hands through the syncopated bits of the doxology…" — Nell Zink, *Doxology*

auto-da-fé ("AW-toh də FAY") ("act of the faith") the public burning of a heretic; or the ceremony for pronouncing judgment on the heretic, followed by execution

"I recalled seeing him… burning a whole stack of [discarded drafts] in the pale fire of the incinerator before which he stood… among the wind-borne black butterflies of that backyard auto-da-fé." — Vladimir Nabokov, *Pale Fire*

sanbenito ("san-bə-NEE-toh") a garment of sackcloth worn by a heretic during the Spanish Inquisition: yellow with red crosses for a penitent, black with painted flames and devils for one who refused to repent and would soon be executed

"I would rather have put on a sanbenito myself than have gone there." — Deborah Alcock, *The Spanish Brothers*

sacerdotal ("sass-ər-DOH-təl") relating to priests

"It was modernism itself, after the collapse of traditional systems of explanation, that invented the 'religion of art' by claiming the sacerdotal functions of spiritual and moral instruction." — from an article in *The New Republic,* 2010, about Nabokov's *The Original of Laura*

oblate ("AHB-late" or "oh-BLATE") a person living in a monastery and following its rules, without taking vows

"Up to the twelfth century, children destined for the monastic life were commonly placed, at seven or thereabouts, in a monastery as 'oblate children,' dedicated to God by their parents." — from an article in the *New York Review of Books*, 1991

This word is also an adjective, meaning "flattened at the poles" (describing a spheroid).

empyrean ("em-PIH-ree-ən") the highest reaches of heaven: to the ancients, a realm of pure fire; to early Christians, the abode of God and the angels; paradise

"In her musings she spread her poor, clipped wings, and flew into the pure empyrean." — D.H. Lawrence, *The Rainbow*

Mammon ("MAM-ən") in the New Testament, riches or avarice personified as a devil (or, with a lower-case M, *mammon:* riches as a false object of worship or an evil influence)

"No man can serve two masters... Ye cannot serve God and mammon." — Matthew, 6:24 (King James Version)

"I was a dope fiend and a dope dealer... a gutless profit-monger and mammon-worshipper." — T.C. Boyle, *Budding Prospects*

Orders of Angels (the hierarchy, in descending order)

seraphim ("SER-ə-fim") possessing three pairs of wings, they sing praises to God continuously

"Where the bright Seraphim in burning row / Their loud up-lifted Angel trumpets blow." — John Milton, "At a Solemn Music"

cherubim (singular: cherub) second in the hierarchy; usually depicted in art as chubby, rosy-cheeked children with wings; by extension, *cherub* can mean any rosy-cheeked, chubby, innocent-seeming person

"So Adam looked at Eve / And she looked back at him. / 'Why don't you let them talk, my Lord?' / Said some bright cherubim." — Anthony Newley and Leslie Bricusse, "Nag! Nag! Nag!" from *Stop the World—I Want to Get Off*

thrones angels who serve as messengers between God and the lower angels

dominions/dominations

virtues

powers/authorities

principalities often shown wearing crowns and carrying scepters

archangels ("ARK-ayn-jəlz") guardian angels of nations

"The idea that Michael was the advocate of the Jews became so prevalent that, in spite of the rabbinical prohibition against appealing to angels as intermediaries between God and his people, Michael came to occupy a certain place in the Jewish liturgy. In the New Testament, Michael leads God's armies against Satan's forces in the Book of Revelation, where during the war in heaven he defeats Satan." — from Wikipedia, "Michael (archangel)"

angels

Among the Archangels, Ronnie had the daintiest feet.

tallit/tallith ("TAHL-əss") a Jewish prayer shawl, with fringes

"Putting on a uniform included pulling a helmet over a yarmulke and strapping padding over a white, tasseled religious shawl, known as a tallit." — from an article in the *New York Times*, 2017, about Yeshiva University's roller hockey team

tzitzit ("TSIT-səss") the fringes on a Jewish prayer shawl

"He carried an iPad and wore a white oxford shirt, navy chinos, a *kipa, tzitzit*, and pleather loafers with no socks." — from a story in the *New Yorker*, 2011

Since *meshuggeneh* means crazy and *tzitzit* means a kind of fringe, extremists in Israel could be called the *meshuggeneh tzitzit*: the lunatic fringe.

Tetragrammaton ("teh-trə-GRAM-ə-tahn") the four consonants of the ancient Hebrew name of God, as revealed to Moses, transliterated as YHWH: used because it was forbidden to speak or write the full name

Though observant Jews still refrain from speaking the full name, others have pronounced it often, as Yahweh or Jehovah.

"[Richard] Powers' 1991 novel, *The Gold Bug Variations*... seems to suggest that Bach's use of four notes in the Goldberg Variations, the four nucleotides in DNA and the tetragrammaton, the four letters in the Hebrew name of God, are all connected in a way that sheds light on our understanding of what it means to be human." — from an article about recent American fiction, in *The Guardian*, 2003

Balaam's ass ("bə-LAHM") Balaam was a Biblical prophet hired to curse the Israelites. While en route to his destination, an angel appeared to Balaam's donkey three times, blocking the way; each time, the donkey stopped, and each time, Balaam beat the donkey. Finally the donkey spoke, saying, "What have I done to you, that you have struck me these three times?" Then the angel appeared to Balaam as well, and reproached him for agreeing to curse the Israelites. (What's the point of the story? Perhaps that even a prophet can be blind.)

Lilith ("LIL-əth") a demonic figure of Jewish folklore: according to some legends, she was Adam's first wife, who refused to submit to his authority and left Eden; Eve took her place and Lilith became an evil spirit.

Reclaiming the name from its origins in patriarchal myth, the creators of a 1990s women's music festival called it *Lilith Fair*. Also, it's no accident that, on *Cheers* and then the eponymous spin-off, Frasier's ex-wife (played by Bebe Neuwirth) was named Lilith.

Asmodeus ("az-mə-DEE-əss") in Jewish lore, the king of demons (appearing in the Book of Tobit)

"It was as if some invisible Asmodeus had revealed to this simple frontiersman a world of which he had never dreamed." — Bret Harte, "In the Tules"

Moloch ("MAH-ləkh," with a throaty final sound) in the Old Testament, a foreign god to whom children were sacrificed by burning; or, by extension, anything regarded as demanding a terrible sacrifice

In Fritz Lang's *Metropolis*, the protagonist witnesses a factory calamity: steam bursts out everywhere and workers fall; the machine then seems to transform into a terrifying god with gaping mouth and ravenous eyes, as bare-chested, handcuffed workers are dragged up the stairs and tossed into the fiery mouth. A title card reads, *Moloch!*

"Progress seems always to involve a trampling underfoot. It is a Moloch whose chariot-wheels spurt blood at every turn." — E.M. Clowes, *On the Wallaby Through Victoria*

Islam

hadj/hajj ("HAHDJ," to rhyme with *dodge*, or "HADJ," to rhyme with *badge*) the pilgrimage to Mecca, a religious duty for all Muslims

"Saudi Arabia... held a largely symbolic hajj earlier this year limited to domestic worshippers..." — from an article on NBC News, 2020 (during the Covid-19 pandemic)

hadji/hajji ("HADJ-ee") a Muslim who has made a pilgrimage to Mecca

After learning the meaning of the word *hadji*, I found myself confused by the fact that Jonny Quest's adoptive brother from Calcutta (on the 1960s Hanna Barbera cartoon) was named Hadji Singh. Others have noticed as well: "But what is the background of Hadji Singh? Hadji is sort of every background... From his dress and surname he appears to be a practicing Sikh, but his name is plainly a Muslim name of religious significance. Arguably this might be a wrongheaded conflation of the two faiths... However, it is going too far to insist that no real person could be born to a Muslim family and be a practicing Sikh... A practicing Sikh named Hadji Singh is very much out of the ordinary, but not completely outside the realm of possibility." — from an essay on Medium.com by Reese Weatherly, 2020

jihad ("jə-HAHD" or "jee-HAHD") a holy war against Islam's enemies or unbelievers: a religious duty for Muslims; or, by extension, any crusade against an opposing belief

"Between 2012 and 2018 over 2,000 French citizens left to take part in jihad in Syria..." — from an article in *The Economist*, 2020

"To the extent that Islam is known about today, it is known principally in the form given it by the mass media: ...the background is populated by shadowy (though extremely frightening) notions about *jihad*, slavery, subordination of women and irrational violence combined with extreme licentiousness." — from an essay by Edward Said in *The Nation,* 1980

giaour ("JOW-ər") (derogatory) in Islam, a non-believer, especially a Christian; an infidel

"Who falls in battle 'gainst a Giaour, / Is worthiest an immortal bower." — Lord Byron, *Giaour*

hafiz ("HAH-fəz") a Muslim who has memorized the Koran

"...the main focus is on learning the Quran, a traditional practice dating to the time of Muhammad. I wanted to document it—not only the discipline required to become a hafiz (one who remembers) but also the way girls retain the essential nature of youngsters." — from an article about religious schools for girls in Turkey, in *National Geographic*, 2022

Sharia ("shə-REE-ə") guidance for Muslims, based on the Koran, encompassing both religious and secular rules (and penalties)

"While it's true that sharia influences the legal codes in most Muslim-majority countries, those codes have been shaped by a lot of things, including, most powerfully, European colonialism." — from an article in the *Washington Post,* 2016

muezzin ("moo-ƏZZ-ən") one who calls Muslims to prayer, from the minaret of a mosque: the call goes out five times a day

"At the moment of interment, as the Jewish prayer for the dead was being chanted, the muezzin from a nearby Palestinian village began the Muslim call to prayer for believers." — from an article in the *Washington Post*, 2020

Buddhism (and sometimes Hinduism)

karma ("KAR-mə") in Buddhism and Hinduism, the sum of a person's actions (and their impact), which will determine the nature of that person's next life; or, in popular usage, the fate you earn by the way you live your life

> "Instant Karma's gonna get you
> Gonna knock you right on the head
> You better get yourself together
> Pretty soon you're gonna be dead." — John Lennon, "Instant Karma"

nirvana ("nər-VAH-nə") in Buddhism, the ultimate goal: a state in which the individual has transcended desire, suffering, and self, and is released from the cycle of death and rebirth; or, in popular use, a perfectly blissful state, free of pain and worry

> "The newspapers said this would result in nirvana for the consumer as prices tumbled in reaction to intense competition." — from an article in *BBC Good Food*, 1998

bodhisattva ("boh-dee-SAHT-və") "enlightened being": in Buddhism, a compassionate being who has attained enlightenment but refrains from reaching nirvana in order to help others become enlightened

> "The Dalai Lamas are Bodhisattvas in whom is incarnate Chenrezi, the God of Mercy." — B.J. Gould, *The Jewel in the Lotus*

samsara ("sahm-SAH-rə") in Buddhism and Hinduism, the cycle of life, death, and rebirth: infinite and laden with suffering

> "The central task of the protagonists is to free themselves and others from enslavement to the illusion of the *Matrix*... Neo and his companions function as bodhisattvas who refuse absolute escape from samsara while others are still trapped." — Anthony Lioi, *Nerd Ecology: Defending the Earth with Unpopular Culture*

mandala ("MAHN-də-lə" or "MAN-") in Buddhism and Hinduism, a symmetrical geometric figure that symbolically represents the universe, to be contemplated during meditation: usually incorporating a square within a circle

> "...the symbol itself is drawn from an old Herero mandala which represented the shape of the tribe's villages." — from an article in the journal *boundary 2*, 1981, about the mandala as a symbol in *Gravity's Rainbow*, by Thomas Pynchon

dharma ("DAR-mə") in Buddhism and Hinduism, the true nature of reality, the fundamental principles of existence; in Hinduism, the word also means each individual's duty, or the "right way of living"; generally, moral law

> Even after offering that definition, I'm still confused about what *dharma* really means. Here's a reason why, from the Wikipedia entry on the subject: "It is difficult to provide a single concise definition for *dharma*, as the word has a long and varied history and straddles a complex set of meanings and interpretations. There is no equivalent single-word synonym for *dharma* in western languages."

samadhi ("sah-MAH-dee") in Buddhism and Hinduism, a state of intense awareness and calm rapture, achieved through meditation on the Absolute, without thoughts or emotions that come from the ego

> "To catch a glimpse of samadhi is not difficult. But to stay there takes years and years." — from an interview with the yoga consultant to Narendra Modi, India's Prime Minister, in the *New York Times,* 2015

Zen Buddhism

satori ("sə-TAW-ree") an awakening into spiritual enlightenment

> "When you have satori you are able to reveal a palatial mansion made of precious stones on a single blade of grass; but when you have no satori, a palatial mansion itself is concealed behind a simple blade of grass." — D.T. Suzuki, *Essays in Zen Buddhism*

> "It was as if Cassady, at the wheel, was in a state of satori, as totally into this very moment, Now, as a being can get…" — Tom Wolfe, *The Electric Kool-Aid Acid Test*

koan ("KOH-ahn") in Zen Buddhism, a paradox, story, or riddle to be meditated upon: its purpose is to confound logical thought and lead the novice toward intuitive enlightenment

> "They might act as Zen koans and cause sudden openings into hitherto unglimpsed regions." — Aldous Huxley, in a letter, 1958

zazen ("zah-ZEN") in Zen Buddhism, meditation practiced in a sitting position: suspending judgment and letting thoughts pass through the mind, with the ultimate goal of gaining insight into the true nature of one's being

> "Zazen, a form of seated meditation, is at the very heart of Zen practice… Zazen is the study of the self… With consistent

practice, zazen transforms our mind, heart and life." — from the website of the Zen Mountain Monastery

Tibetan Buddhism

bardo ("BAR-doh") in Tibetan Buddhism, the state of the existence between death and rebirth

Lincoln in the Bardo — title of a novel by George Saunders, 2017

Hinduism

avatar ("AV-ə-tar") an incarnation of a deity; or a person who embodies a particular quality; or an image representing a person on the internet or in a video game

"If Portnoy has never been outgrown, only grown old, he is, in his present avatar, an everyman..." — from a review of the Philip Roth novel *Everyman,* in the *New York Times,* 2006

Brahma ("BRAH-mə," to rhyme with *drama*) the supreme god: the creator; or, in pantheistic religion, divine reality

"The son of four-headed Brahma and a mortal woman, who begat a water being, [the Brahmaputra River] is among the few male rivers in India." — from an article in *National Geographic,* 2019

Shiva ("SHEE-və") the god who destroys and restores worlds

"Lord Shiva Mantras that will end all of your problems" — headline of feature on the *Times of India* website, 2021

Vishnu ("VISH-noo")the preserver, who protects humans and restores the balance of good and evil in the world

"Purely in terms of power, Vishnu is every bit Shiva's match, though again, appearances can be deceiving... Shiva creates new life by stamping up a storm; Vishnu does it by lying down in a milky sea." — from a review of an art exhibit called "Vishnu: Hinduism's Blue-Skinned Savior," in the *New York Times,* 2011

Shakti ("SHAHK-tee") the dynamic energy of the universe; or the female principle, personified as the wife of a god

"Next door, in a pale-blue classroom decorated with paintings of tropical animals, Bodhisattvas and their bosomy Shaktis, the Lower Fifth were having their biweekly lesson..." — Aldous Huxley, *Island*

the Vedas ("VAY-dəz") the oldest scriptures of Hinduism; the texts, in Sanskrit, contain philosophy and guidance on ritual and meditation

"…nearly 2,000 scholars have gathered for the first time in centuries to chant the timeless message of the Vedas, the bedrock of Hinduism." — from an article in the *New York Times*, 1973

asana ("AH-sə-nə") the seated position used when meditating; or, in hathayoga, one of the poses practitioners assume

If you've ever taken a yoga class in which the leader gave the Sanskrit names of the various poses, you may have noticed that they all ended in *asana*. Now you know why. (My favorite is Savasana, or Corpse Pose, when you lie flat on your back with your eyes closed at the end of the class. Ahhh.)

mantra ("MAHN-trə") in Hinduism, a word or phrase repeated continuously during meditation; or, in popular use, any slogan or phrase that's repeated often, expressing a person or group's core beliefs

"I forgot my mantra." — Jeff Goldblum, distressed on the telephone, in *Annie Hall*, 1977

chakra ("TCHAHK-rə") one of the focal points in the body, believed to be a center of spiritual energy; Hinduism teaches that there are seven major chakras, each related to a different organ or gland

"Sitting between the root chakra and belly button is the sacral chakra, which governs the sex organs… It can get bogged down with the feelings of guilt and shame… It is possible to clear sacral chakra blockages by forgiving yourself and others, and accepting yourself as a sexual being." — from an article on the website MindBodyGreen.com, 2019

kundalini ("koon-də-LEE-nee") in yoga, divine feminine energy, believed to be concentrated at the base of the spine; or a form of yoga that aims to release this energy, so that it can travel to the brain and yield enlightenment

"You see, marijuana tends to unlock my Kundalini in the worst way and the energy just gets stuck in my lower Chakra." — from Spalding Gray's monologue *Swimming to Cambodia*, excerpted in *High Times* magazine, 1986

purdah ("PURR-də") the practice, in some Muslim and Hindu communities, of secluding females—behind a curtain, in separate rooms, or in clothes that cover them completely—in order to keep them out of sight of men

"'You would have allowed me to see her?'
'Why not? I believe in the purdah, but I should have told her you

were my brother, and she would have seen you..."" — E.M.
Forster, *A Passage to India*

"Other"

numen ("NEW-mən") the divinity or spirit that presides over a place
or that dwells within a thing

"[D.H. Lawrence] was always intensely aware of the mystery of
the world, and the mystery was always for him a numen, divine."
— Aldous Huxley, Introduction to *The Letters of D.H. Lawrence*

auspice ("AWSS-pəss") an omen, especially a favorable one; or the
art of finding omens in the flight of birds

"I hated ceremonies... [T]here would be no feast, merely the
usual ritual sacrifice of a ram whose entrails would then be
examined to see whether the auspices were favourable." —
Robert Graves, *I, Claudius*

We're more accustomed to seeing this word in the plural,
auspices, meaning "guidance, supervision, sponsorship" as in "I
have prepared this lexicon under the auspices of the North
American Logophiles Guild." (Not true, by the way. They won't
even return my phone calls.)

mana ("MAH-nə") in the religions of the South Pacific islands, a
supernatural power inherent in sacred objects and certain people

"Warhol has always provided a good example of the kind of
mana which emanates from certain chosen individuals in modern
society." — from an article in *The Listener*, 1965

Dianetics in Scientology, the system by which mental and physical
health is achieved by clearing the mind of negative images left behind
by painful experiences: created by the founder of the Church of
Scientology, L. Ron Hubbard

"A new cult is smouldering through the U.S. underbrush. Its
name: dianetics. Last week its bible, *Dianetics*: *The Modern
Science of Mental Health*, was steadily climbing the U.S.
bestseller lists." — from an article in *Time* magazine, 1950

From Myth and Legend

phoenix ("FEE-niks") a bird resembling an eagle, which lives for
centuries, then burns in flames ignited by the sun, and rises from its
ashes to live again; or a person of great beauty or excellence

In the Harry Potter books, Dumbledore has a phoenix named Fawkes, a companion and defender. Fawkes helps Harry defeat the basilisk in the Chamber of Secrets.

"Here it was; a human being perfect of its kind,
a phoenix amongst barnyard fowls." — John Braine, *Room at the Top*

chimera ("ky-MEE-rə" or "kə-MEE-rə") a fire-breathing monster with a lion's head, a goat's body, and a serpent's tail (slain by Bellerophon, while riding on Pegasus); or a creation of the imagination; or an impossible or foolish fancy

"Simphiwe Ndzube… made a new sculpture for the biennial informed by South African folklore. It's a 6-foot-tall, 20-foot-long creature, a chimera, made of clay and featuring fake eyelashes and dentures, which speaks to both healing and the future." — from an article in the *Los Angeles Times*, 2022

basilisk ("BASS-ə-lisk") a mythical serpent whose breath and/or gaze was lethal: supposedly hatched by a serpent from a rooster's egg

"She answers my sudden greeting by turning and averting her black basilisk eyes." — James Joyce, *Giacomo Joyce*

When she was little, my daughter Helen, a Harry Potter fan, would announce, "The basilisk emerges from the Chamber of Secrets." She would then hold a thin paper napkin in front of her mouth and poke through it with her tongue.

cockatrice ("KAHK-ə-triss") a basilisk; or (archaic) a prostitute

"So, if she has been called a woman of the town, … a buttered bun, a cockatrice, a cock-chafer… it is not surprising." — Erica Jong, *Fanny*

griffin/gryphon ("GRIFF-ən") a mythical creature with a lion's body and an eagle's head and wings

"They very soon came upon a Gryphon, lying fast asleep in the sun… 'Up, lazy thing!' said the Queen, 'and take this young lady to see the Mock Turtle…' Alice did not quite like the look of the creature, but on the whole she thought it would be quite as safe to stay with it as to go after that savage Queen…" — Lewis Carroll, *Alice's Adventures in Wonderland*

sphinx a monster with a woman's head, a lion's body, and wings: it posed the same riddle to all who passed, and killed those who couldn't answer it; when Oedipus answered the riddle correctly, it killed itself

The word also means "a mysterious person."

"Much like the mythological sphinx, Taylor Swift is prone to speaking—and posting on Instagram—in elaborate riddles, tantalizing her fans with esoteric clues about the new projects she's got in the works." — from an article in *Marie Claire,* 2020

hippogriff (or −gryph) ("HIP-ə-griff") a mythical creature with an eagle's head and wings and a horse's hind legs and tail: born of the union of a male griffin and a mare

> "After the hippogryph has won such height,
> That he is lessened to a point, he bends
> His course for where the sun... descends..." — Ludovico Ariosto, *Orlando Furioso* (translated by William Stewart Rose). (Ariosto invented the hippogriff for this poem.)

dipsas ("DIP-səs") a mythical serpent whose bite was said to produce great thirst

> *Dipsa* is Greek for *thirst; dipsomaniac,* another word for *alcoholic,* comes from the same source.

> "A dipsas is a worm accurst,
> From whose bite follows raging thirst." —*The History of Reynard the Fox,* adapted by F.S. Ellis

faun ("FAWN") in Roman mythology, a lustful rural deity with the body of a man and the horns, ears, tail, and sometimes the legs of a goat

> "Prélude à l'après-midi d'un faune" ("Prelude to the Afternoon of a Faun") is the title of a brief orchestral work by Debussy, based on a poem by Mallarmé. The piece inspired a ballet, choreographed by Nijinsky and controversial in its time for its portrayal of sexual desire.

satyr ("SAY-tər") a drunken, lusting god of the forest: usually portrayed as a faun, chasing a nymph; or a lustful man

> A couple of associations:

> • *satyriasis*: a prolonged or painful erection; or an excessive desire for sex, usually in a man (the male equivalent of nymphomania)
> • *The Satyricon,* a Latin satire by Petronius, made into a movie by Fellini, with erotic passages. In one section, the protagonist attends a lavish dinner hosted by Trimalchio, a wealthy, vulgar man; as you may know, Fitzgerald's original title for *The Great Gatsby* was *Trimalchio in West Egg.*

sylph ("SILF") an invisible being with no soul, living in the air (another invention of Paracelsus); or a slender, graceful woman

"Her vest and train of white satin did not conceal
her sylphlike form and delicate feet." — Benjamin Disraeli,
Sketches

dryad ("DRY-əd" or "DRY-ad") a wood nymph, dwelling in a forest
or in a tree

"After all, how big was the Flood? Perhaps a few dryads and
fauns had just run into the hills and the farther valleys and woods,
frightened..." — D.H. Lawrence, *The Rainbow*

hamadryad ("ham-ə-DRY-əd") a wood nymph who dies when the
tree she inhabits dies

naiad ("NY-ad" or "NAY-ad") a nymph living in and presiding over a
river, lake, spring, fountain, or waterfall

If you have a hard time remembering the difference between a
naiad and a dryad, just remember that dryads inhabit *dry* things
(i.e., trees), and Diana Nyad is a renowned long-distance
swimmer.

"The lovely Arcadia region... bears traces of the virgin
wilderness where nymphs, naiads, and the horned god Pan once
frolicked." — from an article about vacationing in Greece, in
National Geographic, 2019

"Yes, I know, I look like a naiad.
But Sir! I can't swim!"

nereid ("NEER-ee-id" or "NAIR-") a sea nymph: one of the 50
daughters of the sea-god Nereus

"It pleased Ursula to think of the naiads in Asia Minor meeting
the nereids at the mouth of the streams... and calling to their

sisters the news of Noah's Flood." — D.H. Lawrence, *The Rainbow*

undine ("UN-deen") a female water-spirit who, according to Paracelsus, could only earn a soul by marrying a mortal and bearing his child: but if he were unfaithful to her, she would die

> *Undine,* a popular German romantic novel published in 1811, tells the story of a knight who falls in love with a mysterious girl who turns out to be a mermaid. Does that remind you of anything? It should: the book inspired Hans Christian Andersen's fairy tale, "The Little Mermaid."

maenad ("MEE-nad") a female worshipper of Bacchus/Dionysus, god of wine: during their rites, possessed by the god, maenads performed frenzied, ecstatic dances in the woods

> "Manson's maenads—dirty, barefoot examples of Dionysian abandon—provide the most fascinating sequences of [Quentin Tarantino's] career." — from a review of *Once Upon a Time in Hollywood,* in the *National Review,* 2018

The Muses: the nine goddesses who inspire practitioners of the arts and astronomy: daughters of Zeus and Mnemosyne (goddess of memory)

> A *muse* (lower-case M) is a source of inspiration to an artist (usually a woman, often a lover).

> "Sing in me, Muse, and through me tell the story
> of that man skilled in all ways of contending..." — opening lines of *The Odyssey* (translated by Robert Fitzgerald)

> "[Salvador Dalí] was... married to one of the greediest harpies in Europe: Gala, who made him the indentured servant of his lost talent even as he treated her as his muse." — from an article by Robert Hughes in *Time* magazine, 1994

Calliope ("kə-LIE-ə-pee") epic poetry

> Because Calliope's voice was said to be divinely harmonious (the name itself means "beautiful-voiced"), she lent her name to the organ-like instrument heard at traveling fairs and carousels, which uses steam-whistles to produce its sounds.

> "Fond of the sound of locomotive whistles, Stoddard affixes 15 of them of varying sizes on a steam chest... Though his hometown quickly bans it, the calliope becomes the signature sound of riverboats and circus parades." — from an article in *Smithsonian* magazine, 2005

Thalia ("thə-LY-ə," the TH pronounced as in *with*) comedy and pastoral poetry

Melpomene ("mel-PAH-mə-nee") tragedy

When you see the paired masks that symbolize theatrical comedy and tragedy, you're seeing masks of Thalia and Melpomene.

Clio ("KLEE-oh" or "KLY-oh") history

Erato ("ERR-ə-toh," the first syllable pronounced like the word *err*) love poetry and mime

Euterpe ("yoo-TER-pee") lyric poetry and music

Polyhymnia sacred poetry and hymns

Terpsichore ("terp-SIK-ə-ree") dancing and choral singing

Her name gives us the adjective *terpsichorean,* "relating to dance"

Urania ("yoo-RAY-nee-ə") astronomy

The Three Graces sister goddesses who dispense charm and beauty

Aglaia ("ə-GLAY-ə")

Euphrosyne ("yoo-FRAH-sə-nee")

Thalia ("THAYL-yə" or "thə-LY-ə," the TH pronounced as in *with*)

Same name as the Muse; different goddess.

The Furies the goddesses of vengeance: three winged goddesses who pursue perpetrators of unavenged crimes, especially murder and offenses against the gods (They're known as the *Erinyes* in Greek.)

"I was most drawn to the figures of the Furies, or Erinyes, particularly at the end of the *Orestia.*" — Lauren Groff, in an interview about her novel, *Fates and Furies,* 2016

Alecto ("ə-LEK-toh")

Megaera ("mə-JEER-ə")

Tisiphone ("tih-SIH-fə-nee")

Erebus ("ERR-ə-bəs") the dark region beneath the earth's surface, through which the dead must pass before they reach Hades; or a deity who personifies darkness

"The man that hath no music in himself, / Nor is not moved with concord of sweet sounds, / Is fit for treasons, stratagems, and spoils. / The motions of his spirit are dull as night, / And his affections dark as Erebus. / Let no such man be trusted." — William Shakespeare, *The Merchant of Venice*

Triton ("TRY-tn") a son of Neptune/Poseidon: his lower half is that of a fish; or, with a lower-case T, a mollusk with a cone-shaped shell

> "I'd rather be / A Pagan suckled in a creed outworn; / So might I... / Have glimpses that would make me less forlorn; / Have sight of Proteus rising from the sea; / Or hear old Triton blow his wreathed horn." — William Wordsworth, *The World Is Too Much With Us*

Momus ("MOH-məss") the Greek god of blame and ridicule, banished from Olympus because he criticized the gods; or a person who always finds fault

> The Knights of Momus, founded in 1872, are the second oldest Mardi Gras krewe in New Orleans. (Krewes put on parades and balls during Carnival season.)

Castor and Pollux ("CAST-ər" and "PAHL-əks") (also called the Dioscuri) sons of Leda, protectors of sailors

> The most common version of the myth says that Castor was the son of Leda and Tyndareus, a king, and therefore mortal; Pollux was the son of Leda and Zeus (who came to her as a swan), and therefore immortal. When Castor was killed, Pollux chose to share half of his immortality with him. In some versions, they became the constellation Gemini.

Penthesilea ("pen-thə-sih-LAY-ə") in Greek mythology, Queen of the Amazons, brave, skillful, and wise: she sided with Troy in the Trojan War and was killed by Achilles

> Heinrich von Kleist wrote a play called *Penthesilea* in 1808, in which the Amazon queen falls in love with Achilles. It's gory and tragic; Goethe called it "unplayable." The play was first performed in 1876, nearly seventy years after it was written.

Ixion ("ik-SY-ən") a king who tried to seduce Hera: he was punished by Zeus by being tied to a perpetually revolving wheel of fire in Hades

> "...so long as we are given up to the throng of desires with their constant hopes and fears, so long as we are the subject of willing,—we can never have lasting happiness nor peace... The subject of willing is thus constantly stretched on the revolving wheel of Ixion..." — Arthur Schopenhauer, *The World as Will and Idea* (translated by R.B. Haldane and John Kemp)

the Parcae ("PAR-ky," the second syllable rhyming with *eye,* or "PAR-see") in Roman myth, the three Fates: three old women who spin the threads of human destiny (singular: *Parca*)

"We worship not the Graces, nor the Parcae, but Fashion. She spins and weaves and cuts with full authority. The head monkey at Paris puts on a traveller's cap, and all the monkeys in America do the same." — Henry David Thoreau, *Walden*

Lares (pronounced like *Larry's*) in Roman myth, guardian deities associated with specific places; they are often associated with the Penates (see next entry), and defined as the spirits of departed ancestors who preside over a household

Penates ("pə-NAY-teez") in Roman myth, household gods who watched over the home

> "I am returned to my own Lares and Penates—
> to my dogs and cats." — Horace Walpole, in a letter, 1775

ichor ("EYE-kor") the fluid said to flow through the veins of the Greek gods; or the watery discharge from a wound

> "She [Venus] spoke, and with her palms wiped off the ichor from her hand: the hand was healed, and the severe pains mitigated." — Homer, *The Iliad* (translated by T.A. Buckley)

theurgy ("THEE-ər-jee," the TH pronounced as in *with*) the act of invoking divine intervention in human affairs; or such an intervention

> "We stand here at a juncture in [*The Iliad*], where its theurgy supersedes its human mechanism." — William Gladstone, *Studies on Homer and the Homeric Age*

Mithras ("MITH-rahss") a god of the ancient Persians, and later the Romans and other Europeans

> Mithras was a god of light, or of the sun; Mithraism was a mystery cult in the late Roman Empire.

> "Three places of worship each built on the same site, one on top of the other. Beneath the earliest church there is also… a pagan 'sacred' site, dedicated to the god Mithras." — from an article about the Basilica of San Clemente on the website Educated-Traveller.com, 2019

manticore ("MAN-tə-kor") a mythical beast with a man's face, a lion's body, and a scorpion's stinging tail (origin: Persia)

> In 1973, the progressive rock group Emerson, Lake & Palmer founded their own label, and called it Manticore Records. I looked up the word at the time, didn't find it in my dictionary, and was baffled—until now.

banshee ("BAN-shee") in Gaelic folklore, a female spirit said to wail outside a house as a warning that a death will occur soon in the family

> "With its banshee call, dark eyes, and bright white face, a barn owl could pass for a winged ghost, moving silently against the night sky." — from an article in *National Geographic*, 2020

kelpie ("KEL-pee") in Scottish folklore, a shape-shifting water spirit (often in the form of a horse) that drowns people (or, alternately, that warns people in danger of drowning)

> "…water-kelpies haunt the foord / By your direction, / An' nighted trav'lers are allur'd / To their destruction." — Robert Burns, "Address to the Devil"

Cuchulain ("koo-KULL-in") in Celtic myth, the tribal hero of Ulster who singlehandedly defended it against an invading army

> "Again the fighting sped, / But now the war-rage in Cuchulain woke, / And through that new blade's guard the old blade broke, / And pierced him." — William Butler Yeats, "Cuchulain's Fight with the Sea"

Finn MacCool in Irish myth, a giant hunter/warrior; according to legend, he built the Giant's Causeway as a path to Scotland

> Finn appears as a character in the novel *At Swim-Two-Birds*, by Flann O'Brien (1939).

Maeve/Medb ("MAYV") in Irish myth, the Queen of Connacht: a strong-willed, cunning warrior

> "Maeve the great queen was pacing to and fro… / Though now in her old age, in her young age / She had been beautiful in that old way / That's all but gone; for the proud heart is gone…" — William Butler Yeats, "The Old Age of Queen Maeve"

dybbuk ("DIB-ǝk" or "DIB-ook," to rhyme with *book*) in Jewish folklore, a malevolent spirit that enters and possesses a living person

> A play called *The Dybbuk*, later made into a Yiddish-language film, tells the story of a young woman possessed by the spirit of her dead beloved.

> "They prescribed high doses of Prozac and lithium to subdue whatever dybbuk had possessed him." — from an article about Philip Roth in *New York* magazine, 2000

golem ("GO-lǝm") in Jewish folklore, a figure made of clay, brought to life by kabbalist ritual, and functioning as an obedient servant, sometimes with unwanted consequences

In the most famous golem story, a rabbi in Prague creates a golem that protects the Jews of that city from persecution.

In Michael Chabon's novel, *The Amazing Adventures of Kavalier & Clay*, a refugee from Nazi-occupied Czechoslovakia travels to America in a coffin, which he shares with The Golem. (What a concept!)

Valhalla ("vahl-HAH-lə" or "val-HAL-ə") in Norse mythology, the hall of Odin, where heroes killed in battle feast in glory; or, figuratively, any heavenly place of glory or perfect happiness

"To Valhalla, to Visit Mr. Ibsen" — headline of humorous essay by Arnold M. Auerbach in the *New York Times*, 1971, which ends this way: "I, after all, merely created Hedda Gabler. But New York has given the world Bella Abzug."

Valkyrie ("VAL-kə-ree" or "val-KEER-ee") in Norse mythology, one of the beautiful deities who watch over battlefields and choose the most heroic among the slain, whom they bring to Valhalla

Wagner's "Ride of the Valkyries," from his opera *Die Walküre*, is the most famous of his melodies; you may know it from the helicopter attack scene in *Apocalypse Now*, or from Elmer Fudd's version, with the lyrics "Kill the wabbit, kill the wabbit…"

the Norns in Norse mythology, the three goddesses (Past, Present, and Future) who control the fates of both gods and men: the Norse equivalent of the Fates in Greek mythology

Loki ("LOH-kee") a Norse god who creates mischief and harm for the other gods: he can change shape

You may know Loki from the Marvel Comics movies, in which, played by Tom Hiddleston, he's constantly at odds with his adopted brother, Thor. (They're not brothers in the original myths.)

Asgard ("AHSS-gard" or "AZZ-gard") in Norse mythology, the fortress home of the Aesir (the principal Norse gods), connected to earth by the rainbow: Valhalla is here

"From afar, the confab known as the World Economic Forum in Davos looked a little like Asgard, the mythical home of the Norse gods." — from an article on TheDailyBeast.com, 2014

Yggdrasil ("IG-drə-sill") in Norse mythology, the huge, sacred ash tree whose trunk is at the center of the cosmos; its roots connect earth to heaven and hell

In Neil Gaiman's *Norse Mythology*, he describes Ratatosk, a malicious squirrel who runs up and down Yggdrasil, "the most perfect and beautiful of all trees," delivering messages between the eagle at the top and the serpent at the bottom.

Isis ("EYE-siss") in Egyptian mythology, the goddess of fertility: a powerful magician, and sister and wife of Osiris

You may have been wondering how the gods Osiris, Isis, Horus, and Ra fit together. Here's a synopsis, from the website UNRV.com: "…Osiris, the first god-king of Egypt, introduced laws and agriculture to humankind. He was then deceived and murdered by his scheming brother Seth, god of chaos. Seth hacked Osiris' body into pieces… Isis collected the pieces and magically revived her brother-husband Osiris, who became King of the Underworld. She also magically conceived a son, Horus… Osiris ruled the underworld, Horus ruled Egypt… and Ra the sun god ruled the heavens."

Anubis ("ə-NOO-biss") the Egyptian god of the dead, who leads the dead to judgment: portrayed as a man with a jackal's head

A children's picture book called *Anubis Speaks!* bears the subtitle: A Guide to the Afterlife by the Egyptian God of the Dead.

Thoth ("THOHTH" or "TOHT") the Egyptian god of the moon, of wisdom, and of learning: he is said to be the inventor of writing and creator of languages; his sacred bird was the ibis

"The ancient Egyptians considered [*The Book of the Dead*] as inspired by the gods, who caused their scribe, Thoth, to write it down." — Arthur Mee and J.A. Hammerton, editors, *The World's Greatest Books*, Volume XIII

Apis ("AY-piss") a bull deity worshipped by the ancient Egyptians

"The Apis mummy, or sacred bull, can be found in no other Egyptian Museum. Here there are three, very large, and beautifully preserved." — from an article about an Egyptian museum in Manhattan, in the *New York Times*, 1860

Hermes Trismegistus ("HƏR-meez triss-mə-JIST-əss") the Greek name for a legendary figure, a composite of the Greek god Hermes and the Egyptian god Thoth: the name means "Hermes the Thrice-Greatest"

He is the purported author of the *Hermetica*, a collection of writings from before the time of Christ. The writings cover astrology, medicine, alchemy, philosophy, and other subjects.

In the novel *Tristram Shandy,* the protagonist's name results from a mistake: his father wants him named "Trismegistus," after the legendary mystic, but the chambermaid mispronounces the name and therefore the curate christens him "Tristram."

Tiki ("TEE-kee") in Maori myth, the first man ever created; or a Polynesian god, considered the creator of man; or a carved image of a Polynesian god, in wood or stone

"Tiki carving is one of the oldest art forms known to man... Tiki statues carved by high-ranking tribesmen were considered sacred and powerful... Tiki statues carved by anyone other than a high-ranking tribesman were used simply as decoration." — from a web article on Tiki culture, on the website HomeWetBar.com, 2019

feast of Barmecide ("BAR-mə-side") a feast at which no food—or only make-believe food—is served

The phrase comes from a tale in the *Arabian Nights*, in which a wealthy prince (named Barmecide) invites a poor, hungry man to a feast, and serves only imaginary food.

(Not to be confused with Barbicide®, the blue disinfectant, which you'll find in a tall jar at the barber shop, usually with a comb or two inside.)

From Law

amicus curiae ("ə-MEE-kəs KYOO-ree-eye" or "-ee") "friend of the court": a person or group that is not party to a case but submits a brief advising the court

The Onion, the satirical website, filed an amicus curiae brief with the Supreme Court in the case of *Novak v. City of Parma*, which involves a citizen who was arrested for parodying a local police department's Facebook page. Explaining The Onion's interest in the case, the brief said, "As the globe's premier parodists, The Onion's writers... have a self-serving interest in preventing political authorities from imprisoning humorists." (2022)

bill of attainder ("ə-TAIN-dər") a legislative act declaring a person (or group) guilty of a serious crime, such as treason, and pronouncing sentence without a trial

"No Bill of Attainder or ex post facto Law shall be passed." —
U.S. Constitution, Article I, Section 9, Clause 3

"If you discover a law against calling you a twit,
Mr. Gribble, please let me know!"

blue sky laws in the U.S., state laws that regulate the sale of
securities, intended to protect buyers from fraud

According to Brittanica.com, the term derives "from concerns
that fraudulent securities offerings were so brazen and
commonplace that issuers would sell building lots in the blue
sky."

"MANY STATES PLAN NEW 'BLUE SKY' LAWS; Existing
Statutes in Several Instances Held Inadequate to Protect
Investors." – headline in the *New York Times*, 1933

change of venue (*venue* rhymes with *menu*) transfer of a trial to a new location, often because impartial jurors can't be found in the original judicial district

> "There is one bad reason and one good reason to grant a change of venue in the Boston Marathon trial of Dzhokhar Tsarnaev." — from an opinion essay in the *New York Times*, 2015

chattel ("TCHAT-əl") personal property, as distinguished from "real property," i.e., land and buildings; chattel can be living (such as livestock) or inanimate

> This word is seen most often in connection with slavery: "The federal government offered to pay slave owners close to market rates for each of their human chattel, thereby bring slavery to an end without a resort to armed conflict." — from an article in *Rolling Stone*, 2021

codicil ("KAH-də-səl") a legal document that adds to or modifies a will

> "In 1990 Donald [Trump] secretly enlisted a lawyer to draft a codicil to the will of his father, Fred Sr." — from an article in the *New York Review of Books*, 2020

corpus delicti ("KOR-pəs də-LIK-tie") "body of the crime": tangible evidence that a crime was committed, e.g., the body of a murder victim

> "An enthusiastic trooper, one of a party investigating river, dam and hollow log in search of the corpus delicti, found some important evidence in a fallen tree." — from an article in the *Sunday Mail Magazine* (Brisbane), 1964

de facto ("DEE FAK-toh" or "DAY-") existing as a fact or reality, though not officially recognized by the law: describes common practice

> "The Federal Government is making a quiet but potentially significant effort to ease the hitherto intractable problem of de facto segregation in the North." — from an article in the *New York Times*, 1967

de jure ("DEE DJOO-ree" or "DAY YOO-ree") according to law: the opposite of *de facto*, i.e., existing in accordance with the law, or as a result of it

> "Biden in response relied on a 1970s-vintage policy distinction between de jure and de facto school segregation." — from an article on Vox.com, 2019

easement the right to enter, cross, and/or use property one doesn't own; or a parcel of land that may be used in this way

"The West Essex Trail follows a short distance... of the former rail bed of... the old Erie-Lackawanna Railroad... The property is now a conservation easement." — from a trail description on the website TrailLink.com

ex post facto "after the fact": retroactive, i.e., describing a law that criminalizes an act that wasn't a crime when the law was written (Such laws are forbidden under the Constitution.)

"[In] the recent 6th Circuit decision in *Doe v. Snyder*... the court voided application of the Michigan Sex Offender Registration Act (SORA) on the grounds that it imposes retroactive punishment on previously convicted sex offenders in violation of the constitutional prohibition against Ex Post Facto laws." — from an essay in the *Washington Post,* 2016

gravamen ("GRAHV-ə-mən" or "grə-VAY-mən") the essential or most serious part of an accusation

"The gravamen of Nick Paumgarten's article... on the measles vaccine is his argument that the people he derisively terms 'anti-vaxxers' are irrational since the risks of vaccines are so low and the rewards so enormous. In my experience, virtually all so called 'anti-vaxxers' are parents of vaccine-injured children whose personal tragedies provoked them to look closely at the complex science supporting that risk/reward assertion..." — from Robert F. Kennedy, Jr.'s response to a *New Yorker* article, published on the website Children'sHealthDefense.org, 2019

habeas corpus ("HAY-bee-əss KOR-pəss") "you shall have the body": a writ of habeas corpus requires law enforcement authorities to bring a prisoner before a judge; it can be used to challenge a purportedly unlawful detention and secure the prisoner's release, unless the detention is found to be lawful

"Nevertheless, Gitmo's status as a strange carve-out to the American justice system remains worthy of attention, given that habeas corpus rights are denied to foreign nationals held prisoner there." — from an article in *National Review,* 2021

in loco parentis ("in LOH-koh pə-REN-təss") "in the place of a parent": acting in place of a parent (Examples include teachers and child-care providers.)

"Colleges instead are practicing a new version of 'in loco parentis'—they are expected to be stand-in parents..." — from an article in the *Washington Post,* 2015

nolo contendere ("NOH-loh kən-TEN-də-ree" or "-ray") a plea of no contest: meaning that the defendant will not contest a criminal charge, and agrees to accept punishment without admitting guilt

Why not just plead guilty? Because a plea of nolo contendere can't be used as evidence in a related civil suit.

"On behalf of the defendant, your honor, I enter a plea of nolo contendere." — Vice President Spiro Agnew's attorney, quoted in an article about Agnew's tax evasion case, in the *New York Times*, 1973

nolle prosequi ("NOH-lee [or NAH-lee] PROH-sə-kwy" or "-kway") "unwilling to pursue": a prosecutor's motion declaring that a criminal case is being abandoned, either before trial or before a verdict

In 1977, I was arrested in Baltimore along with three friends while celebrating the end of our grad school classes at Johns Hopkins, because one of them was throwing firecrackers out the car window. When the case came to trial, the prosecutor entered a motion of nolle prosequi, to our great relief.

prima facie ("PRY-mə FAY-shee") "at first appearance": adequate to establish a fact, unless disproved (usually refers to evidence)

"[The failure of La Reunion, a commune in Texas, in the 19th century] has also been understood as prima facie evidence of the futility of socialist politics." — from an article in the *Dallas Morning News*, 2020

proviso ("prə-VY-zoh" or "proh-") a condition or stipulation in an agreement

"Elgin Police Department's contract… to provide police officers in schools will be extended one year with the proviso that police officials look for ways to address the inequity in Black student arrests and citations." — from an article on ChicagoTribune.com, 2020

quillet (archaic) a quibble; or a subtle distinction; or an evasive or frivolous argument

"A barrister at home in the courts and in the purlieus and quillets of the law." — *The Dictionary of National Biography*, 1912-21

surety ("SHOOR-ə-tee") a guarantee by a person or organization that another person will fulfill a duty or pay a required sum: if the other person fails to do what is required, the guarantor will be responsible for the debt, etc.; or the person or organization making this guarantee

"Ten freeholders… were sureties or free pledges to the king for the good behaviour of each other." — William Blackstone, *Commentaries on the Laws of England*, 1765

tort an action, whether intentional or not, that harms a person or property and entitles the victim to payment of damages; common examples include negligence, physical assault, inflicting of emotional distress, and damage to property

> "In the casino that tort law has become, wild wagers are becoming routine. A family sues the Weather Channel for not forecasting the storm during which a family member on a fishing trip drowned... [T]he need for tort reform is obvious." — from an essay by George Will in the *Washington Post*, 2002

usufruct ("YOOZ-ə-frukt" or "YOOS") the right to use someone else's property, usually for a limited period of time

> "The earth belongs in usufruct to the living." — Thomas Jefferson, Letter to James Madison, 1798

voir dire ("VWAHR DEER") the process of questioning prospective jurors to ensure that they are competent to serve, and not biased for or against a defendant or plaintiff

> "At trial, local prosecutors successfully shuffled almost all of the prospective Black jurors out of the top of the jury pool, and then struck the only remaining Black juror during voir dire, resulting in an all-white jury." — from an article in *The New Republic*, 2022

writ of certiorari ("SƏR-shee-ə-RAIR-eye" or "-ee") an order issued by an appellate court, directing a lower court to deliver its records so that the superior court can review them

> "[T]he respondents... filed a brief requesting the Supreme Court to deny the president's petition for a writ of certiorari..." — from an article in *Newsweek,* 2018

Diacritical Marks (also called Diacritics)

acute accent é: in Spanish, Italian, and many other languages, this mark indicates that the syllable is stressed; in other languages it signifies different things

grave accent ("GRAHV") è: in French, this mark changes the sound of the letter E; over an A or a U, it distinguishes words that are spelled the same way (Other languages use this accent in other ways.)

tilde ("TILL-də") ñ: in Spanish, a tilde changes the sound of the letter N to "nyuh"

> For example, *año* ("year") is pronounced "AN-yo."

In Portuguese, a tilde indicates that a letter is to be pronounced nasally.

cedilla ("sə-DILL-ə") ç: in French and Portuguese, indicates that the letter C is to be pronounced like an S, as in *façade*; it is also used, though differently, in Turkish

umlaut ("OOM-laot") ü: in German, Swedish, and several other languages, indicates that the vowel is to be pronounced a different way

háček ("HAH-chek") č: used in Slavic languages, e.g., Czech

circumflex ("SƏR-kəm-flex") ô

> "The French are notoriously touchy, or sentimental, about their language but on realising that the circumflex accent was at risk of disappearing from 2000 French words... they reacted with anger." — from an article on BBC.com, 2016

macron ("MAY-krahn" or "MA-krən," the A pronounced as in *cat*) ō: in English pronunciation guides, indicates a long vowel sound, like the I in *kite* or the O in *so*; the mark is also used in Latin and other languages

breve ("BREEV") ŏ: in English pronunciation guides, indicates a short vowel sound, like the I in *kit*; the mark is also used in Latin and other languages

diaeresis/dieresis ("dy-ER-ə-səss") oö: indicates that the marked vowel is to be pronounced as a separate syllable, e.g., as in *naïve*

Alloys

steel iron with a small amount of carbon; often includes other elements as well, to give it specific properties

bronze copper with a smaller amount of tin

brass copper with zinc

pewter ("PYOO-tər") tin with a smaller amount of antinomy and copper (formerly, tin plus lead)

sterling silver silver with other metals, usually copper (accounting for 7.5% of its weight): the alloy is harder than pure silver

nickel silver copper with smaller amounts of nickel and zinc: it has a silvery appearance, but contains no silver (unless plated)

pinchbeck copper with zinc: a form of brass that imitates gold, used for costume jewelry and watches

Because of its appearance and use, *pinchbeck* has also come to mean "something that appears valuable but isn't really."

"... he had heard that those pearls were artificial—that those golden locks were only pinchbeck." — William Makepeace Thackeray, *The Virginians*

Poker Hands, Ranked*

five of a kind four cards of the same rank, plus a Joker

royal flush Ace, King, Queen, Joker, 10, all in the same suit

straight flush five cards consecutive in rank, all in the same suit

four of a kind four cards of the same rank, i.e., in all four suits

full house three of a kind plus two of a kind

flush five cards in the same suit

straight five cards consecutive in rank

three of a kind three cards of the same rank, in different suits

two pairs

one pair

high card if no player has any of the above hands, the player with the highest-ranking card wins

*This list refers to the poker game Five Card Draw.

A Potpourri of Etceteras

You may vaguely know what these mean, but could you explain them?

cellulose ("SELL-yoo-lohs" or "-yə-lohs") the main substance in the cell walls of plants: a carbohydrate, it is used industrially in the manufacture of paper, plastics, and many other products

"In order to make the pregnancy test flushable and compostable, the founders of Lia chose natural, cellulose fibers, which allows the product to disperse in water and disintegrate in soil easily." — from an article in *Forbes*, 2021

heuristic ("hyoo-RISS-tik") relating to "mental shortcuts," or using intuition or common sense to make decisions; or (especially in computing) employing informal trial-and-error or experiment to solve a problem or to calculate an approximate answer; or moving step by step, choosing the best answer at each stage, and basing the next step on that answer; or, in education, using a method that lets students learn by making their own discoveries

> When a word has this many shades of meaning, it's no wonder I can never remember its definition.

> "The availability heuristic is a cognitive short-cut used when people easily retrieve information from memory and perceive it as relevant evidence... Although this heuristic is sometimes useful, it can... result in illusionary correlations." — Janet E. Davidson, in *The Psychology of Human Thought* (Sternberg and Funke, editors), 1988

tranche ("TRAHNSH") a portion, or slice: in finance, one part of a larger pool of securities

> This word—derived from the French word *trancher*, to cut— appeared often in articles about the 2008 financial crisis, as reporters tried to explain how the financial industry had divided pools of mortgages, etc., into tranches representing different levels of risk, and then sold them to investors.

Measurements and solids

ell an obsolete measurement of length, often used to measure textiles

> It's different in different countries. In England, an ell equaled 45 inches.

> "...tearful women wetting whole ells of cambric in concert..." — Thomas Carlyle, *The French Revolution*

verst ("VƏRST") a Russian unit of distance, approximately equal to 2/3 of a mile (or a bit more than a kilometer)

> "Muscovite lords commonly go fifty and sixty versts... to make visits to each other." — Nathaniel Wraxall, *Cursory Remarks Made in a Tour through Some of the Northern Parts of Europe* (1775)

parsec ("PAR-sek") in astronomy, a distance roughly equal to 3.26 light years

> I can quote the O.E.D. on this one, even if I can't understand it: "A unit of length equal to the distance at which a star would have a heliocentric parallax of one second of arc."

> "You've never heard of the Millennium Falcon? It's the ship that made the Kessel Run in less than twelve parsecs." — Han Solo to

Ben (Obi-Wan) Kenobi, in *Star Wars* (He's confusing units of distance with units of time, but nobody's perfect.)

dol ("DOHL") a unit for measuring the intensity of pain, based on the sensation of heat rays on the skin (from *dolor*, the Latin word for pain)

> In 1940, researchers "focused the light of a 100-watt projection lamp with a lens on an area of skin that had been blackened to minimize reflection... They developed a pain scale... with 10 gradations, or 10 levels. They assigned the name of 'dols' to these levels." — from the Wikipedia entry on the *dolorimeter,* an instrument for measuring pain.

frustum ("FRUST-əm") a solid that remains after the upper part of a cone or pyramid has been sliced off; the upper surface is parallel to the base

> You may have seen an elephant standing on a frustum at the circus.

parallelepiped ("par-ə-lell-ə-PY-pid," the first A pronounced as in *arrow*) a solid with six faces, each of which is a parallelogram, each parallel to its opposite face

> "Johnny, I see you've built a parallelepiped with your Erector set." "It was a cube, but Sally sat on it."

> Or, for a more serious use of the word: "At the Joint Mathematics Meetings, researchers reported the first sightings of 'perfect parallelepipeds,' bricks whose sides are allowed to be parallelograms rather than strict 90° rectangles and all 13 of whose edges and diagonals are exact integers." — from an article in *Science* magazine, 2010

Earthy language

orogeny ("or-AH-jə-nee") the process of mountain-building, especially by folding or faulting of the earth's crust; or a mountain-building event of this type

> "In the contest between erosion and orogeny, erosion never loses." — from an article in the *New Yorker*, 1986

> (Admit it, you thought this word had something to do with sex.)

rhumb line ("RUM") an imaginary line that crosses all lines of longitude at the same angle: when navigators plot a ship's course on a chart, they use a rhumb line

> "The distance run was 820 leagues (roughly 2,624 miles), which was very close to the rhumb-line distance of 2,610 miles." —

Samuel Eliot Morison, *The Second Voyage of Christopher Columbus*

bathyseism ("BATH-ə-size-əm") an earthquake occurring at great depths

> "…while the immediate origin of the [1906 California] earthquake proper may be traced to occurrences… in the outermost parts of the earth's crust, these are but the secondary result of a deep-seated origin, or bathyseism…" — from an article in the journal *Nature*, 1922

Tanks and pools

cistern ("SIS-tərn") a tank for storing water, especially rainwater; or a tank on top of a building that supplies water to the apartments or offices below

> If only I could have found an engraving that showed monks near one of these: the caption would have read, *Brethren and Cistern.*

septic tank an underground tank that collects household wastewater and sewage; the solids settle to the bottom and decompose through bacterial action

> "When hurricanes or major storms hit the state [of South Carolina], well water is contaminated with pesticides and septic tank residuals, among other toxic matter." — from an article on NBCNews.com, 2021

cesspool an underground receptacle that receives household wastewater and sewage; figuratively, a place characterized by corruption or filth

> "His social media feeds are a cesspool of misogyny, bigotry and bizarre fringe conspiracy theories." — from an article in the *Salt Lake Tribune*, 2022

If you see these words, you're probably reading something very old

anent ("ə-NENT") (archaic, Scottish) about; regarding

> "…nor is it worth while to vex one's self anent what cannot be mended." — Sir Walter Scott, *The Abbot*

quotha! ("KWOH-thə," the TH pronounced as in *with*) (archaic) indeed! forsooth! (often sarcastic, indicating mild contempt after quoting someone else)

"Learning, quotha! A mere composition of tricks and mischief."
— Oliver Goldsmith, *She Stoops to Conquer*

maugre ("MAW-ghər") (archaic) in spite of

"Maugre the fact that there were two of ye, instead of one, she had no more mouths to feed than breasts to feed 'em with." — John Barth, *The Sot-Weed Factor*

hight ("HITE") (archaic) called

"Childe Harold was he hight…" — Lord Byron, "Childe Harold's Pilgrimage"

yclept ("ih-KLEPT") (archaic) named

"We toured the grounds, yclept Erdmann's Cornlot after its former use and owner…" — John Barth, *Letters*

Fancy fabrics

damask ("DAM-əsk," with the A pronounced as in *cat*) a reversible, woven fabric: the pattern is visible on both sides

Originally made in Damascus, Syria, damask is commonly used for tablecloths and upholstery.

"The home… reflects [Evgeny Lebedev's] own peculiar mix of Old and New World interests, with works by modern artists set against acres of mahogany and silk damask." — from an article in *Town & Country*, 2021

chenille ("shə-NEEL") a velvety yarn or fabric with threads that protrude

Chenille is the French word for "caterpillar": the protruding threads supposedly resemble the fur of that critter.

"That silky black chenille keeps coming back to mind. These are elegant, smart-woman clothes designed not to challenge but to flatter." — from an article in *Vogue*, 2020

pashmina ("pash-MEE-nə") a fine material made from the wool of Himalayan goats: a variant of cashmere, made from a different variety of goat

Those shawls and scarfs selling for $10 at the kiosks in your local mall—are they genuine pashmina? Not likely, since the genuine article costs at least $300. But if you really want to know, buy one and burn part of it. If it's real pashmina, it will smell like burnt hair. (Kind of like the Dunk-the-Witch test: if she drowns, she wasn't a witch after all.)

These words have little in common, I'm sorry to say

tack equipment used with horses; common types of tack include saddles, stirrups, bridles, and reins.

> "Joseph Miller, Who Sold Horse Tack to the Well-Heeled, Dies at 93" — headline of obituary in the *New York Times*, 2011 (Miller's shop was on East 24th Street.)

bastinado ("ba-stə-NAY-doh," the first A pronounced as in *cat*, or "-NAH-do") a stick or club used to beat someone; or the beating; or punishment by beating the soles of the feet

> "...from simple fear of pain he did not relish the idea of ritual bastinados on his backside, the administering of which he assumed to be the sailors' object." — John Barth, *The Sot-Weed Factor*

anabasis ("ə-NAB-ə-səss," the second A pronounced as in *cat*) a large-scale military advance, especially moving inland from a coast; or a military retreat

> How can a word mean two opposite things? Xenophon wrote a history of Cyrus the Younger's unsuccessful expedition against Artaxerxes II, and called it *Anabasis*. The history tells of both the offensive march and the arduous retreat.

patronymic ("pat-rə-NIM-ik") a name that comes from the father, usually by the addition of a prefix or suffix, e.g., O', Mac, –son, or -dottir

> In Russia, the middle name is a patronymic: e.g., Anna Arkadyevna Karenina: Anna, daughter of Arkady.

> "Most surnames come ultimately, if not always obviously from one of four sources: place-names... nicknames... trade names... and patronymics." — Bill Bryson, *Mother Tongue*

On death and dying

psychopomp ("SY-koh-pahmp") in Greek mythology, a figure who leads souls to the world of the dead; or a spiritual guide for the living

> "Why... did Botticelli use an outmoded method of pictorial narrative, repeatedly showing the figures of Dante and his psychopomp Virgil more than once in the same 'frame' at the different stages of their journey through Hell and Purgatory...?" — from an article in the *International Herald Tribune*, 2000

necromancer ("NECK-roh-man-sər") one who practices necromancy, a form of magic involving the dead: including reanimation of the dead in order to foretell the future or influence events to come

> "…he suddenly declared that he would make a fiery hand appear on the door; and to the astonishment and terror of the boys in his room, a hand, or something like it, in pale light, did then and there appear. The… young necromancer declared that the same wonder would appear in all the rooms in turn, which it accordingly did…" — Thomas Hughes, *Tom Brown's School Days*

necrology ("nə-KRAHL-ə-jee") a list of those who have died recently; or the science of interpreting mortality statistics

> The *AIA Guide to New York City*, an appreciation of Gotham's most noteworthy architecture, includes a section on demolished buildings, wittily entitled *Necrology*.

thanatologist ("than-ə-TAHL-ə-jist," the TH pronounced as in *with*) a specialist in the needs (practical and psychological) of terminally ill patients and their families; or a scientist who studies the physical process of dying

> "After the first and second World War, many books emerged on the subject of death, grief, and coping with loss. In the 1960s, Elisabeth Kubler-Ross… pushed forward the thanatology movement." — from an article on the website LoveToKnow.com

obsequies ("AHB-sə-kweez") funeral rites

> "A huge black banner, which floated from the top of the tower, announced that the obsequies of the late owner were still in the act of being solemnized." — Sir Walter Scott, *Ivanhoe*

cerements ("SƏR-ə-mənts") cloth coated with wax, formerly used for wrapping the dead

> "The ghost of Athelstane himself would burst his bloody cerements." — Sir Walter Scott, *Ivanhoe*

knell ("NELL") the sound of a bell, especially when rung slowly and solemnly, to announce a death or funeral

> "Being tagged anti-Trump would be a death knell, both with primary voters and the former president, whose endorsement could decide the race." — from an article in the *Washington Examiner*, 2021

barrow a mound of earth or stones built over a grave

> "…steam / Floats up from … the homes / Of happy men that have the power to die, / And grassy barrows of the happier dead." — Alfred, Lord Tennyson, "Tithonus" (The poem tells of a

mythological prince who was granted immortality but not eternal youth, to his sorrow.)

tumulus ("TOOM-yə-ləss") an artificial mound, especially an ancient burial mound

"…the earth is sown with the bodies and the relics of legendary figures… I knew they were lying all about us—the earth tells you so… There are smooth green mounds, hummocks, hillocks, tumuli everywhere, and beneath them, not very deep either, lie the warriors, the heroes…" — Henry Miller, *The Colossus of Maroussi*

catafalque ("KAT-ə-falk," the first and last As pronounced as in *cat*) a wooden structure that supports the coffin when an important person lies in state, or during a funeral

"Benjamin French* designed Lincoln's catafalque, which consisted simply of pine boards nailed together and covered with black broadcloth. Over the years the base and platform have been modified to accommodate the remains of dignitaries who lay in state in the Rotunda and nearby locations." — from an article on the website AbrahamLincolnOnline.org

"[Ruth Bader] Ginsburg lay in state in the National Statuary Hall… her coffin resting on the historic Lincoln catafalque." — from an article in *Vogue*, 2020

* Cousin of Daniel Chester French, who created the monumental sculpture of Abraham Lincoln inside the Lincoln Memorial.

cinerarium ("sin-ə-RAIR-ee-əm") a place where the ashes of cremated bodies are kept

"…he is the superintendent of Tokyo's only locker cinerarium, a three-story concrete building… equipped with 3,950 compartments to hold the ashes of the dead." — from an article in the *New York Times*, 1979

cenotaph ("SƏN-ə-taff, the final syllable rhyming with *half*) a monument or empty tomb honoring a person or people buried elsewhere: especially, a memorial to the war dead

"Near the Cenotaph a middle-aged lady was standing with raised eyes, murmuring a prayer." — Aldous Huxley, *Point Counter Point* (This line refers to London's national war memorial, originally built to honor the dead of World War One.)

exhumation ("eks-yoo-MAY-shən" or "egz-") removal of a corpse from a grave; or digging up something from the ground; or, figuratively, bringing something to light (from the verb *exhume*)

"Exhumation of possible Tulsa massacre victims expected" — headline of a story on a *Washington Post* podcast, 2021

metempsychosis ("me-təm-sy-KOH-səss") reincarnation: the transmigration of the soul into a new body (either human or animal) after death

> "PADDY DIGNAM: Bloom, I am Paddy Dignam's spirit...
> SECOND WATCH: *(Blesses himself.)* How is that possible?
> FIRST WATCH: It is not in the penny catechism.
> PADDY DIGNAM: By metempsychosis. Spooks." — James Joyce, *Ulysses*

End zones

ultima Thule ("ULL-tih-mə TOO-lee" or "THOO-lee" or "TOO/THOO-lə") among the ancients, the northernmost region believed to be inhabited; or, by extension, the farthest place one could voyage; or any far-off, unknown region; or, figuratively, the highest (or lowest) point attainable

> "Before you write off that behaviour as being the ultima thule of ingratitude... try to understand the effect your news... had on me." — from a letter by Malcolm Lowry, 1954

bourn(e) ("BORN") a boundary, terminal point, or goal

> "...death, / The undiscovered country from whose bourn / No traveler returns..." — William Shakespeare, *Hamlet*

The Terminus

The Ones You Really Should Know

Why You Should Know Them

Let's make a bet. If you read today's *New York Times* or *Washington Post*, I predict that you'll find at least one of the words in the following list. As you've already seen, many of the words in this book are still in use, and not ready for retirement. (Kudos to all the novelists, journalists, and others who are helping to keep our language rich. Thank you—and please keep it up!)

You already know some of these words, I'm sure. Familiarize yourself with the others. When you encounter one in your reading, you won't have to stop and think, *What does this mean?* Instead, you'll smile with satisfaction, and a certain pride.

abject ("AB-jekt") wretched, contemptible, lacking self-respect; or (when referring to an undesirable condition) extreme, e.g., *abject poverty*

ablution(s) ("ə-BLOO-shən(s)") cleansing of the body, especially as a ceremonial religious act (sometimes used humorously, for its formality)

abnegation ("ab-nə-GAY-shən") self-denial; renunciation; giving up something

abrogate ("AB-rə-gate") to formally annul or abolish; or to fail to do something one is supposed to do

abstemious characterized by restraint, especially in the consuming of food or alcohol

agoraphobia ("AG-ə-rə-FOH-bee-ə") fear of leaving home, or of going out into open spaces, or of being in a crowd—i.e., of places where you might feel trapped or embarrassed

amicus curiae ("ə-MEE-kəs KYOO-ree-eye") Latin: "friend of the court": a person or group that is not party to a case but submits a brief advising the court

analgesic ("an-əl-JEEZ-ik") a painkiller: a drug that relieves pain (or, as an adjective, having this property)

apostate ("ə-POSS-tait") one who abandons a religious faith—or, by extension, a cause or political belief

apostle ("ə-POSS-əl") someone sent out on a special mission or as a preacher; or (with a capital A) one of the twelve men Jesus sent out into the world to preach his Gospel

apposite ("APP-ə-zit") pertinent; or appropriate

astringent ("ə-STRIN-jənt") tending to constrict or contract tissue; harsh, bitter

auto-da-fé ("AW-toh də FAY") ("act of the faith") the public burning of a heretic; or the ceremony for pronouncing judgment on the heretic, followed by execution

avatar ("AV-ə-tar") in Hinduism, an incarnation of a deity; or a person who embodies a particular quality; or an image representing a person on the internet or in a video game

avuncular ("ə-VUNK-yoo-lər") of or like an uncle, especially a genial, benevolent one

bailiwick ("BAY-lə-wik" or "BAY-lee-wik") one's specific area of authority or expertise

bifurcated ("BUY-fər-kate-əd") split in two; divided into two parts or branches

bilious ("BILL-ee-əss") peevish, bad-tempered; of a sickly color (from "bile")

bombast ("BAHM-bast") cotton batting used to stuff garments in order to make them appear baggy; or, figuratively, inflated language meant to impress, but without substance

cachet ("ka-SHAY") prestige; a quality that earns someone or something respect; originally, an official seal, as on a letter or document

calumny ("CAL-um-nee," the A pronounced as in *cat*) slander: a false, malicious statement (or statements) intended to damage someone's reputation

carapace ("KAR-ə-pace," the first A pronounced as in *cat*) the upper shell of a turtle

caryatid ("carry-A-tid," the stressed A pronounced as in *cat*) in architecture, a supporting pillar carved in the shape of a woman

catheter ("KATH-ə-tər") a slender, flexible tube inserted into a body cavity (the bladder, usually) for draining fluid or distending the passage

cauterize ("KAW-tə-rize") to burn so as to seal a wound or destroy dead tissue and prevent the spread of infection; or, figuratively, to deaden

celerity ("sə-LER-ih-tee") swiftness

centenarian ("sent-ə-NAIR-ee-ən") a person who is a hundred years old, or older

cesspool an underground receptacle that receives household wastewater and sewage; figuratively, a place characterized by corruption or filth

circadian ("sər-KAY-dee-ən") recurring every 24 hours (especially refers to bodily processes such as the cycle of sleeping and waking)

coddle ("KAH-dl") to treat someone with an overabundance of protective care and indulgence; or to cook gently by heating in water that isn't quite boiling (e.g., an egg)

cognomen ("cog-NOH-mən") the name by which one is known: either a surname or a nickname

commodious ("kə-MOH-dee-əss") comfortably spacious

concomitant ("kon-KOM-ih-tənt") accompanying; or occurring along with something else

crepuscular ("krə-PUS-kyə-lər," the second syllable rhyming with *bus*) of or like twilight; or, in zoology, becoming active at twilight, e.g., birds and insects

cupidity ("kyoo-PID-ə-tee") greed; lust for wealth

décolletage ("day-kahl-ə-TAZH") a low neckline

denouement ("day-noo-MAH(N)," pronounced as in French) the conclusion of a story (or film, or play, etc.), when the plot and any subplots are resolved: the final outcome

desultory ("DESS-əl-taw-ree") lacking in order or planning; or, describing a conversation, jumping randomly from one topic to another

diffident ("DIFF-ə-dənt") timid, lacking self-confidence

dissemble ("dih-SEM-bəl") to conceal one's true beliefs or feelings, deceitfully

ebullient ("ih-BOOL-yənt" or "ə-BUHL-yənt") energetically enthusiastic; overflowing with exuberance or excitement

egregious ("ə-GREE-jəss") outstanding in a bad way

emolument ("ə-MAHL-yə-mənt") payment, profits, or perks obtained through one's job

entre nous ("ON-trə NOO") French: "between us": i.e., confidentially

epistemology ("ə-piss-tə-MAHL-ə-jee") the branch of philosophy that examines the nature, origin, and validity of knowledge

eponymous ("ə-PAHN-ə-məss") named after a person; or giving one's name to something, e.g., a city, an era, or a television show

erstwhile former

eugenics ("yoo-JEN-iks") the practice of controlling human breeding in order to improve genes; or the advocacy of this strategy

eulogy ("YOO-lə-jee") any speech of high praise; or, such a speech delivered at a funeral

factotum ("fak-TOH-təm") (Latin: "do everything") an employee or assistant who does all kinds of work

fatuous ("FA-choo-əss," with the A pronounced as in *have*) foolish, or pointless, especially in an oblivious or smug way; can also refer to speech or writing

feckless lacking strength, initiative, purpose, or character; ineffective; irresponsible

fractious ("FRAK-shəss") rebellious; cranky; unruly (often refers to children)

fulminate ("FULL-mə-nate") to issue thunderous verbal attacks or protests

fulsome ("FULL-səm") excessive, overdone, offensive, sickening; when describing praise, it also implies that the praise is insincere

gaffe ("GAFF") an embarrassing social blunder, or faux pas

hadj/hajj ("HADJ," to rhyme with *badge*) the pilgrimage to Mecca, a religious duty for all Muslims

harridan ("HAR-ih-dən," the first A pronounced as in *cat*) an unpleasant, aggressive, scolding old woman

hauteur ("hoh-TƏRR") snobbery, haughtiness, disdainful pride

impecunious ("im-pə-KYOO-nee-əss") poor; having little or no money, either chronically or temporarily

importune ("im-por-TUNE" or "-pər-") to request or demand urgently and persistently

incandescent ("in-kan-DESS-ənt") shining intensely with heat; very bright; or passionate

inchoate ("in-KOH-ət" or "IN-kə-WAIT") not completely formed, because still at an early stage

inveigh ("in-VAY") to protest strongly or bitterly (usually *against* something)

invidious ("in-VID-ee-əss") tending to arouse resentment or animosity; offensive; or containing a slight

jeremiad ("jer-ə-MY-ad") a long lamentation; a catalogue of complaints; a tale of woe; or an angry harangue

jihad ("jə-HAHD" or "jee-HAHD") a holy war against Islam's enemies or unbelievers: a religious duty for Muslims; or, by extension, any crusade against an opposing belief

karma ("KAR-mə") in Buddhism and Hinduism, the sum of a person's actions (and their impact), which will determine the nature of that person's next life; or, in popular use, the fate you earn by the way you live your life

koan ("KOH-ahn") in Zen Buddhism, a paradox, story, or riddle to be meditated upon: its purpose is to confound logical thought and lead the novice toward intuitive enlightenment

limpid ("LIMP-id") transparently clear, like clean glass or water

lubricious ("loo-BRISH-əss") lewd, intended to arouse lust; lecherous, showing sexual desire; smooth or slippery, especially with oil

malediction ("mal-ə-DICK-shən") a curse, intended to bring harm to its target

Manichaean ("man-ə-KEE-ən") one who believes in Manichaeism, the dualistic philosophy that views all of history as a struggle between light and dark, good and evil; or, pejoratively, one who sees everything as black or white, good or bad; or, as an adjective, adhering to this worldview

metastasis ("mə-TAH-stə-səss") the spread of a disease (usually cancer) from its original site to other parts of the body

minion ("MIN-yən") an underling, especially an unimportant or servile one

miscreant ("MISS-kree-ənt") a lawbreaker, evildoer, villain, or one who behaves badly (The word can also be used as an adjective.)

mollify ("MAHL-ə-fy") to placate, soothe, or appease

mot juste ("MOH ZHOOST") French: the right word or expression; the perfect word for the occasion

mullah ("MULL-ə" or "MOOL-ə") a Muslim teacher or interpreter of religious law; a general title of respect for a man learned in Islamic theology

nascent ("NAY-sənt") in the process of emerging

nave ("NAYV") the central part of a church, where most of the congregation sits

neologism ("nee-AHL-ə-jiz-əm") a word or phrase that is newly coined

nirvana ("nər-VAH-nə") in Buddhism, the ultimate goal: a state in which the individual has transcended desire, suffering, and self, and is released from the cycle of death and rebirth; or, in popular use, a perfectly blissful state, free of pain and worry

nostrum ("NAH-strəm") a remedy without proof of effectiveness, the contents of which are kept secret; or a questionable plan for solving a problem

obsequies ("AHB-sə-kweez") funeral rites

olfactory ("ohl-FAK-tə-ree") pertaining to the sense of smell

oncology ("ahn-KAHL-ə-jee") the study of tumors, or their treatment in medicine

paladin ("PAL-ə-dn") a paragon of knighthood, heroic and chivalrous; or a strong defender of a cause

palindrome ("PAL-in-drome") a word, phrase, or sentence that's spelled the same backwards and forwards — famous examples include *Able was I ere I saw Elba* (Napoleon's complaint); and *Madam I'm Adam* (on meeting Eve)

parochial ("pə-ROH-kee-əl) having a narrow outlook; or limited in scope; or relating to a church parish

pediment ("PED-ə-mənt") the triangular part of a classical building's façade, above the columns and the entablature

penury ("PEN-yə-ree") an oppressive degree of poverty

perdition ("pər-DIH-shən") in Christian theology, eternal damnation after death, as punishment for unrepented sin; or hell itself; or complete ruin

phoenix ("FEE-niks") a bird resembling an eagle, which lives for centuries, then burns in flames ignited by the sun, and rises from its ashes to live again; or a person of great beauty or excellence

piquant ("PEE-kənt" or "PEE-kwənt") provocative, in an appealing way; or pleasantly sharp-tasting

polymath one who is learned in many fields

potable ("POH-tə-bəl") safely drinkable; or, as a noun, such a liquid

prehensile ("prə-HEN-səl") adapted for holding or seizing, e.g., a monkey's tail

prescient ("PREH-shənt") having knowledge of what will happen before it happens

preternatural ("preh-tər-NATCH-ər-əl" or "pree-") outside the normal course of nature (less occult than *supernatural*, but more mystical than *abnormal*)

pulchritude ("PUL-krə-tood," with the first U pronounced as in *nut*) (literary) beauty, especially a woman's

quid pro quo ("KWID PROH KWOH") Latin: "something for something": a thing given with the expectation of getting something in return

quintessence ("kwin-TESS-ənss") the most essential aspect of something: its purest form; or the perfect example of a certain type (Originally, the word referred to a "fifth essence": in alchemy, that which remained when the four elements had been distilled away.)

quotidian ("kwo-TID-ee-ən") recurring daily; or commonplace, ordinary

rarefied ("RAIR-ə-fide") very thin (referring, especially, to air at high altitudes); or extremely refined or elevated (in manners, intellect, etc.), and therefore remote from the lives of most people

recalcitrant ("ree-KAL-sih-trənt") stubbornly uncooperative; defiant of authority

redact ("rə-DAKT") to edit (a document) for publication; or to censor part of a document

redoubtable ("rih-DOWT-ə-bəl" or "ree-") formidable; illustrious; worthy of awe or reverence

refractory ("rə-FRAK-tə-ree") stubborn, hard to manage

restive unable to keep still; impatient with restraint; on edge; hard to control

ribald ("RIB-əld" or "RYE-bald") bawdy: referring to sex, in an amusing or coarse way

risible ("RIZZ-ə-bəl") laughable, ridiculous; or pertaining to laughter

saturnine ("SAT-ər-nine") gloomy, surly, sluggish, and/or taciturn

Schadenfreude ("SHAH-den-FROY-də") German: pleasure taken in someone else's misfortune (often an antagonist or rival)

schwa ə: the symbol used in phonetics to indicate the common vowel sound "uh," e.g., the sound of the *a* in *announce*

scintillate ("SIN-tə-late") to throw off sparks, or to flash; to be animated or brilliant

screed a long, tiresome speech or written text, usually a rant, often tedious

sentient ("SEN-shənt") capable of perception through the senses; conscious

spawn the small eggs of fish, frogs, or other aquatic animals, usually produced in large numbers; or the offspring of something

specious ("SPEE-shəss") seemingly plausible but actually false or fallacious; deceptive

sybarite ("SIB-ə-rite") a person devoted to luxury and sensual pleasure: the word sometimes implies effeminacy

synergy ("SIN-ər-jee") the action of two or more organisms, substances, or organizations, resulting in an effect greater than the sum of their individual effects

temerity ("tə-MER-ə-tee") foolish boldness, reckless audacity, overconfidence

temporal ("TEM-pə-rəl") secular, as opposed to ecclesiastical; or pertaining to worldly life, as opposed to spiritual matters or the afterlife; or pertaining to time

tendentious ("ten-DEN-shəss") biased; written or said to promote a cause, especially a controversial one

theocracy ("thee-AHK-rə-see," the TH pronounced as in *with*) a form of government in which religious leaders (presumed to be interpreting God's will) hold the ultimate power

trifecta ("try-FEK-tə") a bet that correctly predicts the first three finishers in a race, in order

trompe l'oeil ("TRAHMP l(e)oy," but with a French accent) (literally, "deceive the eye") a style of painting that deceives the viewer into believing that the image is a real, three-dimensional object

trope a word or expression used in a figurative way; or, more commonly now, a theme or character type that has become a cliché

unctuous ("UNK-chew-əss") insincerely flattering, ingratiating, or pious, in an oily way

untenable ("un-TEN-ə-bəl") not defendable, not justifiable

venal ("VEEN-əl") corruptible; willing to accept a bribe

verdigris ("VƏR-də-gree" or "VƏR-də-greese") the green patina that forms on copper or bronze exposed to the elements over time

vicissitudes ("vih-SISS-ə-toods" or "-tyoods") unpredictable changes in fortune, especially for the worse; ups and downs

Weltanschauung ("VELT-ahn-shao-oong," the third syllable rhyming with *Mao*) German: worldview: one's conception of life

Zeitgeist ("TSITE-geyst," to rhyme with *kite heist*) German: "the spirit of the time": the beliefs and general spirit that define an era

"Shall we have a little quiz now?"